BEARING WITNESS
TO THE HOLOCAUST
1939-1989

Edited by

Alan L. Berger

Symposium Series
Volume 31

The Edwin Mellen Press
Lewiston/Queenston/Lampeter

Library of Congress Cataloging-in-Publication Data

Bearing witness to the Holocaust, 1939-1989 / edited by Alan L.
  Berger.
      p. cm. -- (The Symposium series ; v. 31)
      Proceedings of the 19th annual Scholars' Conference on the
  Holocaust and the Church Struggle, held in Philadelphia, March 5-7,
  1989.
      Includes bibliographical references.
      ISBN 0-7734-9644-0
      1. Holocaust, Jewish (1939-1945)--Influence--Congresses.
  2. Holocaust (Christian theology)--Congresses. 3. Holocaust (Jewish
  theology)--Congresses. 4. Holocaust, Jewish (1939-1945), in
  literature--Congresses. I. Berger, Alan L., 1939- .
  II. Scholars' Conference on the Holocaust and the Church Struggle
  (19th : 1989 : Philadelphia, Pa.) III. Series: Symposium series
  (Edwin Mellen Press) ; v. 31.
  D804.3.B42 1991
  940.53'18--dc20   91-28678
                                                                    CIP

This is volume 31 in the continuing series
Symposium Series
Volume 31 ISBN 0-7734-9644-0
SS Series ISBN 0-88946-989-X

A CIP catalog record for this book
is available from the British Library.

The Edwin Mellen Press   The Edwin Mellen Press
Box 450   Box 67
Lewiston, New York   Queenston, Ontario
USA 14092   CANADA L0S 1L0
                    The Edwin Mellen Press, Ltd.
                      Lampeter, Dyfed, Wales
                  UNITED KINGDOM SA48 7DY

Printed in the United States of America

Dedicated to the Memory of the Victims, the Lives of the Survivors, and the Work of the Annual Scholars' Conference

TABLE OF CONTENTS

Introduction

The Nineteenth Annual Scholars' Conference on the Holocaust and the Church Struggle was held in Philadelphia, March 5-7, 1989. A distinguished group whose numbers included both witnesses and non-witnesses gathered in order to discuss a variety of issues arising from the Holocaust's wounding of humanity. In addition, this meeting also marked the tenth anniversary of the Yad Vashem courses for Educators from Abroad and the Vidal Sassoon International Center for Studies in Antisemitism (The Hebrew University of Jerusalem). Many alumni of these programs participated in the deliberations. At the Conference Dinner, Dr. Elisabeth Maxwell gave a special address "Remembering for the Future," in which she emphasized the importance to humanity of learning the lessons of the Holocaust (*Shoah*). Temple University conferred Honorary degrees on the Maxwells: Dr. Maxwell received the *Doctor of Humane Letters* while Robert was awarded the *Doctor of Laws*. These degrees were in recognition of the Maxwells' contributions to furthering the study of Holocaust and genocide.

The Annual Scholars' Conference was founded in 1970 by Professors Franklin H. Littell and Hubert G. Locke. It was the first such organization whose purpose was to study the *Shoah* and to attempt to delineate the lessons of the catastrophe. Since its inception, The Annual Scholars' Conference has been committed to the principle that effective study of and reflection upon the *Shoah* requires interdisciplinary, interfaith, and international efforts. The Conference has had an enormous impact on those who study, teach, and write about the Holocaust and the Church Struggle.

For example, *The German Church Struggle and the Holocaust,* edited by Professors Littell and Locke, and containing selected papers from the initial conference held at Wayne State University, has become a standard reference in the field.

The papers assembled in this volume bear witness to the massiveness of the *Shoah*'s assault on both the divine and human image. Increasingly recognized as a watershed event in history, the catastrophe of European Jewry raises profound questions both for the religious world-view and for secular culture. The *Shoah* raises with agonizing clarity issues concerning God and history, the fate of humanity and the role of technology. The role of modernity in encouraging murder of the *other* is revealed in the flames of the death camps. Education itself, so prized by modernity as the means of freeing humanity from the fetters of religion, is put in the dock of history. For example, many of the murderers were university-trained professionals. This sad fact has prompted Franklin Littell to wonder about the multiple credibility crises of modernity: the crisis of christianity, of the professions, and of the university. For example, Littell wonders if universities are training what he terms "technically competent barbarians," and whether contemporary American higher education is doing any better than German universities did. It is against this background that these essays should be read and their messages pondered.

This book is divided into five sections: Survivor Testimonies, Philosophical Responses, Religious Responses, Literary and Artistic Responses, and The Aftermath. The bibliographically-rich essays treat the *Shoah* from a variety of disciplinary perspectives, each of which reveals a portion of the enormity of the crime and its continuing impact. These essays shed light on both the unique and universal dimensions of the catastrophe of European Jewry.

Survivor Testimonies reveal the diversity of survivors' experience both during and after the *Shoah*. Professor Herbert Hirsch's essay traces Primo Levi's remarkable literary career. An assimilated Jew and a chemist, Levi was quite at home in his native Italy prior to the Nazi invasion. Hirsch sensitively discusses Levi's stages of survival as revealed through his many writings, ranging from his first memoir *Survival in Auschwitz* to the posthumously published *The Drowned and the Saved*. While not consumed by hatred, Levi insisted that "Every man must answer for Auschwitz." Yet, as Hirsch reveals Levi ultimately died from "survivor's disease," the constant memory of Auschwitz. Doctor Emanuel Tanay, a Polish-born survivor, eloquently writes of the stages of his own re-entry into the world of freedom. He appeals for recognition of different types of survival, e.g., refugees, displaced persons, survivors, resident aliens, and "greenhorns." Any meaningful definition of survivor, he writes, "should have situational and psychic dimensions." Tellingly, he notes the qualitative experiential difference between a survivor and a refugee. Elie Wiesel is a survivor. Bruno Bettelheim is a refugee. Dr. Tanay shares the pain he felt when first applying for a psychiatric residency in the United States. He was told that survivors are shrewd and unscrupulous, therefore unfit for the psychiatric profession. His comments reveal the great distance travelled between initial perceptions of the survivor as anti-hero and the hard-won recognition that they embody a lesson about the meaning of survival in the nuclear age.

Nechama Tec, whose own tale of survival is grippingly revealed in her memoir *Dry Tears*, addresses a different aspect of Holocaust historiography in her essay. She writes of "autonomous altruists" in Poland, the major killing center of the Jewish people. Autonomous altruists are those whose life-saving actions are undertaken in the face of a hostile environment. Focusing on the remarkable career of Oswald Rufeissen, the Jewish-born rescuer of Jews who later became Brother Daniel a Carmelite monk, (the subject of her recently published biography *In the Lion's Den: The Life of Oswald Rufeisen*), Professor Tec sketches a profile of shared characteristics of rescuers. These six characteristics are: 1) individuality; 2) self-reliance; 3) long-lasting commitment to stand up for the needy; 4) helping Jews in an unassuming way; 5) an unpremeditated beginning of Jewish rescue; and 6) universalistic perceptions that defined Jews not in religious terms but as "helpless beings" "totally dependent on the protection of others." Extrapolating from her data, Tec opines that "mutual self-help and support in the camps might well have contributed to survival." She concludes that study of the Holocaust instructs both "about man's inhumanity to man and about man's humanity to man."

The second section deals with Philosophical Responses to the *Shoah*.
Roberta Kalechofsky's paper is a chilling study of nineteenth-century
vivisection. Attitudes and practices at that time were a harbinger of far
worse to come under National Socialism. Her study underscores a
fundamental flaw in modernity, the radical imbalance between the
intellectual and moral aspects of life. Vivisectionists eagerly embraced the
notion that skills be sharpened irregardless of values. Indifference to the
sanctity of life itself emerged as the dominant motif of nineteenth-century
medicine. The physiologist Claude Bernard attested that medicine was a
science and not an art. Consequently, in the practice of vivisection massive
indifference to the suffering of unanesthetized animals was countenanced.
As experimentation moved from animals to humans, special groups which lay
outside the protection of the law; orphans, the poor, and soldiers were
increasingly victimized. Through it all was the specter of "silent public
approval." Two essays discuss genocide comparatively in demonstrating the
unique character of the *Shoah*. Professor Robert Melson analyzes the
Holocaust of the Jewish People and the genocide of the Armenians. While
Melson finds that both exemplify "total domestic genocide," and both were
carried out under the cover of world war, significant differences exist.
Nazism had distinctive ideologies concerning the Jewish People. Chief
among them was a "bio-medical racism" which, in reality was a form of
manicheanism. Moreover, Nazism was informed by a quasi-theodicy,
whereas the Turks were prompted by nationalism. The Nazis had specific
intentions for the Jewish people which were not shared by the Turkish
campaign against the Armenians. Melson argues that just because the
Holocaust was unique and extreme, "it is possible to assert (and warn) that
the threshold for genocide, including total domestic genocide, may be
ordinary, familiar nationalism and that the mass destruction of human groups
need not depend on the rise of Nazi-type ideologies."

Steven Katz's essay deals with the dissimilarities between the moral
and political evils of Auschwitz and the Gulag. He finds that the Nazi
murder camps differed from Stalin's gulag in a multiplicity of ways: design,
empirical facticity, intentionality, and teleology. Professor Katz persuasively
demonstrates that Stalin's mass murder campaigns were undertaken for

economic and national reasons. Hitler, on the other hand, acted on the basis of ontological fantasies. His destruction of the Jewish people was for "metaphysical" reasons, i.e., creating a new world which would be bereft of Jews and Jewish ideas. Consequently, Katz argues that the Gulag was predictable, "an endpoint of a spectrum of Soviet labor exploitation." Moreover, the Gulag "killed people distributively." No single group was to be completely destroyed. Auschwitz, for its part, was unpredictable, being "discontinuous with its immediate past history." The intent of Auschwitz was, however, clear and unprecedented; "All Jews must die." Katz's essay does not relativize evil. On the contrary, he views the task of scholarship as studying "variegated forms of evil and to recognize differences as well as similarities between them."

Professor Roger Smith deals with the complex issue of apocalyptic fantasies and their relationship to genocide. His is an analysis of ideological genocide based on a careful reading of the work of Norman Cohn. Smith demonstrates that where "gross delusions" of past and present exist, one has optimal condition for genocide. In order to counter this distortion of reality, Smith argues for "civic education." This type of education can "instil a sense of personal responsibility" that would cause us "to break with executioners and that through social consciousness and a sense of humanity would ally us with victims." In this way it is perhaps possible to overcome the "power of fantasy and the quest for a new and pure age." One who did not overcome the power of fantasy was the German philospher Martin Heidegger. Professor Richard Rubenstein examines Heidegger's call for authentic existence against the background of his unabashed embrace of Nazism. Heidegger was convinced of the "total absence of any higher authority as guide or source of norms." Moreover, those who, like his contemporary Karl Barth, seek such guidelines are inauthentic. Yet, Rubenstein finds that it was Barth who refused the oath of allegiance to Hitler. No philosemite, Barth was able to make moral judgements. This leads Rubenstein to conclude that although "Christian anti-Semitism was a precondition for the Holocaust, the Christian Church never sanctioned an unremitting program of extermination against the Jews." However, he finds "no comparable moral barriers for much of secular philosophy." Heidegger never expressed any regret either for his espousal of Nazism or for the murder of the Jewish people. Rational thought is no guarantee of moral behavior.

Religious responses to the Holocaust display great variety. Professor Jack Fischel's study of the American Mennonite response to the *Shoah* reveals an all too typical behavior. When Mennonites, who themselves had been subjected to European persecution, expressed concern for the suffering of the Jewish People it was in the context of asserting that only conversion could alleviate their plight. Fischel reports that in the years 1941-1945 only nine articles in six important Mennonite journals dealt with the Jewish plight. In part, he argues that the millenialist view of history which Mennonites embraced led them to believe that the *Shoah* might well be part of God's plan. Fischel notes that the Mennonites position is not unique. Rather, it is symptomatic revealing the "overall failure of much of American Protestant denominations to transcend their sectarian loyalties in behalf of European Jewry." Professor Robert Ross's paper echoes this lesson. When Northern Baptists spoke of racism during World War II, they rightfully mentioned Black people but omitted any reference to the extermination of the Jews. Southern Baptists, for their part, did mention the Jewish People, but in terms that called for their conversion. Jacob Gartenhaus, a Jewish convert, and leader of the Southern Baptists, in fact contended that the Holocaust was God's punishment of the sinful Jews of Europe.

Gershon Greenberg illuminates the fascinating and very different religious response of Lubavitch Hasidim to the *Shoah*. Led by Rabbi Joseph Isaac Schneersohn, Lubavitch established the "Camp of Israel" (*Mahane Israel*) in Brooklyn. The camp functioned as a "Goshen," a refuge from "the contemporary plagues of *khurban* (a Yiddish word used to refer to the destructions of the Jerusalem Temple). The Lubavitch group embraced an esoteric understanding of the final words of the biblical Joseph: "I die and surely God will remember (*pakod yifkod*) you and bring you out of the Land (of Egypt) unto the land which He swore to Abraham, Isaac and Jacob" (Genesis 50:24). Professor Greenberg's study reveals how the *pakod yifkod* functioned paradigmatically, revealing a "transition from exile/death to land-redemption/life." Based on this paradigm, Rabbi Schneersohn taught that destruction (*khurban*) implied redemption (*geula*). Consequently, Rabbi

Schneersohn pleaded that Jews should not despair no matter how bleak things might appear. The dark times of the *Shoah* were in fact the birth pangs of the Messiah. Redemption could occur through penitence (*teshuva*) which, in turn, would be hastened by constant repetition of mishnas and living a life of Torah (study) and mitzvah (commandment/good deed). This group of Hasidim felt obligated to make public their esoteric understanding of events.

Dr. Paul Marcus and Professor Alan Rosenberg urge greater sensitivity for psychotherapists treating religious survivors. The authors argue that the corrosive effects of a secular world may cause analysts to diminish the religious dimension. Overcoming this obstacle requires of the therapist "quiet listening and patience." One thing that the therapist can do for religious survivors is to "broaden their conception of God." This broadening is actually a "replacement" of the personal biblical God by an impersonal deity who refrains from intervening in history. What remains paramount, the authors wisely attest, is the need to "develop trust. The survivor needs to construct a helpful image of the human person."

Literary and artistic responses to the *Shoah* express what perhaps is ultimately inexpressible. Beverly Asbury's essay treats the work of survivor artist György Kádár. Kádár, an assimilated Polish Jew, survived Auschwitz and four other camps. Through what Dr. Asbury terms the artist's "visionary narrative," illustrated in the essay by representative drawings, the viewer is invited to enter the kingdom of night. Kádár's Holocaust imagery then "enters our consciousness." As a consequence of viewing Kádár's work, Asbury argues that people "live beyond but not without the curse of mass murder and the vision of total annihilation." Susan Pentlin's study of Mary Berg's Warsaw Diary brings to light a too little known yet invaluable Holocaust document. Mary Berg (Wattenberg) was an American teenager who lived in the Warsaw Ghetto. Faithfully keeping a diary of events, her book was "the first published (1945) eyewitness testimony from an inhabitant of the ghetto and the first account to testify that gas was being used to kill Jews at Treblinka." The American Wattenbergs were permitted to leave Warsaw after a period of imprisonment. Returning to America, Mary published her diary. She, like Jan Karski, the Polish non-Jew, intended to inform America about Nazi atrocities. Unfortunately, the message of both witnesses was too late. Yet, as Professor Pentlin writes, Mary Berg's diary demonstrates the "vitality and perseverance of the human spirit, even on the brink of destruction." The diary provides a wealth of details concerning ghetto life, including the fact that Mary and her friends formed a theatre group, gave performances, and contributed to the orphanage headed by the saintly Dr. Janus Korczak. Readers can share Pentlin's hope that Mary's diary will soon be reissued and assume its rightful place in "contemporary American courses on the Holocaust."

The two other essays in this section deal with post-Holocaust literary reflections. Professor Rachel Brenner addresses the problematics of post-Holocaust poetics in her insightful study of A. M. Klein and Mordecai Richler. The two Canadian writers embrace very different views of post-*Shoah* diaspora Jewish identity. Klein was among the earliest to attest that, after the Holocaust, all Jews are survivors. Consequently, he believed that "post-Holocaust redemption was predicated upon reception of the victim's story." Richler adopts a very different position. Brenner demonstrates that his works reveal that the "North American Jew dissociates himself from Jewish suffering." The pervasiveness of Jewish vulnerability and anxiety underscore the need to assimilate. These two positions still describe a polarity in the Jewish diaspora. Iwona Irwin-Zarecka's essay treats the novelist as historian. She analyzes the novels of two contemporary Polish non-Jewish writers in order to assess the role of memory and the outcome of what happens when "non-Jewish Poles begin to reflect on the Holocaust." Public reception of Andrzey Szcezypiorski's *The Beginning* and Jaroslaw Morek Rymkiewicz' *Umschlagplatz* speak of a distorted view of the past. Professor Irwin-Zarecka argues that *The Beginning* received both national and international attention because of its reassurance." The Holocaust was a genocide, one among many. The story has a "good" German and a "bad" Jew, while presenting a picture of the Poles solely as victims of the Germans. The novel presents a "correct" picture of the past. *Umschlagplatz*, for its part, received little attention. Arguing that moral responsibility is universal, the author, who has a Jewish wife and is therefore *not one of our own*, attempts to "bring the Umschlagplatz within the lexicon of Polish memory." His novel challenges the view of Poles as passive observers to the destruction of the Jewish People. Irwin-Zarecka's study raises serious questions about the power and responsibility of novelists as they increasingly turn towards the Holocaust.

The Aftermath presents a mixed image. Professor Zev Garber's essay is a midrash on the meaning of the choice of 27 *Nisan* as the date commemorating the *Shoah*. He articulates a linkage between providential design and history in this choice. In an appendix to his paper Garber also presents a complete translation of the Knesset decree formalizing 27 *Nisan* as *Yom HaShoah*. Richard Pierard's paper reveals the depths of antisemitism among the religious and political right. Analyzing the content of and reception accorded to John Beaty's antisemitic *The Iron Curtain Over America* (1951), Professor Pierard sheds light on the current phenomenon of the antisemitism of intellectuals and pseudo-intellectuals. Domestic politics in America were shaped by MacCarthyism and other political witchhunts. Yet, there were effective counter-measures taken against the hatred and lies in Beatty's book. Pierard rightly contends that there is a "useful lesson" to be learned from the Beatty episode. People must be "ready and prepared to counter the Jewish khazar legend with solid historical arguments." Moreover, "when it comes to antisemitism, old ideas never seem to die."

Two papers specifically address the *Shoah*'s impact on Christian theology and liturgy. Professor A. Roy Eckardt's illuminating essay addresses the issue of Christian triumphalism and supersessionism by focusing on the relationship between the *Shoah* and affirming the resurrection. Autobiographically, Eckardt shares the stages of his own thinking on whether the resurrection was an historical or metahistorical act. These stages conform to the Hegelian Thesis, Antithesis, and Synthesis model. Eckardt attests that both he and his wife Alice were led to the study of the *Shoah* by "the anti-Jewish problematic within Christianity and Christian history." Concerning the Holocaust and the resurrection, Eckardt sees "the primary Christian Challenge" as consisting of "demythologizing the Christian tradition." This, in turn, requires one to "deideologize" Christianity. This latter demands that Christians of good conscience "wage war upon (Christianity's) supersessionist elitism" and reject triumphalism. Eschewing a triumphalist or somatic view of resurrection, Eckardt advocates a "nontriumphalist or anti-triumphalist resurrection." Consequently, the resurrection will be "spiritual" but not spiritualized.

Dr. Eugene J. Fisher's essay presents an insider's view of the Catholic Church's reaction to the *Shoah*. Eloquently observing that "memory should be a uniting and sobering experience, not one of triumphalism," Fisher identifies *Nostra Aetate* as a turning point in Catholic-Jewish relations. The Holy See's statement on "The Church and Racism" specifies the Holocaust while terming antisemitism "the most tragic form that racist ideology has assumed in our century." Fisher notes that this document can be utilized by Catholic teachers as a foundation for developing Holocaust education. Two crucial American documents appeared in the late eighties. *Criteria for the Evaluation of Dramatization of the Passion* (1988) deals with how to portray Christ's death without implying "collective guilt." *God's Mercy Endures Forever: Guidelines on the Presentation of Jews and Judaism in Catholic Preaching* (1989) is designed for homilists and rejects supercessionism, the deicide charge, and triumphalism Moreover, for the first time bishops recommend joint Jewish/Christian memorial services for victims of the Holocaust while offering specific liturgical examples. In addition, the document contains a list of nine "general principles" applicable to homilies year round. The significance of this document is revealed in Dr. Fisher's assertion: "I would like to see this list posted on bulletin boards of every Catholic seminary and parish rectory in the country." It is important to note Fisher's contention that many of the themes initially raised at the Annual Scholars' Conference are now becoming embedded in the official teachings of the Roman Catholic Church.

Professor Maria Rosenbloom, survivor from the Polish Ukraine, writes of the survivors' unending need to bear witness and the many contributions which survivors make to the mental health profession. For example, survivors are intimately acquainted with the dangers of ethically unanchored professional skills. Moreover, the survivor testifies to the extreme range of human behavior in extreme conditions. Perhaps most significant is the reminder to mental health professionals of the vital role of "accident" in survival. It is not the "ego strength" theory so favored by mental health workers which was vital to survival. More often than not, one survived quite by accident. Moreover, Rosenbloom explores the continuing implications of the *Shoah* in discussing the following groups: child survivors, members of the second generation, aged survivors, and family. Her discussion of the phenomenon of survivor guilt makes a crucial distinction between the moral and psychological aspects of guilt.

Throughout these essays one sees the interweaving of a world-historical event and very personal and intensely human response to the *Shoah*. The papers reveal mastery of their topics but demand much more. Study of the Holocaust and its aftermath time and again illumine the danger of skills without values. Those whose work is contained herein are sensitive to this truth. Underlying all of the papers is an awareness of the persistence of antisemitism. No social pathology has lasted longer. None is more deadly. Concerning this phenomenon, Elie Wiesel has observed that, "At Auschwitz the victims died, but not the disease." Taken as a whole, the present collection informs as it sensitizes, making the reader aware of the enormity of Auschwitz and both the fragility and the hope of post-Auschwitz humanity. Finally, these discussions reveal that ultimately all questions about the *Shoah* are moral questions.

Alan L. Berger
Conference Chairman
19th ASC

ACKNOWLEDGEMENTS

I wish to thank the conference Planning Committee for their assistance. Professors Harry James Cargas, F. Burton Nelson, Alice E. Eckardt, and Hubert G. Locke were especially involved in providing the benefit of their wisdom and insight in planning for the 19th Annual Scholars' Conference. Dr. Marcia S. Littell's expertise as a Conference Director was invaluable to me. Dr. Franklin H. Littell, whom I have known for fifteen years, has been a teacher and a friend. He is one of the American pioneers of Holocaust and genocide research. I am especially pleased to thank Ariel Berger, my oldest son, whose insight provided the inspiration for the cover design of this volume. Special thanks go to Mr. Joseph H. Fink, Esquire, Vice-President and Counsel of the Annual Scholars' Conference. Mr. Fink is retired senior partner of the Chicago law firm of Antinow and Fink. His generosity and support have helped make this publication possible.

The essay by Professor Richard L. Rubenstein first appeared in *Modern Judaism*, vol. 9, number 2, 1989 and is reprinted here with permission of the author. The essay by Dr. Paul Marcus and Professor Alan Rosenberg is reprinted by permission of Greenwood Publishing Group, Inc., Westport, CT, from *Healing Their Wounds*, co-edited by Paul Marcus and Alan Rosenberg, 1989. Györy Kádár's drawings are reproduced by permission of The Committee on the Vanderbilt University Holocaust Art Collection.

SURVIVAL AND SUICIDE : PRIMO LEVI AND THE CRISIS OF THE TWENTIETH CENTURY

Herbert Hirsch

"...He was assured and coherent in his rejection of life. He was found nearly dead a few days later, and died in the hospital alone. He, who was not a survivor, had died of the survivors' disease" (Levi, 1987, p. 160).

"If we had to and were able to suffer the sufferings of everyone, we could not live" (Levi, 1988, p. 56).

Introduction

Primo Levi, who survived Auschwitz, may also have died of the "survivors disease." As a writer of great humanity and sensitivity whose life was devoted to bearing witness to the past and continuing horrors of the twentieth century, Levi's very existence requires any observer of the continuing crisis of genocide and mass murder to pause to ask a most depressing question: "Is it possible for great humanity and sensitive intelligence to survive the inhumanity and massive destruction of human life, both actual and potential, which appear to dominate the twentieth century?"[1]

Primo Levi's life and writings cast a harsh but moving and compassionate light on our troubled and troubling epoch. One of the tragic heroes of this century, Levi does not fulfill the traditional image of the hero as a person who gains martyrdom through death (Des Pres, 1977, p. 3). Rather, Levi's life validates the persuasive arguments put forth by Des Pres and Lifton[2] (1987) who note that the successful struggle to survive and bear witness to evil is an act of heroism. The survivor preserves life in order to testify, and perhaps to suffer, often speaking, in the manner of the Just Man in the tale recounted by Elie Wiesel,[3] to unhearing ears. In short, to tell unconscious humanity what it does not wish to hear and to live a life, and in Levi's case to write words, that might force confrontation with the guilt of indifference.

Life and Work

Primo Levi is a writer of immense humanity whose powerful evocation of human character in inhuman settings establishes him as a true teacher, one of the just, from whom we are able to learn much about the human spirit. The details of Primo Levi's life are quite well known.[4]

Born in Turin in 1919, Levi was raised in a middle-class assimilated Jewish family. As a young man he studied to be a chemist, receiving his doctorate in 1941. Following the Fascist takeover of Italy, Levi joined a group of partisans in September, 1943. He was arrested in December and deported to Auschwitz in 1944. His stories of his year in Auschwitz, his adventures returning home, and his remembrance of these events form the core of his literary achievement. Their particular power derives from Levi's ability to evoke and describe human character and from, in the words of Irving Howe, his "special gift for the vignette."[5] This gift is apparent throughout his work, and never more so then when Levi reflects on how he came to write about his experiences.

In an "Afterword" to the 1986 combined edition of his first two works, *Survival in Auschwitz* and *The Reawakening*, Levi talks about his first book.[6] He writes about *Survival in Auschwitz*, that this book has a destiny, a distant "birth certificate" found where one reads that "I write what I would never dare tell anyone" (p. 375). Auschwitz gave to Levi the need to tell his story--a need "so strong" that "in the Camp" he began "describing my experience there, on the spot, in that German laboratory laden with freezing cold, the war, and vigilant eyes; and yet I knew that I would not be able under any circumstances to hold on to those haphazardly scribbled notes, and that I must throw them away immediately because if they were found they would be considered an act of espionage and would cost me my life" ("Afterward," p. 375).

The memories, however, "burned so intensely" that within a few months of his return to Italy he wrote *Survival in Auschwitz*. The story of the book is itself dramatic. As Levi describes it:

> The manuscript was turned down by a number of important publishers; it was accepted in 1947 by a small publisher who printed only 2,500 copies and then folded. So this first book of mine fell into oblivion for many years: perhaps also because in all of Europe those were difficult times of mourning and reconstruction and the public did not want to return in memory to the painful years of the war that had just ended ("Afterward," p. 375).

It was not until 1958 that a large publisher, Einaudi, republished *Survival in Auschwitz*. Since then the book has achieved public and critical acclaim, has been translated into eight languages, and adapted for radio and theatre. It is an amazingly humane account of inhumanity.

Captured on December 13, 1943 at the age of 24, Primo Levi describes himself as "with little wisdom, no experience, and a decided tendency--encouraged by the life of segregation forced on me for the previous four years of the racial laws--to live in an unrealistic world of my own, a world inhabited by civilized Cartesian phantoms..." (*Survival in Auschwitz*, p. 9). He was soon to be confronted with another experience and to emerge with wisdom. That he was to retain his humanity is a tribute to this great writer, for he had, in his own words, "reached the bottom" (*Survival*, p. 22).

> Then for the first time we became aware that our language lacks words to express this offense, the demolition of a man. In a moment, with almost prophetic intuition, the reality was revealed to us: we had reached the bottom. It is not possible to sink lower than this; no human condition is more miserable than this, nor could it conceivably be so. Nothing belongs to us anymore; they have taken away our clothes, our shoes, even our hair; if we speak, they will not listen to us, and if they listen, they will not understand. They will even take away our name; and if we want to keep it, we will have to find in ourselves the strength to do so, to manage somehow so that behind the name something of us, of us as we were, still remains (*Survival*, p. 22).

Thus Levi began his descent to the bottom, to experience the ultimate dehumanization. It was the most complete example of a program designed by human beings to dehumanize other human beings to prepare for their ultimate extermination.

In order to understand this process, it is important to hear Levi's description. He continues:

> Imagine now a man who is deprived of everyone he loves, and at the same time of his house, his habits, his clothes; in short, of everything he possesses: he will be a hollow man, reduced to suffering and needs, forgetful of dignity and restraint, for he who loses all often easily loses himself. He will be a man whose life or death can be lightly decided with no sense of human affinity, in the most fortunate of cases, on the basis of a pure judgement of utility. It is in this way that one can understand the double sense of the term "extermination camp," and it is now clear what we seek to express with the phrase: "to lie on the bottom" (*Survival*, p. 23).

So Primo Levi descended to hell, and began his adjustment for survival. Even in this hell people, Levi notes, "gain a certain equilibrium after a few weeks..." (*Survival*, p. 51). Yet, it is the equilibrium of humanity's ability to adjust to the most horrible and degrading circumstance, and it is an equilibrium punctuated by tantalizing dreams:

> One can hear the sleepers breathing and snoring; some groan and speak. Many lick their lips and move their jaws. They are dreaming of eating; this is also a collective dream. It is a pitiless dream which the creator of the Tantalus myth must have known. You not only see the food, you feel it in your hands, distinct and concrete, you are aware of its rich and striking smell: someone in the dream even holds it up to your lips, but every time a different circumstance intervenes to prevent the consummation of the act. Then the dream dissolves and breaks up into its elements, but it reforms itself immediately after and begins again, similar, yet changed; and this without pause, for all of us, every night and for the whole of our sleep (*Survival*, p. 55).

The nightmare continued in the waking hours as Levi describes the days of useless and grueling work; the cruelty and inhumanity of the Nazis and the Guards; the written chemistry examination which ultimately allowed him to work as a chemist, in a warm laboratory, and helped him survive; and, finally, the liberation, or more precisely, the German desertion of the camp. Through it all Levi provides sketches of a series of marvelously human characters. For example, take his "friend," Lorenzo:

> The story of my relationship with Lorenzo is both long
> and short, quiet and enigmatic; it is the story of a time and
> condition now effaced from every present reality, and so I do
> not think it can be understood except in the manner in which
> we nowadays understand events of legends or of the remotest
> history.
>
> In concrete terms it amounts to little: an Italian civilian
> worker brought me a piece of bread and the remainder of his
> ration every day for six months; he gave me a vest of his, full of
> patches; he wrote a postcard on my behalf to Italy and brought
> me the reply. For all this he neither asked nor accepted any
> reward, because he was good and simple and did not think that
> one did good for a reward (*Survival*, p. 109).

Imagine in Auschwitz, a "good and simple" person who did not operate on the principles of selfishness so routinely institutionalized in contemporary society and so necessary for survival in extraordinary circumstances. Levi believes that "it was really due to Lorenzo that I am alive today; and not so much for his material aid, as for his having constantly reminded me by his presence, by his natural and plain manner of being good, that there still existed a just world outside our own, something and someone still pure and whole, not corrupt, not savage, extraneous to hatred and terror; something difficult to define, a remote possibility of good, but for which it was worth surviving" (*Survival*, p. 111).

Lorenzo appears again in a later and moving little book, *Moments of Reprieve: A Memoir of Auschwitz* (1987). Here Levi provides a more complete portrait and adds to the earlier story. The soup Lorenzo supplied helped Levi and his friends by furnishing additional calories which allowed them to survive. The soup, it seems, was

> ...weird soup. In it we found plum nuts, salami peels, once
> even the wing of a sparrow with all its feathers; another time a
> scrap of Italian newspaper (*Moments*, p. 155).

Both Lorenzo and Levi returned to their homes in Italy after the war and Levi went to Lorenzo's town "to see him again and bring him a woolen sweater for the winter" (*Moments*, p. 159). Levi found a man who was "tired":

> ...not tired from the walk, mortally tired, a weariness without
> remedy. Lorenzo no loner worked as a mason but went from
> farm to farm with a small cart buying and selling scrap iron.
> He wanted no more rules or bosses or schedules. The little he
> earned he spent at the tavern; he did not drink as a vice but to
> get away from the world. He had seen the world, he didn't like

it, he felt it was going to ruin. To live no longer interested him
(*Moments*, p. 159).

Levi attempted to help Lorenzo by finding him a mason's job, but
Lorenzo refused. Finally he told Levi "...something which in Auschwitz I
hadn't suspected."

> Down there he helped not only me. He had other proteges,
> Italian and not, but he thought it right not to tell me about it:
> we are in this world to do good, not to boast about it. In 'Suiss'
> he had been a rich man, at least compared to us, and had been
> able to help us, but now it was over; he had no more
> opportunities (*Moments*, pp. 159-160).

Having lived through Auschwitz, Lorenzo was adrift. He became ill,
and after Levi took him to a hospital, he ran away. "He was assured and
coherent in his rejection of life. He was found nearly dead a few days later,
and died in the hospital alone. He, who was not a survivor, had died of the
survivor's disease" (*Moments*, p. 160).

Neither a military hero, nor a political leader, Lorenzo is actually
much more. One of those moral men whose lives enhance ours by their
simple existence. Without Levi's sense of humanity expressed through his
power of description, we would have never become acquainted with Lorenzo
or with the other marvelous characters with which Levi's writing is populated.

Surviving by luck, by chance, by perseverance and intelligence, as well
as with the help of Lorenzo, Levi chronicles his miraculous journey back to
humanity and back to Italy.

The journey to humanity began in the deserted camp. Abandoned by
the Nazis, confined to the infectious disease ward, waiting for the Russian
troops, Levi and two companions repair a broken window, secure and light a
stove, and, as the

> ...stove began to spread its heat, something seemed to relax in
> everyone, and at that moment Towarowski (a Franco-Pole of
> twenty-three, typhus) proposed to the others that each of them
> offer a slice of bread to us three who had been working. And
> so it was agreed.
>
> Only a day before a similar event would have been
> inconceivable. The law of the Lager said: "eat your own
> bread, and if you can, that of your neighbor," and left no room
> for gratitude. It really meant that the Lager was dead.
>
> It was the first human gesture that occurred among us.
> I believe that moment can be dated as the beginning of the
> change by which we who had not died slowly changed from

Haftlinge [inmates or prisoners] to men again (*Survival*, p. 145).

Levi had travelled directly to Auschwitz aboard a train. His journey back to Italy, chronicled in *The Reawakening*, was much less direct.

The publication and success of Levi's first book, *Survival in Auschwitz*, encouraged him to write *The Reawakening*. The journey from Auschwitz to his home in Turin was often tragic, sometimes comic. It took Levi through Eastern Europe, to the Soviet Union, and then back through Eastern Europe to Italy. Once again he fills his story with remarkable and seemingly improbable characters and events.

The "vignettes" can be prophetic and moving such as the scene in which Levi and his companions happen upon a group of 12 German soldiers in the Soviet Union, dressed in rags, without their military hierarchy. Levi describes the following scene:

> They saw us, and some of them moved towards us with the uncertain steps of automata. They asked for bread; not in their own language, but in Russian. We refused, because our bread was precious. But Daniele did not refuse; Daniele, whose strong wife, whose brother, parents and not less than thirty relatives had been killed by the Germans; Daniele, who was the sole survivor of the raid on the Venice ghetto, and who from the day of the liberation had fed on grief, took out a piece of bread, showed it to these phantoms and placed it on the ground. But he insisted that they come to get it on all fours; which they did, docilely (*Reawakening*, p. 286).

The Reawakening is filled with such events. Many of the people exude great strength as they find mechanisms to adapt to their liberation. They appear, disappear and reappear. As specters they enter Levi's life, influence his vision of the world, and then depart never to be seen again. Through it all Levi maintains his sense of humor. Some of the events are almost comical.

Imagine two Italians in rags appearing late at night in a small Russian village of about 30 houses. They wish to negotiate to buy a chicken from the Russian peasants. The peasants speak no Italian and Levi and his companion speak no Russian. Levi and his friend have with them six plates which they wish to exchange for the chickens. The scene in which Levi's companion acts out the role of a chicken is quite incredible. Unable to accept the fact that not everyone spoke Italian, Levi's travelling companion became ever madder as he attempted to talk with the Russian peasants. Beginning to grumble and curse, the following ensued:

> Was it possible that it was so difficult to understand what a chicken is, and that we wanted it in exchange for six plates? A chicken, one of those beasts that go around pecking, scratching and saying "coccode-e-eh"; and rather half-heartedly, glowering and sullen, he put on a very second rate imitation of the habits of the chicken, crouching on the ground, scraping first with one foot and then with the other and pecking here and there with his hands shaped like a wedge. Between one oath and the other, he also cried "coccode-e-eh"....
>
> ....Hopping mad by now, Cesare even tried to lay an egg, pouring far-fetched insults on them all the while, so rendering the meaning of his performance even more obscure (*Reawakening*, pp. 299-300).

Finally, after 20 months, after Auschwitz, after an incredible journey, Levi crosses the border to Italy and describes the moment:

> ...our less tired companions celebrated with a cheerful uproar; Leonardo and I remained lost in a silence crowded with memories. Of 650, our number when we had left, three of us were returning. And how much had we lost in those twenty months? What should we find at home? How much of ourselves had been eroded, extinguished? (*Reawakening*, p. 372).

Unlike most of the survivors, when he arrived home on October 19th Levi found his house still standing, and all of his family alive. He describes himself as

> ...swollen, bearded and in rags, and had difficulty in making myself recognized. I found my friends full of life, the warmth of secure meals, the solidity of daily work, the liberating joy of recounting my story. I found a large clean bed, which in the evening (a moment of terror) yielded softly under my weight. But only after many months did I lose the habit of walking with my glance fixed to the ground, as if searching for something to eat or to pocket hastily or to sell for bread; and a dream full of horror has still not ceased to visit me, at sometimes frequent, sometimes longer, intervals (*Reawakening*, p. 373).

Levi dreamt he was in chaos. In this chaos

> ...everything collapses and disintegrates around me, the scenery, the walk, the people, while the anguish becomes more intense and more precise. Now everything has changed to chaos; I am alone in the centre of a grey and turbid nothing, and now I know what this thing means, and I also know that I have always known it; I am in the Lager once more, and nothing is true outside the Lager. All the rest was a brief

pause, a deception of the senses, a dream; my family, nature in flower, my home. Now this inner dream, this dream of peace, is over, and in the outer dream, which continues, gelid, a well-known voice resounds: a single word, not imperious, but brief and subdued. It is the dawn command of Auschwitz, a foreign word, feared and expected: get up, "Wstawach" (Reawakening, pp. 373-374).

People respond to horrific experiences in many ways. Some withdraw into silence as they attempt to block out all memory. Others become bitter and vengeful. Levi's response was to continue to attempt to untangle the puzzles of life and to devote the remainder of his life to communicating his thoughts to the rest of us. His struggle with his past and with the events of the late twentieth century are to be found in his most recent books. That it had been a struggle to continue to survive and to maintain his humane perspective cannot be in doubt.

The Monkey's Wrench[7] is a book of reminiscences of a metal rigger who travels to remote parts of the world. His adventures are recounted as stories told to the author--stories he has never told before--about work, life, love. The rigger, Libertino Faussome, is a composite of men and, as with all of Levi's work, the character portrayal stands out. This is, however, the least significant of Levi's works. More moving and engrossing is his novel, *If Not Now, When?*[8]

A story of the Jewish resistance in Eastern Europe, this book chronicles the adventures of Jewish partisans who made their way from Russia to Italy to Palestine. Levi calls upon his travels through Eastern Europe and the Soviet Union chronicled in *The Reawakening*. Many of his descriptions of character and place are obviously related to his own journey from Auschwitz to the Soviet Union and back to Italy.

It is impossible to capture the flavor of *If Not Now, When?* without a large bite and long taste of Levi's prose. Who were these partisans? Armed bands?

Ghostly bands, cloudlike bands: here today, blowing up the railroad track, and forty kilometers away tomorrow, looting the silos of Kolkhoz. And the faces were never the same. Russian faces, Ukrainian, Polish; Mongols, who had come from no telling where; Jews, too, yes, some; and women, and a kaleidoscope of uniforms: Soviets dressed as Germans, in police uniforms; Soviets in tatters, still with their Red Army tunics; even some German deserters....How many? Who knows? Fifty here, three hundred there, groups that formed and broke up: alliance, quarrels, sometimes even shooting (*If Not Now, When?*, p. 39).

It is the people, seemingly improbable, yet believable and, no doubt, real, who give to Levi's tale its power and who sustain the narrative. *If Not Now, When?* is a hopeful, but hesitant, book. The people here fought. They exerted their humanity and they not only survived, but created, in the end, new life. For, at the conclusion of the book a baby is born, but Levi in the end asks, what sort of world faces this new child? Having fought through one of the most horrible periods in human history, the new life emerges into a new world:

> ...the newspaper, consisting of a single sheet, bore a very big headline, whose meaning he couldn't understand. That newspaper bore the date of Tuesday, 7 August, 1945 and carried the news of the first atomic bomb, dropped on Hiroshima (*If Not New, When?*, p. 346).

For a survivor of Auschwitz the fact of nuclear weapons must have come as a horrible shock of recognition. People who every day faced the possibility of extinction by gas and fire were now "liberated" into a world in which all people were to be confronted by that possibility. Faced with this realization what does a survivor, or any person, do? How does one cope with the horrible possibility that, after surviving one Holocaust, another awaits? Can memory serve as a warning? Can it function as an inoculation against further destruction? Even in the face of repeated mass death we all cling, perhaps naively, to the hope that this will be the last incident, that this warning will be heeded. Levi certainly hoped as he continued to dig into his past to reconstruct a memorable cast of characters to bear witness to the seemingly perpetual crisis of the twentieth century. Levi's sense of character, his pleasure, his wit and joy of living come together once again in *The Periodic Table*.[9]

The Periodic Table is filled with the poetry of memory brought to life via the analogy of Mendeleev's Periodic Table. For Levi, the elements of the periodic table serve as a metaphor for people and experience, or they play an important role in actual events in his life. The personality profiles are incisive for Levi has the ability to describe with great depth in a few words.

Yet, as with all of his work, *The Periodic Table* is more than a book of individual profiles. In Levi's deft hands, chemistry becomes a metaphor for life and an avenue for philosophical rumination. Take, for example, zinc. Zinc is not, according to Levi, "an element which says much to the imagination, it is gray and its salts are colorless, it is not toxic, nor does it produce striking chromatic reactions; in short, it is a boring metal" (p. 33). Yet, its reaction to acid, especially in a pure state, prompts Levi to consider "two conflicting philosophical conclusions: the praise of purity which protects from evil like a coat of mail; the praise of impurity, which gives rise to changes, in other words, to life" (p. 34). After dismissing the first philosophical conclusion as "disgustingly moralistic," Levi lingers on the second which he finds more "congenial."

> In order for the wheel to turn, for life to be lived, impurities are needed, and the impurities in the soil, too, as is known, if it is to be fertile. Dissension, diversity, the grain of salt and mustard are needed. Fascism does not want them, forbids them, and that's why you're not a Fascist; it wants everybody to be the same and you are not (p. 34).

Vivid personalities and philosophical speculations leap from these pages and are fit into the context of important historical events. The rise of Fascist states, the ascent to power of Hitler and Mussolini, the accompanying anti-semitism and ultimate attempt to destroy the European Jews, are all part of Levi's story. Finally, he brings events full circle.

In the next-to-last section of *The Periodic Table*, "Vanadium," Levi is a chemist working for a varnish company that has purchased vanadium from a German company. When a shipment appears defective Levi corresponds with a German chemist. He begins to suspect that this person may be the same man who was his superior in Auschwitz. Perhaps the same man who, when Levi arrived for his assignment in one of the labs at Auschwitz, gave him a pair of shoes. The man who showed this minimal kindness turned out to be the man with whom Levi was communicating.

This German chemist maintained that he did not know that Jews were being killed at Auschwitz where, not incidentally, over two million were exterminated. He did not ask questions. He utilized, as Levi states, the "common technique" of trying to know as little as possible. He "had not demanded explanations from anyone, not even from himself, although on clear days the flames of the crematorium were visible..." (p. 221). He was, as were most people, "Neither infamous nor a hero; after filtering off the rhetoric and the lies in good or bad faith there remained a typically gray human specimen, one of the not so few one-eyed men in the kingdom of the blind" (pp. 221-222). This one-eyed man, this German chemist, wanted to meet Levi. Perhaps for forgiveness or for salvation. Eight days after agreeing to meet, before the consummation of that event and in the sixtieth year of his life. "Doktor Lothar Muller" died unexpectedly. He was no hero, but he was not a sadistic killer either. Levi says he was "honest and unarmed."

> A world in which everyone would be like him, that is honest and unarmed would be tolerable, but this is an unreal world. In the real world the armed exist, they build Auschwitz, and the honest and unarmed clear the road for them; therefore every German must answer for Auschwitz, indeed every man, and after Auschwitz it is no longer permissable to be unarmed (p. 223).

Despair, Suicide and the Crisis of the Twentieth Century

Even after the repeated warnings of Primo Levi and other survivors much of the world appears to remain unarmed, unhearing and uncaring. So, forty-two years after surviving Auschwitz Primo Levi plunged down the stairwell of his apartment building in Turin, Italy. Having devoted his life to the preservation of memory and the fight against evil, Primo Levi could not help but despair as he watched the events of the late twentieth century. Robert J. Lifton has in fact written that suicide may well, in the twentieth century with its massive destructive forces, be a "quest for the future," a search for meaning born of despair.[10] According to Lifton: "In despair, one feels unable to maintain or envision any larger human connections or significance--any ongoing link in the great chain of being."[11] Despair is fed by "radically negative expectations of the future" and the person experiencing despair may perceive that the only way to create a future is by taking their own life.[12]

As I noted earlier, Levi began to signal his increasingly negative expectations in the moving conclusion to *If Not Now, When?* That he was haunted by the past and anguished by negative expectations for the future is most clearly revealed in *The Drowned and the Saved*.[13] Levi's goal, as he states, is "to answer the most urgent question, the question which torments all those who have happened to read our accounts: How much of the concentration camp world is dead and will not return, like slavery and the dueling code? How much is back or is coming back? What can each of us do so that in this world pregnant with threats at least this threat will be nullified?" (*The Drowned*, p. 21). And when he casts his gaze upon the technology and efficiency of destruction massed in the hands of the modern nation state, his vision is bleak because he sees that the "pressure that a modern totalitarian state can exercise over the individual is frightful" (*The Drowned*, p. 29). Given this reality, Levi pushes forward to ask how secure we, at this moment, may be when

> We have been told, and there's no reason to doubt it, that for every human being on the planet a quantity of nuclear explosives is stored equal to three or four tons of TNT. If even only 1 percent of it were used there would immediately be tens of millions dead, and frightening genetic damage to the entire human species, indeed to all life on earth, with the exception perhaps of the insects (*The Drowned*, pp. 165-166).

Confronted with this horrible possibility, face to face with the suggestion that, as the physicist Isidor Rabi put it "the nations are now lined up like people before the ovens of Auschwitz, while we are trying to make the ovens more efficient,"[14] how could a survivor of the original Auschwitz not despair for the future? And what, Levi asked, are we all doing, any one of us, to prevent the horrible repetition?

> So then? Are today's fears more or less founded than the fears of that time? When it comes to the future, we are just as blind as our fathers. Swiss and Swedes have their anti-nuclear shelters, but what will they find when they come out into the open? There are Polynesia, New Zealand, Tierra del Fuego, the Antarctic: perhaps they will remain unharmed. Obtaining a passport and entry visa is much easier than it was then, so why aren't we going? Why aren't we leaving our country? Why aren't we fleeing "before"? (*The Drowned*, p. 166).

How fitting to turn back on *all* of us the questions so often asked of the Jews, "Why did you stay in Germany?" "Why did you not fight back or resist?" "Why did you not die as a martyr instead of living to write words we do not wish to hear?"

And so Primo Levi died because, as he wrote: "If we had to and were able to suffer the sufferings of everyone, we could not live" (*The Drowned*, p. 56). Left behind is a chronicle of memory, a landscape peopled with the most remarkable characters. Levi introduces us to these people and invites us into their lives and into his life. He provides an example, but he also leaves us with a vision and a warning. A vision of kindliness and compassion, of humanity, and a warning to be considered seriously:

> Few countries can be considered immune to a future tide of violence generated by intolerance, lust for power, economic difficulties, religious or political fanaticism, and racialist attritions. It is therefore necessary to sharpen our senses, distrust the prophets, the enchanters, those who speak and write "beautiful words" unsupported by intelligent reasons (p. 200).

As I once again read Levi's words I find myself growing ever sadder. Sad because I will never again be introduced to the people in Primo Levi's mind. Sad because I can no longer look forward to such words of wisdom and humanity. Sad because he is dead. Even though I never met Primo Levi, I felt infinitely better knowing that he existed. Now, I wonder how? How such a person could survive Auschwitz? How he could "cope" with life after Auschwitz--with the continuing destructive evil of this century? How he could write so humanely about his fellows? Did he really exist or did we have to create him in order to provide us with the exception that enables us to grasp at straws of hope? Was he our Lorenzo? I miss him but I know I will never forget what I have read and never ever forget the last paragraph in *Moments of Reprieve* which is repeated in *The Drowned and the Saved*:

> Like Rumkowski, we too are so dazzled by power and money as to forget our essential fragility, forget that all of us are in the ghetto, that the ghetto is fenced in, that beyond the fence stand the lords of death, and not far away the train is waiting (p. 172 and p. 69).

REFERENCES

Primo Levi. (1987). *Moments of Reprieve.* Penguin Books.

_____. (1988). *The Drowned and the Saved.* Summit Books.

ENDNOTES

[1]Terrence Des Pres, *The Survivor* (New York: Pocket Books, 1977, p. 3.

Indeed, Roger Smith portrays the twentieth century as "an age of politically sanctioned mass murder, of collective, premeditated death intended to serve the ends of the state. It is an age of genocide in which 60 million men, women, and children...have had their lives taken because the state thought this desirable." Please see: Roger Smith, "Human Destructiveness and Politics: The Twentieth Century As An Age of Genocide," in Isidor Walliman and Michael Dobkowski (eds.), *Genocide and the Modern Age* (New York: Greenwood Press, 1987), p. 21.

[2]In particular see the series of essays in: Robert Jay Lifton, *The Future of Immortality* New York: Basic Books, 1987).

[3]See: Elie Wiesel, *One Gereration After* (New York : Pocket Books, 1978), pp. 94-95.

[4]Irving Howe, "Primo Levi: An appreciation." Introduction to Primo Levi, *If Not Now, When?* (N. Y.: Penguin Books, 1985), pp. 3-16. Howe draws his information about Levi from Levi's memoir, "Beyond Survival," translated into English in *Prooftexts* no. 4, 1984 and from H. Stuart Hughes, *Prisoners of Hope* (Cambridge: Harvard University Press, 1983).

[5]Howe, *op. cit.*, p. 12.

[6]Primo Levi, "Afterward: The Author's Answers to His Readers' Questions." in Primo Levi, *Survival in Auschwitz* and *The Reawakening* (N. Y.: Summit Books, 1986), pp. 375-397.

[7](N. Y.: Summit Books, 1978, English translation, 1986).

[8](N. Y.: Penguin Book, 1986).

[9](N. Y.: Schocken Books, 1984).

[10]Robert J. Lifton, *op cit.*, p. 5 and 224.

[11]*Ibid.*

[12]*Ibid.*, p. 225

[13](N. Y.: Summit Boks, 1988).

[14]Quoted in Gregg Herken, *Counsels of War* (N. Y.: Oxford University Press, 1987), p. 346.

ON BEING A SURVIVOR

EMANUEL TANAY

I. REFUGEE OR SURVIVOR?

In February, 1986 I spoke to a high school class in Ferndale, Michigan about my experiences as a Holocaust survivor. After my talk, one of the students wanted to touch me, and others followed. They viewed me as if I were a visitor from another planet.

We survivors are uniquely unique--to borrow a phrase from Alice and Roy Eckhardt.[1] Not only did we succeed in remaining alive, we are the last living members of an extinct culture. In November, 1987 I attended a performance of the Jewish Theater in Warsaw. Jewish songs and dialogue were delivered in Yiddish by Polish actors. Earphones were available at every seat to provide simultaneous translation. I was the only person in the audience who did not need them. I felt like a prehistoric reptile visiting a dinosaur museum.

The Holocaust has been studied extensively, but the survival of individual Jews has received less attention. We do not even have terminology to describe Jews who remained alive after the Holocaust.

Living through the Holocaust took many forms. Some of us held on tenaciously to life in death camps. Others smelled the dangers early and emigrated before the killers began their grisly work. Some ran away from ghettos or jumped from death trains, and a few escaped from Auschwitz or Treblinka. Some were hidden in barns, attics or holes dug in the ground. Others assumed false identities and lived as Christians.

Some of us were deported to Siberia from Poland and managed to endure the hardships of that desolate land. Survivors of Treblinka, Stuthof and Bergen-Belsen are unlike those of Theresienstadt. Living on Aryan papers and living in death camps were opposite ends of the spectrum. Concentration camp inmates acquired a distinct identity. They called themselves Katzetniks.

"He survived in hiding," is applied to those who remained out of sight, concealed in a shelter, and those who lived on false papers, hiding their identity. These two experiences have little in common.

There are various groups within the community of survivors. The mode of survival is part of a survivor's identity. Anyone wishing to understand survivors must recognize these differences. It is true that the grotesque diversity of our experiences cannot be adequately reflected in language. However, this is no reason to bury us in a semantic mass grave.

Terrence Des Pres, in his outstanding book *The Survivor: An Anatomy of Life in the Death Camps*, refers in the same paragraph to Eli Cohen and Bruno Bettelheim as survivors. Cohen survived a death camp, Bettelheim left Germany in 1939. At that time Buchenwald was a terrible place, but it was light years away from Auschwitz.[2]

Failure to differentiate between survivors and refugees was illustrated by a paper presented at the International Scholars' Conference in Oxford, England in 1988. Judith Hassan, of the Jewish Welfare Board of London, described two case histories: The first client, Mrs. H., was identified as a refugee. She had come to England from Germany to escape Nazi persecution during which her mother had been killed. The second client, Mrs. A., was a woman in her 80's. Of her the case history relates, "In her attempts to understand these feelings, it emerged that this survivor felt increasingly badly about not having done enough to save her family who were killed in a concentration camp." We are then told that Mrs. A. "... came to this country on a domestic permit just prior to the war." It would be more accurate to describe Mrs. H. as a survivor and Mrs. A. as a refugee. Both were victims of Nazi persecution who suffered the loss of family members due to the Holocaust.

An encyclopedia of World War II has the following entry:

Fermi, Enrico (1901-1954): Italian-born nuclear physicist. He won the Nobel Prize for physics in 1938, but became a fugitive from Hitler because he was Jewish. Fermi was instrumental in research in the U.S. Manhattan Project that resulted in the atomic bomb.[3]

Was Fermi a fugitive? A refugee? A survivor? Was he a Jew or Jewish? Was he an Italian or Italian-born? Did he become an American or merely an American citizen?

In January, 1952 I disembarked the U.S. Navy ship General Blechford in the port of New York and was welcomed by American social workers as a "refugee." When I had stepped aboard the same ship in Hamburg, Germany, I was called a "displaced person." The United States Immigration Service gave me a card designating me as a "resident alien." The old immigrants called me a "greenhorn." I called myself a "survivor."

Survivor of what? The term Holocaust has gained widespread acceptance and I have little choice but to call myself a Holocaust survivor.

What is survival? The American Heritage Dictionary defines survival as "the act of surviving or the fact of having survived." To survive is "to remain alive or in existence; continue life or activity." Black's Standard Law Dictionary, 5th Edition, defines a survivor as "one who survives another; one who outlives another; one who lives beyond some happening; one or two or more persons who lives after the death of the other or others." According to this definition one becomes a survivor because some significant other died. That is not what we have in mind in the context of the Holocaust.

Experientially, a survivor is someone who has had a near-death experience. Individuals who undergo such exposure are set apart. The return-from-death theme is found in many religions. It occurs in the Judeo-Christian tradition and in Islam. Apocalyptic literature portrays the encounter with death as a life-altering event. Clinical experience with persons who have had near-death experience confirms this view. In *Otherworld Journeys*, Carol Zaleski writes:

It is an axiom of medieval vision literature that those who return from another world are never the same again. As we saw in Chapter Two, Drythelm revives from death with the conviction that 'from now on I must live not according to my old habits, but in a much different manner.'[4]

The survivor's dilemma is the imperative to bear witness to the otherworld experience and the wish to restore life as it was. The life of Elie Wiesel is the survivor's dream and nightmare. Wiesel's immersion in the Holocaust represents the fulfillment of the mission to bear witness. But the survivor also dreads the reminders of his terrible past. He is torn between his sacral duty to tend the memory of the dead and the need to rebuild his life.

I was astonished upon being introduced to Elie Wiesel's wife as I had not expected that this "messenger of the dead" would have a family. In religious literature those who have returned from the dead lead a life devoid of worldly pursuits.

A definition of a survivor should have situational and psychic dimensions. Without exposure to the danger of being killed a person is not a survivor. All survivors of near-death experiences suffer from what R. J. Lifton and E. Olsen call the "death imprint"--intense and unforgettable images of death and destruction.

A *survivor of the Holocaust* is a person defined by the Nazis as a Jew and marked for extermination for that reason. This individual faced the actual danger of being killed but remained alive until liberation.

A *Jewish refugee from Nazi persecution* is a person designated by the Nazis to be a Jew who fled from Nazi control before genocidal measures were instituted. Bruno Bettelheim and Elie Wiesel were both inmates of Nazi concentration camps. Wiesel is a survivor, Bettelheim is a refugee. Bettelheim could not be a survivor of genocide, according to the above definition; he left Germany before the genocidal plan became operational. Individual German Jews were at risk of being killed by the Nazis from the very beginning of the Nazi movement. The murders committed during Kristallnacht were harbingers of the Holocaust but were not part of the genocide.

In my definition of a refugee I stressed the act of removing oneself from persecution. A significant number of European Jews avoided being killed by the Nazis without taking deliberate evasive action. In 1939 many Polish Jews found themselves under the control of the Soviets as the result of the secret agreement between Stalin and Hitler which placed the eastern part of Poland under Soviet occupation. During the short-lived German-Polish War many Jews from western Poland escaped the advancing German Army by moving to the east. After the collapse of Poland some of these Jews registered with the Soviets for return to their homes which were under German occupation. The Soviet authorities deported these Jews to Siberia. This turned out to be the biggest "rescue" operation of Polish Jews during World War II.

Some Jews eluded Soviet deportation and returned to General Gouvernement, the name given to German-occupied Poland. Shortly thereafter these Jews faced genocidal measures. Many of the Jews who survived in Russia returned to Poland in 1945 and then left Poland for the Western-occupied zone of Germany.

At the end of the war the Allies established displaced persons camps in Western Germany. These facilities provided temporary housing for the homeless people liberated from Nazi oppressions. To be admitted to a displaced persons camp in 1945 one had to state that one had been liberated by American or British forces. For a brief period there was an effort to repatriate victims of Nazi persecution to their native countries. Jews who survived on false papers in Eastern Europe and who had come to the Western zone of occupation in 1945 had to declare that they had been liberated in a concentration camp. A Polish Jew who survived in Russia had to make the same false claim. Thus, statistics on survival in concentration camps are distorted by these initial administrative requirements. To this day we do not have a term describing those who were saved by having been deported to Siberia. They do not fit the above definitions of refugee or survivor.

II. WHY DID THEY NOT FIGHT?

The will to live was not the only reason for my survival. I wanted to defeat the enemy's purpose. There was an element of spite in my efforts. I must live because they wanted me dead--was my slogan. The wish to live was a declaration of war. Liberation did not bring joy, it merely removed me from death row. I was alive, but around me there were ruins and mountains of ashes. The stench of death was everywhere. The danger of being killed by the Germans was replaced by the risk of starving to death or being killed by Poles. When some months later I ended up in the U.S. zone of occupied Germany, safe and free of hunger, I became depressed. At long last I could mourn. I spent weeks in bombed out Munich lying on a U.S. Army cot. I slept, ate and cried. There was no one to help me deal with my losses. There was no one who said, "I am glad you survived." They were too busy asking why I and my fellow survivors did not offer armed resistance.

The expectation of armed resistance represents lack of comprehension and empathy for Jewish victims of the Nazi extermination effort. It is a psychosocial equivalent of anthropomorphism in the study of animal behavior. Armed resistance was not appropriate; it was a suicidal gesture which played into the hands of the Nazis.

A war with the enemy implies a hope of victory. Winston Churchill, upon his election as Prime Minister of Britain, told the House of Commons:

> I have nothing to offer you but blood, toil, tears, and sweat....You ask what is our aim? I can answer in one word: it is victory, victory at all costs, victory in spite of terror, victory however long and hard the road may be....[5]

Confronted with the Nazi machine of extermination, we, the Jews of Europe, did not have the option to wage war. Our only hope to achieve victory over the lethal enemy was to preserve life. Every one of us represents a victory. We are living symbols of the will to live which remains the only hope for the survival of mankind in an age of total annihilation.

Winston Churchill was the mastermind of the great escape at Dunkirk. Was the evacuation of troops at Dunkirk a shameful chapter in the history of British armed forces or a heroic rescue operation? I believe "Operation Dynamo," as the Dunkirk evacuation was called, is a glorious chapter in the history of the British armed forces. In the House of Commons on June 4, 1940 Churchill did not speak of how many Germans were killed but rather of the purpose of the Dunkirk operation:

> We must be very careful not to assign to this deliverance the attributes of victory. Wars are not won by evacuation. But there was a victory inside this deliverance which should be noted. It was gained by the Air Force....This was a great trial of strength between the British and the German Air Forces. Can you conceive a greater objective of the Germans in their air than to make evacuation from these

beaches impossible and to sink all these ships which were displayed almost to the extent of thousands? Could there have been an objective of greater military importance and significance for the whole purpose of the war than this? They tried hard, and they were beaten back; they were frustrated in their task. We got the army away...."[6]

"They did not do something which they should have done," was the charge directed at survivors. The underlying assumption is that the victims of Nazi persecution had the ability to choose something other than trying to keep alive. On closer examination the accusation of passivity turns out to be a projection of guilt.

L. H. Gann wrote in the January, 1989 issue of *The American Spectator* about his memories of witnessing the burning of a synagogue in his home town of Mainz on November 10, 1938 (Kristallnacht):

> Kristallnacht was a German as well as a Jewish catastrophe. This is how it seemed to that crowd of onlookers who stared in bewilderment at the burning temple....Certainly among the bystanders in Mainz who watched the temple burn there was no merriment. Far from it! It was terror by order from above. The crowd, as I remember it, was not only embarrassed but incredulous and filled with gloomy forebodings.[7]

This image conveys the passivity of Germany and the world at large, and yet Gann recalls that it was he and other "refugees" who, upon arrival in England, were accused of passivity:

> How often did I hear, in England, observations such as the following: 'You refugees whine and snivel. But why did you not defend your freedom when you had a chance? Now you tell us hard-luck stories and expect the British Army to do your fighting for you. The British Army has better things to do.' Such remarks were addressed to me not only as a Jew but also as a German. I had no answer then. I have found none since.[8]

The answer is simple. The Jewish victims of Nazi persecution did not have the option to "defend their freedom."

In 1942 there was more knowledge in America and England about Nazi plans and efforts to exterminate Jews than was known in my town of Miechow and other similar ghettos which were about to be annihilated. We had no knowledge of the dangers and no resources with which to fight.

Yael Danieli, studying survivor families in New York, categorized these families as either victims or fighters. Thus, being a victim and a fighter seemed mutually exclusive to this Israeli sociologist. Were the British and French troops waiting in orderly lines on the beach at Dunkirk victims or fighters? Many men stood for hours in water up to their chins waiting to be taken aboard rescue vessels while Germans were attacking. Is the fight for survival less admirable than the fight to cause death?

Nazi values contributed to the reaction to the Holocaust victims. It has taken decades to gain perspective. The victims have been blamed for what they did not do and were not honored for what they have done.

The survivors achieved what seemed unreachable--their own survival. Most of them succeeded in rebuilding their shattered lives and some became parents. The children of survivors are living monuments to the indomitable spirit of the survivors. The survivors and their children have risen out of the ashes--which, in this context, is unfortunately not merely a metaphor.

Historians of the Holocaust often fail to differentiate between collective and individual behavior. Raul Hilberg, in a chapter entitled "The Victims," writes:

> When confronted by a force, a group can react in five ways: by resistance, by an attempt to alleviate or nullify the threat (the undoing reaction), by evasion, by paralysis, or by compliance. Let us consider each in turn.[9]

He then provides a mixture of examples dealing with both collective and individual behavior. The responses of the Jewish social structure and the reactions of individuals are related but obviously are not identical.

Some historians make psychological statements based upon sociological data. The life course and behavior of individuals in ghettos and concentration camps was not determined exclusively by historical and sociological phenomena. Individual psychology of perpetrators and victims of the Holocaust played a critical role in victimization and survival. Hilberg writes:

> Compliance is a course of action that becomes increasingly drastic in a destruction process. It is one thing to comply with an order to register property but quite another to obey orders in front of a grave. The two actions are part of the same habit. The Jews who registered their property were also

the ones who lined up to be killed. The Jews who lined up on the killing site were the ones who had registered their property. Yet, these two actions are very different in their effects. Submission is altogether more burdensome in its last stages than in its beginning, for as one goes on, more and more is lost. Finally, in the supreme moment of crisis the primeval tendency to resist aggression breaks to the surface. Resistance then becomes an obstacle to compliance, just as compliance is an obstacle to resistance. In the Jewish case the cooperation reaction was the stronger one until the end.[10]

This is an example of do-it-yourself psychology which explains complex adaptive mechanisms with the concept of "habit."

III. THE SURVIVOR AS ANTIHERO

My experience as an adolescent victim of Nazi oppression acquired new meaning after I was liberated. I discovered that we had not been rescued. Our freedom was merely a by-product of the defeat of our oppressors. Worse than that, our survival had to be justified and explained. In 1945, at gunpoint on a Budapest street, I had to explain to a Russian soldier that I survived by my wits and courage and not by collaboration with the Germans. He took my leather coat and let me go. Some of my underground friends were not so lucky. They were among those deported to Russia.

In the same year, at the age of 16, I travelled from liberated Budapest to my home town of Miechow, Poland in search of my father and other relatives and friends. To say I travelled is an overstatement. I had to make my way across war-torn Europe without funds, food or means of transportation. I walked, rode on the roofs of military trains, hid in boxcars, and climbed into military trucks. Upon reaching Miechow, I was told by family friends that surviving Jews were not being treated kindly. A number of them had been killed by the Polish population. I was cautioned to stick to the large cities.

Eight years later, in the United States, I was being interviewed by Dr. Louis Steinberg, Superintendent of Elgin State Hospital, for the position of psychiatric resident. Also present were Dr. Daniel Haffron, Assistant Superintendent, and Dr. Alan Liberman, Clinical Director. All three were American Jews. I was then an intern at the prestigious Michael Reese

Hospital in Chicago. A few questions dealt with my training and interest in psychiatry, but many were asked about my survival. I explained that I had survived on false papers. Dr. Steinberg asked casually, "What papers did you falsify to be accepted as an intern at Michael Reese Hospital?"

A few years after this encounter, Dr. Mina Emch, a grand lady of American psychoanalysis and my supervisor in psychotherapy, encouraged me to apply to the Chicago Analytic Institute for training. She recommended my acceptance wholeheartedly. I was interviewed by three analysts who questioned me, mostly about my survival, and who concluded that my ability to control anxiety made me unfit for psychoanalysis. I was not accepted. After many years of psychoanalysis for anxiety, I was encouraged by my analyst, Dr. Harry August, to apply to the Michigan Psychoanalytic Institute. The senior interviewer spent most of the time discussing my survival. He told me candidly that someone who survived the Nazi ordeal had to be shrewd and unscrupulous and therefore unsuitable to become a psychoanalyst. He emphasized that he admired me and that there was nothing personal in his comments. This man was a Jew who had been brought to the United States from Poland as a child.

The Russian soldier on the street in Budapest and the Jewish psychiatrists in America displayed in different ways their ambivalence toward survivors.

Jews survived in death camps, on death marches, hidden in "bunkers," or living as Christians on the Aryan side. Some survived by living in forests and others formed or joined partisan units. Survivors, in their autobiographical accounts, vary in the attention they devote to the survival process. They rarely acknowledge their own contribution to being alive. Some accounts begin with liberation while others barely mention the post-liberation period.

Over the years I have interviewed hundreds of survivors and have read many of their autobiographical accounts. The moment of liberation was rarely remembered as a joyful experience. It was an end of one form of suffering and the beginning of another. It took many years for survivors to be able to again experience the joy of living.

Primo Levi's book, *Survival In Auschwitz: The Nazi Assault On Humanity*, was originally published under the title *Se Questo è Un Uomo (If This Is A Man)*. Why was the title changed? Presumably Primo Levi agreed to it. The final chapter, entitled "The Story of Ten Days," describes the final phase of the struggle for survival of the men in the "Infektionsabteilung" of the camp. Levi recounts the superhuman efforts of a small group to maintain life under grotesque circumstances. The story ends on January 27, 1945, the day of liberation. The liberation itself is not described. Why not? Was it too painful? Too anticlimactic? Too disappointing?

Professor Michael Lustigman, in his paper "Reading Ashes: The Holocaust and the Question of Beginning," quotes a survivor:

> How can I possibly say how I survived? ... Three days before liberation Hessler came into the barracks and I was sick in bed, I could not go to work and the kapo even told me to stay in bed. And Hessler asks: 'Why are you in bed?' I told him that I was sick and the kapo said the same. Hessler's response: 'If I see you here tomorrow, you are dead, I'll shoot you down like a dog.' Two days later, he was in jail, it was liberation already....[11]

Why did a kapo tell him to stay in bed? Why did Hessler depart from the routine of shooting a sick Jew? These are questions I would ask. Did the sick inmate contribute to the solicitude of a kapo and the deviance of an S.S. man?

Samuel Pisar, in his book *Of Blood and Hope* published in 1981, describes his survival as a youngster in Auschwitz and his fabulous success as an international lawyer and diplomat in the United States. The book is an inspiring tribute to the human spirit. Out of destruction and degradation we see the creative regeneration of a person. Sam is a survivor. He was able to adapt to life in the man-made hell of the extermination camps and in the post-war world. The Auschwitz kid and the Paris diplomat are found between the covers of the same autobiography.

The book has three central figures: Niko, Sam and Ben. Niko is most able to adapt to the psychotic world of the extermination camp but was unable to succeed in post-war "normal" life. Sam barely survived the camp but became a great success in the post-war world. Ben falls somewhere between the two extremes. Sam not only survived the Holocaust, he survived the liberation. He became bigger than life, a one-man tidal wave of vitality, roaming the globe in quest of success, understanding and peace. He describes his suffering during the Holocaust, but there is almost nothing said about his anguish, nightmares and depression in the post-Holocaust period. Did Sam survive without Survivor Syndrome? I doubt it.

I understand Sam because we have much in common. He and I are successful victims. My Holocaust experiences were not as severe as his. My post-Holocaust achievements are not as great as his, but there are significant similarities. We are the same age and were born only miles apart. After the war we were in the same places. No doubt we encountered each other in Landsberg, Germany where we both spent time immediately after liberation. We have aunts and uncles in Australia who supported us in the post-war period. We pursued professional careers with success and maintained interest in our dreadful past. Sam has written his book about the Holocaust, and I have been thinking of doing it for the last 40 years. Sam believes that his major achievement is a scholarly book he has written on political science. I disagree. Many another brilliant lawyer or political scientist could have written it. Only Sam could have written *Of Blood and Hope*.

To remain alive as a Jew during World War II required courage to endure. Survival was a personal achievement and a triumph over the mortal enemy. Surviving the Holocaust was a miracle which happened only to those who pursued it.

To say "I am a hero" evokes the rather unheroic image of Idi Amin who so described himself. When I was first so characterized by my analyst, my response was indignation. Like most survivors I felt that I was spared by accident, the result of luck or fate. I understand why Simon Schochet began his book with the seemingly incongruous quotation:

And the Lord spoke unto the fish
And it vomited Jonah upon the dry land.[12]

We survivors could not accept credit for our survival because we suffered from survivor guilt. If my own ingenuity rescued my mother, my sister, myself, and others, why did I not save my father from being killed? Realistically this question is easily answered. Emotionally, it remains a burden to this day. Every survivor struggles with this burden. We do not feel like heroes. We felt more like villains. The world did not welcome us as heroes; on the contrary, we met with reproaches. "Why did you not fight? Why did you not die with honor? What dishonorable deeds did you commit to remain alive?" These were the questions that greeted us.

On January 20, 1945 I was liberated from Nazi oppression. The Nazi law which had consigned me to the status of vermin fit only for extermination was no longer a threat to my life. Suddenly I was a free human being. January 20th is a memorable day in my life. We traditionally commemorate birthdays, anniversaries and similar momentous occasions. Forty years later I decided to celebrate the day of my liberation.

In January of 1985 I sent out printed invitations to my friends asking them to join me in a "celebration of my liberation." The first page of the invitation depicted an eagle with the word "Freedom" in its claws. Underneath bold letters proclaimed "40 Years of Freedom."

My friends knew my history well and yet a number of them misunderstood the purpose of the gathering. One friend asked if I was observing the 40th anniversary of my arrival in the United States. Another commented, "January 20th is not the day when the war in Europe ended." My family and close friends know the date of my birthday, but they were uninformed about the day when I was reborn. Some of them did not even realize that I am a born-again human being, having been declared non-human in my childhood.

Why did it take 40 years to decide that the day of my liberation should be a day for reflection and festivity? The answer is simple. It took 40 years to fully understand the meaning of this day. I have always commemorated the end of World War II as the day when mankind was freed from the Nazi menace. I have shared with countless millions admiration and gratitude to the countries and individuals who made victory of the Axis powers possible. Without their sacrifices civilization as we know it would not have endured, and we, the victims of Nazism, would never have known liberation.

It took four decades for me to understand that my liberation had required not only the sacrifices of millions but also my own efforts. My liberation was a combination of deliverance and personal achievement. The liberators and the survivors both deserve to be celebrated. It took ten years of psychoanalysis to understand this simple fact and an additional fifteen years to be able to celebrate it.

Throughout the war there were many episodes when my own efforts saved me from certain death and yet I chose to believe that I was a passive recipient of rescue by others. This is typical for nearly all survivors.

Guilt is the survivor's inevitable companion. I could not have survived without the aid of many self-sacrificing people who extended a helping hand. The heroic helpers took great risks and are themselves survivors. Helpers, like survivors, have mixed feelings about the dreadful past. We all have reasons to feel both proud of our achievements and guilty for not having done more for victims of oppression. Avoiding memories does not solve the conflict or diminish the pain. Celebrating a joyful occasion strengthens life-enhancing forces.

I am grateful to my rescuers and healers. But I am also mindful of my contributions to my survival and to the good life that followed.

My liberation celebration was a great success. It took place at the renowned Bayview Yacht Club which looks out on the Detroit River and Lake St. Clair. It was a beautiful, sunny winter day. Jan Wojnar, a Pole who survived in Saxenhausen Concentration Camp, played the piano. Large logs burned in the big fireplace. Good food and wine were served. Bayview is a beautiful place, and I was its first Jewish member.

ENDNOTES

[1]Eckhardt, Alice L. and A. Roy, *Long Night's Journey Into Day* (Detroit: Wayne State University Press, 1988), p. 13.

[2]Des Pres, Terrence, *The Survivor: An Anatomy of Life in the Death Camps* (New York: Washington Square Press, 1988).

[3]McCombs, Don and Worth, Fred L., *World War II Super Facts* (New York: Warner Books, 1983), p. 183.

[4]Zaleski, Carol, *Otherworld Journeys* (Oxford University Press, 1987), p. 1.

[5]Maule, Henry, *The Great Battles of World War II* (London: Hamlyn Publishing Group, Ltd., 1972) quoting Winston Churchill.

[6]*Ibid.*

[7]Gann, L. H. in *The American Spectator* (January, 1989).

[8]*Ibid.*

[9]Hilberg, Raul, *The Destruction of the European Jews*, 3 vols. (New York: Holmes & Meier Publishers, Inc., 1985), III, p. 1030.

[10]*Ibid.*, p. 1039.

[11]Lustigman, Michael, "Reading Ashes: The Holocaust and the Question of Beginning" (Pergamon Press, 1988), p. 1105.

[12]Schochet, Simon, *Feldafing* (Vancouver: November House, 1983).

JEWISH RESCUE DURING THE HOLOCAUST

Nechama Tec

What did the rescuing of Jews mean during World War II? Who was likely to engage in such life-threatening behavior?

Till recently Holocaust literature paid little attention to the selfless protection of others. This prolonged silence is not surprising. World War II was dominated by extreme suffering and devastation. The compassion and help that were a part of this cruel environment were atypical, easily overshadowed by the enormity of the Nazi crimes. It is only expected that those who studied these events would focus first on the typical experiences rather than the rare exception. Only when the basic story had been told, would chroniclers begin to notice the less visible, the less obvious; namely, the selflessness and compassion that were expressed in the readiness of some few to die for others. Once noticed, however, the contrast between the cruelty of the time and the ability of some to rise above it to save the helpless underlies the nobility of their deeds.[1]

For more than ten years, I have been conducting research about compassion, self-sacrifice, and help, particularly as these touch on Jewish rescue by Christians. My research has concentrated on Poland, a country designated by the Nazis as the center of Jewish annihilation; most European Jews were sent there to die. It is also a place to which the Nazis introduced their measures of destruction ruthlessly and without regard to human cost. I believe that as the center of Jewish annihilation, Poland provides the key to an understanding of the Holocaust in general and to the rescuing of Jews in particular. As a country in which the Holocaust drama was played out in the most gruesome ways, Poland can teach us about similar but less extreme cases.[2]

Within this cruel environment, selfless protection of Jews seems to fit into the definition of altruistic behavior. And so, bypassing the many definitions of this concept, I rely on one that describes altruism as behavior "carried out to benefit another without anticipation of rewards from external sources."[3] When dealing with the rescue of Jews, a distinction between two types of altruism seems appropriate: normative and autonomous.

Normative altruism refers to helping behavior demanded, supported, and rewarded by society. In contrast, autonomous altruism refers to selfless help that is neither expected nor rewarded by society. Autonomous altruism may be opposed by society and at times even involve grave risks to the helper.

Society demands that a mother should donate a kidney to her child, that a child should aid an ailing parent. However, society does not ask its members to sacrifice their lives for strangers, particularly not for those whom society despises. For Christians, then, saving Jews was an act beyond and above the call of duty, in that it put the actor in conflict with society's expected values. And so, then, those who without regard for external rewards risked their lives to protect Jews belong to the category of autonomous altruists.[4]

In 1978, research on Jewish rescue by Christian Poles took me to the Jewish Historical Institute in Warsaw. There I examined the unpublished testimonies of Jews who survived by living illegally among Christians, and Poles who were willing to risk their lives to save them. As I studied these cases, I wanted to know who the rescuers and the rescued were, what did the Jews receive, and what did the Christians give them, what was the relationship between the rescuer and the rescued. All along, I had no problems differentiating between the Jews and the Christians, the rescuer and the rescued. However, when I came upon Oswald Rufeisen's case, I was not sure whether to treat him as a rescuer or as a Jewish survivor.

Oswald Rufeisen, a Jewish youth of seventeen, when World War II began, survived the war by pretending to be part Polish and part German.

Through an unusual set of circumstances he became an interpreter and a secretary to the head of a German gendarmerie in Mir, a small town in Western Belorussia.

With the acceptance of this position came a determination to help all prospective Nazi victims. Oswald took advantage of the opportunities offered to him by his official position and saved an entire Belorussian village, a large number of Russian partisans and hundreds of Jews. He armed Jews in the ghetto Mir and arranged a ghetto breakout. Later, denounced by a Jew he ran away, found shelter in a Polish convent, in Mir, next door to the Gendarmerie. In the convent Oswald converted to Catholicism but after 16 months left to join the Russian partisans. After the war Oswald became a Carmelite monk and a priest. Yet, he continues to identify himself as a Jew and a Zionist.

When in 1958 he came to settle in Israel he challenged the Israeli Law of Return because he wanted to be officially identified as a Jew. He lost his case but was offered Israeli citizenship.

A Carmelite monk, a priest, and an ardent Zionist, he lives in the Carmelite monastery Stella Maris in Haifa and devotes his life to bridging the gap between Judaism and Christianity and to charitable work.

Not only does Oswald fit into the category of rescuer and survivor, but he even seemed to qualify for the Yad Vashem distinction of the righteous.

Yad Vashem was established in 1953 in Jerusalem as a memorial to European Jews who perished during World War II. This memorial also pays tribute to Christians who, during this period, saved Jews. The formal Hebrew title for these saviors is *Hasidei Umot Ha-Olam*, literally the Righteous Ones of the Nations of the World. In English they are called righteous Christians or righteous Gentiles. Attached to the Yad Vashem institution is a special committee that deals with requests for this distinction. Applications come directly to Yad Vashem or indirectly through a foreign embassy. It is difficult to receive this title without a request from Jewish beneficiaries; survivors usually petition the committee to honor their protectors.[5]

Because Oswald Rufeisen's actions are well-documented, I asked Mordechai Paldiel, director for the Department of the Righteous at Yad

Vashem, why they did not recognize Oswald as one of the righteous ones. Paldiel explained that this honor extends only to non-Jews and that as a Jew Oswald had an obligation to protect his fellow Jews. Implied in this answer is the distinction between normative and autonomous altruism, with Oswald assigned to the normative category.

But not all those who had benefited from Oswald's help were Jewish. As noted, he had rescued a Belorussian village from destruction and countless numbers of Russian P.O.W.s and partisans. Shouldn't he be rewarded for that? Yad Vashem has no special provisions for honoring Jews who had risked their lives for others. As far as I know, no other ethnic group or nation offers distinctions to outsiders who were risking their lives for its people. Israel seems to be the only country that has provisions for such recognitions.

Intrigued by Oswald Rufeisen's testimony, I had to set it aside and continue with my research on the rescuers and the rescued. Only later, when I began to concentrate on Oswald Rufeisen's life, did I become aware that many of the Jewish survivors in my study, though in less dramatic ways than Oswald, had also offered aid to others.[6] When I examined them earlier, I had overlooked their acts of kindness. Why? Did I, because the Jews were the main targets of Nazi measures of destruction, expect them to concentrate on their own survival? Did I assume that self-preservation took precedence over the need or desire to protect others?

These assumption make sense. And yet, some of the survivors in my study, while struggling for their own lives, were also devoting themselves to the protection of others. Did their concern about others mean that they were defying the principle of self-preservation? How did their help compare to the aid offered by Christian rescuers?

To rescue Jews, Poles had to overcome several barriers. Foremost among them were the Nazi policies of Jewish annihilation. In Poland, these policies were introduced early and with a high degree of ruthlessness.

Among the various measures aimed at Jewish extermination was a 1941 decree that made any unauthorized move out of a ghetto a crime punishable by death. The same punishment applied to Poles who were helping Jews move into the forbidden Christian world, the so-called Aryan side.[7] This law was strongly enforced, and executions of Christians and Jews followed.[8] The names of the executed were widely publicized. Moreover, the Nazis followed the principle of collective responsibility, which meant that the same punishment applied to the family of the arrested Poles. There are many cases on record where entire families of Poles were murdered, including infants, only because one of them had protected Jews.[9]

In addition, the cultural climate of Poland was antagonistic toward Jews. That is, the pervasive Polish anti-Semitism became an obstacle to Jewish rescue. Those eager to save Jews knew that by following their inclinations they would be inviting the censure of their fellow countrymen.

Though an integral part of the Polish culture, not all forms of anti-Semitism were explicit. The form I call diffuse cultural anti-Semitism remained vague and free-floating. In contrast to direct and explicit anti-Jewish images and actions, this vague and yet all-encompassing sort of anti-Semitism has been taken for granted. It attributes to the Jew any and all negative traits, but it calls for no special action.

People would accept this form of anti-Semitism without much thought or awareness. It was expressed in such generally accepted and widely used utterances as "Be a good boy or the Jew will get you." "You are dirty like a Jew." "Don't be a calculating Jew!" and many, many others.

In the Polish language the very term Jew (Zyd) is something polite people are reluctant to use. Still, it is the only correct term; others such as "a person of Mosaic faith" or "an Israelite" sound archaic, pompous, and downright phony. But, one can easily insult a person by simply calling him a Jew (Zyd). The term evokes strong negative images.

Unobtrusive and latent though it is, this diffuse cultural form of anti-Semitism acts as an insidious foundation for all other forms. Many Poles, and particularly the rescuers, find objectionable other more explicit expressions of anti-Semitism, but this almost subconscious type they tend to shrug of as insignificant and anything that reflects this form of anti-Semitism they dismiss as mere jokes.[10]

When helping Jews, then, Poles had to overcome layers of obstacles. The outer and strongest part was the Nazi prohibition that made helping Jews a crime punishable by death. Next came the explicit anti-Jewish ideologies and the pervasive anti-Semitism that made help to Jews both a highly dangerous and disapproved-of activity. Last, these Poles had to overcome their own diffuse cultural anti-Semitism.[11]

Before these Christians became rescuers, their lives were not as endangered as the lives of the Jews. Because their lives were not as threatened did they become more aware of the sufferings of others? Can we assume that those whose lives are endangered become insensitive to the dangers faced by others? Are such expectations justified?

Some students of the concentration camp experience say that only after inmates felt that immediate threats to their lives had diminished and only after they had "adjusted" to the concentration camp conditions could they even begin to think about the needs of others.[12]

Clearly, very few concentration camp inmates felt that their lives were not endangered. Similarly, only very few had adjusted to the concentration camp experience. In fact, most inmates perished and only a handful succeeded in overcoming the horrors of the concentration camp experience. It follows that only a small minority had reached the stage where they could think about the welfare of others. It seems, however, that those who did live through the concentration camp imprisonment were involved in some kind of activities that had to do with mutual help, compassion and caring. It stands to reason that in a devastating environment like the concentration camp one could not survive without some kind of cooperation. Therefore, the mutual help and support which the concentration camp survivors did experience might have contributed to their survival.[13]

I know of no study that systematically describes rescuers and helping behavior within the Nazi camps. I can only tentatively compare the characteristics of the Christian rescuers in my earlier study to the Jewish rescuer Oswald Rufeisen.

Results of my early research have shown that Poles who rescued Jews came from a variety of social backgrounds and differed greatly in terms of education, religion, and political involvement. In terms of generally used conventional categories, such rescuers were very heterogeneous.

Only a close-range analysis of these selfless helpers yielded a cluster of shared characteristics and conditions. Highly interrelated, these common factors refer to the rescuers: (1) individuality or separateness, which means that they did not quite fit into their social environments; (2) independence or self-reliance to act in accordance with personal convictions, regardless of how these were viewed by others; (3) broad and long-lasting commitment to stand up for the helpless and needy; (4) the tendency to perceive their help to Jews in a matter-of-fact unassuming way. This came together with consistently strong denials of heroic or extraordinary qualities; (5) an unpremeditated, unplanned beginning of Jewish rescue, which could either have happened gradually or suddenly, even impulsively; and (6) universalistic perceptions that defined the Jews only as helpless beings and as totally dependent on the protection of others. Closely connected to this is the ability to disregard all their attributes except those that expressed extreme suffering and need.

Tentatively, the theoretical formulations that grew out of my research suggest the following set of interrelated hypotheses.

The less integrated into a community people are, the less constrained and controlled they are by the community's norms and values. Thus freed of constraints, people are more able to resist the community's pressures and act independently.

Independence implies a greater freedom to act in accordance with personal inclinations and values. Personal inclinations of Polish rescuers had to do with moral imperatives, which were expressed as a desire to help the needy. The wish to stand up for the downtrodden was a powerful, compelling force, capable of overshadowing the particulars of the needy, except those which had to do with the dependence on aid. At times this wish to help others could overcome personal dislikes and prejudices.

The longer people act in accordance with such strong moral imperatives, the more likely are such actions and values to become traditional patterns. The more firmly established these actions become, the easier they are to follow and the greater the likelihood that they will be taken for granted and defined as natural reactions and as a duty.

Once such actions become well established and are viewed in a matter-of-fact way, their extraordinary or heroic qualities are more likely denied.[14]

Oswald Rufeisen seems to resemble the Polish rescuers. Like they, throughout his life he has been an outsider. He is very independent. Similarly, he has had a long history of doing good deeds. Just like other rescuers, Oswald sees his aid in a matter-of-fact way, as nothing extraordinary. Like they, as he continued to support and protect prospective victims, he would improvise and rely on different opportunities of rescue. Finally, he, too, had universalistic perceptions of the victims, and offered help to whoever needed it, regardless of who they were.

These similarities between Oswald Rufeisen and the Christian rescuers support some broader theoretical assumptions; namely, as a historical period, the Holocaust was reduced to the most fundamental aspects of human existence, with life reflecting its bare essentials. It was a time in which most conventional and decorative features of society had lost their power. This conventional stripping in turn offers an uncluttered view of the fundamental human condition. And precisely because life at that time was reduced to its basics the study of that period creates the opportunity to better see and understand the meanings and implications of essential human conditions.

Moreover, the very presence of people willing to risk their lives for the persecuted and the helpless shows that extreme situations can lead to reactions of extreme evil and extreme goodness. The study of the Holocaust, then, can instruct us both about man's inhumanity to man and about man's humanity to man. Such a study in turn is capable of moving beyond the particular time, place, events, and people.

ENDNOTES

[1]A few recent examples of such studies are: Phillip Hallie, *Lest Innocent Blood Be Shed* (New York: Harper and Row, 1979); Peter Hellman, *Avenue of the Righteous* (New York: Atheneum, 1980); Samuel P. Oliner and Pearl M. Oliner, *The Altruistic Personality, Rescuers of Jews in Nazi Europe* (New York: The Free Press, 1988); Kazimierz Iranek-Osmecki, *He Who Saves One Life* (New York: Crown Publishers, Inc., 1971); Alexander Ramati, *The Assisi Underground: The Priests Who Rescued Jews* (New York: Stein and Day Publishers, 1978); Nechama Tec, *When Light Pierced The Darkness: Christian Rescue of Jews in Nazi-Occupied Poland* (New York: Oxford University Press, 1987).

[2]Tec, *When Light Pierced The Darkness*, p. 11.

[3]Jacqueline R. Macaulay and Leonard Berkowitz, "Overview," pp. 1-9 in Jacqueline R. Macaulay and Leonard Berkowitz, eds., *Altruism and Helping Behavior* (New York: Academic Press, 1970).

[4]This theoretical distinction has been suggested by David L. Rosenhan, "The Natural Socialization of Altruistic Autonomy," pp. 251-268 in Macaulay and Berkowitz, eds., *Altruism and Helping Behavior*.

[5]See Hellman, *Avenue of the Righteous*, p. ix. Also, the *Encyclopedia Judaica* mentions four kinds of distinctions, by differentiating between a "certificate of honor" and "a letter of esteem." See *Encyclopedia Judaica*, Vol. 14, p. 184. The kinds of distinctions are by no means set. Discussions about their number and quality are still continuing. Personal communication, Dr. M. Paldiel, director of the Department for the Righteous, Yad Vashem, Jerusalem, Israel.

[6]Nechama Tec, *In The Lion's Den: The Life of Oswald Rufeisen*, (New York: Oxford University Press, 1990).

[7]Lucy S. Dawidowicz, ed., *A Holocaust Reader* (New York: Behrman House, Inc., 1976), p. 67.

[8]Wladyslaw Bartoszewski, "Egzekucje Publiczne W Warszawie W Latach, 1943-1945" [Public Executions in Warsaw], *Biuletyn Glownej Komisji Badania Zbrodni Niemieckiej W Polsce*, no. 6 (1946): 211-224; Ringelblum, *Notes from the Warsaw Ghetto* (New York: Schocken Books, 1975), p. 236; Tatiana Berenstein, *et al.*, eds., *Exterminacja Zydow Na Ziemiach Polskich W Okresie Okupacji Hitlerowskiej* [Jewish extermination in Poland during Hitler's Occupation] (Warszawa: Zydowski Instytut Historyczny, 1957), pp. 121-122; Dawidowicz, ed., *A Holocaust Reader*, pp. 67-68.

[9]Tec, *When Light Pierced The Darkness*, Chapter 3, pp. 52-69.

[10]*Ibid.*, p. 56.

[11]*Ibid.*, p. 69.

[12]H. O. Bluhm, "How Did They Survive?", *American Journal of Psychotherapy*, Vol. 2, No. 1., 1948, p. 26; Elie A. Cohen, *Human Behavior In Concentration Camps* (London: Johnatan Cape, 1954), p. 182.

[13]Shamai Davidson, "Human Reciprocity in the Nazi Concentration Camps," pp. 555-572 in Yisrael Gutman and Avital Saf, eds., *The Nazi Concentration Camps* (Jerusalem: Yad Vashem, 1984); Terrence des Pres, *The Survivor: An Anatomy of Life in the Death Camps* (New York: Oxford University Press, 1976), pp. 121, 136, 153, 197-198; Alexander Donat, *The Holocaust Kingdom* (New York: Holt Rinehart & Winston, 1965), p. 237; Eugen Kogon, *The Theory and Practice of Hell* (New York: Berkley Publishing Corporation, 1980), pp. 311-315.

[14]The description and discussion of rescuers follows closely my book, Tec, *When Light Pierced The Darkness*, pp. 188-191.

THE SOCIAL AND MEDICAL ANTECEDENTS TO THE MEDICAL EXPERIMENTS IN THE NAZI CONCENTRATION CAMPS

Roberta Kalechofsky

The nineteenth century was pivotal in the development of modern medicine, in the transformation of medicine regarded as an "art" into a profession regarded as a "science." The words "art" and "science," in their application to this profession, were understood by nineteenth-century doctors to suggest very different philosophies, which engaged different procedures and different technologies in the healing process. The words aroused venomous internal debate in the medical profession, for at issue were the moral problematics of vivisection, human and animal, and what many conceived of as the destiny of the medical profession.

"Art" for physiologists such as Claude Bernard was equivalent to everything that was indeterminate and diffuse in life, and which involved intuition, collective memory and tradition in order to resolve questions. "Science" was determinate; it expelled uncertainty. Claude Bernard wrote: "...the realm of the indeterminate is the occult and the marvellous ... the real and effective cause of a disease must be constant and determined....anything else would be a denial of science in medicine." In the case of a problematic profession such as medicine, necessarily occupying the realm of ambiguity, Bernard, accredited as the "Father of Modern Medicine," a brilliant physiologist and an eloquent writer, threw down the gauntlet to the profession: one must choose "science" or "art" in the practice of medicine.

No one was more influential in shaping the destiny of modern medicine than Claude Bernard (1813-1878). His writings, his life as a physiologist, his views on medical science and vivisection were decisive. (His classic, *An Introduction to Experimental Medicine* [1865], was required reading as part of the philosophy program for the baccalaureate in French schools up to 1957.) As Reino Virtanen wrote of him, "...his physiology was...a fulfillment of Cartesian mechanism. It contains the current leading from the Beast-Machine through La Mettrie's Man-Machine...." Following the Cartesian path, Bernard excoriated vitalism in medicine. It was for him "...a kind of medical superstition--a belief in the supernatural....(which) encourages ignorance and gives birth to a sort of unintentional quackery....In living bodies and in organic bodies, laws are immutable."[1]

Such views were not stated without opposition. Gerdy, a famous surgeon and professor in the Faculté de Médicine at the Charité, attacked Bernard at a meeting, saying: "Your conclusion would be correct for inert nature, but it cannot be true for living nature." Elizabeth Blackwell, one of the first women doctors, expressed the problem thus: "The first law of good Science and all morality is to know the distinction between the organic and the inorganic." But Bernard also knew that unless he submitted the organic to the model of the inorganic, medicine would not be accepted as a science, a status much coveted.

The healing profession suffered from a tradition of anxiety that was centuries old, and from a strenuously contradictory relationship between doctor and patient, one founded on authority and presumed benevolence on the part of the doctor, and mistrust on the part of the patient that was often suppressed hostility.[2] The doctor was indispensable--like the gravedigger-- but his presence always augured something nasty. His status was at the mercy of a force--disease--over which he had little control. Aptly, Peter Gay has called medicine, "A Profession of Anxiety."[3] "Gradually, the doctor, long the buff of hostile jokes, became a folk-hero of bourgeois culture." Men of science and medicine, like Pasteur, Koch and Bernard, became national heroes, their funerals attended by the pomp reserved for victorious generals and royalty. The transformation was electrifying, and the medical profession grasped the brass ring with what Gay sardonically called "The Flight Into Knowledge."

Experimentation--which meant vivisection--became the accepted methodology: it became an orthodoxy. Vivisection--both human and animal--had been practised haphazardly and intermittently for centuries. Galen used to collect the bodies of the dead--and perhaps the dying--gladiators. Dr. Henry Beecher tells us that, "Celsus, practising in Alexandria in the third century B.C. cried out against the dissection of living men."[4] Descartes cut up living unanesthetized animals and made the practice acceptable, at least to some. There were always considerable voices of dissent and, to an important extent, the history of the rise of the medical profession since 1850, is the history of the silencing of these dissenting voices.

Human experimentation was incipient in the experimental method. Claude Bernard had reservations, but wrote: "The right to experiment on humans cannot be denied as a matter of principle."[5] In 1892, Lord Lister acknowledged, "A serious thing to experiment on the lives of our fellow-men, but I believe the time has now come when it may be tried...."[6] By the turn of the century, the American chemist, E. E. Slosson proclaimed, "...a human life is nothing compared with a new fact...the aim of science is the advancement of human knowledge at any sacrifice of human life."[7] By the beginning of the twentieth century, a considerable amount of human experimentation was being practised in England and in France, and soon in the United States, but not so much that it threatened public tranquility, though it had become a class issue which led to anti-vivisection riots in Great Britain. For several decades in Edwardian England, the anti-vivisection movement was composed of members from all the social classes, including the poor and the working-class who knew that it was their graves that were being robbed for bodies, their orphans and their people in the charity wards and asylums who were the victims of this new practice.[8] Their protests were so marked that Stephen Paget, founder of the Research Defense Society, an English pro-vivisection lobby, accused the anti-vivisection movement of being a Marxist conspiracy.[9]

The problem of the "material," or population to be used for human experimentation vexes modern ethicists. Unfortunately, and invariably, those used for such purposes remain the same: the unpropertied, the unintellectual, the unwanted.[10] The problem of human experimentation is a civil rights issue of unacknowledged but imposing magnitude. The opposition determined Bernard to advise vivisectors, in his last work published posthumously, to practise their discipline secretly, and soon after the turn of the century, vivisection or "biomedical research" as it is now called, went underground and a new era in experimental medicine was born.

But prior to the turn of the century, vivisection was practised openly, indeed often in theaters where men and women could watch living, unanesthetized dogs strapped down and dismembered. The literature of the day attests to the forcible impressions made on many of those who watched a vivisection experiment. Jung, in a diary notation, wrote that he was sickened by one such exhibition and vowed never to go again. "...horrible, barbarous, and above all unnecessary."[11] Dr. William Sharpey, testifying at the First Royal Commission Into Vivisection in 1875 said:

> When I was a young man studying in Paris, I went to a series of lectures which Magendie gave upon experimental physiology, and I was so utterly repelled by what I witnessed that I never went back again. In the first place, they [the experiments] were painful and sometimes they were very severe, and then they were without any sufficient object....He [the experimenter] put the animals to death in a very painful way.[12]

Such citations are numerous. I quote this one for its reference to Magendie, who was Bernard's teacher and whom he called, "mon maître," and for the observation which Dr. Sharpey expressed, similar to Jung's, that this dreadful procedure was "without any sufficient object."

Between 1870 and 1900, when vivisection gained a foothold in the academic world, its medical relevance was not at all established and often refuted. In defiance of Koch's announcement that he had isolated the cholera bacilli and had proven that it made animals sick by injecting them into dogs, hens, mice and cats, Professor Pettenkofer of Munich heroically drank a glass of water swarming with cholera bacilli and triumphantly survived. It was noted that epidemics of cholera and smallpox came and went in cycles that defied the logic of medical determinism. Anna Kingsford, an outspoken opponent of vivisection, asked Professor Leon Le Fort at the Faculté de Médicine of Paris, where she was taking her degree in medicine, why vivisection is insisted upon when its conclusions seem unsound. His response echoed that of other vivisectors of the nineteenth century.

Speaking for myself and my brethren of the Faculté, I do not mean to say that we claim for that method of investigation that it has been of any practical utility to medical science, or that we expect it to be so. But it is necessary as a protest on behalf of the independence of science against interference by clerics and moralists. When all the world has reached the high intellectual level of France, and no longer believes in God, the soul, moral responsibility, or any nonsense of that kind, but makes practical utility the only rule of conduct, then, and not till then, can science afford to dispense with vivisection.[13]

This view, archaic as it may strike us now, was echoed liberally at the turn of the century by others, such as Dr. Mary Putnam-Jacobi of the Women's College of the New York Infirmary. Opposing all regulations of vivisection, she declaimed, "We have repudiated the right of the church to control the procedures and conclusions of science. Why should we now make over this right to men immersed in business and politics. Are they any more fitted than priests."[14] Dr. Putnam-Jacobi did not hesitate to perform toxicological experiments on "a very healthy Irish boy," who had suffered a fracture of the skull, and whose case "offered a unique opportunity for the study of conditions affecting inter-cranial pressure." She administered to him quinia, brandy, belladonna, bromide of potassium, and injected atropia under his skin, for the purpose of demonstrating its effects on the subject to her students.

Such sentiments as Professor Leon Le Fort and Dr. Putnam-Jacobi expressed were echoed elsewhere throughout the latter part of the nineteenth century, stated openly, with little censure. Charles Richet, an eminent physician, wrote in his published writings:

I do not believe that a single experimenter says to himself when he gives curare to a rabbit, or cuts the spinal marrow of a dog, or poisons a frog, 'Here is an experiment that will relieve or cure the disease of some man.' No, in truth, he does not think that. He says to himself, 'I shall clear up some obscure point; I will seek out a new fact.' And this scientific curiosity which alone animates him is explained by the high idea he has formed of science. This is why we pass our days in foetid laboratories, surrounded by groaning creatures, in the midst of blood and suffering, bent over palpitating entrails.

We find no hypercritical pretence here whether of utility or anesthetics, or of the comparative non-sensibility of the animals. The operator addresses himself to the public as frankly and as confident of their sympathy as we might conceive a devil addressing his fellow-devils to be, taking it for granted that the sentiments of humanity are as extinct in them as in himself.[15]

Such an avowal did not speak wholly for all the practitioners of vivisection, but the new practice was embraced as an ideology and a discipline in the service of cybernetic man by many, and as a necessary discipline for those who wished to be acolytes in the new science of medicine. The grotesqueries were excused under the rubric "pour la science," and in its name an "esprit de corps" was enforced. Magendie performed deliberately cruel experiments to prove that "the sentimental instincts" were extinct in him as he believed they should be. Claude Bernard expressed credit that he could perform ghastly experiments without feeling anything, and wrote, "The physiologist is not an ordinary man: he is a scientist possessed and absorbed by the scientific idea that he pursues. He does not hear the cries of animals, he does not see their flowing blood, he sees nothing but his idea...." A gratuitous sadism was inevitable. One experiment by Bernard is suggestive. In wishing to determine the rate of decomposition from the digestive juices of a dog, he made a fistula in the side of a dog and struck the head of a living frog into the opening and watched it decompose. The frog wriggled and struggled for three days until it died. With macabre wit, Bernard referred to the frog as "the Job of the laboratory." In protest of such a discipline in the name of science, John Galsworthy wrote in a letter to *The Times*, 1913, "No man ever became a stoic and acquired the virtues of fortitude and courage by inflicting pain on others."

Human history often develops specialized types of personalities, such as the shaman or types of priesthoods, often justified by an esoteric knowledge and practice, by a strenuous discipline, and by the lofty goal of saving the human race from corruption or disease. The "physician-scientist," became such a specialized type of person, and quickly evolved into what Robert Lifton has eloquently formulated as "the healer-killer."[16] To Professor Lifton's psychological analysis, however, must be added the history and sociology of the medical profession. The personality of "the healer-killer" did not arise in a social vacuum, but had its roots in nineteenth-century vivisection practice, philosophy and discipline. By 1916, in a critique of the vivisection practice, Dr. Albert Leffingwell commented: "...rarely, if ever, in the history of the world has a transformation of ideals been more completely attained."[17] In the process, our civilization became transformed as well.

Dr. Leffingwell, a crusader against outrages in human and animal vivisection--though not an anti-vivisectionist--recorded as an experiment to measure the relationship between pain and blood pressure:

> The means taken to depress the vital powers were as varied as the ingenuity of the vivisectors could devise. Sometimes it was accomplished by skinning the animal alive, a part of the body at a time, and then roughly 'sponging' the denuded surface. Sometimes it was secured by crushing the dog's paws, first one and then the other. Now and then the dog's feet were burnt, or the intestines exposed and roughly manipulated; the tail crushed, the limbs amputated, the stomach cut out. Then came the 'stimulation' of the exposed nerve, carried on and repeated sometimes until Nature refused longer to respond, and death came to the creature's relief.[18]

Dr. Leffingwell tells us that the experiment was conducted on "a little dog, weighing only 11 pounds," and that he is quoting directly from the published report of the experiment so that no one should conclude that he is fantasizing.

What astonished contemporaries who witnessed the rise of vivisection was the joining together of education and cruelty. It was not only what was being done in the name of science, but who was doing it. John Graham, principal of Dalton Hall in Victoria University, Manchester, in his testimony before the Second Royal Commission Into Vivisection Practices in 1906, expressed the disquiet of many when he said of vivisection: "This is a new incursion of reaction into human life. In the very highest part of human life, namely, the intellectual side, the moral side is outraged...."[19]

Leffingwell's efforts to arouse the public against the excesses of animal and human experimentation were joined by other eminent figures of his time such as William James, but went unheeded. In 1907, Leffingwell published a booklet, entitled *Illustrations of Human Vivisection*. If the experiments on humans were not as grotesque as those upon animals, they equally embraced the new ethos. Dr. Sydney Ringer, of the University Hospital of London, experimented with poison on children and openly wrote "using healthy children for our experiments." The patients often suffered severe headaches, vomiting, and spasmodic twitching of limbs. In several of these cases, the children had been brought in already sick, some suffering from pneumonia, one from belladonna poisoning, and were subjected to experiments after they had been cured of their original illness, or in addition to their original illness. "Dr. Ringer's scientific enthusiasm was so great that he could not forbear making experiments upon hospital patients with a poison for which there appears to be no recognized medical use, and so rare that he was obliged to have it specially manufactured for the occasion." His experiments were published openly in a text, *Handbook on Therapeutics*, in which he described using overdoses of salicin, nitrate of sodium, gelseminum, and other toxic agents on charity children, many under the age of ten. The only criticism the publication of this book elicited was from *The Lancet*, which complained that such experiments would inflame the anti-vivisectionists. Dr. Leffingwell comments that Dr. Ringer already had the support of Dr. Keen, Dr. Mitchell and Dr. Morehouse, distinguished American doctors who had laid down "the rule that in the study of poisons 'in order to appreciate properly any toxic agent, we must follow its effects through a wide range of created existence from vegetable to man.'"[20] *The Handbook on Therapeutics* was not an erratic episode in human experimentation: it went through eight editions.

What disturbed Dr. Leffingwell, perhaps as much as the experiments, is that there seemed to be silent public approval. He noted experiments made in Europe which were quoted in "an American work without expression of disapprobation," though,

> A distressing feature of many of these experiments is the fact that the men and women upon whom they were performed were not only ignorant, but under constraint. In this horrible case certain patients in the hospital were not merely poisoned once, but were obliged 'on compulsion,' to undergo the convulsive paroxysm and all the other agonizing symptoms a second time.[21]

He comments that, "it is certain that human vivisectors have given certain poisons up to a point just short of collapse.[22]

His short book is a dismal account of suffering inflicted upon the unsuspecting, often for purposes of mere curiosity, by a profession which by now assumed this right as its prerogative. What exhausted his indignation was the fact that these experiments were published not only in esoteric journals, but frequently in newspapers without disapproval, and he indicted human vivisection as "the greatest vice of modern science."

It was a short step before wholesale populations, such as soldiers, the poor, the mentally retarded and the imprisoned for whatever purpose, were being used for experimentation, done in league with or with the knowledge of eminent institutions such as The Rockefeller Institute and The League of Nations. The defense of the Nazi doctors rested, for example, on the argument that human experimentation had not been considered a crime but was accepted as a norm of medical practice. In support of this position, their attorney exhibited three volumes recording human experimentations conducted internationally by scientifically oriented countries. Of the dilemma of the Nazi doctors, Dr. W. B. Bean observed that "The degradation of physicians in Germany exemplifies the decline and fall of a group whose moral obligations went by default in a single generation. The house would not have fallen had not many of the timbers been rotten."[23] The prosecution correctly rebutted the argument that such crimes committed elsewhere excused these crimes, but the rotten timbers were spread far further than in Germany. Human experimentation was then, and continues to be, acceptable practice in medical science, and all efforts to restrain it against incursions into human rights and human dignity have proven futile.[24] Dr. Leffingwell ended his book on *Human Vivisection*, in 1907, with these words:

> At the beginning of a new century, we are confronted by great problems. One of these is human vivisection in the name of scientific research. We appeal, then, to the medical press of America to break that unfortunate silence which seems to justify or, at least, to condone it. Now and henceforth, will it not join us in condemning every such vivisector of little children, every such experimenter upon human beings? We make this appeal to it, in the name of Justice and Humanity and for the sake of millions yet unborn.

ENDNOTES

[1]Reino Virtanen, *Claude Bernard and His Place in the History of Ideas*, University of Nebraska Press, 1960, p. 29.

[2]For a brief history of this issue, see Dr. Jay Katz, *The Silent World of Patient and Doctor*, The Free Press, 1984.

[3]*The Bourgeois Experience: Victoria To Freud: Education Of The Senses*, Oxford University Press, 1984. For a discussion of the *Anxieties of the Medical Profession in the 19th century*, see Chapter Four.

[4]*Research and The Individual*, Little, Brown & Co., 1970, p. 10.

[5]Reino Virtanen, p. 20.

[6]E. Westacott, *A Century of Vivisection and Anti-Vivisection*, C. W. Daniel Co., 1949, p. 236.

[7]John Vyvyan, *The Dark Face of Science*, Micah Publications, 1989, pp. 20-21.

[8]Coral Lansbury, *Women, Workers, and Vivisection in Edwardian England*, University of Wisconsin Press, 1985.

[9]*The Dark Face of Science*, pp. 92-94. The Research Defense Society was founded in 1908.

[10]For contemporary discussions, see Bradford H. Gray, *Human Subjects in Medical Experimentation*, John Wiley & Sons, 1975; and *Experimentation With Human Subjects*, ed. Paul A. Freund, Braziller, 1970.

[11]*Memories, Dreams, Reflections*, Collins, 1963, p. 104.

[12]E. Westacott, pp. 166-167.

[13]*Ibid.*

[14]Dr. Albert Leffingwell, *Illustrations of Human Vivisection*, Vivisection Reform Society, 1907, p. 16.

[15]*Ibid.*, p. 180.

[16]*The Nazis Doctors: Medical Killing and the Psychology of Genocide*, Basic Books, 1986.

[17]*An Ethical Problem*, G. Bell and Sons, 1916.

[19]Westacott, p. 239.

[20]*Human Vivisection*, p. 11.

[21]*Ibid.*, p. 14.

[22]*Ibid.*, p. 15.

[23]M. H. Pappworth, *Human Guinea Pigs*, Beacon Press, 1967, p. 187.

[24]There are now thirty-three codes relating to human experimentation. None prove adequate because one of the essential problems has not been addressed, and that is that all judgment of such ethical questions is left solely to the medical profession itself to arbitrate.

ON THE DISTINCTIVENESS OF THE HOLOCAUST
AND THE ARMENIAN GENOCIDE

Robert Melson

The Problem

The massacre and extermination of peoples based on their ethnicity, nationality, race, religion, language, class, or political beliefs were not unknown in the past, but they have become emblematic of the exercise of power by the contemporary state. Indeed, following the shock of the Holocaust, we have become aware of mass destruction that preceded and followed the Second World War. One thinks, for example, of the Armenian genocide of 1915-1923, of the Stalinist Gulag, Burundi, Biafra, Indonesia, Sudan, Ethiopia, and of the Cambodian "autogenocide."

Tragically because other genocidal events have occurred in our era, it is possible to compare the *Shoah* in order to get a better understanding of some of its causes, or its etiology. Indeed, given the possibility of a variety of mass destructions it is possible to pose two important questions: 1) Is there some underlying pattern, a set of empirically grounded explanations that might apply to the Holocaust and similar catastrophes such as the Armenian genocide? And 2) If such an etiology exists, what about the distinctive features of particular genocides? Do these undermine the causal analysis or do they demonstrate how the process of mass destruction varies in individual instances?

This essay makes reference to the Armenian genocide in particular because it seems in its essential features most closely to resemble the Holocaust, and together with the *Shoah* it differs in important ways from other instances of mass destruction. Distinguishing these two cases of genocide from other events and comparing one genocide to the other may shed light on both and on the process of genocide in general. An earlier paper focused on their common etiology.[1] This essay will direct itself to their significant differences.

Distinguishing the Holocaust and the Armenian Genocide from Other Instances of Mass Destruction

There may be other instances to which the Holocaust may be compared but none presents itself as readily as the Armenian genocide. Assuming that the term "genocide" implies a policy process whose end is the intended destruction in part or in whole of a human community such as a communal group or class, there are at least two reasons why the Armenian genocide and the Holocaust are distinct from other instances of genocide. 1) Both destructions were the products of state-initiated policies whose intentions and practical results were the total destruction of the two groups as viable communities in the Ottoman Empire and Central Europe respectively. These were not only massacres, pogroms, or mass murders. The Armenian genocide and the Holocaust were clear instances of what the UN has called "genocide-in-whole" in distinction to less thorough killing which it called "genocide-in-part."[2] 2) Both victimized groups were ethno-religious communal minorities that had been partially assimilated, integrated, or, as in the case of the Jews, emancipated in the wider society. The mass destructions of the Armenians and Jews originated as attacks against domestic components of the victimizing state's own society. This is in distinction to genocides that have been carried out by perpetrators against foreign groups of "infidels" or "savages" living abroad, often far from the state's own people. Indeed, this essay will refer to these two instances as illustrations of "total domestic genocide," in order to distinguish the Armenian genocide and the Holocaust from other instances of mass murder and human destruction.[3]

Some examples may clarify these points. The Armenian genocide of 1915-23 in which some one-and-one-half-million people were killed out of a population of approximately two million bears some resemblance to the Armenian massacres of 1894-96, where it is estimated that tens of thousands of Armenians were murdered under the regime of Sultan Abdul-Hamid II.[4] There is no evidence, however, that the Sultan's regime wanted to eliminate the Armenians as a viable millet or communal group from the Ottoman Empire. By the same token there is strong evidence that the Young Turks, led by the Committee of Union and Progress (CUP), intended to destroy the Armenian community in the Turkish lands.[5] It was the Young Turks' policy intentions, methods, and results as compared to those of the Sultan's regime that differentiated the mass murders of 1915-1923 from the massacres of 1894-96 and converted them into "total domestic genocide."

A similar distinction between massacre or "genocide-in-part" and total domestic genocide may be drawn between Nazi policies directed against Poles, Ukrainians, and Russians, on the one hand, and those against Jews and Gypsies, on the other hand. The Nazis used massacre and other means such as not permitting education past primary schooling in an attempt to reduce the Slavic peoples to slaves of the "master race." There was, however, no apparent plan to exterminate the Polish, Ukrainian, and Russian communities as such. In contrast, the Final Solution meant to exterminate all Jews and most Gypsies.[6] The willingness to work under slave-like conditions for the German army did not save the inhabitants of the Lodz ghetto from destruction.

Furthermore in distinguishing the Armenian genocide and the Holocaust from other instances of mass murder and genocide one needs to recall that history is full of instances of peoples being slaughtered by invading armies wanting to seize their lands, to enslave some of them, or to convert them to their religions. One need only to recall the depradations of the Athenians against Melos, of the Romans against Carthage, of Tamarlane, Ghengis Khan, and of the Europeans in Africa, Tasmania, and the New World. In none of these instances, however, did the state turn against a major communal component of its own society and condemn it to destruction. The men of Melos were not Athenians. The Carthagenians were not Romans. The Europeans were not Africans. But the Armenians had been a millet integral to the Ottoman Empire and the Jews had become emancipated citizens of Germany in 1871. To destroy such partially integrated and assimilated domestic communities, the perpetrators had to devise ideological rationalizations like integral nationalism or racism and methods like mass deportations and the death camp that had not been used in previous mass murders. These are some of the things that differentiate the Armenian genocide and the Holocaust from other instances of group destruction and make them the quintessential examples of total domestic genocide in the modern world.

However, to point out that the Armenian genocide and the Holocaust bear certain striking similarities and that they differ from other cases of genocide is only of passing interest unless it leads to a better understanding of each case and of the process of total domestic genocide. This can be done by examining their similar origins as well as emphasizing their significant differences. Identifying similar causes should tell us something about the process of genocide, but their differences are of crucial theoretical importance as well. Indeed, it is only by spelling out the differences between the two cases of total domestic genocide that it is possible to identify how that process may vary under different conditions. In what follows this essay continues with a brief discussion of some of their similar causes as well as their differences.

Similar Causes

Some of the similarities between the origins of the Armenian genocide and the Holocaust may be listed:

1. Under the old regimes of the Ottoman Empire and Germany, Armenians and Jews were ethno-religious minorities of inferior status that had experienced rapid social progress and mobilization in the nineteenth century. These circumstances helped to create what were known as the "Armenian Question" and the "Jewish Problem" respectively.

2. Under the old regimes, Armenians may have suffered persecution and Jews may have experienced discrimination, but in neither

case was a policy of genocide formulated or implemented to solve "questions" or "problems." Genocide followed in the wake of revolutions in the Ottoman Empire and Germany.

3.   Following the reversals of 1908-1912, the Committee of Union and Progress rejected Pan-Islam and Ottomanism as ideologies and political myths linking state to society and turned to Turkish nationalism and Pan-Turkism. The CUP identified the Turkish ethnic group as the authentic political community, and by implication it excluded Armenians and others from the Turkish nation. Once Ottoman Turks came to view themselves not in religious but in nationalist terms, the Armenians especially were in danger of being perceived as enemies of Turkey and the Young Turk revolution. This is so because the Armenians, unlike the Greeks and the Jews of the Ottoman Empire, for example, occupied lands which were claimed by the Turkish nationalists to constitute the Turkish heartland.

As in the case of the CUP in the Ottoman Empire, a revolutionary situation in Germany allowed the Nazis to recast their society's identity and political myth. When they came to power they had the opportunity to redefine the German political identity in terms of their racialist antisemitic ideology. To do so they first systematically excluded and expelled the Jews from what they called the "Aryan" community.

4.   When the First World War broke out, the CUP brought the Ottoman Empire onto the side of the Germans and against the Russians. This permitted the CUP to claim that the internal Armenian enemy was in league with the external foe. These were the circumstances then that were used to justify the deportation and destruction of the Armenian community which was said to constitute a "deadly threat."

Like the CUP, the Nazis used general war to try to improve their nation's standing in the international arena and implement a policy of genocide. Indeed, they perceived the Soviet Union, their principal foreign enemy, as being ruled by a "World Jewish Conspiracy." Together with the invasion of Russia they put the "Final Solution" into effect.

Thus did ideological vanguards use the opportunities created by revolution and war to destroy ancient communities which were judged to be "problematic" under the old regimes and "enemies of the revolution," and "deadly threats" under revolutionary and wartime circumstances.

Significant Differences

A comparison of the Holocaust with other instances of genocide such as the Armenian genocide may be suggestive in uncovering some of their causes and illuminating the process of genocide in general. But this demands our recognition that although the origins of these two instances of genocide were similar in some essential ways they were also significantly different. Indeed, there were two major differences that need to be pointed out. The first pertained to the specific ideologies of the Nazis and the CUP and the second to the methods of destruction, especially massacre and the death camp.

Distinctive Ideology

A major difference between the Holocaust and the Armenian genocide pertains to the distinctive ideologies of the Nazis and the committee of Union and Progress. Hitler's pathology became the ideology of a mass movement that came to rule the most potent country in Europe. Nazi racialist ideology--what Lifton has aptly called the bio-medical vision--was a form of manicheanism that divided the world into the Aryans, carriers of the seeds of virtue and civilization, and the Jews, progenitors of evil and destruction.[7]

Enver and Talaat, and the other members of the CUP did not view the Armenians in the same manner. They were not millenarian racialists. The Young Turks became nationalists, believing that without radical change the Ottoman empire could not survive the centrifugal forces of ethnic self-determination and the pressures of the great powers. After the defeats of 1908-12, they rejected Ottomanism and Pan Islam as rival ideologies and adopted Pan-Turkism.

The Young Turks aimed to replace the Ottoman empire with a new Turkish national state stretching from Anatolia to Central Asia. From their perspective the Armenians had to be destroyed as a people not because they were the carriers of an evil seed, or because they threatened to control the world, or because their destruction would bring on a thousand-year racial utopia, but because they were identified as an alien nationality, living in the heartland of Turkey and creating an obstacle to the formation of the expanded Turkish state. Once the Ottoman Empire joined Germany, and Russia became a wartime enemy, the Armenians--living on both sides of the border--were identified as siding with the Russians. These were some of the ideological and structural conditions leading to the destruction of the Armenians. Thus ideology played as significant a role in the Armenian genocide as it would play in the Holocaust, but, as one might expect, the content of the specific ideologies in the two instances were clearly distinct from each other.

The difference in ideology between the Nazis and the CUP had implications for the scope of the destruction. The project of exterminating the Jews became a twisted crusade against an imaginary evil. The result was that not only German and Austrian Jews had to be killed, but all Jews everywhere on earth were to be annihilated in order that the world might be purified and redeemed. Indeed, Jews were sentenced to death by the Nazis not only in Europe under direct German jurisdiction, but the attempt was made to carry out that verdict in places like Japan where the Germans had influence but no jurisdiction.[8] In the event, the Japanese refused to carry out their allies' genocidal policies, but the example illustrates the difference between the Nazis' millenarian racialist vision--in essence a theodicy--and the nationalist vision of the Young Turks.

Indeed, not even the Committee of Union and Progress which had set out to destroy the Armenians in Turkey and the Ottoman empire was motivated by such grandiose visions. Thus, for example, although Armenians were deported from most parts of the Ottoman Empire and massacred and starved en route, the Armenian populations in Lebanon and Palestine were not destroyed.[9] It was possibly felt that these Armenians were far enough from the central areas of Turkish interest that they could be left alone.

This would have been perfectly sensible from a Turkish nationalist perspective. Moreover, because the definition of a Turk was a Muslim whose native tongue was Turkish, some Armenians who spoke Turkish fluently and had converted to Islam were able to save themselves or to be saved by sympathetic Turks.[10] Such "oversights" because they would have challenged racialist theory would not have been tolerated by the Nazis.

From this analysis it can be seen that part of what made the Holocaust distinct from the Armenian genocide, and from other cases even of total domestic genocide, were the specific intentions of the Nazi perpetrators.[11] It should be noted that this is an empirical and not a moral nor a legal observation. Moreover, it is a distinction with a difference: the Nazi worldview accounts in part for the extraordinary scope of their mass murder. They were not satisfied with deporting or killing only German Jews. All Jews in their sphere of influence, and even beyond their sphere of influence, were sentenced to death.

Ironically, because the intentions of the Nazis were so bizarre, that aspect of the Holocaust is less useful for a comparison with other like cases than is the Armenian genocide. In their single-minded and murderous nationalism the Young Turks have more to teach us about current massacres and partial genocides in parts of the contemporary Third World, for instance, than does the Holocaust.

Thus, for example, recent events in Biafra, Indonesia, Burundi, Pakistan, Ethiopia, and the Sudan have a certain comparability to the Armenian genocide of 1915. In each of these cases armed vanguards seized power after the fall or departure of a regime that had been set up by an imperial power, and they perpetrated massacres against communal groups which seemed to be opposed to the national aspirations of the dominant ethnic group. Nationalism, or ethnic chauvinism, not millenarian racialism was the governing ideology, just as it had been in Turkey.

However, in the other cases cited above, the policy of the state was conquest or subjugation not destruction of the communal group as such. In none of these instances did communal massacre or partial genocide add up to total domestic genocide. It was the policy of total destruction of a national group as such that differentiates the Armenian genocide from communal massacres and links it to the Holocaust. Finally it needs to be stressed that the Armenian genocide demonstrated that radical nationalism was quite enough to justify total domestic genocide. The Nazi ideology of millenarian antisemitic racialism was certainly unique, but it is not uniquely necessary in order that a regime commit total domestic genocide.

Distinctive Methods

There were some significant similarities but also differences in how both genocides were implemented. Unlike the Armenian genocide, which evolved rapidly once the First World War started, the Holocaust as a set of policy initiatives took longer and went through at least three stages before it reached the Final Solution. These were the pre-war stage (1933-39), the interim stage (1939-41), and the final stage (1941-45). Each stage can be characterized by different policy goals and distinctive but overlapping processes of victimization and destruction.

The goals and processes characterizing the first stage (1933-39) were the definition of the Jews and the Aryans, the exclusion of the former from the institutional and social life of Germany, their expropriation and their expulsion. The second interim stage (1939-41) was characterized by some vacillation in the machinery of destruction. What to do with the Jews in the conquered Polish territories? Should they be resettled in Madagascar? On a reservation in the Lublin district? Should they be exterminated? The policy of the Final Solution had not yet gelled. In the meantime, Jews were being terrorized and deported from the countryside into the cities where they were concentrated in ghettoes and immured behind their walls. In the third and last stage (1941-45) of the Holocaust, the Final Solution was formulated and initiated. Coinciding with the millenarian war against Russia, the decision to exterminate the Jews was implemented.

In the case of the Armenian genocide, things moved much more swiftly. The Great War commenced in August 1914. By February 1915 Armenians in the Turkish army were disarmed and turned into labor battalions. By April the Armenian leadership was seized and the expropriations, deportations, massacres, mass shootings, and starvation of the Armenian population at large began. By 1916 some million Armenians had perished. At war's end another half million were added to the slaughter.

The decision to kill the Armenians was taken in conjunction with the outbreak of the First World War and the danger and opportunities that wartime provided. It did not have the quality of experimentation with various solutions to the "Armenian Problem" that the Holocaust had with respect to the "Jewish Problem." Thus the first two stages of definition, expropriation, expulsion, and concentration that required extensive bureaucratic involvement on the part of the German judiciary, police, Nazi party, and SS were not present in Turkey. These stages were telescoped into one process of identification-expropriation-deportation-destruction.

Massacre and Death Camp

A number of writers have pointed to the invention of the death camp as being especially emblematic of the Holocaust.[12] Whereas other massacres and genocides may have been implemented by shootings, pogroms, and starvation, the death camp was different because it adopted modern industrial methods to the process of killing. Auschwitz Birkenau was primarily a factory for the destruction of Jews and Gypsies and for their cremation. The implication here is that only a modern industrialized society like Germany could have invented and implemented this method of mass destruction.

There is an important element of truth in this view, but it overestimates the differences between the relative development of Germany and Turkey, and the methods used in the two genocides. It is true that compared to Germany, Turkey was an industrially backward country; nevertheless, it used effectively those industrial facilities that were at its disposal to carry out the genocide.

Extensive use was made of the telegram to coordinate activities and the railroad system to deport Armenians to the Syrian desert. Indeed, Talaat himself was a former official in the telegraph office. Consequently, a hallmark of modern genocide, namely the depersonalization and bureaucratization of the crime, could already be seen. By the same token it should not be forgotten that millions of Jews perished by shooting, forced marches, and starvation, just as the Armenians had done before them. Thus although the death camp and its extraordinary universe were a hallmark of the Holocaust, the difference in the killing process of the two genocides should not be exaggerated.

Just as the death camp is emblematic of the Holocaust, the recurrent massacre of columns of Armenian deportees as they made their way from the eastern vilayets in Turkey to the Syrian desert near Aleppo is a hallmark of the Armenian genocide. Toynbee estimates for example that on the average some 50 percent of such columns were destroyed on the way.[13]

Although mass shootings and the stimulation of massacre was also utilized by the Nazis, especially in the Baltic states and the Ukraine, a much smaller percentage of Jews perished in this manner than in the death camps. Moreover it is significant that massacre was never used in Germany itself. This suggests that there was a predisposition for massacre present in the Ottoman Empire and the Caucasus that was not available to the same degree to the Nazis in Germany and the occupied countries.

One can only speculate about the reasons for such a potential for massacre. It may be noted, however, that massacres had been used against Muslims in Russia, Greece, Cyprus, and the Balkans before the onset of the Armenian genocide. Moreover, it is significant that thousands of Turkic and non-Turkic Muslim refugees fleeing Russia and the Balkans in the nineteenth century had been resettled precisely in those areas of the eastern vilayets populated heavily by the Armenians. It follows, therefore, that they and their descendants may have been stirred by passions of revenge and displaced aggression against their helpless neighbors.[14] The CUP's role was to initiate, encourage, coordinate, and tolerate popular violence against the Armenians. In such a situation popular massacres complemented the tasks of special killing units, and there was less need for factories of destruction.

As in the CUP's destruction of the Armenians, the Nazis utilized massacre and "spontaneous" actions against Jews in the Ukraine, Hungary, Rumania, and the Baltic states. It is important to stress, however, that genocide could occur in Germany and in other "advanced" countries, even in the absence of a potential for massacre. All that was needed was a genocidal regime, a willing bureaucracy, and the acquiescence of a silent majority.

Conclusion

This essay asserted that the Armenian genocide and the Holocaust in being total domestic genocides were significantly different from other cases of genocide and mass destruction in the modern era. It went on to list some of their similarities and differences. The analysis pointed out that both genocides may have been the products of revolutionary transformations in the Ottoman Empire and Imperial Germany, respectively; that the victims targeted for mass murder were ethno-religious groups of traditionally low status who had dramatically improved their social and economic position in the modern world; and that both genocides occurred in the midst of world wars. This was said to make up their similar etiology.

There were also significant differences between the two genocides. In particular, the intention of the perpetrators and the methods of destruction were singled out. Nazi millenarian racialism and the device of the death camp were significantly different from the ideology of Turkish nationalism and the process of massacre and starvation characteristic of the Armenian genocide.

However, these differences did not vitiate a meaningful comparison of the two instances of total domestic genocide. To the contrary it was precisely because the two cases varied in their etiology and methods that it was possible to gauge how total domestic genocide proceeded under distinct conditions. Thus it was seen that because of the wider reach of the Nazis' millenarian racism as compared to the CUP's integral nationalism, the scope of the Holocaust was broader than that of the Armenian genocide. By the same token because the CUP's intentions were shaped by nationalism and not racism, it is possible to assert (and warn) that the threshold for genocide, including total domestic genocide, may be ordinary, familiar, nationalism and that the mass destruction of human groups need not depend on the rise of Nazi-type ideologies. Similarly a comparison of the methods of destruction demonstrates that although the death camp was a successful adaptation to the exigencies of mass murder in the Third Reich, less sophisticated methods including repeated massacres and mass starvation can also prove to be effective in perpetrating total domestic genocide. Indeed, they have proved to be so in the contemporary world.

Finally, since genocide is a crime against humanity and not simply a historical event like the French Revolution, its occurrence raises many juridical, moral, and existential issues that a comparative empirical analysis cannot resolve. Nevertheless, by helping to identify the causes of genocide and their variation an empirical work might help in laying the groundwork for more informed philosophical discussion.[15]

ENDNOTES

[1]Robert Melson, "Revolutionary Genocide: On the Causes of the Armenian Genocide of 1915 and the Holocaust," *Holocaust and Genocide Studies*, 4, 2 (1989): 161-174. Also see Helen Fein, "A Formula for Genocide: A Comparison of the Turkish Genocide (1915) and the German Holocaust (1939-1945)," *Comparative Studies in Sociology*, 1 (1978): 271-293 and *Accounting for Genocide* (New York: The Free Press, 1979), pp. 3-30 Vahakn N. Dadrian, "The Convergent Aspects of the Armenian and Jewish Cases of Genocide: A Reinterpretation of the Concept of Holocaust," *Holocaust and Genocide Studies*, 3, 2 (1988): 151-170.

[2]According to the widely accepted UN definition formulated in 1948, genocide means actions "committed with intent to destroy *in whole or in part* a national, ethnic, racial, or religious group as such". See United Nations, *Yearbook of the United Nations, 1947-48*, pp. 595-599. For an important discussion of the UN definition see Leo Kuper, *Genocide* (New Haven: Yale University Press, 1981).

[3]This essay suggests that the Armenian genocide and the Holocaust were "total" genocides in that they were genocides "in whole" according to the UN definition. They were "domestic" in that Armenians and Jews constituted communal segments of Ottoman and German society respectively. It will be noted below, however, that although the early stages of the Holocaust commenced as a "domestic" genocide, with the invasion of Poland it also became an "international" genocide.

[4]Robert Melson, "A Theoretical Inquiry into the Armenian Massacres of 1894-96," *Comparative Studies in Society and History*, 24, 3 (1982): 481-509.

[5]Robert Melson, "Provocation or Nationalism: A Critical Inquiry into the Armenian Genocide of 1915," in Richard G. Hovannisian, ed., *The Armenian Genocide in Perspective* (New Brunswick, N.J.: Transaction Press, 1986), pp. 61-84.

[6]On the genocide of the Romany peoples or Gypsies see Donald Kenrick and Grattan Puxon, *The Destiny of Europe's Gypsies* (London: Cox and Wyman, 1972) and Leita Kaldi, "Gypsies and Jews: Chosen People," in Israel W. Charny, ed., *Toward the Understanding and Prevention of Genocide* (Boulder and London: Westview Press, 1984), pp. 113-118. According to Himmler's "Regelung" of October 13, 1942, racially pure Gypsies of the Sinti tribe were to be segregated from the rest while the other Romany people were to be exterminated. In fact two-thirds of the Sinti tribe were also killed, most at Auschwitz. Kenrick and Puxon estimate that out of a European Gypsy population of 937,800, approximately 219,700 or 23 percent were murdered by the Nazis.

[7]See Robert J. Lifton, *The Nazi Doctors* (New York: Basic Books, 1986) and especially Eberhard Jäckel, *Hitler's World View*, (Cambridge: Harvard University Press, 1981).

[8]See Marvin Tokayer, *The Fugu Plan: The Untold Story of the Japanese and the Jews in World War II* (New York: Paddington, 1979).

[9]See Avedis K. Sanjian, *The Armenian Communities in Syria Under Ottoman Dominion* (Cambridge: Harvard University Press, 1965), pp. 274-288.

[10]See for example the survivor's memoir: Kerop Bedoukian, *Some of Us Survived* (New York: Farrar, Straus, Giroux, 1978).

[11]This point was earlier stressed by Yehuda Bauer, "Is the Holocaust Explicable?" *Holocaust and Genocide Studies*, 5, 2 (1990): pp. 145-155.

[12]See Alan Rosenberg, "Was the Holocaust Unique?" in Isidor Walliman and Michael N. Dobkowski, eds., *Genocide and the Modern Age* (New York and London: Greenwood Press, 1987), pp. 145-162.

[13]See Arnold Toynbee, "A Summary of Armenian History up to and Including 1915," in Great Britain, *The Treatment of the Armenians in the Ottoman Empire: Documents Presented to Viscount Grey of Fallodon, Secretary of State for Foreign Affairs* (London: H.M.S.O., 1916), p. 650.

[14]See Vahakn N. Dadrian, "Factors of Anger and Aggression in Genocide," *Journal of Human Relations*, 19, 3 (1971): 394-417.

[15]Franklin H. Littel refers to the Holocaust as an epochal event and sees it as creating a crisis of meaning for all persons and institutions including Jews and Christians, churches and universities. See his "Fundamentals in Holocaust Studies," *The Annals of the American Academy of Political and Social Science*, 450 (July 1980): 213-217. For a bitter but moving Jewish religious response to the Holocaust see Richard L. Rubenstein, *After Auschwitz* (Indianapolis: Bobbs-Merrill, 1966). For similar sentiments articulated by writers on the Armenian genocide see Dadrian, "The Convergent Aspects," *op. cit.*, and Leo Hamalian, "The Armenian Genocide and the Literary Imagination," in Richard G. Hovannisian (ed.), *The Armenian Genocide in Perspective*, pp. 153-166.

AUSCHWITZ AND THE GULAG: DISCONTINUITIES AND DISSIMILARITIES

Steven T. Katz

I

Scholars and others have, for various reasons, been likening Auschwitz and the Gulag since the 1940's, and the comparison has become "canonical" since its powerful employment by Hannah Arendt in her *Origins of Totalitarianism*, first published in 1951.[1] Today this linkage is again at the center of the historical and normative discussion due to its vital role in the "Historical Debate" generated in Germany by the obscene nationalist apologetics of Ernest Nolte and his supporters.[2] But is this accepted historical piety correct? I think not. In contradistinction to Arendt and Nolte,[3] and others, I want to argue that the usual analogies drawn between these two evil phenomena are largely and essentially misleading, even fundamentally incorrect.

Before proceeding, however, let me be very clear about what I am and what I am not saying. The disjunctiveness that I will argue for is not moral--that one environment was more evil than the other (though this may also be the case)--but phenomenological, that is that the two contexts were created by, organized through, and employed in and for vastly different purposes, with nearly wholly different regulative ideologies. In their design, empirical facticity, intentionality and teleology they are radically alternative forms of manipulation, violence, and death. Both Auschwitz and the Gulag perpetrated monstrous acts of inhumanity and it is the recognition of this fact that leads to the intuitive assertions regarding their commonalty. But on other than ethical grounds, and the unsparing moral condemnation of both, the comparison is misleading. That is to say, the awareness of this primal ethical similarity must serve as the beginning of a conversation not its conclusion if we are not to lapse into intellectual barrenness, into that type of conceptual sterility that is a corollary of an inability to make necessary, if hard, distinctions. And it is to the making of such repercussive phenomenological discriminations as a moral obligation, as a debt to the truth, that we must now turn, inquiring in what way the Gulag is comparable to Auschwitz, in what way is it not.

II

The intriguing, not altogether transparent, exposition of the larger social-historical contexts out of which Nazism and Stalinism respectively grew is where we must begin.[4] Nazism emerged out of the turmoil of the post World-War I years, out of the inability of Germany to admit its own responsibility for defeat, out of the lack of viable democratic traditions in Germany, exacerbated by the inherent weaknesses of the Weimer state,[5] and out of the economic chaos created by the combination of reparations required by the Versailles Treaty and the "Great Depression." Yet it occurred in a highly modernized, technologically and culturally advanced society.[6] By contrast, Stalin came to power in the wake of a violent revolution wrought by an ideological, urban minority whose achievement of political control was in direct violation of those very Marxist theories in whose name it seized power. The revolution and Stalin's eventual triumph occurred in a society which was generally backward[7] and underdeveloped in every sense and, importantly, that was accustomed to harsh autocratic government maintained by force, secret police agencies, and detention camps, chronicled so powerfully by Dostoevsky.[8] A society without any tradition of political freedom or human rights. It was, perhaps, therefore not altogether unexpected that Bolshevism should, once it had seized political power, replace one menacing dictatorship with another.[9] Certainly the revolutionary leadership was not averse to the use of force to maintain itself as the Kronstadt[10] uprising and its suppression showed. Or again as the coming into being of the Checka revealed. Indeed Lenin seems to have felt such repression was a necessary condition for the maintenance of a proletarian revolution.[11] Thus, the ground for a bureaucratic, centralized, dictatorial, if not murderous, regime was established,[12] to be exploited to its full potential for evil, as well as transmuted in unprecedented[13] ways, by Lenin's successor, Comrade Stalin.

Stalin, with his immense energy, uncanny cunning, total unscrupulousness, and eccentric psychology, which included considerable native intelligence, would exacerbate, in central areas even recreate and transmogrify through a quantitative radicalness, all existing problems.[14] His parochial Russian nationalism[15] would bring him into conflict with Russia's minorities; his uncompromising drive towards rapid industrialization would produce the terrible, ravaging collision with the peasants (not only the wealthy Kulaks); and his egomaniacal hunger for absolute power would cause his paranoic fear of any and all holders of power, no matter how marginal or delimited, within the state and lead thereby to the many bloody party and army purges that mark his tenure as the leader of the Soviet Union.[16] Together these factors, always combined with his heightened political instincts and total lack of political morality, would sweep away all real and imagined opposition leaving him not only the undisputed ruler of Russia, but the greatest murderer, in quantitative terms, history has ever known.[17]

Of great importance is the fact that the historical context, the political culture and socioeconomic realities, out of which Stalinism emerged and in which it functioned, were markedly different[18] from that of Nazism. In Nazi Germany, because of its virulent antisemitic legacy (shared with most of Europe), and, even more, due to its own contemporary ideological constructions which led to genocide, the Jews were singled out for "metaphysical," i.e., racial and manichean, reasons. There was, neither in 1933 nor subsequently, any fundamental political or economic[19] gain in persecuting them, despite much widespread misunderstanding to the contrary. In Russia the Terror was, in contrast, a function of politics and economic policy (industrialization) plus Stalin's mental instability--a murderous quirkiness[20] he shared with Hitler.

Put another way, Hitler could have pursued all the dominant goals in his political revolution, e.g., national renaissance, *lebensraum*, even the disemancipation of western Jewry, without the "final solution"--assuming for the moment that killing Jews *per se* was not his major goal, as it seems finally to have been.[21] In contrast, Stalin could not have succeeded in his push towards rapid collectivization and the transformation of the fundamentals of the Soviet economy as part of the overall socialist transmogrification of Russian society without a direct clash with the peasantry as well as a deadly collision with the remaining elements of the pre-revolutionary socioeconomic structure that still survived.[22] He could, of course, have taken a different tack on economic policy, as Lenin and others had thought the better course, but once he decided on radical socialization and industrialization, or as he might argue in his own self-defense, with some modest justification, once these policies were forced by events upon him, extensive, pervasive conflict was inevitable. Isaac Deutscher has sensitively described the inherent confrontation in these terms:

> It would be easy for the historian to pass unqualified judgement on Stalin if he could assume that in his fight against Bukharin, Rykov, and Tomsky he pursued only his private ambition. This was not the case. His personal ends were not the only or the most important stakes in the struggle. In the tense months of 1928 and 1929 the whole fate of Soviet Russia hung in the balance.
> On the face of things, the opening of the crisis was so undramatic as to appear irrelevant. The peasants had failed to deliver a few million tons of grain to the towns. Prosaic as the event was, there was real drama in it. In refusing to sell food, the peasants had no clear political motives. They did not aim at the overthrow of the Soviets, although some of the politically minded elements among the well-to-do peasantry hoped for such an ending. The mass of the peasants was driven to apply that peculiar form of "sabotage" by economic circumstances. Most of the small farms did not produce more than was needed to feed their owners. After more than ten years the agricultural upheaval of 1917 was now taking its revenge. The splitting up of large estates into tiny holdings had given the Bolsheviks the support of the peasantry in the civil war; but in consequence the productivity of farming, or rather its capacity to feed the urban population, deteriorated. The big farmers,

on the other hand, demanded high prices for food, prices intolerably burdensome to the townspeople; and they also pressed for further concessions to capitalist farming. Stalin was, indeed, confronted with a most complex dilemma. If he yielded more ground to the peasants he would dangerously antagonize the urban working classes, which, on the whole, now again stood behind the Government, especially after the Government had about 1927, succeeded in rebuilding industry to its pre-war condition. But the refusal to yield to the peasantry also entailed the threat of famine and unrest in the towns. The problem demanded a radical solution. If the Government had begun to curb the big farmers and to encourage gradual collectivization earlier, as Trotsky and Zinoviev had counselled, it might not have needed now to resort to drastic emergency measures in order to obtain bread. As things stood, Stalin acted under the overwhelming pressure of events. The circumstance that he was not prepared for the events precipitated him into a course of action over which he was liable to lose control.[23]

Survival, economic and national, not ontological fantasies, was the key determinant. That is to say, the contextual consideration of the terror in Russia suggests that Stalin was confronting, to some degree at least, real[24] enemies both politically and in class terms during the 1920's, and possibly up until 1934-36.[25] By contrast, the Jews of Germany (and Europe) were not, except by definition, an authentic, political "enemy."

Still more, despite scholarly claims to the contrary,[26] Stalinism is not a complete *novum* in Bolshevik (and earlier Russian) tradition; it is, for all its radicalness, even recognizing its innovativeness, intimate with the Russian past. Not so the Nazi death camps. Auschwitz was unpredictable before it occurred, while having occurred it is not accounted for, nor explained, by precedents, despite the many terrible antisemitic precedents that do exist. A student of Czarist coercion and Leninist ideology would not be totally surprised, as the vast secondary literature proves, to encounter the phenomenon of the Gulag, though its sheer magnitude would still ravage one's sensibilities. By contrast, no study of pre-1933 German or modern western European history would suggest, or *ex post facto* explain, Treblinka and *Einsatzgruppen*. Looking back one can find "roots," but no amount of such "backward looking" historiography is sufficient to the reality. What occurred not only so exceeds what was "predictable," but in its qualitative dimensions is so discontinuous with its immediate pre-history as to represent its antithesis. The uncompromising, revolutionary evil of Auschwitz as compared to the massive, unceasing, primitive immorality of the Gulag, therefore conjures a different mood, a dissimilar cognitive response. The Holocaust remains always "beyond comprehension," an event as much revealed as mysterious, much as we must insist that it be open to scholarly investigation and ordinary rules of historical and philosophical enquiry. It is these very qualities that lead to the constant temptation--*to be resisted*--to remove it altogether from history. By contrast, the Gulag generates rage and dread, anger and sorrow, but not mythification. One is prepared, alas, to find it all too believable.

III

It may be that this impression, this disjunctive response, rests ultimately on the assimilability of the Gulag to two not unfamiliar historical categories, penal detention and slavery, that mix together in a particularly better way to create the Stalinist camps. Penal institution, including the use of special incarceration centers for political "dissidents," is an all too common historical phenomenon.[27] For example, the Nazi use of internment camps from 1933, e.g., Dachau, for political enemies such as Communists and liberals, is a parallel occurrence belonging to this general history and need not detain us.[28] The same may be said of the schematic role and temporal evolution of Czarist prison institutions into Bolshevik ones. Dostoevsky's *The House of the Dead* leaves us no innocent illusions on this subject. The relation of Stalin's Gulag to the normative structures of slavery,[29] however, requires a closer, adequately nuanced, look. The basic, compelling comparability of the two oppressive configurations lies in their purposeful, aggressive exploitation of human labor, i.e., both are rooted in and maintained by specific economic and social needs that are held to be best met by unfree labor.[30] Stalin's policy of the forced acceleration of industrialization was "aided"[31] by reducing a significant percentage of Russia's population into, effectively, "slaves," if by another name. Through this coercive labor policy, rooted in the Czarist past,[32] the inmates of the camps were made to provide crucial cheap labor for all forms of Soviet industrialization ranging from the mining of raw materials to the building of transportation networks.[33]   Representing, at its peak, on some accounts, more than 1/6th[34] of the male adult population, this "enslaved" group comprised the largest single industrial working class in Russia.   Moreover, this captive class was able to be set tasks that were: (a) necessary to the economy as a whole, yet which were situated in places where labor on the free market would have been very costly to procure;[35] and (b) that could be accomplished by the calculated substitution of a large work force in place of expensive machines, machines that could only be procured through foreign currency that the Soviet Union did not have.[36]

What requires particular recognition is that this slave labor system was not created as the result of the devastation wrought by the First World War, nor the consequences of special short-term problematics, aberrations, in the life of the Stalinist regime, though the numbers of such workers did vary from period to period.   Rather, and unmistakenly, it was inherent, as Solzhenitsyn has so dramatically emphasized, in the very fabric of Stalinism *per se*.[37]   The abiding constitutive excess which was a dominant feature of Stalinism was predicated upon, enacted within, an already grotesque, authoritarian, order.   Not only in the Gulag empire, but throughout the Soviet economy coercion was the norm after 1929.   The brutalities of agricultural collectivization form an essential ingredient in our schematic deconstruction, and to them must be added the extensive reorganization of (regular) industrial labor in 1930 that led, for example, in December 1938, to the system of industrial passports and in October 1940 to the introduction of severe penalties for lateness, absenteeism, and curtailment of the workers' freedom in job selection.[38]   Even more significant, analogous in intent to slave labor, is the system of State Labor Reserves[39] established by Stalin in October 1940 which, in effect, created large-scale pools of young, *unfree* industrial workers.   According to this scheme, as many as 1 million male teenagers, the majority off the farms, would be "drafted" into technical industrial apprenticeships deemed necessary by the State economic planners. After a training period lasting between 6 months and 2 years depending on the job for which one was being prepared, the young man would be assigned a task to which he was legally bound for 4 years.   In this way a novel method of industrial serfdom was instituted.   The Fourth Five-Year Plan called for

4,500,000 such recruits, a major percentage of all industrial employees. And as in the Gulag such unfree labor was expected to provide, in particular, 70% to 80% of the new workers in the heavy industries, e.g., coal mining, the mining of ferrous metals and machine building.[40] In this sense, then, the Gulag can be identified as the endpoint of a spectrum of Soviet labor exploitation rather than as a discontinuous and radical alternative to the "normal" Stalinist social order.

Upon reflection it becomes unarguably clear that those who project a mythical "Stalinism without excess" are twice deluded, once because the notorious extremes were the very stuff of Stalin's regime, and secondly, because the excesses were built into a normative, abiding structure that, in and of itself, was barbarously abusive. Hitler, or perhaps more precisely Himmler and Speer,[41] would create, during the war, a somewhat comparable slave empire comprised of captured prisoners of war, overrun Slavic peoples, and even citizens of conquered countries in western Europe, not to mention the industrial complexes utilizing Jewish labor at Auschwitz and elsewhere. However, Hitler's use of slave labor, whatever its overall qualitative comparability to Stalin's, differed with respect to the expropriation of Jewish labor. Jewish manpower resources were not utilized as slave-labor either in the classical, or Stalinist, sense,[42] but rather as, in Benjamin Ferencz's telling phrase, "less than slave [labor]," i.e., the German intent was not to foster economic efficiency, or substantive production gains, but instead, sought to establish the disutilitarian equation that balanced labor utilization with necessary guarantees that Jewish workers be worked to death in a very specific, highly inelastic period of time.[43]   Stalin's system, in contrast, theoretically at least, and more often than not in practice, was predicated on a fixed period of forced labor. The dominant concern of the regime being the realization of the labor quotas, while at the same time being callously, cynically *indifferent* to the survivability of its prisoner labor force. Whether Kolyma workers lived or died was a matter of little moral or practical import, aside from its bearing on productivity, to Stalin or the camp bureaucracy. If inmates could survive under the prevailing execrable conditions, well and good, but their individual fate was not primary--*neither that they survive nor that they die.* The Gulag, in the main, during most of the Stalinist era, vis-à-vis the majority, was uncaring, its state-dictated attitude towards its wards expressed in a skeptical, perverse disinterest in their particularity. Without doubt there was in the organization of the Gulag much malice, sadism, murder. Brutality was normal, the norm brutal. What was absent, however, was a specific, unambiguous, national policy of mass murder. That is to say, despite the high death toll in the Gulag, with the exception of that exceptional year 1938, the major causes of death in this environment were corollaries of the dolorific natural condition and the official attitude of unconcern which had the impact of ramifying the negative consequences of the ecological habitat. No less a critic of Stalin's Camps than Robert Conquest has summarized these circumstances in the following terms:

> Previous years [pre-1938] had seen, on occasion, massive casualties. But these had been due to inefficiencies in supply, attempts to carry out assignments in impossible conditions, and in fact--if in exaggerated form--the normal incompetence and brutality of Soviet life. When the difficulties could be overcome, conditions, as we have seen, were tolerable. But above all, prisoners were not subjected to lethal conditions on purpose.[44]

Even in that cruelest of years, 1938,[45] when Stalin and his new chief henchman for the Kolyma region, Major Garanin, ordered an unprecedented wave of shootings, increased every manner of abuse, and saw to it that conditions went from bad to unbearable, even then, for the entire year, the whole Kolyma district witnessed "only" 40,000[46] shootings, i.e., planned, directly sponsored, intentional, official murders.[47] And, even now, 1938, executions were still coupled to work quotas[48]--and generally unconnected to any other ideological or normative category, e.g., Kulaks, old Bolsheviks, or Jews. This is not to argue that Stalin's new ferocity towards the Gulag's population did not take its considerable, if more oblique, toll during this year. Figures are uncertain, but estimates ranging from 200,000 to 400,000 deaths caused by cold, starvation and overwork are commonly accepted. For this one year, under these exceptional conditions, the *Gulag* approached Auschwitz *asymptotically*. Asymptotically because even in this worst of years the Gulag did not operate under the same equation of life[49] and death as did Auschwitz. The priorities of labor versus death, of productivity vs. dehumanization, did shift towards a heretofore unprecedented near equality;

yet, even at its nadir, the demands of life, even if translated and reduced to economic units, still had at least equal weight.[50] In this matrix exploitation and annihilation certainly became too casually contraposed while the original dominant economic drive saw itself paralleled by a corrupt desire to debase, even destroy, many of the Camp inmates. However, even amidst this rueful reevaluation of purposes, at no time was the equation so wholly inverted that death was all; the highest, supreme unchallenged good. Moreover, and elemental to the Nazi vs. Gulag comparison, the Gulag killed people distributively, i.e., taking its toll on all groups, singling none out for "special treatment."[51] Then again, the powerful streak of harsh realism in Stalin's perception of reality caused him to recognize the need for "compromise" between actual economic requirements and the primitive desire to "punish" real or imagined enemies, while his Marxist-Leninist ideology allowed for such mediation. Alternatively, Hitler's severe biocentric "idealism" encouraged no comparable compromise on the Jewish question, while his immolating racial metaphysics permitted none.

As a consequence, Himmler's SS empire manifested no such mediating dispositions, nor did it represent similar, primarily utilitarian, priorities, at least not where the *Judenfrage* was concerned. In this arena it was primordially committed not only to Jewish submissiveness, to the exploitation of frightfully controlled Jewish labor, but also, and more rudimentarily, to the unenigmatic biological extinction of each and every Jew trapped within its parameters. Hitler and his Aryan elite were neither skeptical about nor disinterested, *contra* the controlling rationality of the Gulag, in the fate of "their" Jews--they were, rather, passionate advocates of the universal imperative that all Jews *must* die. Under no conditions, no matter how economically advantageous their efforts and no matter how politically co-operative Jewry proved itself to be, could it be left to survive. *Mere* Jewish survival was the active enemy. Compared to 40,000 shootings in total in the Kolyma in 1938, 10,000 Jews a day died at Auschwitz in 1944, Treblinka consumed 1.5-2 million Jews in 18 months, and the *Einsatzgruppen* efficiently murdered at least 1.5 million Jews in about the same period of time.

IV

In pointing out the sociological, historical, economic and ideological factors that operated distinctively and disjunctively in the Gulag and Auschwitz we have no desire to relativize one at the expense of the other, or to deny the immense evil of both. However, evil comes in many forms and it is the task of scholarship, distasteful as it might be, to study these variegated forms and to recognize differences as well as similarities between them. When one looks closely at the Gulag and Auschwitz in all their destructive complexity, one cannot but be profoundly aware of how very dissimilar they are.[52]

ENDNOTES

[1]Hannah Arendt, *The Origins of Totalitarianism* (New York, 1951; revised edition New York, 1966).

[2]Fuller details of this debate are provided by Charles Meier, *The Unmasterable Past: History, Holocaust, and German National Identity* (Cambridge, 1988); and Historikerstreit: *Die Dokumentation der Kontroverse um die Einzigartigkeit der Nationalsozialistischen Judenvernichtung* (Munich, 1987).

[3]In mentioning these two individuals together I do not mean to equate Arendt's employment of this connection with that of Nolte's.

[4]The particulars of the Nazi onslaught against Jewry will be described and analyzed exhaustively in my forthcoming study of the *Holocaust in Historical Context* (tentative title) to be published by Oxford University Press.

[5]On the growth and importance of antisemitism in the Weimar Republic, consult my essay, "1918 and After: Antisemitism in Weimar," in S. Katz and S. Gilman (eds.), *Antisemitism in Times of Crisis* (New York University Press, 1990).

[6]The many complex issues of the post-1918 situation in Germany will be analyzed in much greater detail, especially as they bear upon questions of German and Nazi antisemitism, in Vol. Three of my forthcoming study, *The Holocaust in Historical Context*.

[7]For example only 33% of the population could read in 1920. See, for more, Jean Elleinstein, *The Stalin Phenomenon* (London, 1976), pp. 15-16.

[8]Note especially his *The House of the Dead* (1861-62). See also D. Dallin and B. Nicolaevsky, *Forced Labor in Soviet Russia* (New Haven, 1947), pp. 299-305; and particularly Richard Pipes' extreme view of the origin of and continuity between the Soviet police state and its Czarist predecessor, *Russia Under the Old Regime* (New York, 1974). The work of Solzhenitsyn is, of course, relevant here as well.

[9]We note that the White Russian army and its short-lived terror was not very much different. Consider, for example, the pogroms in the Ukraine that caused thousands of casualties. It was a case of terror on the right and terror on the left. For fuller analysis of the Ukrainian situation see James Mace, *Communism and the Dilemmas of National Liberation, National Communism in Soviet Ukraine, 1918-1933* (Cambridge, 1983); and J. Borys, *The Sovietization of the Ukraine* (Edmonton, 1980).

[10]The entire Kronstadt experiment has been described in the recent excellent study by Israel Getzler, *Kronstadt 1917-1921: The Fate of the Soviet*

Democracy (Cambridge [England], 1983); and the earlier work by Paul Avrich, *Kronstadt, 1921* (Princeton, 1970).

[11]*Cf.* Lenin's 1917 essay *Can the Bolshevites Retain State Power?* For discussion of the early history of the *Checka* and *GPU* see Ronald Hingley, *The Russian Secret Police: Muscovite, Imperial Russian and Soviet Political Security Operations 1565-1970* (London, 1970); Boris Lewytzkyj, *Die rote Inquisition: die Geschichte der sowjetischen Sicherheitsdientse* (Frankfurt A.M, 1967); Simon Wolin and Robert M. Shesser, *The Soviet Secret Police* (New York, 1957); and Elleinstein, *The Stalin Phenomenon*, pp. 20-29. Reference should also be made to Solzhenitsyn's treatment of, and quotation from, Lenin in the *Gulag Archipelago*.

[12]On the meaning of the Civil War for later Soviet policies, see Sheila Fitzpatrick's interesting essay, *The Civil War As A Formative Experience* (The Wilson Center, Washington, DC, 1981). See also on this important issue Ronald Gregor Suny, *The Baku Commune 1917-18* (Princeton, 1972); David Lane, *The Roots of Russian Communism* (Assen, 1969); Robert Service, *The Bolshevik Party in Revolution, 1917-1923: A Study in Organizational Change* (New York, 1979); T. H. Rigby, *Lenin's Government, Sovnarkom 1917-1922* (Cambridge, 1979); and Sheila Fitzpatrick, *The Russian Revolution* (Oxford, 1982).

[13]There can be no doubt that Stalinism, in its use of mass murder, transcends the Czarist past. Czarist policy was oppressive in the extreme, but judging by all available statistics *not* murderous to any marked degree as A. Solzhenitsyn points out in his *Gulag*. In the 50 years before the revolution the Czarist regime, with all the provocation of the anarchists and other revolutionaries, executed less than 15,000 individuals. On this issue see also R. Conquest, *Kolyma*, (New York, 1979), pp. 229-230.

[14]This claim, of course, depends on how one understands the relation of Stalin and "Stalinism" to previous events in Russian history both Czarist and Bolshevik, an issue too complex to enter into in detail here.

[15]Stalin's Russian nationalism represented something very different from Lenin's attitude to other nationality groups. The brief encouragement of minority national identities under Lenin (d. 1924) and for a brief period thereafter, e.g., the brief flourishing of Ukrainian, Armenian, Muslim, Tatar, and Yiddish culture, was soon eclipsed by a militant, homogenizing Russian cultural imperialism.

[16]On these purges, see Robert Conquest, *The Great Terror: Stalin's Purge of the Thirties* (New York, 1968), and the additional sources cited in the next note.

[17]For a more detailed investigation of this highly complex problem see, among many relevant sources, Robert Conquest, *The Great Terror idem.*, *Kolyma idem.*, "Forced Labor Statistics: Some Comments," *Soviet Studies*, Vol. 34, No. 3 (July 1982): 434-439; *idem., The Harvest of Sorrow: Soviet Collectivization and the Great Famine* (New York, 1986); Josef G. Dyadkin,

Unnatural Deaths in the USSR, 1928-1954 (New Brunswick, 1983), to be used with care, cf. the review by Michael P. Sacks in *Slavic Review*, Vol. 43, No. 1 (Spring, 1984), pp. 119-120; Frank Lorimer, *The Population of the Soviet Union: History and Prospects* (Geneva, 1946); Mikhail Heller and Aleksander Nekrich, *Utopia in Power: The History of the Soviet Union from 1917 to the Present* (New York, 1986); Jerry Hough and Merle Fainsod, *How the Soviet Union is Governed* (Cambridge, 1979); Moshe Lewin, *Russian Peasants and Soviet Power* (Evanston, 1968); Robert A. Lewis, *et al.*, *Nationality and Population Change in Russia and the USSR: An Evaluation of Census Data, 1897-1970* (New York, 1976); Murray Feshbach, "The Soviet Union: Population Trends and Dilemmas," *Population Bulletin*, Vol. 37, No. 3 (August, 1982): 3-44. The most intense debate on the issue has been carried out since 1981 between Steven Rosefielde who favors very high mortality estimates for the Stalinist era "Collectivization, Gulag forced labour and the terror apparatus that sustained the Stalinist system appear to have claimed the lives of 21.4 to 24.4 million adults and 7.2 to 8.0 million children. An additional 14.4 million unrealized births unrelated to the war may also be included in this inventory, bringing the total population deficit attributable to Stalin's forced industrialization policies to 43.8 to 46 million people; figures more than double the 20 million civilian and military casualties incurred during the war," in "Excess mortality in the Soviet Union," (full bibliographical citation below) and S. G. Wheatcroft who has been aggressive in defending much lower estimates. For the acrimonious dialogue between these two see Steven Rosefielde, "The First 'Great Leap Forward' Reconsidered: Lessons of Solzhenitsyn's *Gulag Archipelago*," *Slavic Review*, Vol. 39, No. 4 (December 1980): pp. 593-602; Steven Rosefielde, "An Assessment of the Sources and Uses of Gulag Forced Labor 1929-1956," *Soviet Studies*, Vol. 33, No. 1 (January 1981): 51-87; Stephen G. Wheatcroft, "On Assessing the Size of Forced Concentration Camp Labour in the Soviet Union, 1929-56," *Soviet Studies*, Vol. 33, No. 2 (April, 1981): 265-295; *idem.*, "Towards a Thorough Analysis of Soviet Forced Labour Statistics," *Soviet Studies*, Vol. 35, No. 2 (April, 1983): 223-237; Steven Rosefielde, "Excess Mortality in the Soviet Union: A Reconsideration of the Demographic Consequences of Forced Industrialization 1929-1949," *Soviet Studies*, Vol. 35, No. 3 (July, 1983): 385-409; *idem.*, "Excess Collectivization Deaths 1929-1933: New Demographic Evidence," *Slavic Review*, Vol. 43, No. 1 (Spring 1984): 83-88; Stephen G. Wheatcroft, "New Demographic Evidence on Excess Collectivization Deaths: Yet Another *Kliuvkva* from Steven Rosefielde," *Slavic Review*, Vol. 44, No. 3 (Fall, 1985): 505-508; and Steven Rosefielde, "New Demographic Evidence on Collectivization Deaths: A Rejoinder to Stephen Wheatcroft," *Slavic Review*, Vol. 44, No. 3 (Fall, 1985): 509-516.

A further evaluation of the issues discussed by Rosefielde and Wheatcroft, favoring Wheatcroft's position in general, can be found in Barbara A. Anderson and Brian D. Silver, "Demographic Analysis and Population Catastrophe in the USSR," *Slavic Review*, Vol. 44, No. 3 (Fall, 1985): 517-536. In this context one should also read Stephen Wheatcroft's two complementary papers, "Famine and Factors Affecting Mortality in the USSR: The Demographic Crisis of 1914-1922 and 1930-33" and "Famine and Factors Affecting Mortality in the USSR: The Demographic Crisis of 1914-1922 and 1930-33, *Appendices*," both published in The Soviet

Industrialization Project Series, pamphlet numbers 20 and 21, University of Birmingham, Birmingham, England. The basic work done in Russia has been that of B. Urlanis, whose major demographic studies are, unfortunately, still not translated.

[18]Hannah Arendt's attempt in *The Origins of Totalitarianism*, and the derivative efforts of those many others who have followed her lead, to portray Stalinism and Nazism as two forms of a common political reality called "Totalitarianism" is seriously flawed and leads to more distortion than illumination in the final analysis of these two movements.

[19]The "economics" of antisemitism are complex, but I would argue that economic justifications are "bad reasons for what people believe on instinct." Jews did *not* control the German national economy as the antisemites claimed, and their purge would not "free" the economy in any appreciable way.

[20]Robert Tucker has described both Stalin and Hitler as "warfare personality" types, a category he defines as follows:

> The warfare personality shows paranoid characteristics as psychologically defined, but what is essential from the standpoint of our discussion is that it represents a *political* personality type. The characteristically paranoid perception of the world as an arena of deadly hostilities being conducted conspiratorily by an insidious and implacable enemy against the self finds systematized expression in terms of political and ideological symbols that are widely understood and accepted in the given social milieu ("The Dictator and the Totalitarian," *World Politics*, Vol. 17, No. 4 [July, 1964]: 555-583).

[21]See his "Last Testament," for example.

[22]The intimate relationship between modernization and conflict in the Stalinist era has been amply studied. Among the more reasoned analyses are N. Valentinov, *The NEP and the Party Crisis* (Stanford, 1971); Cyril E. Black (ed.), *The Transformation of Russian Society: Aspects of Social Change Since 1861* (Cambridge, 1967); Alex Inkeles, *Social Change in Soviet Russia* (New York, 1971); E. H. Carr and R. W. Davies, *Foundations of a Planned Economy, 1926-1939*, 3 Vols. (New York, 1969-71); Nicholas Lampert, *The Technical Intelligentsia and the Soviet State* (New York, 1971); Alexander Ehrlich, *The Soviet Industrialization Debate, 1924-1928* (Cambridge, 1960); and R. V. Daniels, *The Conscience of the Revolution: Communist Opposition in Soviet Russia* (Cambridge, 1960). On the economic situation under NEP see V. N. Bandera, "The New Economic Policy (NEP) as an Economic System," *Journal of Political Economy*, Vol. 71, No. 3 (June, 1963): 265-279.

[23]Isaac Deutscher, *Stalin: A Political Biography* (New York, 1949), pp. 317-318.

[24]"Real" does not mean I approve, nor that Stalin was the "good" guy and the enemies the "bad" guys. It means only that Stalin had cause to be concerned with, for example, Trotsky and his faction on the one hand and the peasants on the other.

[25]See A. Ulam, *Stalin*, p. 295, for more on this issue.

[26]Consider, for example, the argument of S. Cohen, "Bolshevism and Stalinism." See also Robert Tucker's revisionist thesis in the same general direction though much more subtly and dialectically stated, and therefore also perhaps embodying a more profound contradictoriness, "Stalinism as Revolution from Above," in R. Tucker (ed.), *Stalinism*, pp. 77-110.

[27]The history and character of such penal institutions has been described in Michel Foucalt's interesting, but limited, *Discipline and Punish: The Birth of the Prison* (New York, 1977); U.R.Q. Henriques, "The Rise and Decline of the Separate Systems of Prison Discipline," *Past and Present*, Vol. 54 (1972): 61-93; and George Ruschke and Otto Kirchheimer, *Punishment and Social Structure* (New York, 1939).

[28]It should, however, be remembered that so-called "concentration camps" are to be clearly distinguished from Death Camps, i.e., places created primarily, if not solely, to kill people, e.g., Treblinka and Auschwitz. The existence of industrial complexes at these Death Camps should not be misunderstood, i.e., as mitigating their overall genocidal charge, for all their workers were scheduled to die as part of the process.

[29]The salient, complex comparative questions raised by the historical institution of slavery will be taken up in detail in Volume One (Roman Slavery) and Volume Two (Black Slavery) of my forthcoming study, *The Holocaust in Historical Context*.

[30]A sad story with many earlier chapters. One such abuse which is paradigmatic of many is that of sixteenth-and seventeenth-century galley slavery on which see Paul Bamford, *Fighting Ships and Prisons: The Mediterranean Galleys of France in the Age of Louis XIV* (Minneapolis, 1973).

[31]I use this term in quotation marks in light of the counter-claim advanced in many, and in particular, more recent studies, particularly of the agricultural sector, that contend that this policy was counter-productive even on the basis of strict economic rationality. For myself, I am not altogether convinced by these arguments against the strictly economic benefits of this activity which, vis-à-vis industrialization, seem positive and real. It seems to me that while this collectivized labor was not efficient it did produce modest results when all elements are factored in which were exaggerated enormously by Stalin and the ruling elite. This however, of course, does not mean that I would agree that this was the best way to achieve such results.

[32]The use of criminal proceedings and institutions to assure needed labor is an old policy not only in Russia but elsewhere in Europe.

[33]A full list of camps and the type of work carried on in them is given in David J. Dallin and Boris Nicolaevsky, *Forced Labor in Soviet Russia*, pp. 58-72.

[34]All demographic statistics provided in this paper are provisional and the subject of great scholarly debate. For an introduction to the problematic aspects of this basic issue see: Dallin and Nicolaevsky, *Forced Labor in Soviet Russia* who give a figure of 5-6 million slave workers in 1937 and 8 million 'slave' workers in 1941; Steven Rosenfielde who provides very high estimates of 8 million Gulag workers in 1937, 10 million in 1940, and 12-15 million in 1946-50; "An Assessment of the Sources and Uses of Forced Labor, 1929-1956," *Soviet Studies* No. 1, (January, 1981): 51-87; Stephen Wheatcroft concludes that "some four to five million is the maximum number of concentration camp labourers who could have existed in 1939," "On Assessing the Size of Forced Concentration Camp Labor in the Soviet Union, 1931-1956," *Soviet Studies*, No. 2 (April, 1981): 286, the entire essay covers pp. 265-295; *idem.*, "Towards a Thorough Analysis of Soviet Forced Labor Statistics," *Soviet Studies*, No. 2 (April, 1983): 223-237; R. Conquest, *The Great Terror*; and *idem.*, "Forced Labor Statistics: Some Comments," *Soviet Studies*, No. 3 (July, 1982): 434-439. Conquest seems to put the figure of slave laborers at 8 million or above, *Great Terror*, Appendix A. On Soviet manpower note, in addition, Warren W. Eason, "Forced Labor," in Abram Bergson and Simon Kuznets (eds.), *Economic Trends in the Soviet Union* (Cambridge, 1963), pp. 38-93; N. S. Timasheff's much lower estimate (2.3 million) of forced labor in 1937 in his "The Post War Population of the Soviet Union," *The American Journal of Sociology*, Vol. 54 (1948): 148-155; and N. Jasny "Labour and Output in Soviet Concentration Camps," *Journal of Political Economy*, Vol. 59, No. 5 (October, 1951): 405-491, who gives a lowish figure of 3.5 million Gulag workers in 1941.

[35]More details in support of this view can be found in Roy Medvedev, *Let History Judge*, p. 394.

[36]Dallin and Nicolaevsky, *Forced Labor in Soviet Russia*, pp. 88-90, discuss this issue more fully. Also note the comments of Robert Conquest, *Kolyma*, p. 39; and the observations of A. Ciliga, *Sibërie, terre de l'exil de l'industrialisation* (Paris, 1960).

[37]It may well be that part of this problematic is structural, i.e., it is part of the larger problem of trying to re-form Russia on the basis of a Marxist theory ill-suited to the industrial and agrarian realities of Russia in the 1920's. Ulam suggests: "One cannot find out from Marx how to build socialism in a prevailingly agrarian society, any more than one can learn how to build a nuclear reactor by reading the works of Newton," *Stalin*, p. 294.

[38]This labor reorganization and its implications are analyzed by Solomon M. Schwarz, *Labor in the Soviet Union* (New York, 1952), pp. 209f. This issue and relevant sources was called to my attention by Barrington Moore Jr., *Terror and Progress in the USSR* (Cambridge, 1954), pp. 54-55.

[39]On this program see Harry Schwartz, *Russia's Soviet Economy* (New York, 1950), pp. 449f.

[40]Solomon M. Schwarz, *Labor in the Soviet Economy*, pp. 77-83.

[41]Himmler's entrepreneurial ambitions are narrated in Speer's study entitled *Infiltration: How Heinrich Himmler Schemed to Build an SS Industrial Empire* (New York, 1981).

[42]Jerzy Gliksman, an inmate in the Gulag, gives us this accurate understanding of the Stalinist slave labor system:

> The Soviet *lagers* are in fact institutions practicing slave labor. They are closely tied to various industrial or other enterprises which, in turn, are part of the over-all Soviet economy. They are expected to fulfill their part in the general economic plan, and are a tremendous source of cheap labor for this plan. Openly and cynically, without any trace of concern for appearances, the camp inmate is therefore treated simply as a forced supplier of needed work (*Tell the West* [New York, 1948], p. 244).

[43]Raul Hilberg, *The Destruction of European Jewry* (Chicago, 1967), pp. 334-345, discusses the relation of slave labor to survival in detail. His important conclusion: "The Polish Jews were annihilated in a process in which economic factors were truly secondary" (p. 345).

[44]R. Conquest, *Kolyma*, p. 47.

[45]On these events see R. Conquest, *Kolyma*, pp. 49-66.

[46]R. Conquest, *Kolyma*, p. 58.

[47]By comparison the Nazis were killing more Jews in one week at Auschwitz in late 1943 and 1944 than is represented by this Gulag total for the entire year 1938.

[48]Further details of this deadly activity are provided by R. Conquest, *Kolyma*, pp. 51-52.

[49]This conclusion becomes incontrovertible when one examines in detail the day-to-day conditions in the two environments. I.e., matters of "selections," work assignments, health care, living conditions, sex, women, children and release all reveal fundamental differences.

[50]Even Robert Conquest, in his most telling indictment of the Stalinist enterprise, does not claim more than this.

> All in all, these conditions reflected one main truth. In the minds of its creators and organizers the conscious purpose of Kolyma, which had originally been the production of gold,

with death as an unplanned by-product, had become the production, with at least equal priority, of gold and death (*Kolyma*, p. 124).

[51]I.e., in the generality of Gulag life itself.

[52]The full examination of these differences will be found in my forthcoming *The Holocaust in Historical Context*.

THE PHILOSOPHER AND THE JEWS:
THE CASE OF MARTIN HEIDEGGER

Richard L. Rubenstein

Martin Heidegger was one of the most important Western philosophers since Hegel. At least for a time, he was also a confirmed Nazi and, perhaps, a convinced anti-Semite who, unlike so many of his fellow Germans, never expressed a word of regret for the horrors perpetrated by the Third Reich. Moreover, even after ceasing to be visibly active as a Nazi, he retained his membership in the Nazi party (#312589 Gau Baden) until the very end of the war, faithfully paying his dues and assessments.

Debate concerning Heidegger's alleged anti-Semitism and his commitment to National Socialism has been carried on since the end of the war. Recently, the debate has been renewed with the publication of Victor Farias' book, *Heidegger et le nazisme*.[1] Were Heidegger a lesser figure, his involvement in National Socialism would be of little concern save to historians with a special interest in twentieth-century German philosophy. Unfortunately, such is not the case. If, as some students of Heidegger contend, Heidegger was an unrepentant follower of a political movement whose most distinctive institution was the death camp, with its factory-like capacity for the extermination and incineration of as many as 25,000 human beings a day, one must either come to understand philosophy in a radically new light or one must seriously question the value of Heidegger's contribution.

Some of Heidegger's defenders insist that there is no intrinsic connection between his thought and his politics. This is a position Heidegger himself rejected. Whatever his political commitments after resigning as Rector of the University of Freiburg, he did maintain contact with a few of his former Jewish students including the philosopher Karl Löwith. Löwith has written of a conversation he had with Heidegger during a reunion of the Heidegger and Löwith families in Rome in 1936 in which Heidegger "left...no doubt concerning his faith in Hitler" and acknowledged that this commitment to National Socialism was an intrinsic expression of his philosophy. Löwith also reported that Heidegger saw nothing "out of place" in wearing a swastika lapel pin during the entire Rome visit.[2]

Moreover, as early as 1927 in his major work, *Sein und Zeit*, Heidegger implied that there is an intrinsic connection between authentic existence, thought and politics. In that work Heidegger's readers are called to "authenticity," which is characterized as honest acceptance of man's own being and which Heidegger further identifies as "resoluteness" (*Entschlossenheit*), that is, the authentic response to the call of conscience.[3] In that call man, who is referred to by Heidegger as *Dasein*, is summoned out of his accepted, routine ways toward openness to the uncertainty and groundlessness of human existence.[4]

As understood by Heidegger, authentic existence in our era presupposes Nietzsche's "death of God" and the total absence of any higher authority which could serve as a guide or source of norms. Those who seek this guidance, such as Heidegger's contemporary, theologian Karl Barth, are regarded as leading an unauthentic existence. It should, however, be noted that Barth, who was as important to Christian theology as Heidegger was to philosophy, was never in doubt concerning the evil of National Socialism. Barth later wrote about his experiences during the turbulent period of the Nazi seizure of power: "[I] knew where I stood and what I could not do. In the last resort, this was because I saw my dear German people beginning to worship a false God."[5] In 1934 Barth refused to take the oath of allegiance to Hitler required of all German professors even though his refusal cost him his job. By contrast, during his tenure as rector of the University of Freiburg, Heidegger compelled his faculty colleagues to take the oath. Barth's rejection of National Socialism is all the more notable because it was by no means motivated by any kind of philosemitism, personal or theological. In a letter to Dr. Freidrich-Wilhelm Marquardt of Berlin dated 5 September 1967, Barth wrote

> I am decidedly not a philosemite, in that in personal encounters with living Jews [even Jewish Christians] I have always, so long as I can remember, had to suppress a totally irrational aversion, naturally suppressing it at once on the basis of all my presuppositions, and concealing it totally in my statements, yet still having to suppress and conceal it. Pfui! is all I can say to this in some sense allergic reaction of mine. But this is how it was and is. A good thing that this reprehensible instinct is totally alien to my sons and other better people than myself (including you). But it could have had a retrogressive effect on my doctrine of Israel.[6]

The aversion may very well have influenced his doctrine of Israel. Barth discerned the hand of God in the Holocaust. In 1942 he wrote, "And there is no doubt that Israel hears; now less than ever can it shelter itself behind the pretext of ignorance and inability to understand. But Israel hears--and does not believe."[7] Barth reiterated the same message in 1949, asserting that "the evil that had come to the Jewish people was the result of its unfaithfulness."[8] For Barth Israel's alleged "unfaithfulness" was, of course, its failure to accept Christ as Israel's messiah. Nevertheless, in spite of Barth's identification of the Holocaust as God's punishment of the Jews for their unbelief, he steadfastly opposed National Socialist racism on Christian grounds. We shall return to the contrast between the philosopher and the theologian below.

Absent any transcendent authority, Heidegger's categories of resoluteness and authenticity appear to have an abstract, formal quality which can easily lead to sheer arbitrariness and nihilism in which anything, including the most radical National Socialist programs, is permissible. Nevertheless, *Dasein* cannot exist in the world without constantly being confronted with the necessity of responsible choice and decision. In *Sein und Zeit* Heidegger sought to escape from nihilism by seeking authority in "repeatable possibilities of existence," that is in the past.[9] Unfortunately, Heidegger offered no criteria by which those aspects of the past deemed worthy are to be recognized. Instead, he identified "authentic repetition" with "the possibility that *Dasein* may choose its hero."[10] Who that hero might be or how he might be identified was not specified.

Nevertheless, Heidegger did suggest criteria by which heroes are to be recognized. Having rejected all possibility of transcendence, Heidegger also rejected modern subjective individualism, characterizing *Dasein* as being-in-the-world-with-others.[11] Such being-in-the-world has, of necessity, an historical dimension which *Dasein* shares with his fellows of the same *Volk*:

> Our fates have already been guided in advance, in our Being with one another in the same world and in our resoluteness for definite possibilities....*Dasein*'s fateful destiny in and with its 'generation' goes to make up the full authentic historizing of *Dasein*.[12]

For Heidegger authenticity thus entails the individual's historical involvement in the destiny of his community and his generation. With the advent of National Socialism, Heidegger's choice of a hero and his involvement in the destiny of his community were to take on a sinister dimension. By his own admission, Heidegger found his hero in Hitler at least for a time. Unfortunately, as Karsten Harries has pointed out, "Due to its formal character, *Being and Time* invites a...readiness to commit ourselves without prior assurance that there is a cause worthy of our commitment."[13] Unlike Heidegger, Karl Barth was capable of discerning which causes are worthy of our commitment.

The question of the relation between Heidegger's thought and his politics, including the issue of anti-Semitism, can thus be seen as consistent with Heidegger's own views. Victor Farias, the most recent researcher to explore this question in a systematic way, has concluded that Heidegger's anti-Semitism and his Nazi commitments were neither a sport nor an aberration but were intrinsic to his development as a thinker. Farias argues that these attitudes were preceded by a long period of gestation going back to the anti-Semitic Christian Social movement of Austria and the region in which Heidegger began his studies, Messkirch and Constance.

The subject of Heidegger's earliest published writing was Abraham a Santa Clara (1644-1709), a court preacher of the baroque era who had attended the same Latin school as did Heidegger in his time. The occasion for Heidegger's initial writing was the dedicatory ceremonies for a monument to Abraham a Santa Clara at Kreenheinstetten, a village close to Messkirch, on August 15, 1910. The monument itself proved beyond the resources of the village and could only be completed with the assistance of a contribution from the office of the anti-Semitic Mayor of Vienna, Karl Lueger, concerning whom Hitler expressed his indebtedness in *Mein Kamf*.[14]

Santa Clara was violently anti-Jewish and ultra-nationalist. He wrote, "Outside of the Devil, humanity has no greater enemy than the Jews....For their beliefs, they deserve not only the gallows but the funeral pyre."[15] In Heidegger's time that pyre was finally lit. The young Heidegger saw the preacher as offering a counter-model to the relativistic culture of urban modernity with its rapidly changing mores and its absence of fixed values. At the time Heidegger was preparing to enter the Jesuit order and become a priest.

The inauthenticity and corruption of urban, secular life, a theme effectively used by the Nazis, was to be an abiding idea for Heidegger. A persistent theme in Heidegger's thought from start to finish was the idea of authentic existence as rooted in one's local *Heimat*. This theme was linked to a profound distrust of the world of technology. Like so many other Germans and Austrians whose roots were outside of burgeoning, multi-ethnic cities like pre-Hitler Vienna and Berlin, Heidegger had a profound distaste for the modern world of asphalt and concrete and the alienating, relativising culture it engendered. Heidegger twice turned down an invitation to become Professor of Philosophy in Berlin. On the second occasion (1934), he expressed disdain for the "world of the city" and explained that his philosophical work "belongs right in the midst of the peasant's work."[16] Heidegger's friend, Heinrich Petzet, has commented on Heidegger's distaste for urban life:

> If a certain type of urban life was repugnant to him, and all that pertained to the big city appeared strange to him, this was especially true of that mundane spirit of Jewish circles that dominate the great capitals of the West. But this attitude must not be understood as anti-Semitism, although it has often been interpreted that way.[17]

In spite of Petzet's claim that Heidegger's repugnance of urban life and the "mundane spirit of Jewish circles that dominate" was not the view of an anti-Semite, this same repugnance was characteristic of virtually every German anti-Semite in the twenties and thirties. In the Weimar era, right-wing Germans tended to regard the *Volk* as "diseased" by the "polluting" presence of Jews in their midst. As Robert J. Lifton has demonstrated, this was a "disease" which an important segment of the German medical profession came to believe could only be "cured" by the "surgical" removal of the polluting social elements. Lifton has shown that such ideas became the basis for the interpretation of extermination of "undesirables" as a therapeutic tool in the service of racial hygiene.[18] Moreover, as we shall see, Heidegger's life-long friend, Eugen Fischer, was an intellectual leader of Nazi "racial science."

Heidegger's distaste for the pluralistic, modern world--epitomized by the Weimar Republic in the eyes of a decisively influential group of German intellectuals and academics--was also shared by such prominent German Protestant theologians as Gerhard Kittel, Paul Althaus and Emanuel Hirsch.[19] Like Heidegger, these men lent their wholehearted support to National Socialism when it came to power. One is struck, for example, by the similarity between Petzet's description of Heidegger's attitude toward urban life and the Jews and a 1937 statement by Paul Althaus, the mildest anti-Semite of the three theologians, on the Jewish problem:

> It does not have to do with Jewish hatred--one can reach an agreement directly with serious Jews on this point--, it does not have to do with blood, also not with the religious beliefs of Judaism. *But it does involve the threat of a quite specific disintegrated and demoralizing urban spirituality, whose representative is now the Jewish* Volk.[20]

Heidegger returned to writing about Abraham a Santa Clara toward the end of his career. On May 2, 1964 Heidegger gave a lecture entitled "Concerning Abraham a Santa Clara" on the occasion of a reunion of alumni of the Messkirch Latin School. On that occasion, Heidegger praised Santa Clara as a master of language and a man of destiny. However, in spite of the Holocaust and Santa Clara's prescription of the "funeral pyre" as the "solution" of the Jewish problem, Heidegger passed over Santa Clara's virulent anti-Semitism in silence.[21] As we shall see, this was typical of Heidegger's post-war indifference toward the *Shoah*. Heidegger held that "Dasein is historical," but had almost nothing to say concerning the bloodiest and most destructive action ever perpetrated in the name of the German *Volk*.

After the war, Heidegger claimed that he had ceased to participate in Nazi party activities in 1934. This claim can no longer be supported by the available evidence.[22] Before turning to that evidence, however, we must take note of Heidegger's most overtly Nazi period, his term as rector of the University of Freiburg. Undoubtedly, the best source of information concerning Heidegger's political activities as rector is to be found in the university's archives. Unfortunately, the archives have been declared unavailable to the public and are likely to remain so for a long time.[23] The refusal of the university to open its archives more than fifty years after Heidegger's tenure as rector inevitably raises the question of why a research institution sees fit to hamper rather than foster historical research on this question. Nor is Freiburg the only institution that has withheld relevant historical material. Farias reports that he encountered considerable difficulty in getting material on Heidegger from a number of German archives.

Because of Heidegger's international reputation and his widely known pro-Nazi views, Heidegger was elected rector three months after the Nazi seizure of power. The appointment was considered an event of international importance. The faculty had hoped that Heidegger would be able to serve as an effective mediator between the university and the new National Socialist state, preserving as much of the university's autonomy as was possible under the circumstances. Heidegger disappointed these expectations.

Heidegger's inauguration on May 27, 1933 was a ceremonial event with all of the customary Nazi trappings, including an abundance of swastikas, the presence of members of the Nazi student movement in their SA uniforms and the singing of the Nazi anthem, the "Horst Wessel Lied." Heidegger's inaugural lecture, the notorious *Rektoratsrede*, was entitled "The Self-Assertion of the German University."[24] The address is usually taken to be one of the most explicitly pro-Nazi addresses he ever gave. For example, he expressed satisfaction in the end of academic freedom in the German university, declaring:

> The much celebrated "academic freedom" is being banished
> from the German university; for this freedom was not genuine,
> since it was only negative. It meant primarily freedom from
> concern, arbitrariness of intentions and inclinations, lack of
> restraint in what was done and left undone. The concept of the
> freedom of the German is now brought back to its truth.[25]

Heidegger concluded with words of praise for "the splendor and greatness" of
the current "setting out" of the German people to "fulfill its historic mission,"
a matter decided by "the young and the youngest strength of the people." In
the context of the upheavals taking place in Germany in the spring of 1933, it
is difficult to understand these words as other than an enthusiastic public
endorsement of the National Socialist *Machtergreifung*.

Nevertheless, a word of caution is in order. It is important to note
that the body of the lecture is devoted less to Nazi politics than to the
question, "what is science?" and the role of the German university in
fostering it. In attempting to answer that question Heidegger goes back to
the beginnings of science in Greek philosophy and shows how that beginning
is related to the destiny of the university and the German people. The
interpretation of the *Rektoratsrede* as an overtly pro-Nazi document cannot
be dismissed. Heidegger was a committed Nazi at the time. However, this
interpretation should be read together with that of scholars such as Karsten
Harries and Graeme Nicholson.[26] Harries points out that "Heidegger's
concern in the address is directed not so much towards the individual as
towards the threatened autonomy of the German university."[27] Still, Harries
observes that Heidegger "was willing to fuse his own philosophical
terminology with Nazi jargon." He cites as one example the "three bonds" of
the German student which are to replace the now banished "academic
freedom," namely, *Arbeitsdienst, Wehrdienst* and *Wissensdienst*, Labor Service,
Military Service and Science Service.[28] Nicholson sees the *Rektoratsrede* as
an expression of Heidegger's attempt to put "the mark of his philosophy" on
National Socialism.[29] This is in keeping with Heidegger's later explanation
in which he acknowledged that in 1933 he saw "in the movement that had
gained power the possibility of an inner recollection and renewal of the
people and a path that would allow it to discover its historical vocation in the
Western world."[30] Heidegger thus discerned at least a partial coincidence of
aim and aspiration between this thought and that of the Nazi movement at

the time. Later in the year, Heidegger made matters worse in an address to the students of Freiburg in his capacity as rector in which he told them, "Let not theories and 'ideas' be the rules of your being. The Führer himself and he alone is German reality, today and henceforth."[31] The philosopher-theologian Emil Fackenheim has commented that when Heidegger endorsed the Führer's actions, he was impelled neither by fear nor by opportunism, "but rather deliberately and with the full weight of his philosophy behind it."[32]

On October 1, 1933 Heidegger was appointed Führer of the university. Unlike his appointment as rector, this appointment was made by the Nazi Minister of Education rather than the faculty senate in accordance with the Nazi Führerprinzip. In a letter dated December 20, 1933, Heidegger declared that his goal had been, "the fundamental change of scientific education in accordance with the strengths and the demands of the National Socialist State."[33] Heidegger's efforts towards the transformation of the university into a Nazi institution were especially evident in his dismissal of "non-aryan" professors and the application of Nazi discriminatory laws to Jewish students. Heidegger himself refused to accept Jewish students even during the period in which, though discriminated against, they were still permitted to attend German universities. Among the other changes was the institution of the compulsory Nazi salute at the beginning and conclusion of each class session, and the organization of a Department of Race in the university managed by the SS and offering courses taught by a specialist from the Institute of Racial Hygiene in Berlin. Heidegger himself remained a lifelong friend of Eugen Fischer, director of the Institute of Racial Hygiene since 1927 and an officer in the SS. Fischer's published works include volume seven of *Forschungen zur Judenfrage*, the annual journal of Walter Frank's *Reichsinstitut für Geschichte des neuen Deutschlands*, co-authored with Gerhardt Kittel, Professor of New Testament Theology at Tübingen from 1926 to 1945 and Nazi party member as of May 1945. Fischer and Kittel observe:

> Always, at all times, whether in the first or the twentieth century, the dream of world Jewry is sole domination of the world, now and in the future.[34]

Apparenly, Fischer's career as a leader in the movement to endow biological anti-Semitism with an aura of "scientific" legitimation constituted no impediment to Heidegger's continuing friendship. In 1960 Heidegger sent Fischer an inscribed copy of one of his books as a Christmas gift.[35]

It should, however, be noted that Heidegger claimed that he was never wholeheartedly a Nazi. He has written that his first act as rector was a refusal to permit the posting of the anti-Semitic *Judenplakat*, the "Jew Notice," of the Nazi *Deutsche Studentenbund* in any of the university rooms. He incurred further party displeasure by failing to appoint party members as deans and by seeking the retention of Jewish professors, Georg von Hevesy and Siegfried Thannhauser. Von Hevesy emigrated to Sweden and won the Nobel prize for chemistry in 1943.[36] Heidegger further claimed that he resigned as rector when "it became clear that a rift separated the National Socialist conception of university and science from my own, which could not be bridged."[37]

In reality, Heidegger was less than forthcoming in his publicly available explanations of his activities as rector. A particularly nasty aspect of Heidegger's attempts to reform the university along National Socialist lines was his secret denunciations of academic colleagues to Nazi authorities. On September 29, 1933 Heidegger informed the office of the Ministry of Education at Karlsruhe that Hermann Staudinger, Professor of Chemistry at Freiburg, had been a pacifist during World War I. Heidegger recommended that Staudinger be fired without pension.[38] Heidegger later moderated his position because of fear of international repercussions. In 1953 Staudinger received the Nobel prize in his field.

On December 16, 1933 Heidegger wrote to Dr. Vogel of Göttingen concerning Dr. Eduard Baumgarten, a specialist in American philosophy at Göttingen who had formerly been Heidegger's close friend and student at Freiburg.[39] Baumgarten had also taught for several years in the United States. Heidegger complained that Baumgarten was "anything but a National Socialist," that he came from a "circle of liberal-democratic intellectuals around Max Weber," that he had studied with "the Jew Fraenkel who had been active at Göttingen before being expelled from here [Freiburg]," and that he had become "very Americanized" as a result of his sojourn in the

United States. Although a convinced Nazi, Vogel refused to act on Heidegger's denunciation. He filed the letter with the notation, "Unusable, charged with hatred."[40]

As is well known, after the war Heidegger was denied the right to teach and forbidden to take part in the public activities of the university. However, by 1951 he was accorded the status of a Professor Emeritus and once again permitted to teach.

Heidegger's claim to have become disenchanted with National Socialism did not in any way mitigate his hatred of both the United States and the Soviet Union. Heidegger was convinced that Americanism and Bolshevism were the two greatest dangers of the twentieth century. By contrast, he saw the Germans as the only people capable of bringing about the renewal of the West. In 1935 he depicted the German *Volk* as the "metaphysical *Volk*" par excellence. He enlarged upon the claim in the interview he gave to *Der Spiegel* on September 25, 1966 for posthumous publication. In the interview Heidegger asserted that there is a "special inner kinship between the German language and the language and thought of the Greeks." "Being speaks German," Heidegger insisted, arguing that when the French begin to reflect on the mystery of Being, "they speak German."[41] Given his exaggerated opinion of the importance of the German *Volk* and their language, it is hardly surprising that in 1943 he told his students that only Germany's victory in the war "can save the West for its history."[42] However, for Heidegger the West could only be saved if Nazi Germany was triumphant over both the United States and the Soviet Union. This was at a time when knowledge of the death camps was widespread within Germany. Heidegger saw the Germans before, during and after the war as caught "in the pincers between Russia and America." He described both countries as exhibiting "the same desolate frenzy of a rootless and groundless organization of mediocre humanity."[43] Both countries were in the minds of Nazi ideologues unduly influenced by Jews and Judaism, each in its own distinctive way. Convinced of Germany's spiritual and moral superiority in spite of the death camps, he could see no real difference between the United States and Stalinist Russia. Incidentally, such ideas are once again becoming popular in the Federal Republic.

Moreover, in 1953 Heidegger made the claim that Germany's defeat had settled nothing:

> What has World War II decided? (Let us be silent about its terrible consequences for our *Vaterland*, and in particular its split through its middle.) This world war has decided nothing. If we take the term "decision" in so high and wide a sense as to concern solely the essential destiny (*Wesengeschick*) of man on this earth.[44]

In spite of Heidegger's oracular pronouncement, there were millions of people for whom World War II settled a great deal. These included millions of Eastern Europeans who were treated by the Germans as *Untermenschen* to be enslaved and/or annihilated. Above all, the Allied victory decided a great deal about the Nazi death camps, a matter of more than a little consequence both to the survivors and to the moral health of the German nation. Apparently, Heidegger was incapable of understanding that the division of the *Vaterland*, which he lamented, was a direct consequence of the Third Reich having launched and lost a war of aggression, enslavement and annihilation.

While Heidegger had no difficulty in expressing pain and sorrow for the sufferings endured by his fellow Germans, he was incapable of even a remote suggestion of compassion for their victims. In one of the few instances in which he commented on the Holocaust, he trivialized it. On January 20, 1948, Heidegger responded to an inquiry from Herbert Marcuse concerning his silence on the subject by stating:

> I can only add that instead of the word "Jews" [in your letter] there should be the word "East Germans," and then exactly the same [terror] holds true of one of the Allies, with the difference that everything that has happened since 1945 is public knowledge world-wide, whereas the bloody terror of the Nazis was in fact kept a secret from the German people.[45]

Heidegger's silence concerning the *Shoah*, the supreme example of technological and bureaucratic dehumanization, is especially ironic in view of the philosopher's preoccupation with the negative aspects of technical civilization and the dimension of the historical.

Nevertheless, there is another side to the story. Although Heidegger's attitudes and behavior during the Nazi era were well known to the philosopher Karl Jaspers, the latter asserted in a letter to his former student,

Hannah Arendt, that Heidegger "*selber nie AntiSemit.*"[46] In the 1920's and early 30's, Jaspers and Heidegger had been very close friends. However, Jaspers' wife Gertrud was Jewish and Jaspers broke with Heidegger over National Socialism in 1933. Moreover, even in his *Rektoratsrede* Heidegger took issue with the Nazi assertion of the supremacy of race and biology by asserting that while the people's strengths "are tied to earth and blood....Only a spiritual world gives the people the assurance of greatness."[47]

Jaspers and Arendt had a special reason for a keen and abiding interest in Heidegger. Hannah Arendt first met Heidegger as an eighteen-year-old entering student at the University of Marburg in 1924.[48] She was Jewish; he was of Roman Catholic background, married and the father of two sons. His father had been the sexton of the village church in Messkirch. Heidegger and Arendt became and remained secret lovers until 1930 when Heidegger's growing commitment to National Socialism precluded a continuation of the relationship.

In the first years of their relationship, Heidegger was her most important academic mentor. In some respects he remained so until the end of her life. However, both recognized that he could not serve as her *Doktorvater* because of their relationship. Heidegger suggested to Arendt that she complete her work at Heidelberg, doing her thesis under Heidegger's then good friend, Karl Jaspers. Following Heidegger's advice, Arendt proceeded to Heidelberg where she completed her thesis, *Augustine's Concept of Love*, in 1929.

Arendt had no contact with Heidegger from 1930 to 1948 when she visited Freiburg and sent him an unsigned note summoning him to her hotel. Heidegger came immediately. Arendt later wrote to her husband, Heinrich Blücher, concerning the encounter that "we really spoke to each other, it seemed to me, for the first time in our lives."[49] It is difficult to believe that they avoided the issue of Heidegger's Nazi involvements or that Arendt could have been deceived by him. She was, after all, the author of *The Origins of Totalitarianism* and *Eichmann in Jerusalem*.[50] The next day Heidegger told his wife Elfriede, who remained a convinced Nazi, that Arendt had been "the passion of his life" and the inspiration for his work. Frau Heidegger's anger was understandable. Nevertheless, Heidegger saw Arendt again, giving her copies of his manuscripts and letters. Later that year Arendt visited Freiburg and Heidegger for a second time and wrote that her experience, which does not appear to have compromised her marital relationship, offered confirmation of her decision to remain loyal to their friendship in spite of everything that had happened. By contrast, Jaspers was never able to be reconciled with Heidegger in spite of Arendt's attempts to bring about a reconciliation between the two men who were Germany's greatest philosophers in their time.

Arendt's renewed relationship with Heidegger was not without its ups and downs.[51] She consented to contribute to the Festschrift published on the occasion of his eightieth birthday in which she gave a moving appreciation of the thinker and offered what many have regarded as a questionable defense of Heidegger's involvement with Nazism.[52] Arendt represented Heidegger as politically naive and characterized his involvement with Nazism as an episode which lasted "ten short hectic months."[53] In the light of what is now known about Heidegger, it is obvious that Arendt was mistaken about the duration of Heidegger's Nazi commitment. Nevertheless, Arendt's lifelong relationship with Heidegger was not that of a woman whose judgment had been distorted by a youthful love affair. Arendt was an internationally famous political philosopher and, as noted, an authority on both Nazism and the Holocaust. Conceivably her judgment about Heidegger could have been distorted. However, before we conclude that Heidegger was an unregenerate anti-Semite, we would do well to keep in mind the Heidegger-Arendt relationship and Arendt's lifelong loyalty to the man.

Arendt has called Heidegger, "the last romantic." He was certainly a provincial. Because of their lack of rootedness in the traditional German world, Jews were far more likely to feel at home, insofar as they could feel at home anywhere in Germany and Austria, only in the very cities romantics like Heidegger so deeply distrusted. At the very least, the circles in which Heidegger was born and educated regarded the Jews as a politically, religiously, and culturally disruptive alien presence. Preferring the culture of the peasant to that of the city-dweller, Heidegger made it amply clear that he had little use for cultural pluralism, which was the only basis on which a Jewish demographic presence encompassing modern political rights could have been possible in Germany. Incidentally, this was clearly understood by Gerhardt Kittel. Even after 1945 Kittel remained committed to undoing the political legacy of the Enlightenment and the French Revolution with its program of Jewish emancipation. In the 42-page document he wrote to defend himself after his incarceration by French authorities as a leading Nazi ideologue in May 1945, Kittel wrote that the Jewish question was for him a crucial element in the *Weltanschaungskampf* between his Christian, Germanic and *völkisch* worldview and the secular legacy of the Enlightenment.[54] In the case of Heidegger, a thinker who placed so much stress on identification with and spiritual appropriation of one's origins, the feeling that Jews were both alien and even threatening could easily have been pre-theoretical, as it was for Karl Barth. It would therefore not be surprising if Heidegger regarded Jews with the suspicion and hostility that so often confronts an alien presence. His behavior towards Jews during the Nazi years was fully consistent with Nazi norms.

Even Heidegger's affair with Arendt may not have been inconsistent with strong anti-Semitic attitudes. He was, after all, not her husband committed to a shared family life with her but her married lover. The very alien character of so brilliant and, at eighteen, attractive a Jewish woman could have been an unsettling attraction. This is, of course, only speculation, but, if this line of thought has any merit, Heidegger would not be the first anti-Semite to be drawn to a Jewish woman.

Moreover, while there is little direct evidence that he approved of or advocated extermination, he actively supported and lent his prestige to a movement which committed mass extermination, a deed for which he never publicly expressed regret. We do, however, have a report that on at least one occasion Heidegger did express regret that some of the Jewish professors who had escaped the Holocaust were not exterminated. Maurice Friedman has written that Abraham Joshua Heschel imparted this information to him in 1965.[55] Admittedly, this is not hard documentary evidence. Nevertheless, as Friedman observes, Heschel was not the sort of person to indulge in gratuitous defamation, a judgment with which this writer, a former student of Heschel, concurs. One could cite yet other witnesses, such as Karl Jaspers, but that is hardly necessary.[56] It is difficult to believe that a man of

Heidegger's epoch-making importance in the history of philosophy was incapable of grasping the real meaning of National Socialism, the most radically anti-Semitic movement in human history. Incidentally, Emil Fackenheim holds that Heidegger became a problematic anti-Nazi at some point after 1935. That judgment may have been correct given the evidence available to the theologian when he wrote. It now seems difficult to maintain. In any event, even today Fackenheim can be judged correct in asserting that Heidegger's thinking, "while not responsible for his surrender to Nazism, had been unable to prevent it."[57] Still, we are left with the puzzling question of his relationship with Hannah Arendt.

I came away from my inquiry into Heidegger's politics with a heightened appreciation for Karl Barth and a renewed awareness of the difference between philosophy and religion. Barth came from the same world that saw the Jews as alien and threatening as did Heidegger. In spite of Heidegger's reflections on authenticity, it was Barth, not Heidegger, who had no difficulty in identifying National Socialism as worship of false gods. At the risk of his academic career Barth refused to go along with National Socialism. When the Nazi nightmare was over, Barth had nothing to regret and nothing to explain after the fact. Moreover, Barth left no doubt where he stood on the issue of racism and anti-Semitism. Nor was Barth the only major Christian theologian to refuse to compromise with Nazism. Although the vast majority of the clergy and theologians in Germany and Austria approved of or made their peace with National Socialism, Paul Tillich refused to give the movement his allegiance and voluntarily left his homeland for the United States. There is no doubt that Christian anti-Semitism was a precondition for the Holocaust. Nevertheless, the Christian Church never sanctioned an unremitting program of extermination against the Jews. There were moral barriers which the Church as an institution refused to transgress.

Unfortunately, there are no comparable moral barriers for much of secular philosophy. Every time I read Hegel's calm reflections on the course of human history, I wonder how that great philosopher would have regarded the Holocaust. For example:

When we see the evil, the wickedness, and the downfall of the
most flourishing empires the human spirit has created...we can
only end with a feeling of sadness at the transience of
everything....We can only harden ourselves against it or escape
by telling ourselves it was ordained by fate and could not have
been otherwise....But even as we look upon history as an altar
on which the happiness of nations, the wisdom of states and the
virtue of individuals are slaughtered, our thoughts impel us to
ask: to whom, or to what end have these monstrous sacrifices
been made? From the beginning we proceeded to define those
same events...as no more than the means whereby...the
substantial destiny, the absolute and final end, or in other
words, the true result of world history, is realised.[58]

For Hegel, the Holocaust could easily be seen as one more example
of "the happiness of nations" being offered up on the "altar of history." For
Heidegger, history is ultimately the story of the self-concealment and the self-
unveiling of Being, a self-unveiling which begins to manifest itself in our
times in Heidegger's own philosophy. It would thus not be inconsistent with
Heidegger's thought to interpret the Holocaust as a necessary stage in the
self-unveiling of Being. As late as 1966 Heidegger insisted that because of
"the special inner kinship between the German language and the language of
the Greeks and their thought," Germans have "a special task" in the
overcoming (*aufgehoben*) of an exhausted metaphysical tradition which had
culminated in nihilism and the modern technical world.[59] Implicit in
Heidegger's thought is the idea that Being once spoke Greek and now speaks
its kindred Aryan language, German. National Socialism was for no mere
political movement but, at least in its early years in power, a world-historical
movement restoring the German *Volk* to its true vocation. Heidegger's
identification with the movement was so complete that a 1934 photograph
shows him actually looking like Hitler with his Hitler-type mustache and a
swastika lapel pin.[60] Under the circumstances, Heidegger may have
regarded the elimination of the Jewish element in German language and
thought as both a spiritual and an ontological necessity so that Being might
finally uncover itself and bring modern nihilism to an end. How that
elimination was to take place could be left to other, more practical men.
After all, the philosopher's "abode" was the domain of thought.

There is in any event an extraordinary arrogance in both philosophers.
Implicit in Hegel's thought is the claim that the World Spirit arrives at

Absolute Knowledge in and through his philosophy. In the case of Heidegger, Being is interpreted as having begun to emerge from the long historical winter of its forgetfulness and self-concealment through his thinking. As Hans Jonas has pointed out, by insisting that the thinker no longer thinks about Being but is *grasped by Being*, thereby shifting the initiative from the thinker to Being, Heidegger asserts that "the very essence of things itself" speaks through the philosopher, thereby claiming "an authority which no thinker should ever claim."[61] No religious person convinced of the infinite qualitative difference between God and humanity would ever make such a claim. Moreover, a thinker making such a grandiose, world-historical claim would hardly be likely to confess that he had been in error on a subject such as the fate of the Jews.

In spite of all attempts to diminish Heidegger's stature as a thinker, he nevertheless remains one of the century's greatest philosophers. Unfortunately, it was possible for Heidegger to have been both a great philosopher and, at the same time, an anti-Semite who secretly denounced colleagues, implemented National Socialist racial laws which, in retrospect, can be seen as having been an indispensable part of "the twisted road to Auschwitz," and remain utterly indifferent to the cold-blooded destruction of millions of innocent men, women and children by a movement to which the philosopher had given, at least for a time, his highly visible and extremely valuable allegiance. There is absolutely nothing in the purely formal character of Heidegger's analysis of *Dasein* that would permit him to say, "this action is forbidden...this movement is evil." By contrast, in spite of Nietzsche's "death of God," which Barth took very seriously, and in spite of his instinctive personal aversion toward Jews, which he strove to overcome, the theologian had no doubt concerning what was evil and how to behave when confronted with the unholy.

ENDNOTES

[1]Victor Farias, *Heidegger et le nazisme* (Lagrasse, 1987).

[2]Karl Löwith, *Mein Leben in Deutschland vor und nach 1933* (Stuttgart, 1986), p. 57, cited by Thomas Sheehan, "Heidegger and the Nazis," *The New York Review of Books*, June 16, 1948, p. 38.

[3]Martin Heidegger, *Being and Time* (New York, 1962), pp. 335-344, corresponding to the pagination of the German edition, *Sein und Zeit*, 7th ed. (Tübingen, 1953), pp. 289-297. Henceforth the German pagination, which appears in the margins of the American edition, will be preceded by the letter "H.", as, for example, H. 289-297.

[4]Henceforth, we use the word *Dasein* where appropriate.

[5]Cited by Eberhard Busch, *Karl Barth: His Life from Letters and Autobiographical Texts* (Philadelphia, 1976), p. 223.

[6]Karl Barth, *Letters: 1961-1968*, (ed.) Jurgen Fangmeir and Hinrich Stoevesandt (Grand Rapids, 1981), p. 262.

[7]Karl Barth, *Church Dogmatics* (Edinburgh, 1957), Vol. II, 2, p. 235.

[8]Karl Barth, "The Jewish Problem and the Christian Answer," in *Against the Stream* (London, 1954), pp. 193 ff. For this citation I am indebted to Emil L. Fackenheim, *To Mend the World: Foundations of Future Jewish Thought* (New York, 1983), p. 133.

[9]*Being and Time*, p. 443, H. 391.

[10]*Ibid.*, p. 437, H. 385.

[11]Heidegger's failure to transcend subjective individualism, is discussed by Buber in *Eclipse of God: Studies in the Relation Between Religion and Philosophy* (New York, 1952), pp. 70-78. See David Novak, "Buber's Critique of Heidegger," *Modern Judaism*, (Spring, 1985): 125-140.

[12]*Being and Time*, p. 436, H. 385.

[13]Karsten Harries, "Heidegger as a Political Thinker," in Michael Murphy (ed.), *Heidegger and Modern Philosophy: Critical Essays* (New Haven, 1978), p. 309.

[14]Adolf Hitler, *Mein Kampf*, trans. Ralph Manheim (Boston, 1971), pp. 55, 98-101.

[15]Victor Farias, *op. cit.*, p. 41. Farias cites as his source, *Abraham a Santa Clara*, Abrahamische Lauberhutt, 1721, p. 383, but omits the publisher and place of publication.

[16]"Warum bleiben wir in der Provinz?" *Der Alemanne*, March 7, 1934. *Der Alemanne* was a National Socialist publication. English translation: "Why Do I Stay in the Provinces? (1934)," in Thomas Sheehan (ed.), *Heidegger, The Man and the Thinker* (Chicago, 1981), pp. 27-30.

[17]Heinrich Weigand Petzet, *Auf einem Stern zugehen* (Frankfurt, 1983), p. 40. cited by Farias, *op. cit.*, p. 248. Thomas Sheehan rejects the translation "Jewish circles that dominate..." and offers instead "Jewish circles that are at home...."

[18]See Robert J. Lifton, *The Nazi Doctors: Medical Killing and the Psychology of Genocide* (New York, 1986).

[19]The anti-Semitism and Nazism of these men is authoritatively explored by Robert P. Ericksen, *Theologians Under Hitler* (New Haven, 1985).

[20]Paul Althaus, *Kirche und Volkstum: Der völkische Wille im Lichte des Evangeliums* (Gutersloh, 1928), p. 34, cited by Eriksen, *op. cit.*, p. 108.

[21]Farias, *op. cit.*, p. 293. Farias discerns an approving reference to the death camps on Heidegger's part in a sentence the philosopher quotes from Santa Clara: "The peace [we enjoy] is as far from war as Sachsenhausen is from Frankfurt," This was Santa Clara's way of saying that war was not very distant. As Farias indicates, the Sachsenhausen to which Santa Clara refers was a seventeenth-century suburb of Frankfurt, now a part of the metropolis. Farias mistakenly assumes that this was the site of the notorious Nazi concentration camp of the same name. That Sachsenhausen was, however, considerably to the north of Berlin and nowhere near Frankfurt. Nevertheless, Heidegger's choice of a sentence in which the violently anti-Semitic Abraham a Santa Clara makes mention of the name of the site of the future concentration camp leads Farias to speculate on the possibility that Heidegger, in defiance of public opinion, wanted to indicate his approval of the death camps. Farias attempts to buttress his argument by pointing to the fact that Heidegger gave that lecture as an old man returning to his place of origin and addressing those whom he had so often identified as "the forces of the future," namely, the youth of the local *Heimat*. Nevertheless, even Farias admits that this argument remains a conjecture and awaits further documentation. It is important to note that Thomas Sheehan, an authoritative and critical student of Heidegger, regards Farias' interpretation as "absurd." See Sheehan, "Heidegger and the Nazis," pp. 38-39, n. 5.

[22]See Martin Heidegger, "The Rectorate 1933/34: Facts and Thoughts," trans. Karsten Harries, *The Review of Metaphysics*, Vol. 38, No. 3, (March, 1985): 481-502. This is a translation of "Das Rektorat 1933/34. Tatsachen und Gedanken." According to Hermann Heidegger, the philosopher's son, this document was written by his father "shortly after the collapse of the

National Socialist regime in 1945." Heidegger later gave the manuscript to his son with the request that it be published "at the appropriate time."

[23]Farias, *op. cit.*, p. 123.

[24]Martin Heidegger, "The Self-Assertion of the German University," trans. Karsten Harries, *Review of Metaphysics*, Vol. 38 (March 1985), pp. 468-480.

[25]*Ibid.*, pp. 475-476.

[26]See Karsten Harries, "Heidegger as a Political Thinker," in Michael Murphy, *op. cit.*, pp. 304-328.

[27]Harries, *op. cit.*, p. 313.

[28]Martin Heidegger, "The Self-Assertion of the German University," trans. Karsten Harries, pp. 476-477.

[29]Graeme Nicholson, "The Politics of Heidegger's Rectorial Address," *Man and Word*, Vol. 20 (1987): 174.

[30]See Martin Heidegger, "The Rectorate 1933/34: Facts and Thoughts," trans. Karsten Harries, p. 483.

[31]See Guido Schneeburger, *Nachlese zu Heidegger* (Bern, 1962), p. 136, cited by Farias, *op. cit.*, p. 130; English translation in Maurice Friedman, *The Worlds of Existentialism* (Chicago, 1964), p. 530.

[32]Emil L. Fackenheim, *op. cit.*, p. 169.

[33]Hugo Ott, "Martin Heidegger als Rektor der Universität Freiburg i. Br. 1933/34," *Zeitschrift der Breisgau-Geschichtsvereins*, Vol. 103 (1984): 116, cited by Sheehan, *op. cit.*, p. 39.

[34]Eugen Fischer and Gerhard Kittel, Das antike Weltjudentum. Tatsachen, Texte, Bilder," *Forschungen zur Judenfrage*, Vol. 7 (Hamburg, 1943), pp. 10-11; cited by Eriksen, *op. cit.*, p. 65.

[35]Farias, *op. cit.*, p. 79.

[36]Heidegger's explanations are to be found in (a) "Nur ein Gott kann uns retten," *Der Spiegel*, May 31, 1976, English translation by William J. Richardson, S.J., "Only a God Can Save Us Now," in Thomas Sheehan (ed.), *Martin Heidegger, The Man and The Thinker*, pp. 45-67; (b) Martin Heidegger, "The Rectorate 1933/34: Facts and Thoughts," trans. Karsten Harries, pp. 481-502.

[37]Heidegger, "The Rectorate 1933/34: Facts and Thoughts," p. 497.

[38]Farias, *op, cit.*, p. 131.

[39]Rudolf Augstein, *op. cit.*, identifies Vogel as the Rector of Göttingen; Farias, *op. cit.*, p. 235, describes him as the Führer of the Nazi professors at Göttingen.

[40]Farias, *op. cit.*, p. 235.

[41]The Der Spiegel interview, entitled "Nur ein Gott kann uns retten," was published on May 31, 1976. For English translation see note 36.

[42]Martin Heidegger, "Heraklit" (1943), in *Festschrift der 350. Jahresfeier des Humanistischen Gymnasiums in Konstanz* (Constance, 1954).

[43]Martin Heidegger, *Introduction to Metaphysics* (New Haven, 1959), p. 37.

[44]Martin Heidegger, *What Is Called Thinking*, trans. J. Glenn Gray and F. Wieck (New York, 1968), p. 66. I have used Emil Fackenheim's translation of this passage in Fackenheim, *op. cit.*, p. 181.

[45]*"...kann ich nur hinzufügen, dass statt 'Juden' 'Ostdeutsche' zu stehen hat, und dann genau so gilt für einen der Allierten mit dem Unterschied, dass alles, was seit 1945 geschieht, der Weltöffentlichkeit bekannt ist, während der blutige Terror der Nazis vor dem deutschen Volk tatsächlich geheimatgehalten worden ist."* This letter is in the Marcuse archives in Frankfurt. The translation is by Thomas Sheehan, "Heidegger and the Nazis," p. 42.

[46]Jaspers, letter to Hannah Arendt, March 9, 1966, cited by Elizabeth Young-Bruehl, *Hannah Arendt: For Love of the World* (New Haven, 1982), p. 506, n. 39.

[47]See Nicholson's interpretation of this passage, Nicholson, *op. cit.*, p. 481.

[48]The story of the Heidegger-Arendt relationship has been made public by Arendt's former student and biographer, Elizabeth Young-Bruehl, *op. cit.* See especially pp. 42-70 and 246-248.

[49]Letter to Heinrich Blücher, 8 February 1950, Library of Congress, cited by Young-Bruehl, *op. cit.*, p. 246.

[50]Hannah Arendt, *The Origins of Totalitarianism* (New York, 1951) and *Eichmann in Jerusalem; A Study in the Banality of Evil* (New York, 1963).

[51]The details are recounted in Young-Bruehl, *op. cit.*, 302-308.

[52]See, for example, Fackenheim, *op. cit.*, 302-308.

[53]Hannah Arendt, "Heidegger at Eighty," in Michael Murphy, *op. cit.*, p. 303.

[54]Gerhardt Kittel, *Meine Verteidigung*, manuscript dated Tubingen, June 1945, p. 8; cited by Eriksen, *op, cit.*, p. 44.

[55]Maurice Friedman, *Martin Buber's Life and Work: The Later Years, 1945-1965* (New York, 1983), p. 436.

[56]Jaspers reports that in June 1933 Heidegger asserted that there was a "dangerous international alliance of Jews." Karl Jaspers, *Philosophische Autobiographie* (Munich, 1977), p. 101; cited by Sheehan, *op. cit.*, p. 41.

[57]E. Fackenheim, *op. cit.*, p. 181.

[58]G. W. F. Hegel, "Introduction: Reason in History," in *Lectures on the Philosophy of World History*, (ed.) Johannes Hoffmeister, trans. H. B. Nisbet (Cambridge, 1975), pp. 68-69.

[59]Martin Heidegger, "Only a God Can Save Us Now," p. 62.

[60]The photograph appears in *L'Express*, 5 February 1988, p. 48.

[61]Hans Jonas, "Heidegger and Theology," in Hans Jonas, *The Phenomenon of Life: Toward A Philosophical Biology* (New York, 1966), p. 257.

FANTASY, PURITY, DESTRUCTION: NORMAN COHN'S COMPLEX WITNESS TO THE HOLOCAUST

Roger W. Smith

Everyone wants to go to Heaven, but no one wants to die. Yet for centuries many people have tried to use mass slaughter to bring about a heaven on earth. This is, in fact, the central theme in the work of the distinguished British historian Norman Cohn. In *The Pursuit of the Millennium, Warrant for Genocide,* and *Europe's Inner Demons,* Cohn examines closely the "urge to purify the world through the annihilation of some category of human beings imagined as agents of corruption and incarnations of evil."[1]

In so doing, he attempts to elaborate a model of human destructiveness that will illuminate both the Holocaust and other ideological genocides, whether medieval, early modern, or late twentieth century. Those familiar with the *Khmer Rouge* regime and its consequences will recognize, for example, the family resemblances between Cohn's portrait of the medieval quest for purity and salvation *here on earth* and *now*, and the style, motives, and consequences of a regime that managed in three and a half years to destroy a third of its own population. But the shock of recognition works both ways: those of us who have read accounts of the forced, brutal evacuation of Phnom Penh in 1975 will also see clear parallels between that and the forced evacuation of Münster by the Anabaptists and their leader Matthys in 1534:

On the morning of 27 February armed bands, urged on by Matthys in prophetic frenzy, rushed through the streets calling: 'Get out, you godless ones, and never come back, you enemies of the Father!' In bitter cold, in the midst of a wild snowstorm, multitudes of the 'godless' were driven from the town by Anabaptists who rained blows upon them and laughed at their afflictions. These people included old people and invalids, small children and pregnant women and women who had just given birth. Mostly they came from the more prosperous part of the population; but they were forced to leave behind all their belongings and money and spare clothes, even their food was taken from them and they were reduced to begging through the countryside for food and shelter....By the morning of 3 March there were no 'misbelievers' left in Munster; the town was inhabited solely by the Children of God.[2]

I

COHN'S MODEL OF HUMAN DESTRUCTIVENESS

Cohn's model involves several distinct, but related, ideas: *fantasy, tradition, an apocalyptic style of mind, the social preconditions for the appearance in history of this type of genocidal movement,* and *the ways in which a combination of fanaticism and indifference allow genocide to take place.*

I should like, first, to look briefly at each of these ideas, ideas which are part of Norman Cohn's complex witness to the Holocaust, but also are intended to help us understand ideological genocide more generally. Then I shall ask what the implications of Cohn's analysis are for the prevention of ideological genocide--the type of political/religious mass murder that tends to claim the largest number of victims.

FANTASY

Most scholars who study genocide view it as a rational, calculated act, involving cruelty without passion.[3] There is much to be said for this approach, but it tends to leave out any assessment of the end, focusing instead on genocide as a means only. Cohn, on the other hand, focuses on genocide as an end and says relatively little about the means used to destroy human lives. Nevertheless, his approach is a valuable corrective, for it calls attention to the irrational basis of much genocide, resting as it does on fantasies that are contrary to reality. Cohn also calls attention to the imaginative element in human beings and our susceptibility to blind passions and delusions. In speaking about the irrational in history and how fantasies often involve an impulse to cleanse the world of some assumed evil, Cohn brings to our attention precisely that which is often left out in discussions of genocide.

I must point out for the sake of clarity that Cohn actually has two notions of fantasy (I shall call them Fantasy I and Fantasy II) which he does not always distinguish. Fantasy I involves the human capacity to believe and act upon that which is contrary to reality. Examples of this include, in medieval society, the belief that kings long dead will be resurrected and usher in an age free from corruption and oppression; in the sixteenth century, the belief in a conspiracy of witches; and in the medieval and modern periods, the belief that Jews are demons bent on world domination. Such fantasies, although without foundation, often become widely accepted and even begin to seem self-evident. Given a certain content, they can become warrants for genocide. That there is this propensity in human nature to succumb, under certain conditions, to fantasy seems as important a fact about human nature as that other, better known propensity--to obey orders. No wonder Cohn quotes Ovid at the beginning of *Warrant for Genocide*: "How much blind night there is in the hearts of men!"[4]

Fantasy II is a specific type of belief and it is this that is likely to become genocidal in practice: the apocalyptic, messianic fantasy. The basic form of this fantasy of social salvation, repeated over time and place, whether in the language of religion or the pseudo-science of the right or left in modern totalitarian movements, is as follows: the world/society is "dominated by an evil, tyrannous power of boundless destructiveness," a power not only cruel, but in some sense demonic. The tyranny of that power will become "more and more outrageous, the sufferings of the victims more and more intolerable." Then, suddenly, the oppressed will rise up with a "final, exterminatory struggle": the world/society will be reborn into innocence.[5] In short, only through massacre can the world be purged of evil and oppression: extermination is the price of virtue and happiness.

TRADITION

The fantasies that lead to attempts to purify the world through extermination of particular groups--heretics, witches, Jews--spring, Cohn thinks, from specific, apocalyptic traditions, many of them centuries old, which, modified by circumstances, are revived in times of social crisis. Thus, for example, Cohn traces the sixteenth-century fantasy of a devil-worshipping, incestuous, child-devouring conspiracy to the Romans, who had used such claims against the Christians, persons suspect as a threat to the State. In the sixteenth century the same charges were used, but now the threat was that of "witches." The result of this fantasy was the death of over 100,000 persons, most of them women.[6] Similarly, the kind of antisemitism that leads to massacre and genocide, Cohn argues, is a modernized, secularized version of the medieval view of Jews as demons who poisoned wells, murdered children, and worked in the service of Satan to destroy Christendom. It is this fantasy, blended with anxieties and resentments over modernization--capitalism, democracy, liberalism, secularism--with which Jews were identified, that led to the myth of a Jewish world-conspiracy. According to Cohn, this fantasy, given widespread expression through the *Protocols of the Elders of Zion*, was a necessary condition for the Nazi drive to exterminate the Jews.[7]

A GENOCIDAL STYLE OF MIND

At bottom, Cohn suggests, those who give themselves to an apocalyptic movement seek a kind of salvation, which they see as collective, earthly, imminent, and total: with the final massacre, society will be transformed for all time.[8] Such thinking is boundless in its aims and premises: a "social struggle is not seen as a struggle for specific, limited objectives, but as an event of unique importance, different in kind from all other struggles known to history, a cataclysm from which the world is to emerge totally transformed and redeemed."[9] Such a mindset is Manichean, lending itself readily to the dehumanization of the victim, but it also tends to overstate vastly the power of the enemy, which it portrays as engaged in a gigantic conspiracy against God, humanity, or the Master Race. In its utter rejection of those it identifies as the source of all evil, it resorts to the most primitive images of evil: disease, the unclean, the loathsome, and a later innovation, the diabolical. It is also a state of mind that lends itself to total absorption in a group, subordination to a leader, and ruthless adherence to its sense of cosmic mission, which becomes a license to destroy men, women, and children with a good conscience, free from guilt.[10]

SOCIAL PRECONDITIONS

Cohn argues that apocalyptic movements appear only in times of mass disorientation and social anxiety. It is not hardship as such that leads people into the quest for total salvation, but rather the collapse of the normative order, the fact that society no longer seems to make any sense.[11] War, famine, plague, the breakdown of authority, rapid social and economic change--all of these can contribute to the breakdown of a familiar, sustaining pattern of life. Under these conditions, many persons will long for "new bearings and new hope" and this is what the leader, or prophet, brings, based on the fantasy of the world redeemed and made new through the removal of groups perceived as the embodiment of evil, both threatening and anti-human.[12]

What the leader offers his followers, then, is escape from their atomized condition, but more than that the prospect of carrying out a mission of unique and ultimate significance. What emerges is a new group obsessed by the apocalyptic fantasy, convinced of its own infallibility, and utterly ruthless in pursuit of its goal.[13] Referring to the Nazis for illustration, Cohn says that "again and again one comes across the same weird, apocalyptic atmosphere, hints of some gigantic final battle in which the demonic hosts will be eliminated, the world released from the strangling octopus, a new age brought to birth."[14] Through the destruction of the lives of others, one restores meaning to one's own.

FANATICISM AND INDIFFERENCE

For those drawn into the apocalyptic movement, the myth provides meaning to their lives, holding anxiety at bay, making them feel both important and powerful. It may do nothing to solve the social dislocations that gave rise to their disorientation in the first place, but the meaning it imparts and the emotional release it provides leads such persons both to live and kill for the movement.[15] For them the myth is a warrant for genocide--it identifies the victims, dehumanizes them, turns them into the embodiment of ultimate evil, and justifies their eradication. Participating in the apocalyptic movement, subordinating their lives to the leader, embracing fully the all-important mission assigned to them, they become capable of the most ruthless acts, with no sense of guilt for the humiliation, torture, and murder of human beings.[16] The conviction of such people, who are, in Cohn's words, "bearers and elaborators of that fantastic view of the world on which the whole murderous enterprise depends for its justification," provides "reassurance and encouragement" to those (quite numerous) who participate in the movement without being fully absorbed into it.[17] The groups that killed Jews in the medieval period, the Black Hundreds of Tsarist Russia, and the Nazis all included *fanatics*, but also *others*: those "who wanted nothing but a chance to torture and murder, and also plenty of looters, whose main interest was in the property of the killed. To these one must add, for the modern period, the opportunists at all levels, for whom organizing and carrying through of massacre was simply a means to a better income, more security, and more prestige than they could otherwise have hoped for."[18] Yet even men like these, Cohn believes, need an ideology to justify and excuse their behavior, for "without it they would have to see themselves and one another as what they actually are--common thieves and murderers. And that is apparently something which even they cannot bear."[19]

The fantasy or myth (Cohn does not distinguish these terms) of a Jewish world-conspiracy served as a warrant for genocide in another way: it encouraged ordinary persons to show no concern for the fate of the Jews, a people, if not hated, at least held in suspicion by Christians for centuries.[20] With indifference, there would be no protest, no attempt to stop the discrimination, persecution, murder. In fact, Cohn notes, in the Nazi era a "mood of passive compliance became general," rooted in indifference: "Antisemitism played only a limited part in bringing Hitler to power, but indifference played an important part in facilitating the subsequent persecution."[21] The unwillingness to act on behalf of the Jews grew stronger as the persecutions grew worse: with the realization that a vast injustice was being committed, many persons began to blame the victims as a way of easing their own consciences. "Just as the organized killers needed the myth of the Jewish world-conspiracy if they were not to recognize themselves as common thieves and murders, so many ordinary people needed some smattering of it if they were not to see themselves as passive accomplices in the persecution and massacre of innocent people."[22]

If the many viewed indifference as a neutral act, Cohn, on the other hand, points out its lethal quality. It was, he says, "precisely the mixture of fanaticism of a minority with the indifference of the many that made possible the whole development, from the first restrictions to the final extermination."[23] Indifference, far from being neutral, is always on the side of the executioner.

II

IMPLICATIONS OF THE MODEL FOR THE PREVENTION OF GENOCIDE

Genocide occurs in a number of different forms; consequently, no single approach to prevention is possible.[24] If Cohn's analysis of ideological genocide, however, is even approximately correct, it has important implications for the prevention of a form of genocide that has already claimed millions of lives.[25]

Current approaches to the prevention of genocide tend to be "institutional," with emphasis on genocide early warning systems, the expansion of international legal institutions, the use of economic sanctions, and the threat of humanitarian intervention.[26] Cohn's approach is compatible with these, but his concern is more "moral" than institutional, with the primary emphasis on education and the maintenance of normative integration within society. Realistically, both approaches are necessary if genocide is to be prevented (and it will not be easy in any case), but it is the moral approach that has been neglected in recent years, hence the importance of considering Cohn's work for the prevention of genocide.

First of all it would seem that the capacity of human beings to believe in fantasies can never be erased completely, but it might be affected at least to some extent by an education that would point out the gross delusions of the past and present, the circumstances surrounding people's acceptance of these beliefs, and the tragic consequences--persecution, massacre, holocaust-- of acting upon such fantasies. It might be possible also to encourage a more skeptical view of ideology, with its sweeping generalizations about nature, history, and society, and its willingness to set a speculative, perfect future above the concrete death and suffering it lends itself to in the present.

This kind of education would, in short, raise serious questions about the ethics and consequences of an apocalyptic politics and the feasibility of a millenarian society, devoid of blemish and conflict. It would remind us, as Isaiah Berlin recently pointed out, that the "first public obligation is to avoid extremes of suffering....The best that can be done, as a general rule, is to maintain a precarious equilibrium that will prevent the occurrence of desperate situations, of intolerable choices--that is the first requirement of a decent society; one that we can always strive for, in the light of the limited range of our knowledge, and even of our imperfect understanding of individuals and societies. A certain humility in these matters is very necessary.[27]

Cohn would agree with Berlin, but would also suggest that by avoiding "extremes of suffering," social stability and normative order would most likely be preserved, providing barren soil for the growth of apocalyptic, millenarian movements that seek salvation through extermination.

The apocalyptic style might also be undercut by an education that prompted tolerance, respect for individuals, and a less rigid, Manichean view of morality and the world. But since mass killing typically takes place only where it has the sanction of government, education would have to encourage the questioning of authority, helping us to recognize that law is not always the same as justice, and that obedience to orders is not always a social virtue, but must be squared with the individual's own conscience. In this way, individuals would be encouraged to accept responsibility for their actions, and where government condoned mass violence against innocent groups, to refuse to support such actions, breaking any links between oneself and governmental crime.[28]

But genocide, Cohn points out, is also facilitated by public indifference to persecution and the violation of the rights of minorities. Here civic consciousness--a recognition of fundamental principles of justice and fairness and the spirit of constitutional democracy--would need to be taught. Beyond this, ways must be found to increase a sense of solidarity between and among human groups--a solidarity that recognizes differences, but in matters of life and death transcends them; a solidarity in which any person whose life is threatened by a genocidal State is our neighbor. At a very minimum, the civic education would instil in us, to the extent possible, a sense of individual responsibility that would lead us to break with executioners and that through social consciousness and a sense of humanity would ally us with victims.

The goal of this kind of education would be to banish the acceptability of the claim, "I was only obeying orders," and to undermine the propensity of too many persons to be bystanders (Elie Wiesel refers to them as "faces in the window") who simply look on in silence as fellow human beings are led to the slaughter in the name of history, God, biology, or peasant simplicity.

In sum, there are a variety of means that can be used to overcome the power of fantasy and the apocalyptic quest for a new and pure age, a quest, as Norman Cohn has demonstrated, that frequently leads to mass destruction of innocent life. The question is: to what extent will we use them?

ENDNOTES

[1]*The Pursuit of the Millennium: Revolutionary Millenarians and Mystical Anarchists of the Middle Ages*, revised and expanded edition (New York: Oxford University Press, 1970); *Warrant for Genocide: The Myth of the Jewish World-Conspiracy and the Protocols of the Elders of Zion* (New York: Harper & Row, 1967); *Europe's Inner Demons: An Enquiry Inspired by the Great Witch-Hunt* (New York: Meridian, 1977). See also Cohn's "Introduction" to Herman Bernstein, *The Truth about "The Protocols of the Elders of Zion": A Complete Exposure* (New York: KTAV, 1971). The quotation is from *Europe's Inner Demons*, p. xvi. I am grateful to Professor Frank Chalk of Concordia University for useful comments on an earlier version of the essay.

[2]*Pursuit of the Millennium*, pp. 262-263. For an account of the forced evacuation of Phnom Penh, see François Ponchard, *Cambodia Year Zero*, trans. Nancy Amphoux (New York: Holt, Rinehart & Winston, 1978), Chs. 1-4. For a comprehensive study of the Cambodian genocide, see Elizabeth Becker, *When The War Was Over: Cambodia's Revolution and the Voices of Its People* (New York: Simon and Schuster, 1987).

[3]See, for example, Helen Fein, *Accounting for Genocide* (New York: The Free Press, 1979), pp. 7-8 and Roger W. Smith, "Human Destructiveness and Politics: The Twentieth Century as an Age of Genocide," in *Genocide and the Modern Age*, eds. Isidor Wallimann and Michael N. Dobkowski (Westport, Conn.: Greenwood Press, 1987), pp. 22-24.

[4]*Warrant for Genocide*, p. 13.

[5]*Pursuit of the Millennium*, pp. 21, 286.

[6]*Europe's Inner Demons*, Ch. I.

[7]See Cohn's "Introduction" to Bernstein, *Pursuit of the Millennium*, pp. 76-88; and *Warrant for Genocide, passim*, but especially pp. 15-18, 21-25, 41-42, 169-193, and 252-255. The idea of a Jewish world-conspiracy may have been a precondition for the Holocaust, but Cohn, in my opinion, attaches undue importance to the *Protocols*, almost suggesting that without this forgery from Tsarist Russia, the Holocaust could not have taken place (*Warrant for Genocide*, pp. 17-18). The question of what had to be present/absent for the Holocaust to occur is a difficult one; it does not lend itself to the precision that Cohn sometimes attempts to impart to it.

[8]*Pursuit of the Millennium*, pp. 15-17, 21.

[9]*Ibid.*, p. 281.

[10]*Ibid.*, p. 85.

[11]*Ibid.*, pp. 59-60, 87-88, 281-283.

[12]*Ibid.*, p. 60.

[13]*Ibid.*, p. 285.

[14]*Warrant for Genocide*, p. 249.

[15]*Pursuit of the Millennium*, p. 88.

[16]*Ibid.*, p. 85.

[17]*Warrant for Genocide*, pp. 264-265.

[18]*Ibid.*, pp. 263-264.

[19]*Ibid.*, p. 264. Here Cohn is partly right, but he underestimates the human capacity for eluding responsibility: some persons may need ideology to excuse their behavior, but there are other devices that can be used, such as, "I was only following orders" or "Who am I to judge?"

[20]*Ibid.*, p. 267.

[21]*Ibid.*, pp. 200 (note 2), 213.

[22]*Ibid.*, p. 268. Again, Cohn is right, but there are also other ways to avoid a sense of guilt: one can point to a conflict of responsibilities between duties to victims and to one's own family, or one can perceive oneself as lacking power to effect change in any way at all, invoking implicitly the notion that "ought" implies "can."

[23]*Warrant for Genocide*, p. 200.

[24]On forms of genocide, see, for example, Helen Fein, "Scenarios of Genocide: Models of Genocide and Critical Responses," in Israel W. Charny, ed., *Toward the Understanding and Prevention of Genocide* (Boulder, Colorado: Westview Press, 1984), pp. 3-31, and Leo Kuper, "Types of Genocide and Mass Murder," in the same volume, pp. 32-50.

[25]Cohn's work, however, is not without some striking omissions: in his discussion of the Nazi extermination of the Jews, for example, he barely mentions the history of European racism and does not consider at all how bureaucracy and technology (and not just ideology) reduce moral awareness and, thus, further guilt-free mass murder. Even so, his model of ideological genocide seems to me to be essentially sound.

[26]On possible means of preventing genocide, see the comprehensive study by Leo Kuper, *The Prevention of Genocide* (New Haven: Yale University Press, 1985) and the thoughtful essay by Helen Fein, "On Preventing Genocide," *Worldview*, Vol. 23 (January-February 1980): 42-45.

126

[27]Isaiah Berlin, "On the Pursuit of the Ideal," *The New York Review of Books*, March 17, 1988, p. 18.

[28]See, for example, Richard Falk, "Ecocide, Genocide, and the Nuremberg Tradition of Individual Responsibility," in *Philosophy, Morality, and International Affairs*, eds. Virginia Held, Sidney Morgenbesser, and Thomas Nagel (New York: Oxford University Press, 1974), pp. 123-137.

AN AMERICAN CHRISTIAN RESPONSE
TO THE HOLOCAUST

Jack Fischel

The performance of American Christian Churches in protesting against Nazi Germany's persecution of the Jews in the 1930's and 40's is not a distinguished one. When church activity did take place it generally occurred in behalf of German Christian refugees. With the notable exception of the Quakers, it would appear that most clergymen, (again with notable exceptions such as Harry Emerson Fosdick), and church institutions missed the opportunity to bring their great moral and material resources to bear in behalf of a small persecuted minority.

It is not as though American churches did not have ample precedents to justify mobilizing their membership against the oppressive acts of Nazi Germany. American Catholics attempted to mobilize support for Catholics being persecuted by the Mexican government in the 1920's. Near East Relief was created in 1915 to meet the relief needs of persecuted Armenians and by 1930 it had raised some $91,000,000.[1] Similarly, in the 1920's against the background of Soviet persecution, North American Mennonites pooled their resources to help their brethren escape from the Soviet Union. The presence of Russian Mennonites in Canada and Mennonite colonies in Paraguay and Brazil testify to the successful relief operations of the Mennonites in behalf of their persecuted brethren.

Because of its own recent history, few American Christian groups were in a better position to empathize with the plight of European Jews than the North American Mennonites in the years between 1933-1945. Like the Jews, the descendants of the sixteenth-century Anabaptists found themselves victims of religious intolerance and were persecuted for their beliefs. Because of their refusal to bear arms and to swear oaths the Mennonites, who originated in the Netherlands, Switzerland and the Palatinate, were forced to migrate in order to maintain their religious practices. In the eighteenth century, many came to British North American and settled in Pennsylvania, Ohio and many other parts of North America. Still other Mennonites were invited to settle in Russia by Catherine the Great, were given religious freedom, and were exempt from military service. Regardless of the new location, however, Mennonites brought with them their devotion to Scripture and their love of German culture. In fact for some Mennonites, the German language and the practice of religious devotional were seen as inseparable.

In Southern Russia, where most Mennonites lived, they maintained a status of "a state within a state" whereby the German language and German culture flourished. When, in the nineteenth century, the Czarist governments began their program of Russification, Mennonites were forced to leave. Towards the end of the nineteenth century, thousands of these Russian Mennonites left the Ukraine and came to North America. A great many settled in Canada and from there attempted to retain their identity with German culture. In the 1920's, Mennonites found themselves victims of both a severe famine and Soviet persecution. In this moment of crisis for the Mennonites of Russia, their brethren in North America came to their aid. In 1920 the Mennonite Central Committee (M.C.C.) was formed to help Russian Mennonites recover from the severe famine that had begun that year. Mobilizing the resources of the main Mennonite Conferences in North America, the M.C.C. was able to implement an effective relief program for Mennonites in the Soviet Union. Thus, like the organizational structure of their Jewish counterparts, Mennonites were able to create through the M.C.C. an efficient organ of mutual aid which linked Mennonites throughout the world.

In 1929-1930, the Soviet government began their persecution of minorities including the Mennonites. North American Mennonites rallied their resources and attempted to help these Russian Mennonites find a haven, and when both the United States and Canada refused to bend their immigration laws to allow these refugees entry, the situation looked hopeless. But it was the Weimar government that offered temporary sanctuary to the Russian Mennonites. For this aid, the Russian Mennonites, who would shortly find their way to South American countries as well as into Canada, would be grateful to the government of President von Hindenburg.

The advent of Hitler to power in January, 1933 brought mixed reactions from Mennonites in North America. Although Mennonites eschewed political involvement of any kind--even to the point that many Mennonites did not vote--nevertheless some Mennonites instinctively reacted to the excess of the Nazis. The influential *Christian Monitor*, an organ of the (Old) Mennonite Church, in its world news column warned "that Germany is riding to her possible judgment and misery."[2] With regard to the Jews,...

> As I'm writing, the Jews of Germany are facing one of their sad days when Germany under Hitler (sic) boycott the Jews....What the future holds in store for the Jews of Germany, we do not know. But this we know, the days of the Jews will be days of sorrow and travail, until he will say from the heart, 'Blessed is He that cometh in the name of the Lord.'...A word as to Germany. It has never paid any nation to misuse the Jews. Nations that kick this ancient and beloved people usually suffer seriously from stubbed toes. Hatred works like a boomerang. Germany beware.[3]

The *Christian Monitor* editorial illustrates a theme frequently found in the Mennonite press in the period 1933-1945 amongst those who were sympathetic to the plight of Europe's Jews. Concern for the Jews would go hand-in-hand with advice that only through conversion to Christianity could Jewish travail be ended. Thus in 1940 the *Christian Monitor* notes the following with regard to the plight of the Jews: In an article entitled "The Jews Awakening From their Age-Long Sleep," the writer states that Jews have begun to realize that they are not wanted in most nations and were only tolerated in others.

> These evil days have made him think. He is asking questions he never has been asking (to large an extent)...this is the hour

for the Christian Church! The Jew is cuddling closer to the Christian Church than any other group of people....Most evangelical Christians who are interested in the prophetic content of the Bible have a place in their hearts for Jews....There is more stir among the Jews concerning Christ than there has been for centuries.[4]

A Mennonite missionary, Kathe Weaver, reporting on "The Suffering Jew" for the (Old) Mennonite publication *Gospel Herald* tells her readers

The Polish Ministry of Information has recently reported that more than 500,000 persons, mostly Jews, have been put to death in a concentration camp at Oswiecim, southwest of Krakow. In a long report on Nazi atrocities the Ministries declared three crematories had been erected inside the camp to dispose of 10,000 bodies a day. Gas chambers were said to have been attached to the crematories...men, women, and children arrived by truckloads and were removed to the gas chambers where from ten to twenty-five minutes were required for execution....[5]

The above reference to the implementation of the Final Solution is one of the very few reports or notices of what was happening to European Jews to be found in the Mennonite press in the period 1941-1945. In fact, in six important Mennonite publications--*Missionary Messenger, Gospel Herald, Mennonites Weekly Review, The Mennonites, Sword and Trumpet* and *Christian Monitor*--in the years 1941-1945, this writer found only nine articles dealing with the plight of Jews in Europe and only two dealings with reports such as the one described above.

Kathe Weaver's account of what was happening to Jews in Poland would have been a service to the Mennonite Community in altering them to the stark realities of the Holocaust had the article not also included the following;

"This is but a part of the price the Jews must apy for saying, when the Lord of glory was crucified "His blood be on us, and on our children." In Moses' farewell address to Israel he told them that continued disobedience to Jehovah would result in their world-wide dispersion...Our Lord Himself...gives an outline of events in Jewish history following His rejection until His return...'Then shall they deliver you up unto tribulation and shall kill you: and ye shall be hated of all the natiions for my name sake.' (Matthew 24:9)"

For Kathe Weaver, even the Jewish return to Palestine is no solution, "for there is abounding evidence that the Jew is returning to Palestine in unbelief

- Zionism is political, not religious." It is true that a few quotations from selected publications do not necessarily lead to the conclusion that Jewish suffering was seen as an opportunity to convert Jews. But the evidence is there, that the plight of European Jewry as described in the Mennonite press is, more often than not, followed by the Evangelical solution to the problem of European Jewry.

On the whole it can be argued that, as evidenced by its periodicals and weekly's, Mennonites were anti-Hitler. Once could also make the case that the evangelical interest in the Jews was well meaning in the sense that Mennonites were sincerely motivated to save Jewish souls. But from the viewpoint of Jews, this misguided "philo-Semitism" didn't help them in their hour of peril, and furthermore the evangelical solution represented an additional problem for Jews. Mennonites were not the only Christian denomination viewing the persecution of Jews in Europe as an opportunity to convert them. What is often overlooked in the sad history of the Holocaust is the point that although it was milder in form and certainly not life-threatening, the missionary activity of Christian groups, both in America and in Europe, was still an additional threat to Jewish existence.

Not all Mennonites concerned about the Jews of Europe were, however, offering the solution of conversion. In the pages of *The Mennonite*, a publication of the General Conference Mennonites, one can find articles on United States Immigration laws, the falsity of the *Protocols of the Elders of Zion* and, in the late thirties, a series on the origins, causes and persistence of anti-Semitism.[6] A letter from a pro-Nazi Mennonite in Germany to Mennonite historian John Horsch, vehemently attacked an article in the *Christian Monitor* which exposed the anti-Jewish slanders of the Hitler regime. In perhaps the most pro-Jewish article found in the Mennonite press in the period 1933-45, the World News Editor of the *Christian Monitor* refuted, point by point, the attempt of the Nazi propaganda machine to link the Jews in Germany with Communism.[7] After "*Kristallnacht*, the *Mennonite* published vigorous denunciations of Hitler's policies towards the Jews. In May of 1939, the *Mennonite* urged that the immigration laws be amended to allow for more Jewish refugees to enter the United States and to perhaps allow them to enter without restrictions on number."[8]

Mennonites in the thirties and forties were primarily a rural people and probably had few contacts with Jews. What they knew of Judaism may have come from their idealization of the Jewish people as they emerged out of the pages of the Old Testament. Especially in the Eastern part of the United States, Mennonites were not only a deeply pious people but also, in different locations, attuned to the Fundamentalist challenge to modernism that swept eastward from places like Kansas and the South. In addition to the Fundamentalism that made inroads amongst Mennonites, pre-millennialism was also a force in many Mennonite communities. The pre-millennial belief that God's plan unfolded in stages or dispensations led many Mennonites to view the persecution of Jews as part of God's plan. Perhaps the persecution of the Jews was God's way of moving the Jew to accept Christ, thus anticipating the "end of days." Mennonites of this kind were not callous to Jewish suffering but rather saw divine purpose behind what was happening. A decade later, this same type of pre-millennialism would anchor supporters of the newly created state of Israel.

Stereotypes, however, work both ways. If some Mennonites connected the Jews with the Hebrews of the Old Testament, others tended to accept negative cultural stereotypes of the Jew and connected the Jews with the worst excesses of materialism and modernity. The thirties produced its share of anti-Semitic clergymen, ranging from Father Coughlin to Gerald L. K. Smith. Amongst Mennonites Gerald B. Winrod, with his mixture of religious fundamentalism and anti-Semitic rhetoric, made significant inroads amongst Mennonites in the Middle-West as well as in the East. Winrod was a gifted orator, and Mennonites in Kansas came to know him by attending his prayer meetings as well as by reading his *Defender*--a militantly anti-Semitic, anti-New Deal and pro-Hitler publication. Reprints of *Defender* articles found their way into publications such as the *Mennonite* and the ultra-conservative Mennonite publication *Sword and Trumpet*. Although one Mennonite historian has argued that Mennonites were attracted more to Winrod's fundamentalist message than to his anti-Semitism,[9] it should be pointed out that often they went together.

The fundamentalist attack on Modernism started out as an argument over the theory of evolution, the literalness of the Bible and the supernatural presence of Jesus.[10] The Modernist Controversy, as it came to be known in Mennonite circles, was linked with the triumph of atheism in the Soviet Union. Furthermore, among a small but influential number of Mennonites, there was a belief that Jews were behind the Communist Revolution in Russia. This type of Mennonite, fundamentalist in outlook, anti-Communist and opposed to those aspects of modernity that threatened his religious "Weltanschauung," found in Adolf Hitler someone who, he believed, was an ally against the forces of atheism and Bolshevism. The following examples illustrate how this type of Mennonite was able to combine support for Hitler with a callous disregard for what was happening to the Jews of Germany. The extracts are taken from the fundamentalist Mennonite publication *Sword and Trumpet* and are illustrative of the influence of Gerald B. Winrod amongst certain Mennonites.

> The Mennonites never persecute their enemies neither do they approve others doing so, but we do...wonder why the American press kept up such an editorial storm...against the heavy hand of Hitler while they can be as quiet as a dove...while the Communist of Russia, the promoters of which are said to be mostly Jews, for fifteen years have kept up a campaign of oppression, enslavement...and extermination against the lovers of religion.
>
> July 1933 p. 23

> Some say that the Protocols of the Elders of Zion are a forgery but it is amazing how world events seem to be shaping themselves to the pattern therein set forth.
>
> Jan. 1934 p. 16

> It is true that Red Communism is of Jewish origin and that its engineers and financiers are mainly Jews. Marx and Engels, the founders of the movement were Jews. It was a Jewish banking concern, Kuhn, Loeb and Co. of New York, that financed the Jews, Lenin and Trotsky, in precipitating the Russian Revolution. And 454 of the original 545 Communist offices of the Moscow dictatorship were filled by Jews. But these have been renegade Atheistic Jews, uncircumcized in heart, and he is not a Jew who is one outwardly only...there are many orthodox Jews who are reputable and useful citizens and we should be careful not to speak distastefully of Jews as Jews--the promise of Abraham has not run out yet.
>
> Oct. 1934

> It is interesting, to say the least, that at least 265 of the 454 Jews in Russia's governing circle come from the East side of N.Y. according to U.S. Senate records.

134

Jan. 1935 p. 36
Finally

The Pathfinder of Oct. 1937 records that an honor society of Jewish students has named 120 persons to a Jewish hall of fame in Chicago and gives leading names as follows: Felix Frankfurter, Albert Einstein, Leon Blum, Sigmund Freud, Paul Muni, Larus Brandeis, Benjamin Cardozo, Henry Morgenthau Jr., Maxim Litvinoff. If this list really expresses the true sentiment of the Jewish people they should not complain when they are charged with being friends, supporters, and promoters of the Communist revolutionary activities of the nation and the world.

Jan. 1938 p. 5

To the credit of mainstream Mennonite publications, some of these inaccuracies were attacked, especially in the columns of C. F. Derstine in the *Christian Monitor*. But for those who saw the Bolshevik Revolution as the triumph of modernism and materialism, Hitler was seen as a savior. John R. Thierstein, the editor of the *Mennonite* extolled Hitler's regime. According to Thierstein, the treatment of the Jews was justified because of the inordinate amount of influence they exercised in Germany. Writing in the *Bethel College Monthly* in 1934, Thierstein states "harm done to the Jews was insignificant by comparison with the great service Hitler had performed in saving Germany from Communism and its Jewish adherents."[11]

In the years between 1933 and 1939, one could argue that whereas most Mennonites were probably anti-Hitler or indifferent to what was going on in Europe, this certainly was not true with regard to some Mennonite leaders and intellectuals. There were Mennonite leaders such as Thierstein who suspected that what was reported with regard to the persecution of the Jews was in fact an exaggeration or a lie perpetrated by American Jews. Responding to his father-in-law John Horsch, the Mennonite historian, Harold Bender challenged Horsch for proof that "wealthy Jews have worked America by propaganda" against Hitler. Bender, at the time Dean of Goshen College, and future author of the *Anabaptist Vision* further adds in his response

Winrod is known to be a great propagandist and has published a great deal of trash and propaganda himself. For instance he has all along upheld the truth of the..."Jewish Protocols," and apparently, in spite of overwhelming evidence to the contrary...believes them to be true....In conclusion, my interest

> in Hitler and Germany...concerns the Christian church...and I feel that the situation has gotten worse. Then too, we must all feel that anti-Semitism in any respect is wrong and should not be tolerated. Hitler's official program includes this, so it can not be merely propaganda when Jews talk about....[12]

Horsch, the author of books attacking modernism and Communism remained unconvinced, until the German invasion of the Netherlands, that anti-Hitler feeling in this country was not a result of Jewish propaganda. Although Horsch's views with regard to Jews, Communism and Hitler was a minority voice in the Mennonite Community, his ideas would have found fertile soil among the Russian Mennonites in Canada.

The Russian Mennonites' gratitude to the Weimar government for providing sanctuary in 1929-30 was transferred to the Hitler regime. It is also not surprising that amongst the colony of Russian Mennonites in Canada, there was not only a hatred for the Soviet Union and Communism but also an admiration for Hitler who was perceived as standing up to Bolshevism.

In the pages of *Der Bote*, the leading Russian immigrant and Mennonite paper in Canada, Jews were credited with having founded Communism. The *Protocols of the Elders of Zion* were seriously discussed and the writings of Gerald B. Winrod were recommended to the paper's readership. In addition, writers from within Germany who were published in *Der Bote* assured the readership that "the maltreatment of Jews in Germany was highly exaggerated by the foreign Jewish-dominated press."[13]

How representative *Der Bote* and the immigrant Russian Mennonite press was of Russian Mennonites in Canada is difficult to determine but one historian of the period, Frank Epp has written...

> the immigrant newspaper was a fairly representative reflection of the Mennonite immigrant mind, which in the 1930's was very strong on nurturing and preserving cultural Germanism, as essential to the Mennonite way of life, strong also in its identification with racial Germanism, and though ambivalent on the question by and large also sympathetic to the political Germanism of the Third Reich.[14]

Epp further argues...

> The pro-German attitude of *many* Mennonites during the 1930's was common knowledge....The close ties with German sources in Germany and Canada, the circulation of National Socialist literature and Adolf Hitler photos, the participation in brownshirt organization and demonstrations...in Winnipeg

there was an actual clash between Communists and brownshirts in which Mennonite blood was spilled--the actual enlistment of a few young men in the National Socialist cause and their return to Germany, the purchase of short wave radios in order to tune in Hitler's speeches and the supporting of a pro-Nazi paper could not be and were not kept a secret.[15]

With the possible exception of the Russian Mennonites, it would appear that most Mennonites were sympathetic to the plight of the Jews in Europe. But this sympathy was not translated into action. Because of their belief in non-resistance and their tradition of non-involvement in politics, most Mennonites would have refrained from pressuring Congress to modify the immigration laws, or by joining a boycott of Nazi Germany demonstrate on behalf of Europe's Jewry in the nation's capitol. (In Germany, parenthetically, some Mennonites helped Jews, others did nothing and most supported the Hitler regime going as far as serving in the German Army--in the Netherlands, Mennonites sheltered Jews.)

But North American Mennonites did have a tradition of relief work. In fact, throughout the thirties and forties, the Mennonite Central Committee was involved in relief work in many parts of Europe. M.C.C. workers aided refugees all the way from Spain to Poland but although its charter called for M.C.C. "to function as a charitable organization in the relief of human suffering and distress and in aiding...Mennonites and other refugees..."[16] its record is striking by its almost total absence of any relief work amongst Jews.

The reports and letters of M. C. Lehman, sent to Poland by the M.C.C. in 1939, for the purpose of organizing refugee relief, are notable for their lack of mention of Jews or awareness of a specific Jewish problem in Europe.[17] The official history of the M.C.C., which deals primarily with Mennonite relief work in Europe during the thirties and where possible, the forties, almost entirely ignores the plight of the Jews.[18]

How is one to account for this omission? Is it possible that the M.C.C., so involved in relief work throughout the world today, was so concerned with helping their own brethren that they simply ignored the suffering of others? Was it possible that M.C.C. was afraid to rupture its good reputation with the German government and perhaps compromise the position of Mennonites in Germany by becoming advocates of the Jews? Or more to the point, was it possible that pro-Nazi Mennonites such as Benjamin Unruh were in charge of relief on the other side of the Atlantic and thus affected the relief priorities of North American Mennonites?[19] Certainly Mennonite relief workers in Europe were in a unique position to witness the immense suffering of the Jews in Europe. That M.C.C. did not offer aid in behalf of Jewish refugees is one of the more perplexing unresolved questions in understanding Mennonite reactions to the suffering of the Jews in Europe.

The response of North American Mennonites to the plight of the Jews was a complex one. If allowances are made to discount the influence of those small number of Mennonites who held anti-Semitic attitudes in the United States and a larger number in Canada, then the conclusion is reached that most Mennonites were both anti-Nazi Germany and sympathetic to the plight of the Jews. But this sympathy was not translated into action. Rather, many Mennonites believed--despite evidence to the contrary vis-à-vis Nazi racial laws--that Jewish suffering would be alleviated by accepting Christ. On an organizational level, the failure of experienced Mennonite relief organizations even to approximate the efforts of the Quakers with regard to Jewish refugees is an unresolved question in evaluating Mennonite attitudes towards Jews. Finally, Mennonite theology simply did not allow for effective coalition politics in tandem with Jewish groups in order to bend the rigidly enforced immigration laws. Mennonites had little history in "working" Congress although there were examples of Mennonites petitioning government in behalf of their own. This last point may be a clue to the failure of not only Mennonites but most Protestant groups in bringing their resources to the aid of persecuted Jews. One cannot help but agree with the conclusions drawn by William Nawyn that Protestant groups in America did not see themselves as Protestants but rather as Baptists, Methodists, Presbyterians, etc.[20] It would appear, especially from the history of the M.C.C., that for the most part Mennonites thought of themselves first. What was happening to the Jews of Europe was only tangentially a Mennonite issue. In the abstract, Mennonites should have followed the motto of the M.C.C. "In the Name of Christ." That it concerned itself primarily with Mennonites caught in the European upheaval and not with refugees in general was not just a failure of the Mennonites but rather symptomatic of the overall failure of much of American Protestant denominations to transcend their sectarian loyalties in behalf of European Jewry.

138

ENDNOTES

[1]William, Nawyn *American Protestantism's Response to Germany's Jews and Refugees, 1933-41* (Ann Arbor: UMI Research Press, 1980), p. 7.

[2]*Christian Monitor*, March, 1933, p. 4.

[3]*Ibid*, May, 1933, p. 19.

[4]*Ibid*, July, 1940, p. 223.

[5]Kathe Weaver, "The Suffering Jew," *Gospel Herald*, May 12, 1944, p. 114.

[6]E. L. Horshberger, "History Views the Jewish Persecutions," *Mennonite*, Feb. through April, 1939.

[7]"Clearing the Atmosphere of Anti-Jewish Slander," *Christian Monitor*, April 13, 1936, p. 120.

[8]*Mennonite*, May, 1939, p. 3.

[9]James Juhnke, *A People of Two Kingdoms: The Political Acculturation of the Kansas Mennonites* (Newton, Kansas: Faith and Life Press, 1975), pp. 132-134.

[10]John Horsch, *The Mennonite Church and Modernism* (Scottdale, Pa.: Mennonite Publishing House, 1924), pp. 7-8.

[11]Nawyn, *ibid*, p. 99

[12]See Harold Bender to John Horsch, March 9, 1935, Hist. MSS 1-8-1, John Horsch Letters, 1934-40, Box 6.

[13]Frank Henry Epp,, "An Analysis of Germanism and National Socialism in the Immigrant Newspaper of a Canadian Minority Group, the Mennonites, in the 1930's" (unpublished Ph.D. dissertation, University of Minnesota, 1965), pp. 120-123.

[14]*Ibid*, p. 220.

[15]*Ibid*, p. 243.

[16]John Unruh, *In the Name of Christ*, (Scottdale, Pa.: Herald Press, 1952), p. 35.

[17]See M. C. Lehman papers which are found in the Archives of Goshen College.

[18]Unruh, *op. cit.*

[19]Epp, *op. cit.*, p. 224. Frank Epp shows the apparent pro-Nazi sympathies of Benjamin Unruh in his brief biographical sketch of the Mennonite Commissioner in Germany.

[20]Nawyn, *op. cit.*, see Introduction and Conclusions.

MAHANE ISRAEL-LUBAVITCH 1940-1945: ACTIVELY RESPONDING TO *KHURBN* *

Gershon Greenberg

Joseph Isaac Schneersohn (1880-1950), the Rav of Lubavitch Hassidism (or "Habad"), established "Mahane Israel" (or "Camp of Israel," see *Exodus* 14/19-20) sect on 20 October 1940, seven weeks after he arrived in America. Based in Brooklyn, New York, it had appeal not only to Hassidim but to Misnagdim, to Sephardi and Ashkenazi Jews as well.[1] In addition to American members, Jews from Canada, England, Australia, the Land of Israel, Shanghai, Paris and the Oswego, New York refugee camp belonged.[2] In terms of numbers, it is known that there were 400 people present at the 24 May 1942 MI Oral Mishna Fellowship lottery, and 670 at the 20 June 1943 concluding ceremony of Mishna study (*Siyyum*).[3]

Refuge in Goshen

MI conceived of itself as a "Goshen" ("Only in the land of Goshen, where the children of Israel were, was there no hail," *Exodus* 9/26). Within its boundaries, contemporary Jews could find refuge from the contemporary plagues of the *Khurbn*, which were the pains preceding the advent of the messiah (*Hevlei Moshiah*) and stand at the threshold to redemption. As the plagues of Egypt once unfolded outside the ancient Goshen at the eve of redemption (*erev der geula*), so the contemporary catastrophe would remain outside MI.

> World-plagues cannot enter into Goshen, [which] means being able to outlive all the troubles and being worthy of redemption ....Only there can Jews await the imminent 'immediate

redemption'! Once settled there [they are] liberated from the omnipresent darkness and from many other plagues as well....The prophet warns us, ['Come, my people, enter thou into thy chambers and shut thy doors about thee;] hide but a little moment, until the indignation passes,' (*Isaiah* 26/20). The prophet means that [Israel] should remain in Goshen, and that Jews who believe in false redemptions have no Goshen and certainly no redemption! May God have pity![4]

JIS hoped that all Jews would join MI. He encouraged the current members to recruit and serve as bridges for others to enter Goshen and thereby diminish the *Hevlei Moshiah*.[5]

Esoteric and exoteric knowledge

MI claimed that it possessed esoteric knowledge of the apocalypse, of the nature of the passage from the *Khurbn* to *Geula*. The "deep secrets of providence" in which the end of World War II was bound up, were available in Goshen.[6] MI knew about the "Jewish secret of conception."[7] The secret knowledge was contained in Joseph's final words: "I die and God will surely remember (*pakod yifkod*) you and bring you out of the land [of Egypt] unto the Land which He swore to Abraham, Isaac and Jacob" (*Genesis* 50/24). The "*pakod yifkod*," as the MI referred to it, contained the paradigmatic reality of transition from exile/death to Land-redemption/life. Thus, because JIS knew the *pakod yifkod* in fall 1940, he could see how overwhelming the war would be, that an American victory would not mean rescuing of Israel, and that victory would come too late for European Jewry.[8]

Joseph shared the secret because the "*pakod yifkod*" had reached the point of no return. Similarly, soon after MI members were told in October 1940 not to spread knowledge of the paradigm among strangers until the exile oppressed them so severely that their very existence was endangered.[9] JIS proclaimed: "Immediate penitent return, Immediate redemption" and seven months later explained the declaration in detail in a *Kol Kore* (proclamation).[10]

The secret message created a secretive aura, and MI members kept their memberships hidden even from close friends and family members,[11] and did not reveal their identities when they carried out MI activities.[12] They also communicated through secret messages in HK, by running lengthy

Yiddish acronymic codes upside down below the monthly "Flying Letters" poetry sections. The messages began with the first issue of 20 October 1940 and ran almost regularly through the forty-eighth issue of 20 July 1943.[13] Two acronyms were decoded. That of 21 September 1941 was decoded on 20 July 1944.

d/ts/h/e/a/z/k/a/s/f/d/f/f/a/a/a/a/y/a/b/z/f/y.a/d/v/g/
z/g/a/e/v/z/v/a/ts/v/k/v/n/n/d/ts.a/z/v/h/z/e/n/e/a/v/f,
a/b/a/f/e/v/z/a/a/z/h/n/d/a/a/.z/a/a/v/a/a/v/z/d/n/e*/
v/z/a/a/a/g/d/d/ts, f/v/h/k/m/d/e/s.

Dem tsorrer Hitlers ende iz zeyn kumender achzariot-diger strashunok far der fornikhtung fun ale Oyropeer un Amerikaner yehidim oyf beyde zeyten fun yam. Ale Deytsehe vilde gvaldthaten, zeyendig groyzam un ekelhaft, velen zeyn vaserdig antkegen tsorendigen vaulkan kokhendiger velt-nekama Nazi-Deutschland tsutsushteren, un zi vet Hitler's ziegreykhe ekelhafte Naziland endlikh arumkhapen vi feyr, ihr befelkerung oysroten fun ekzistents vi zey ale un zeyr Hitlerisher Nazism durshten oystsuroten Iden. Sumer arum Ellul, ven in Amerika velen ziden di November elekshons (1944), velen zikh in Oyropa opshpielen groyse dershiterende durkhgehende tsarot. Folglikh vet Hitler kumen mit Deutschlands ekelhaften strashunok!* (The tyrant Hitler's end is his [own] ongoing cruel threat to annihilate all individuals in Europe and America, on both sides of the ocean. All the violent, horrible German action will be impeded when they confront the furious volcanoes which are now boiling with a vengeance against German Nazism. They will overcome Hitler's victorious and abhorrent Nazi-land like fire. They will annihilate its population's existence as Nazism has thirsted to annihilate Jews. In [August-September] when America will be involved in its November (1944*) [Presidential] elections, there will be great troubles in Europe. Then Hitler will come out with Germany's abhorrent threats.[14]

*Added in 1944.

That of 27 December 1943 was decoded in 21 June 1944:

v/a/f/z/a/b/a/a/s/a/d/g/f/z/a/v/z/a/e/f/h/y/a/d/d/n/a/f
/e/f/d/v/z/d/kh/y/n/b/v/g/b/a/d/v/d/h/a/d/a/s/a/m/z/a

Velt iberkehrenishen fangen zikh on bald, un a sakh, ober der grus fun zeyr onfang vet zeyn arum erev Pessah heyntigen yohr, eygentlikh, dem dreytsenten Nissan: 'Invazie folgt! Ervartet front!' Dos vet zikheren dem 'ki yom nakam be'libi ushenat goali ba'a!' Unzer demokratie vet demolt halb aroylozen ihr invazie-sod, obvohl magerlikh, zehr unbashtimt! (Great world upheavals will soon begin. But the major onset will take place around Passover this year [8-15 April 1944], specifically on 3

April 1944/10 *Nissan* 5704: 'Invasion follows. Expect a [military] front.' This will assure the 'For I had planned a day of vengeance and My year of redemption arrived' [*Isaiah* 63/4]. Half of our democracy's invasion secret will then be revealed-- albeit limitedly and vaguely.)[15]

But the threshold of death had been entered, and the knowledge had to be spread. As the prophet Elijah once came with the knowledge of *pakod yifkod*, telling of imminent divine redemption, and suffered isolation because of his zeal for God (I *Kings* 19/14),[16] so in October 1940 JIS began to proclaim apocalypse, explained it in a series of urgent "calls" (*Kol Kore*, "a voice rings out clear in the desert a road for the Lord," *Isaiah* 40/3) in the pages of HK, and felt alone.[17]

The HK editor[18] prefaced the first call of 26 May 1941 by stating that Jews were then situated a few years prior to (*erev der*) complete redemption. JIS pleaded for the Jews not to despair, no matter how bad matters might become. He assured them that the act of penitent return (*Teshuva*) could ease the *Hevlei Moshiah*, and that if God so willed a great light would follow the intense darkness. JIS also took the opportunity to criticize American Orthodox leaders for being oblivious to the *Ikvassa demeshiha*, and to claim that because they failed to speak categorically of the apocalypse their calls of *Teshuva* and prayer evoked little response.[19]

JIS saw the body of European Jewry burning and the soul of American Jewry being destroyed by coldness and indifference to Tora. Thus, American Jews deduced that if God could not help Tora-true Jews in Europe then Tora in America was useless and it was best to rely on democratic leaders. American Jews, JIS insisted, failed to recognize the choice they faced between life and death ("By thy blood [*or*] live," *Ezekiel* 16/6), between awareness of the apocalypse (*Teshuva*) with removal of impurity (*Tuma*) and *Hevlei Moshiah*. The choice for the first meant redemption, while the second meant sharing the fate which the angel of death would mete out to other nations. JIS ended with a desperate cry:

'Immediate redemption!' is our call, because this is the call which [fits] today. This is not merely a consolation for the despaired. It is our good news about a factual "salvation which is to come soon" (*Isaiah* 56/1). We must prepare ourselves in heart and soul to welcome the righteous redeemer. And we call upon all Jews to join the MI which, with the help of the

Blessed Name, is being organized for this purpose! 'Immediate redemption!' Be ready for redemption soon! It approaches in rapid strides, although you do not see it. It is near at hand! The righteous messiah is already around the corner, and the time for self-preparation is already very short.[20]

In his second *Kol Kore*, 24 June 1941, JIS observed that the prevalent atmosphere of impurity (*Tuma*) characteristic to the point between exile and redemption included the ignoring of messianic faith. Ultimately, the ignoring would be shattered, but by the *Hevlei Moshiah* themselves. Then the souls and bodies of those who ignored the call and introduced "alien fire" into the "holy fire" of messianic belief would burn and die--as happened once even to Nadav and Abbihu, children of Aaron the priest (*Leviticus* 10/1). But there was still time. Every Jew would still choose, and should choose lest the choice be made for him:

> Either *Kol Kore* or 'in the desert' (*ba'midbar*). Ignore the *Kol Kore* and you are left to the desert. And this is a desert without manna, without a pillar of cloud, without a pillar of fire, without Moses and the divine rod in his hand. It is a desert with a new 'And Amalek will come' (*Exodus* 17/8), one in the form of a cruel antisemitic wave, God forbid, the likes of which has never occurred.

JIS wanted every Jew to join MI and build a united fortress of public *Teshuva*, whereupon God would stop the enemy. Once contemporary Jews became a great mass of God's covenant--bearers (*Deuteronomy* 31/25) no storm could touch them. The enemy would become dismayed (*Exodus* 15/15) and so dumb and lame that it could no longer even lift its contaminated hand.[21]

In the third *Kol Kore*, 24 July 1941, JIS sought to impress upon Jews the urgency of ending their resistance, of recognizing the apocalyptic events and seeking protection from the "raging storm" ("The Lord shall come forth from His place to punish the dwellers of the earth for their iniquity, and the earth shall disclose its bloodshed and shall no longer conceal its slain," *Isaiah* 26/21). The apocalyptic moment was near: "We have not said that the messiah will come in a few moments, we have also not postponed the messiah's coming for very long."[22]

On 13 September 1941, JIS called upon his followers to participate in the 14 September fast called by the American Orthodox leadership, the

Agudat Ha'rabbanim. Thousands of Jews in Europe were being tortured and exterminated, and the remainder exposed to famine, prison and exile. When such calamities occurred, fasting, prayer, and acknowledgement that they resulted from disobeying Tora were required. God's mercy upon the people would follow (Maimonides, *MT Hilkhot Ta'aniyot* ch. 1, *Halakha* 4):

> In these days of mercy and *Selihot* a day of fasting has been announced for all of Israel with the unanimous approval of Israel's greatest spiritual leaders, on account of the present terrible condition of the Jewish people....I entreat you, brothers and sisters, have compassion on yourselves, your sons and daughters [and participate] so that you will not be destroyed during the birth pangs of the coming messiah....[23]

On 21 September 1941 JIS stressed that the current troubles needed to be recognized as the consequence of bad deeds, not as accidents within the cosmic process. Yet if Israel cried out to God, the troubles would not befall the entire nation.[24]

On 2 December 1942 JIS issued two open letters, which supplemented the *Kol Kore*'s. In the first, in which he supported the Agudat Ha'rabbanim's call for a fast on 2 December 1942, he observed that the Tannaim and Amoraim had predicted 2,000 years ago that a harsh tyrant like Haman would at some point arise, carrying out God's intention to thereby awaken Israel to *Teshuva* and return to Tora and *Mitzvot*. JIS insisted that the rescue from pain, indeed exile itself, was in Jewish hands. Namely, through *Teshuva*, Sabbath observance, *Kashrut*, family purity and Tora-true education, redemption could be brought closer. In the second letter JIS anguished over the fact that while European Jews were being murdered, most American Jews were too spiritually impoverished to carry on the sacrificial battle for Tora and *Mitzvot* to respond to catastrophe. If they did not change, they themselves would suffer consequences; what God meant when He suspended Mt. Sinai over Israel ("If ye accept the Tora it will be well with you, but if not, there will be your grave," *Avoda Zara* 2b) would become clear for American Jews.[25]

A *Kol Kore* by MI of 21 October 1941 pointed out that the call for *Teshuva* was intended to accelerate the passage of *Hevlei Moshiah* and the messiah's arrival, and that the messiah was expected imminently; the relationship between human action and divine "timing" was not spelled out.

HK itself was planned for a short run, because its sole purpose was to spread that message. Although a history of "messianic" debacles in Judaism coupled with an irreligiosity could explain the indifference to apocalypse, the indifference remained unforgivable in the face of the European destruction and the reality of *Hevlei Moshiah* and imminent messianic redemption. MI was disappointed that the Orthodox (*Yeraim ve'haredim*) were standing aside:

> This by itself means that, win or lose, you really want [to stand] along with those who are total heretics when it comes to the coming of the messiah and who ridicule openly the call of *Admor Shlita*. If the messiah should indeed not come soon, you *win* along with the heretics. If, as *Admor Shlita* says, the messiah does come, you *lose* along with the heretics. This is quite bizarre: that either way the *Yeraim ve'haredim* should stand on one platform with those who are heretical about the messianic coming, but not with the *Admor Shlita* of Lubavitch who stands opposed to those who are heretical about the messiah, *against* them if they win, and *against* them if they lose.[26]

In the fourth and last *Kol Kore*, that of 11 September 1942, JIS declared that the pouring of blood would be followed by redemption. Free nations were already winning, and this was God's doing. Still, the Jew faced a choice: "I have set before you life and death...choose life" (*Deuteronomy* 30/19).[27]

In commenting on the four *Kol Kore*'s the HK editor spoke of the urgency of understanding the meaning of the crisis, that is, hearkening to the esoteric *pakod yifkod* which the Rav enunciated at the point of Israel's death. God, the editor wrote, would offer no further proof to the doubters of the fact that Israel was situated at the brink of redemption (*kodem le'geula*) (*cf. Numbers* 16 on Dathan and Abiram). He concluded that some were destined to hearken and thereby survive for redemption, while others were doomed:

> There are Jews who in their hearts deserve complete redemption. [And] complete redemption wants *them*. These [Jews} will, for one reason or another, ultimately do *Teshuva*, and outlive the troubles. The Master of the world will not rescue any others. They do not need *complete redemption*. And complete redemption does not need them.

Some of those who did not hearken to the Rav's declarations would, the editor thought, be so disappointed in the course of world events that they would become suicidal. Those who heard the Rav's call and understood the "*pakod yifkod*" that redemption followed troubles, would not have to choose between suicide or more suffering but between suicide or *Teshuva* leading to immediate redemption. The editor considered the fourth *Kol Kore* as an addendum to Holy Scripture, concluding a four-chapter book which crystallized the prophetic writing about the end of days.[28]

Thus, those who found refuge in Goshen from the storm had esoteric knowledge about the "*pakod yifkod.*" It impressed upon them the need for *Teshuva* and enabled them to endure the suffering by envisioning redemption and acting accordingly. This knowledge became exoteric at the crisis point when death became imminent. At that point, the *cognoscenti* could no longer withhold the secrets, for they meant life itself. But the bearers of knowledge met resistance--which in turn impelled MI to press forward with its enlightenment with even more urgency in the belief that the resistance spelled doom for the ignorant ones.

MI activities

When asked by MI about how to act in the crisis so as to endure the suffering and even experience redemption, JIS responded: "Do the same as I am doing." First of all, this meant *Teshuva*.[29] When JIS first arrived in America, he had been warned against trying to recreate Eastern European Jewish life in America,[30] but he responded by committing himself to aggressively promoting *Teshuva*. *Teshuva*, MI believed, was the one way to rescue Israel from the severity of the *Hevlei Moshiah*. It also paved the way to redemption.[31] *Teshuva* was not a matter of scholarship, e.g. innovative Tora interpretation (*Hiddushim*). JIS recalled bitterly how some youngsters in Russia once held study sessions in defiance of the law--and they were sent to Siberia to learn.[32] *Teshuva* was more than following positive commandments. It occurred when a heavenly root touched the soul, there was sudden awareness and one became removed from the wrong path on to the path of Tora.[33] JIS passed on his father Shalom Dov Baer's (1866-1920) acronymic explanation:

> T (*Tet*): As in "You must be wholehearted (*tamim*) with the Lord your God" (*Deuteronomy* 18/13). That is, be sincere with God.

S (*Shin*):   As in "I am ever mindful (*shaviti*) of the Lord's presence" (*Psalm* 16/8).

V (*Vav*):   As in "Love (*ve'ahavta*) your neighbor as yourself" (*Leviticus* 19/8). This, according to Habad founder Shneour Zalman of Lliady (1747-1812) was instrumental to loving God: "As the spirit of creatures guides him, so the spirit of God guides him."

B (*Bet*):   As in "In all your paths (*bekhol Derakhekha*) know Him" (*Proverbs* 3/6), meaning that man should serve God in everything he does and be aware of how his life is immersed in divine providence. For example, Shneour Zalman's son Dov Baer of Lubavitch (1773-1837) praised the businessmen for perceiving God in concrete contexts.

H (*Hay*):   As in "Walk modestly (*hatznaya lekhet*) with your God" (*Micah* 6/8), meaning that a person should not make his accomplishments obvious.[34]

Teshuva also took time. The people of Ninevah, the children of Noah himself, needed forty days (*Jonah* 3) and Esther and Mordekhai needed a year.[35] JIS stressed that by calling for *Teshuva* at that moment he was not using redemption just as a ploy but that *Teshuva* was a necessary preparation for the messiah's arrival.[36]

The means of promoting *Teshuva* included various activities. In 1943 JIS' nephew Menahem Mendel Schneersohn, who arrived in America in 1941 and was appointed MI's Executive Director,[37] specified exemplary conduct in the spirit of Tora and *Mitzva*, becoming Shabbat advisors, and forming Oral Mishna and Psalm Societies.[38]

Women had a special role in the process. MI believed that women were always the first victims at times of trouble, that most victims were women, and that women felt the suffering of their children more than men. Women were also able to understand and recognize crisis before men, and they had more religious integrity. Thus, the exodus took place on account of pious women (*Midrash Exodus Rabba* I/12) and God told Moses to offer the Tora to women first (*Midrash Exodus Rabba* 28/2) because of their refusal to worship the golden calf (*Exodus* 32/28; *Midrash Numbers Rabba* 21/10).

When the MI Women's Division was established in summer 1941, it spoke of (1) practicing family purity, (2) organizing Sabbath societies to prevent buying on Sabbath, (3) forming groups for children to tell midrashic stories and to explain the enduring validity of Tora and *Mitzva* to help ease the *Hevlei Moshiah*.[39]

MI worked against Christian missionary efforts. It attacked Reform rabbis for being co-opted by missionaries by renouncing the messianic coming before the nations of the world and surrendering Sabbath, family purity, *Tefillin* and *Tzitzit*.[40] Specific groups were assigned by MI to rescue youths from conversion and to divert Jewish men from the offices of Christian Science.[41] MI delegates were sent to private homes to persuade parents to send their children to proper Talmud Tora's and Yeshivas. Some members spoke in parks and streets about Sabbath observance.[42] At the 20 May 1945 *Mishna Siyyum* JIS established the *Hevra Bikkur Holim* (Society to Visit the Ill). Headed by Yohanan Gordon, the Society offered small stipends to elders to visit hospitals to comfort the sick and strengthen their confidence in God. They provided reading material, including HK and JIS' *Sihot* (*Conversations*), and helped the ill recite prayers and use *Tefillin*.[43] Under Duber Baumgarten's direction, MI sent holiday greetings signed by MMS along with an informational brochure about the holiday to soldiers. Jewish chaplains received information about their religious responsibilities on holidays.[44] In the summer of 1945, following liberation from the camps and ghettos, MI distributed ritual items to the Displaced Persons in American and British zones in Europe.[45] The *Agudat Shiurei Limud Torah* (or "*Eshel*," Organization for Tora Study Sessions), also established at the 20 May 1945 *Mishna Siyyum*, recruited students for Habad's "Tomkhei Temimim" Yeshiva network and recruited businessmen and English-speaking youth who were strangers to *Halakha* and *Aggada* to synagogue study groups.[46] Lastly, MI prepared a special Tora scroll, called the "*Sefer Tora* for welcoming the countenance of the messiah" ("*Kabbalat P'nei Moshiah Sefer Tora*). Work on it was to start on 4 November 1940, the birthday of Shalom Dov Baer, but it was delayed until 19 April 1942, JIS' birthday. JIS recalled on Simhat Tora, 4 October 1942, how a delegation of Jews once appealed to the Baal Shem Tov in 1753, for him to pray for the many critically sick Jews of the town of Medziboz. He referred the petitioners to the phrase "May the worship of Your people Israel always be acceptable to You" in the *Eighteen Benedictions* prayer. There were two ways, he explained, in which worship could evoke (*shaft*) a divine will to annul an evil decree. One was to recite the letters of the Tora and the Psalms and the other was to have all those affected participate in writing a Tora scroll. The petitioners proceeded to prepare a scroll, and as soon as the Baal Shem Tov's own scribe R. Tsevi completed the first two sheets the people of Medziboz began to recover. The HK editor encouraged everyone, male and female, to participate in the preparation of the scroll for alleviating the contemporary *Hevlei Moshiah* and welcoming the messiah. He asked each to fill out one or more letters on the appropriate forms and send them to the Committee--which consisted of Samuel Halevi Levitan, Eliahu Simpson and David Shifrin. They would forward the letters to the special scribe appointed for the task who would inscribe the letters on behalf of the participants.[47]

Psalm and Mishna Fellowship

Within Goshen, the Psalm Fellowship and Oral Mishna Fellowship enhanced *Teshuva* and thereby helped to bring messianic redemption.

JIS established the Universal Psalm Fellowship on 22 May 1942 in the belief that Psalm-recital provided a means to both endure and ease messianic sufferings, and make Jews worthy of speedy redemption. The Fellowship was centered in Jerusalem under the direction of Shlomo Y. L. Eliezerov. It was led by Ashkenazi Chief Rabbi Isaac Halevy Herzog (1888-1959), Ultra-Orthodox Agudat Israel leader Joseph Zevi Dushinsky (1868-1948), Sephardic Chief Rabbi Benzion Meir Usiel (1880-1953) and a group of elders. The elders, serving as representatives (*Sheluhei Tzibbur*) of all Israel, recited all 150 Psalms at the grave of King David near Mt. Zion or at the Western Wall. The recitals, it was believed, would awaken Jews throughout the world to *Teshuva*, make them eligible for redemption, and ease the *Hevlei Moshiah* overall. As JIS observed, God would cherish the recital of Psalms by elders in this era of immediate redemption as He had once cherished the activities of elders at the redemption from Egypt (*Numbers* 11/24-25).

There were Psalm-recital groups in America and Canada, and it was hoped that others would develop in synagogues and *Bathei Midrash* throughout the world. The "elder fellowships" recited Psalms before *Shaharit* in equally divided sections over a seven-day period, the "daily fellowships" recited them after *Shaharit* over a thirty-day period, and the "Sabbath fellowships" recited Psalms 119-150 either before *Shaharit* or between *Minha* and *Ma'ariv* on the Sabbath. On the first day of each *Shavuot* there were worldwide recitals and a celebratory meal (*Seuda Mitzva*) at King David's grave. Women were eligible to become full members--although not to hold office as *Gabbai*, public reader or clerk. The Fellowship functioned at least through *Shavuot*, 28 May 1944.[48]

JIS initiated the MI Oral Mishna Fellowship on 9 April 1942 in order to purify the air through the Tora letters of *Mishna*. Fellowship members were issued cards stating that healthy life was possible only in purified air, and this depended upon uninterrupted Mishna recitation wherever Halakhically permitted: "Exiles are gathered together only by merit of Mishnas! Israel is redeemed only through *Teshuva*! Immediate *Teshuva*! Immediate redemption!" The first lottery to assign tractates took place on 24 May 1942, the second on 24 June 1942, the third on 20 June 1943, the fourth on 18 June 1944. The number of tractates varied. On 9 April 1942 JIS spoke of reciting two to three tractates a week, on 20 June 1943 of ten or at least one in addition to what the regular prayer schedule required. MMS spoke of completing all six divisions in a year. The first ceremony for the completion of the entire Mishna, on 20 June 1943, was led by MMS and addressed by JIS; the second on 18 June 1944 was led by MMS; the third on 20 May 1945 was led by MMS. At the first two there were lotteries and *Seudot Mitzva*, and at the third religious melodies (*Nigunim*) were sung and there were no lotteries.[49]

On 24 June 1942, at the second lottery to assign Mishna tractates for recital, JIS explained that the air had become clouded (*fargrebt*) and was making people sick. To purify it, the letters of Tora, i.e. Mishna, needed to be spoken while walking in the street, travelling by street, car, bus, subway or automobile, and while standing in a store or office. "Mishna," with the same letters as "*Neshama*" (soul), provided calmness of spirit (see *Midrash Vayyikra*

Rabba 21/4). Because Mishna repetition authenticated the life of Tora and *Mitzva*, it brought God to protect the people of Israel from internal and external enemies. JIS concluded with a prayer to God to awaken Jews to do *Teshuva* through Mishna and thereby lighten the *Hevlei Moshiah*.[50] On 31 October 1942 he explained that Tora-study and *Mitzva* observance purified the air and provided a strong sense of divinity. Conversely, when they were absent people would be drawn away from God and into materiality. JIS cited the medieval philosopher Levi ben Gershon (1288-1349) regarding thinking as it affects a second person:

> When a person is walking in the street and suddenly has a good idea about Tora, *Mitzva* or good behavior, it means that he met a person who studied Tora, kept *Mitzvot* and behaved properly. Someone awakened a good [atmosphere] around him. Similarly, if he has a bad idea, it means that a bad person with evil thoughts affected him.[51]

At the 20 June 1943 *Mishna Siyyum* and lottery JIS pointed out that Mishna study, once confined to *Batei Midrash*, should now be brought outside and become a matter of "as thou walkest by the way" (*Shema*). It could rescue an individual and his family from evil. JIS believed Mishna study coalesced with a person's character. For example, Shneour Zalman of Lliady once told a Rabbi Eysel that if he learned *Mishna Kelim* by heart he would develop a wide-ranging intellectual apparatus (*Kelim*) and he did. Shmuel ben Menahem Mendel Schneersohn (1834-1883) called one young man "Shabbat" because he studied *Mishna Shabbat*. Mishna study had the power even to defy Amalek. R. Eleazar observed in the name of R. Yehoshua b. Levi that Mishna was a "pillar of iron" (*Barzel*), numerically equivalent to 240 (actually 239), which neutralized the doubt (*Safek* = 240) brought by Amalek (*Amalek* = 240) (*Midrash Vayyikra Rabba* 21/4).[52] On 20 May 1945 JIS said that the soul struggled to expel dust which stuck to it as with a slingshot (I *Samuel* 25/29) and that memorizing and repeating the Mishna accomplished this.[53]

In summer 1944 MMS offered four points of explanation. First, air was crucial above all for life. While eating and drinking were necessary at certain points in time, without air a person died within the hour (see *Yoma* 75b, Rambam, MT *Hilkhot Deot* ch. 4 beginning, SA *Even Ha'ezer* paragraph 17 part 32, Menahem Mendel Schneersohn (1789-1860), *Tsemah Tsedek*.

She'elot U'teshuvot mi'SA Even Ha'ezer nr. 78). Indeed, Moses survived seven days without eating or drinking (*Exodus* 24/16, *Yoma* 4b, Rambam, MT *Hilkhot Shavuot* ch. 5, *Halakha* 20). Sleep was needed only to refresh man enough to eat and drink (*Sukka* 53a, *Pirke de'Rabbi Eliezer* ch. 12; *Midrash Psalms Rabba* 25). Accordingly, "For every breath [which] man [takes he] should praise the Creator" (*Midrash Genesis Rabba*, ch. 14 end).[54] It followed that air impacted personality. Food and drink had their effect. For example, according to Nahmanides (commentary to *Leviticus* 11/11) animals of prey were prohibited because they instilled cruelty. Or:

> On the Day of Atonement [Elisha ben Abuyya] heard a voice. 'Return, backsliding children' (*Jeremiah* 3/14). 'Return unto Me and I will return unto you' (*Malachi* 3/7). All except Elisha ben Abuyya, who knew My power and yet rebelled against Me! How was it that Elisha acted in this [rebellious] manner?...When his mother was pregnant with him she passed by idolatrous temples. She smelled the dish, they gave her some of it to eat, and it spread through her like the venom of insects (*Midrash Ruth Rabba* 6/4).

If this was the effect of food and drink, MMS reasoned, how much greater was that of air without which one died within the hour? R. Zera, for example, could understand the wisdom of R. Elai because of Palestine's air (*Baba Bathra* 158b). According to the "Book of Rab Hamnuna the Elder," some races looked strange because of air quality (*Zohar* III, 10a).

Second, speech affected the air. Good speech had a positive affect and expelled defilement (*Tuma*):

> Once a certain disciple was mumbling over against R. Judah b. Bathyra. He said to him: 'My son, open thy mouth and let thy words be clear, for words of Tora are not susceptible to uncleanness, as it says, "Is not My word like as fire" (*Jeremiah* 23/29). Just as fire is not susceptible of defilement, so words of Tora are not susceptible of defilement' (*Berakhot* 22a).

Or, Rambam commented that Ezra's enactment that a person defiled by a nocturnal pollution was prohibited from reading Tora never took effect in Israel because words of Tora were immune to defilement: 'Is not My word like as fire? saith God.' (*Jeremiah* 23/29) (Rambam, MT *Hilkhot Keriyyat Shema* ch. 4, *Halakhah* 8). Because abominable words were found least of all in the synagogue and mostly in markets and streets, the mending (*Tikkun*) of purifying air was needed mostly in the latter.

Third, of all Tora letters, Tora-explication in the words of Mishna had the most critical role in purifying the environment. Unlike the Pentateuch, Mishna could be recited even when a text was not available. R. Simeon b. Lakish interpreted "Write thou these words....For according to the mouth of these words" (*Exodus* 32/27) to mean that words of Scripture could not be said by heart while words of oral Tora were not to be recited from the written text (*Gittin* 60b).

Fourth, recitation of Mishna could transform the cosmos from the condition of exile to redemption. Tora rescued Israel from *Gehinnom* and exile together:

> Said R. Isaac, 'Why was the Torah given in fire and darkness? In order to show that he who is constantly and diligently occupied with the study of it will be saved from the fire of hell (i.e. *Gehinnom*) and from the darkness of exile in heathen lands. It was the merit of Abraham which saved Israel from hell fire. According to tradition, the Holy One said to Abraham, 'As long as thy children shall be absorbed in the Torah they will be saved from punishment, but should they turn from her and forget her paths the fire of hell will have dominion over them and they will be subjugated by the nations of the earth' (*Zohar* II, 83b).

The primary instrument of Tora rescue was Mishna. R. Huna said that all exiles would be gathered in only through Mishna study: "Yea, if they engage in the oral law among the nations, I will now gather them up" (*Hosea* 8/10); "For from the rising of the sun even unto the going down of the same, My name is great among the nations; and in every place offerings are presented to My name, even pure oblations" (*Malachi* 1/11)...."The Holy One, blessed be He, said, 'Seeing that you are engaged in the study of Mishna, it is as if you were offering up sacrifices' (*Midrash Leviticus Rabba* 7/3). (Cf. Shneour Zalman of Lliady, "Ve'ele shemot" paragraph 6, *Shemot. Torah Or* 1837 and *idem*, "Tziyyon mishpat" paragraph 3 beginning, *Devorim Likkutei Torah* 1848). Joseph Caro pointed out that Asher's tribe was the only one to respond when someone cried out from *Gehinnom* for help. His tribe was responsible for Mishna--olive oil found in Asher's territory promoted study (*Horayot* 13b, *Menahot* 85b)--and he would respond to the cry with the question: "Did you read Mishna?" If the answer was yes, the person was rescued (Joseph Caro as cited in Elijah ben Solomon Abraham (d. 1792), "Anaf Efod," *Midrash Talpiot*).

Mishna was the key to bringing about redemption. The Temple was not fully restored by miracle upon the return from exile because the distance from Tora which caused the exile had yet to be overcome. The Jews were engaged in Tora, but did not bless it. They did not have the right intention, to study it for its own sake (*Sota* 36a with Rashi, *Nedarim* 81a with Nissim b. Reuben of Gerondi). Mishna study produced the right intention. Ingathering was also conditioned upon removing hatred leading to social disunity. Although the people of Israel were by then engaged in Tora and charity, the second Temple was still destroyed because there was hatred without cause (*Yoma* 9b). Scripture could not promote unity because it contained no *Halakhic* differences which needed to be resolved, the *Gemara* could not because its *Halakhic* differences were not resolved (*Kiddushim* 30b), but Mishna could. It provided incontrovertible bases because its judgments reflected the single tradition traceable to Moses (*Sanhedrin* 33a, Shneour Zalman of Lliady, beginning of chapter 2 and "Kuntres Aharon," SA *Yore Dea. Hilkhot Talmud Torah* 1815/1816 and *idem*, "Ve'ele shemot" paragraph 6, *Shemot. Torah Or* 1837).[55]

Concluding remarks

In response to the unfolding *Khurbn*, Habad Hassidism established MI, a "Goshen" community of refuge and rescue, to ease the pains of the onset of the messiah and provide access to redemption. It was intended for all Jews, but only some--perhaps 1,000--belonged. These Jews shared the esoteric knowledge of the apocalypse, that *Khurbn* implied *Geula*. Included in the knowledge was the responsibility to share it, to make it exoteric. This was to be done when *Khurbn* worsened to the point of catastrophe--beyond which lay redemption for the worthy. At that point the apocalypse could be recognized by all, and it was absolutely urgent that all had the knowledge in order to be saved.

The campaign for enlightenment was led by JIS. He attacked all those who blocked out the knowledge--whether Orthodox, Reform or secular nationalist. He urged them all to confront the either/or choice before all of

Israel, between life and death, between *Khurbn* and *Geula*. Once the choice was confronted, they could--and probably would--choose life.

The esoteric knowledge, sharing in Joseph's *"pakod yifkod,"* implied action. JIS himself provided the paradigm. At the center was *Teshuva*, a *Teshuva* which emerged simultaneously from God and man. The forms of *Teshuva* were ritualistic (Sabbath, *Tefillin*, *Tzitzit*, family purity, *Kashrut*, Psalm recitation); charitable (visiting the sick); informational (providing soldiers with information about holidays, dissuading Jews from paying attention to Christian missionaries); and textual (recitation of Mishna). Habad women had a special role in clarifying the apocalyptic situation and promoting the means of *Teshuva*. The recitation of Mishna belonged to the transition point from catastrophe to the onset of the messiah (*Ikvassa demeshiha*). JIS explained how the process purified the air, stimulated *Teshuva* and eased the pains which preceded the messianic arrival. It defied Amalek and enabled direct access to God. MMS spoke about the fact that air was crucial to personal identity, that speech, above all Mishna speech, affected the air, and even provided the way to pass from *Gehinnom*/exile to redemption.

A full analysis of MI awaits the availability of unpublished materials in the Habad archives. In the meantime, the published materials available in the Habad Library describe an impressive attempt by the people of Israel to respond aggressively to the *Khurbn*. The response took place on the level of intellect and action, prayer and compassion, and was intended for all of Israel. As an action-oriented eschatological community which sought to change the universe for the better through exclusively religious means, it may have been unique to the universe of the *Khurbn*.

ENDNOTES

[*]I am grateful to Morris Faierstein and Nehemia Polen for their advice; and to Nehemia Kessler and Shlomo Krauss of the Levi Yitshak Library and Habad Archives for help in providing the published materials. The unpublished sources, held at the Habad Archives at 770 Eastern Parkway, Brooklyn, New York, were unavailable.

Abbreviations used here include: JIS: Joseph Isaac Schneersohn. MMS: Menahem Mendel Schneersohn. MI: Mahane Israel. IK: *Iggerot Kodesh* (*Letters of Holiness*). KL: *Kovets Lubavitch* (*Lubavitch Collection*). *Admor*: *Adoneinu Moreinu Ve'rabbeinu* (our master, teacher and rabbi). *Shlita*: She'yihiye le'orekh yamim tovim amen (may he live for many good days amen). "*Admor Shlita*" refers to JIS. MT: *Mishne Tora* of Maimonides. SA: *Shulhan Arukh*. Habad's term for Holocaust was "*Khurbn*." HK: *Hakerriya Vehakedusha*. HK issues are dated here according to the masthead's Hebrew date. The name came from the *Ha'aderet veha'emuna* prayer of the Yom Kippur liturgy and was drawn from *Hekhalot Rabbati* (Pietrkov 1884 ed.): ch. 26 paragraph 7. G. Zarhi explained: "Reading and holiness for eternal life (*Ha'keriyya veha'kedusha le'hai olamim*)! [True] reading and study are present only when they follow the will of that which lives eternally, when they are bound with holiness. People who are merely well-read and learned are, as far as God Blessed be He is concerned, hardly anything special." G. Zarhi, "*Ha'aderet veha'emuna*," HK II/21 (16 May 1942): 6, 12, 13 [Hebrew title, Yiddish text].

[1][MI], "Die MI apelirt, ruft, makht bekant un varent," HK I/11 (24 July 1941): 13-14.

[2]Shlomo Duber Levin, *History of Habad in America* (Brooklyn 1988): 306 [Hebrew title, Yiddish text]. [JIS], "Letter 3/375 (27 January 1949)," *IK X 5709-5710* (Brooklyn 1984): 70-71 [Hebrew]. JIS, "Letter 3/384 (8 February 1949)," *IK X 5709-5710* (Brooklyn 1984): 80 [Hebrew]. [JIS], "Letter 3/447 (31 March 1949)," *IK X 5709-5710* (Brooklyn 1984): 138 [Hebrew]. MMS, "Letter 2/467 (10 August 1944)," *IK VIII 5704-5705* (Brooklyn 1984): 375-379 [Hebrew].

[3][Editor], "Hagrala fun Mishnayot be'al pe," HK II/23 (14 July 1942): 4. JIS, "Sunday, 20 June 1943," *Book of Conversations 5703-5704-5705* (Brooklyn 1986): 132-135 [Hebrew title, Yiddish text].

[4][Editor], "Falshe geulot ohn a Goshen!" HK IV/44 (24 March 1944): 1-2.

[5]JIS, "Tsveyter *Kol Kore* fun Lubavitsher Rabbin," HK I/10 (25 June 1941): 9. JIS, "Sunday, 20 June 1943," *supra*. MI, "Immediate redemption," HK I/11 (24 July 1941): 7, 9, 10 [Hebrew title, Yiddish text].

[6][Editor], "Fun der redaktsie. Di propagande vegen dem of fun der milhama," HK V/57 (12 April 1945): 4-5.

[7][Editor], "Fun der redaktsie. Der Idisher sod ha'ibbur," HK III/30 (4 February 1943): 8-10.

[8]MI, "*Kol Kore* to our brethren the children of Israel," HK II/14 (21 October 1941): 11 [Hebrew title, Yiddish text]. [Editor], "Fun der redaktsie, fun 5701 biz 5703," HK III/34 (3 June 1943): 10-11.

[9]Ish Yehudi, "Let there be light," HK I/1 (2 October 1940): 8-10 [Hebrew title, Yiddish text].

[10][Editor], "Fun der redaktsie, fun 5701 biz 5703," HK III/34 (3 June 1943): 10-11. [JIS], "*Kol Kore* fun Lubavitsher Rabbin," HK I/9 (26 May 1941): 15.

[11]JIS, "Discussion of the last day of Passover 5702 [9 April 1942]," *Book of Statements. Tractates* III (Brooklyn 1986): 80-84 [Hebrew title, Yiddish text].

[12]MI, "Immediate Redemption," HK I/11 (24 July 1941): 7, 9, 10 [Hebrew title, Yiddish text]. MMS, "MI. Short outline," *Diary 5703* (Brooklyn, N.Y. 1943?): inside cover [Hebrew]. The English translation is available at the Levi Yitzhak Library.

[13]There were no secret messages in HK issues 28 (8 December 1944), 35 (3 July 1943), 36 (1 August 1943), 40 (27 November 1943), 43 (23 February 1944), 47 (20 June 1944), or in issues 49-61.

[14][Editor], "Nit veyt fun of," HK IV/48 (20 July 1944): 1-2. The original acronym appeared in HK II/13 (21 September 1941): 4.

[15][Editor], "Mir hoben dos gevust," HK IV/47 (21 June 1944): 1-2. The original acronym appeared in HK IV/41 (27 December 1943): 7.

[16][Editor], "*Kol Kore* to our brethren the children of Israel," HK II/14 (21 October 1941): 11 [Hebrew title, Yiddish text].

[17][JIS], "*Kol Kore* fun'm Lubavitsher Rabbin," HK I/9 (26 May 1941): 15.

[18]The editor has not been identified. See Levin, *supra*, pp. 344-346.

[19]See also Ish Yehudi, "Bakent zikh mit der varnung, '*Le'alter Le'geula*,'" HK III/25 (11 September 1942): 15-16 and MI, "Di 'MI' apelirt, ruft, makht bekant un varent," *supra*. Several leaders of Israel Agudat Israel and Agudat Ha'rabbanim (Union of Orthodox Rabbis of America and Canada) did in fact speak of *Khurbn* as prelude to redemption at the time MI levelled its criticism. See for example Eliezer Silver, Israel Halevi Rosenberg and Arye Hacoben Levinthal, "Proclamation of Agudat Harabbanim to the Jews of America," *Hapardes* 14 nr. 7 (October 1940): 2 [Hebrew]. [Nissan Telushkin, ed.], "Contemporary questions. 'And all the first born of my children shall I

redeem,'" *Hamessila* 6 nr. 3 (March-April 1941): 1 [Hebrew]. Jacob Rosenheim, *Jewish Future. Address to a meeting [at] the Jewish Center of New York, 1 February 1942* (Mss. held at Agudat Israel Archives, New York City). Eliezer Silver, "Der Yom Tov fun Idisher eybikeyt," *Idishe Shtime* 2 nr. 3 (April 1941): 1.

[20][JIS], "*Kol Kore* fun'm Lubavitsher Rabbin," HK I/9 (26 May 1941): 15. An English version appeared as [JIS], "To the nearing redemption," HK I/11 (24 July 1941): 2-3. The first *Kol Kore* also appeared as [JIS], "*Kol Kore* fun Lubavitsher Rabbin--Le'alter le'geula," *Der Teglikher Yiddisher Kurier* (30 May 1941): 11 and [JIS], "*Kol Kore* fun Lubavitsher Rabbin--Le'alter le'geula," *Der Morgen Zhurnal* 40 nr. 12,034 (27 May 1941): 8. A slightly altered Hebrew version appeared as JIS, "Immediate Redemption," *Netzah Israel* (Munich) 3 (August 1948): 6-7.

[21]JIS, "Tsveyter *Kol Kore* fun'm Lubavitsher Rabbin," *supra*. Also [JIS], "Tsu di gleykhgiltige!, [letter] 1/455 (11 June 1941)," *IK V 5700-5701* (Brooklyn 1983): 377-386. The first two *Kol Kore's* were recalled in [Editor], "Fun der redaktsie. Fun 5701 biz 5703," HK III/34 (3 June 1942): 10-11.

[22][JIS], "Driter *Kol Kore* fun'm Lubavitsher Rabbin," HK I/11 (24 July 1941): 5-7.

[23][JIS], "Call for prayer and penitence by the Rabbi of Lubavitch," HK I/13 (21 September 1941): 1.

[24]JIS, "*Kol Kore* from the Admor of Lubavitch," HK I/13 (21 September 1941): 4 [Hebrew]. JIS used the language of the Agudat Ha'rabbanim as it appeared in *Hapardes* 18 nr. 12 (March 1945): 3.

[25]The source for the prediction of the Sages was not given. [JIS], "Summary from the writings of *Admor Shlita* ....," HK III/29 (6 January 1943): 10 [Hebrew title, Yiddish text].

[26]MI, "*Kol Kore* to our brethren the children of Israel," HK II/14 *supra*.

[27][JIS], "Ferter *Kol Kore* fun dem Lubavitsher Rabbin Shlita. Sisu ve'simhu be'simhat geula! Der driter front," HK III/25 (11 September 1942): 12-14.

[28]To back up the dangers of doubting the redemption, the HK editor pointed to the fate of Dathan and Abiram who doubted Moses:

> It is a small thing that thou has brought us up out of a land that floweth with milk and honey, to kill us in the wilderness, except thou make a prince over us? ...And Moses rose up and went unto Dathan and Abiram....and he spoke unto the congregation, saying, 'Depart, I pray you, from the tents of these wicked men.'...And it came to pass, as he had made an end of speaking all these words, that the ground clave asunder that was under them. *Numbers* 16/12-31.

Editor, "Fun der redaktsie. Der ferten *Kol Kore* fun Admor Shlita," HK III/26 (11 October 1942): 8-10.

[29][MI], "Immediate Redemption," HK I/11 (24 July 1941): 7, 9, 10 [Hebrew title, Yiddish text]. [Editor], "Falshe geulot ohn a Goshen!" *supra.*

[30][JIS], *Di reyd fun kavod kadsho Admor marana ve'rabbana ha'rav Yosef Yitshak Shlita Schneerohn mi'lubavitsh tsu der finf yoriger hagiga fun Mercaz Ha'yeshivot in Amerika, 11 March 1944* (Brooklyn 1945), pp. 5-6. See also [S. A. Pardes, editor], "The dean, pious one, the *Admor* of Lubavitch *Shlita*," *Hapardes* 13 nr. 12 (March 1940): 4-5 [Hebrew]. Pardes said that "[JIS] left the lands of blood. He came to America to establish the tabernacle of God's holiness....He [will work] to awaken Jews in America to spread Torah and Judaism, while the *Khurbn* of Tora and Judaism in Europe is taking place."

[31]MMS, "Vendung fun 'MI,'" HK III/25 (11 September 1942): 4. In this statement MMS referred to a published collection of JIS' speeches and letters on immediate *Teshuva* and immediate redemptoin which was available through MI. Possibly, [JIS], *Collected Letters and Discussions by the Sanctified Admor Shlita [Concerning] Teshuva, Psalms, Oral Mishnahs, Yeshiva Students* (Brooklyn: Kehot 1943?) [Hebrew]. See [Editor], "Seforim un broshuren tsu bakumen bey dem farlag 'Kehot,'" HK III/34 (3 June 1943): 13. The *Kor Kore's* were published under the title *The Four Kol Kore's of the Admor of Lubavitch* (Jerusalem 1942) [Hebrew title, original Yiddish text with Hebrew translation].

[32]JIS, "Discussion of the last day of Passover," *supra.*

[33]JIS, "Our rabbis will teach us," HK IV/39 (29 October 1943): 2-3 [Hebrew title, Yiddish text].

[34]JIS, *Tractate on the Teaching of Hassidism* (Brooklyn 1945): 23-24 [Hebrew]. See "First day of the holiday of Shavuot at the feast of the day," *Book of Conversations, Summer 5700, 5701-5702* (Brooklyn 1986): 118, 129 [Hebrew title, Yiddish text].

[35]JIS, "Discussion of the last day of Passover 5702," *supra.* I have been unable to trace the Mordekhai and Esther reference.

[36]MI, "He says it in the name," HK II/21 (16 May 1942): 4 [Hebrew title, Yiddish text].

[37]MMS' arrival in America was facilitated by Breckinridge Long of the State Department, whose 7 February 1941 internal memo read:

> Mr. Arthur Rabinowitz [?] advises me that Rabbi Mendel Schneersohn's visa application was transferred from Nice district to Marseilles district, and he is now refused non-quota visa by Marseilles. We authorized issue of visa. Consul at Marseilles suggests immigrant visa. I see no reason why he should not be granted immigrant visa even though we

162

authorized non-quota. As we have communicated several times about Schneersohn and there appears no objection, I see no reason why we should not communicate further to Marseilles on his account.

Library of Congress Manuscript Division, Washington, D.C. A-L:BL:WA.

[38][MMS], "MI. Short Outline," *supra*.

[39][MI], "*Kol Kore* fun der 'MI' tsu di Idishe froyen," HK I/11 (24 July 1941): 12-13. Translated as [Editor], "An urgent call to the Jewish women from the 'Camp of Israel,'" HK II/14 (21 October 1941): 1-2. MI Women's Division, "Sehr geehrte froy," cited in Levin, *supra*, p. 310. See also [JIS], *Reyd tsu froyen, fun Rabbin Shlita* (Brooklyn, N.Y., 1943?), advertised in HK. [Editor], "Seforim," *supra*.

[40][JIS], "Tsveyter *Kol Kore* fun'm Lubavitsher Rabbin," HK I/10 *supra*. On missionizing see Robert W. Ross, "Perverse witness to the Holocaust: Christian missions and missionaries," *Holocaust Studies Annual II. The Churches' Response to the Holocaust*, edited by Jack Fischel and Sanford Pinsker (Greenwood, Florida 1986): 127-139.

[41]MI, "Immediate Redemption," HK I/11, *supra*.

[42]JIS, "Discussion of the last day of Passover 5702," *supra*.

[43][Editor], "MI grindet a khevra 'Bikkur Holim,'" KL I/4 (3 July 1944 - 6 September 1944): 59. [JIS], "Letter 2/698 (10 May 1944)," *IK VIII 5704-5705* (Brooklyn 1984): 603 [Hebrew].

[44][Editor], "'MI' - tsu soldzshers," KL I/1 (16 December 1943 - 4 March 1944): 8. [Editor], "MI shikt oyf Shavuot mesedzsh tsu soldaten," KL I/3 (11 May 1944-3 July 1944): 40. [Editor], "Grupe tsu farvaundete soldaten organizirt bey 'MI,'" KL I/4 (3 July 1944-6 September 1944): 59. See also *The Soldier* (Brooklyn, N.Y. 1943?) advertised in HK. [Editor], "Seforim," *supra*.

[45][Editor], "'MI' shikt tefillin, mezuzot, tallitim un seforim in kontsentratsia lageren," KL II 9(4) (23 June 1945-27 August 1945): 60.

[46][Editor], "'Eshel Tora' bey 'MI,'" KL II/7(2) (1 May 1945): 28. [JIS], "*Di reyd...*," *supra*, p. 18. [Haim Liebermann, JIS' secretary and librarian], "Letter of 2/691 to Menahem Mendel Feldman (29 April 1945)," *IK VIII 5704-5705* (Brooklyn 1984): 597 [Hebrew].

[47][Ed.], "A spetsieler *Sefer Tora* mit velkhen tsu mikabel panim zeyn meshiah tsidkeinu," HK II/14 (20 October 1941): 12. [Ed.], "Committee for the Sefer Tora to welcome the countenance of the messiah," HK III/25 (11 September 1942) [Hebrew title, Yiddish text].

48[JIS], "Letter 1/785 (1 May 1942)," *IK VI 5702* (Brooklyn 1984): 311-312 [Hebrew]. Reprinted in HK II/21 (16 May 1942): 3 [Hebrew]. MI Psalm Fellowship Division, "To the honored rabbis, deans and synagogue leaders, may God grant them life," "[Letter 1/785 supplement undated]," *IK VI 5702* (Brooklyn 1984): 312-317 [Hebrew title, Yiddish text]. Also published as "MI thetigkeyten," HK III/25 (11 September 1942): 4-5. JIS, "Letter 2/459 (6 August 1944)," *IK VIII 5704-5705* (Brooklyn 1984): 367 [Hebrew]. On the elders at redemption see *Numbers* 11/24-25.

49Levin, *supra*, p. 308. JIS, "Discussion of the last day of Passover 5702," *supra*. JIS, "Sunday, 20 June 1943," *supra*. There are traditions of studying *Mishna* between *Minha* and *Ma'ariv* and reading a *Mishna* connected to the weekly *Parasha*, but I have been unable to determine the particular context here. MMS, "Responsa and explanations," KL I/4 (3 July 1944-6 September 1944): 63-65, 68 [Hebrew]. Reprinted in MMS, *Responsa and Explanations* (Brooklyn 1974): 13-21 [Hebrew]. [Editor], "MI Mishnayot be'al pe opteylung," HK II/21 (16 May 1942): 4. [Editor], "Hagrala fun Mishnayot be'al pe," HK II/23 (14 July 1942): 4. [Editor], "MI tetigkeyt. Impozante siyyum Shass-Mishna be'al pe feyerung," HK III/35 (3 July 1943): 3. [Editor], "Feyerlikher siyyum Mishanayot be'al pe," HK I/3 (11 May 1944-3 July 1944): 40-41. "'MI' ruft tsu mobilizatsie fun religieze kohot," KL II/8(3): 38-39. JIS, "Letter 2/710 (20 May 1945)," *IK VIII 5704-5705* (Brooklyn 1984): 615 [Hebrew]. [JIS], "Oystusug fun di reyd fun Rabbin Shlita bey der hagrala Mishnayot [24 June 1942]," HK II/23 (14 July 1942): 5.

50[JIS], "Oystsug...," *supra*.

51JIS, "I will go down now" [*Genesis* 18/21], *Book of Statements 5703 VIII/I* (Brooklyn 1975): 92 [Hebrew]. JIS associated Tora speech and pure air with a good feeling for God and God's hearing man's words. He associated evil speech and poisoned air with God's not hearing the words. When speech was without Tora the air thickened, the heart numbed to the point of being unable to grasp God-related matters, and man became obsessed with materiality. JIS, *Book of Conversations 5703*, p. 64 and *Book of Conversations 5702*, pp. 116, 129 as cited in *Habad Encyclopaedia* II (Brooklyn, N.Y. 1983): columns 236-241 [Hebrew].

52JIS, "Sunday, 20 June 1943," *supra*.

53JIS, "Letter 2/710 (20 May 1945)," *IK VIII 5704-5705* (Brooklyn 1984): 615 [Hebrew].

54JIS said earlier that air was blessed because it was available everywhere. JIS, "Kiruv Hashem," *Book of Statements VIII 5699* (Brooklyn 1976): 152-153 [Hebrew].

55MMS, "Responsa and explanations," *supra*.

THE RELIGIOUS LIFE OF HOLOCAUST SURVIVORS AND ITS SIGNIFICANCE FOR PSYCHOTHERAPY

Paul Marcus and Alan Rosenberg

In a secular age when most psychotherapists tend to diminish the religious dimension of their patients' lives, it is not surprising that the Holocaust survivor's religious experience both during and after the event has been underemphasized.[1] Despite the fact that the significance of the religious dimension has been repeatedly articulated in survivor diaries, testimonies, and contemporary literature, psychotherapists have not adequately appreciated the importance of this element in their work with survivors of the Holocaust.[2] In our readings and professional experience we have observed that many therapists are not sufficiently aware of the variety of conflicts and issues that are of concern, consciously or unconsciously, to the survivor with religious sensibilities and the survivor who came from a religious background but lost faith because of the Holocaust. Therefore, this chapter concerns itself mainly with the survivor's religious realm as it affects the psychotherapeutic process. It will also provide a conceptual framework for helping the therapist understand the significance of religion in the survivor's life.[3]

The process of exploring the varying effects the Holocaust has had on the survivor's faith and religious behavior, at least as it affects the psychotherapeutic experience, touches on some of the most profound questions that emanate from the cataclysm: How did faith in God and religious activity help concentration camp inmates cope with the physical and mental pain experienced during the incarceration? What kinds of Holocaust experiences and pre- and post-Holocaust factors influenced whether a survivor remained a believer or renounced a belief in God after the Holocaust? Has the survivor who still believes in God significantly changed the nature of that belief? How can God be affirmed meaningfully in a world where evil enjoys such power? And finally, what is the effect of a renunciation of faith? These and other questions need to be clarified and elaborated in order for psychotherapists to be better able to help the survivor.

The importance of psychotherapists being sensitive to these issues goes beyond the seemingly straightforward notion that therapists need to "know where their patients are coming from." More to the point is the problem of how psychotherapists work with and conceptualize the impact of a severe trauma on the symbolic world of an individual. In this case, it is the symbolic world of the religious survivor, both the survivor from a religious background who may still have a religious framework or sensibility, and the survivor who is faced with the awesome task of replacing his religious worldview with another perspective. By symbolic world we are referring to a total system of beliefs, values, morals, and knowledge--which for the person are often highly abstract and loom far above everyday life, yet tangibly impose themselves upon everyday life in their capacity to inspire or to give meaning to individual or collective activity, to delegitimate other activity, and to bring to bear the force of social control. Symbolic worlds provide an important ordering impulse to social affairs and to collective views of the world.[4] The importance of these ideas about a symbolic world to the religious survivor lies in the view that socially structured, taken-for-granted meanings enjoy a "stability deriving from more powerful sources than the historical efforts of human beings"[5] and contribute therefore to the creation of ultimately powerful and meaningful notions of reality ("sacred cosmoi"). A symbolic world thus provides a framework of ultimate meaning. It is important to appreciate that a symbolic world refers to more than just a universe of discourse, a going community of meanings and values that rationalize a given way of behavior. The investigation of the symbolic world is centrally concerned with that which makes such a world real, how it penetrates and shapes everyday life. It must be made clear that this is our characterization of the believer's world--the believer might simply view his world as the "real" world--this perhaps is why the collapse of his world is so traumatic.

For many survivors, religion was (and still is) the symbolic world that formed a reservoir of meaning that could be utilized in private--a psychological world of significance that nourished them when the outside world was assaulting their very physical existence and mental integrity. In some sense this "sacred canopy"[6] offered the survivor a certain degree of understanding, predictability, safety, and satisfaction. It was a religious framework of meaning that permitted the survivor to develop and maintain a viable sense of self-esteem, the reflective and intuitive sense that he or she is fulfilling a significant role in a meaningful cosmic drama. In other words, these individuals felt themselves "to be a locus of primary value in a world of meaning."[7]

Now what happens to such a person when this sense of ontological security is radically challenged or breaks down, as was the case with many survivors? What happens when something that the self identifies with so profoundly (i.e., God), and is viewed as necessary to one's well-being, is undermined or destroyed?

It is painfully clear that when the fundamental order in terms of which the individual can "make sense" of his life and recognize his own identity is undermined, the process of psychological disintegration and disorganization begins. It is this issue that draws the psychotherapist into the picture, for it is the task of therapists to help the patient recreate, as far as possible, a feeling of ontological security, to alleviate the pain, chaos, and anxiety associated with the loss of such security and to help the patient reconstruct a symbolic world so that he experiences his life as a more coherent narrative.[8]

RELIGIOUS LIFE BEFORE THE HOLOCAUST

In order to understand better the manner in which religion has an impact on the psychotherapeutic experience with survivors, it is necessary to appreciate the kind of community and social context they were part of prior to the war. Although there were many survivors who significantly altered their beliefs and practices, and others who completely gave up their religion, it is very important to be aware of their pre-Holocaust ways of thinking, feeling, and organizing the world, though their manifest lifestyle today and conscious frames of reference bear little resemblance to those of the past. These earlier patterns and especially theological upbringing may affect the survivor's present worldview in a myriad of taken-for-granted and unconscious ways. For example, there are survivors who were raised to view God as all-seeing and all-knowing, a God who punishes individuals for their sins. In their post-Holocaust world, they may have given up their belief in God but retain a diffuse fear that they will be punished if they don't obey the law. There is a tendency to blame themselves for their problems in living. Moreover, it is the therapist's awareness of the continuities and discontinuities in the survivor's faith and religious behavior that will permit the therapist to appreciate maximally the survivor's experience, especially the manner in which his world was affected by the Holocaust. It is the discontinuities in particular which contribute to the survivor's internal conflict and disrupted sense of self-sameness (i.e., being a locus of primary value in a world of meaning). This impedes his attempt to recreate a meaningful world that incorporates the past in a manner that isn't jarring and debilitating.

As historian Jacob Robinson has estimated, about half of the 6 million Jews murdered during the Holocaust were Orthodox Jews, who strictly observed the *halakhah* (Jewish Law).[9] Reeve Brenner's survey of survivors now residing in Israel further supports the claim that the Jewish communities of Eastern Europe prior to World War II constituted a religiously observant community.[10] Moreover, as Lucy Dawidowicz has pointed out, even in those communities where secularism was most imposing, the Jewish community was still greatly influenced by traditional Jewish values and *halakhah*.[11]

Halakhah dealt with every aspect of a Jew's life, his relationship and responsibilities to God and man. His everyday ordinary existence was made intelligible and was completely determined by this very tightly organized system of religious prohibitions and commandments. More than formal law, halakhah was "the way" in which the Jews walked, which reflected their ethos--the "tone, character, and quality of [their] inner life, its moral and aesthetic style and mood; it is the underlying attitude towards themselves and their world that life reflects."[12] This devotion to the Law was rooted in the conviction that to love God, one had to serve Him through cognition of the Torah, and hallowing life by meticulously following His Law.[13] *Halakhic* man could not accomplish his task in isolation, but viewed himself as part of a communal way of life lived in the presence of God that served as a meaningful matrix and powerful reference point for all his endeavors. As Lichtenstein points out, *halakhah* thus makes the service of God part of a total life that is infused with religious significance, harmoniously organized into a divinely ordained whole and gives man a sense of purpose and a sense of divine purpose.[14]

In the early stages of Nazism, religious Jews usually put their persecution into the historical context of Jewish suffering. The Jews have been persecuted since ancient times, and the Nazis were viewed as another variation on this theme of Jewish suffering and victimization. In other words, Jews were putting their suffering into the familiar category of Jewish scapegoating by the *Goy*. The religious response was maximizing prayer, ritual, and good deeds. In this way God would be more likely to deliver them from their suffering.

RELIGIOUS LIFE DURING THE HOLOCAUST

The variety of religious responses and problems after the Holocaust can be adequately understood only within the context of the survivors' actual incarceration condition and specific Holocaust experiences. The question of the ways religion was used by inmates to help cope with the brutality and degradation during their incarceration is a subject that warrants a book in itself. For our purposes, given the scope of this chapter, some brief comments will suffice.[15]

The manner in which the psychotherapist understands the behavior of the religious concentration camp inmate significantly affects the way he approaches the survivor's current problems. For example, therapeutic technique with the survivor stems, in part, from the assumption underlying the therapist's account of how the presenting problem is linked to his Holocaust behavior, and this in turn is related to the therapist's acceptance of a particular narrative of how the survivor coped with his experience in the first place. As Anna Ornstein points out, for the therapist to empathize accurately with the survivor and protect himself from giving meaning to the survivor's experience from his own idiosyncratic perspectives, it is necessary for the therapist to understand the mode of adaptation to the conditions as they existed during the years of persecution. This, Ornstein says, is "the missing link" that could meaningfully connect the survivor's pre-Holocaust past with her/his recovery and adaptation to a new life.[16]

For the survivor, continues Ornstein, establishing a sense of continuity, a connection between past and present is of central significance in psychological recovery. The understanding of the mode of adaptation to extreme conditions provides the therapist with an in-depth, longitudinal view of the survivor. For the survivor, the reconstruction of his adaptation facilitates the integration of the Holocaust experience into the totality of his life history. It is in relation to establishing a sense of continuity that recounting the circumstances and conditions to which adaptation had to take place has its significance.

Finally, the importance of the therapist being aware of the inmate's successful coping strategies used while incarcerated is that the therapist can more readily sense the manifest and latent strengths of the person--strengths that can possibly be tapped in the present in order to help the survivor more adequately cope with his current problems.

Even in the concentration camp, many inmates with religious convictions made a world for themselves. That is, to some extent they were able to imagine patterns of meaning that transcended the immediacy of the situations they had to endure. Through the capacity for symbolization the religious survivor was able to better cope with the environment and attain a degree of freedom relative to it. For the religious Jew, religion acted as a meaningful reality that comprehended him and all his experiences. This all-embracing fabric of meanings gave sense to his life, especially to the dissonant and painful aspects. By the individual having a plausible theodicy (a vindication of divine justice in allowing evil to exist) in particular, he was better able to integrate the painful experiences of life into a framework that makes him feel that his experience makes sense: "it is not happiness the theodicy primarily provides, but meaning."[17] As Peter Berger points out, and

Viktor Frankl[18] demonstrates, in situations of acute suffering, the need for meaning is as strong as, or even stronger than, the need for happiness. Being able to understand why one suffers, that is to have a convincing theodicy, is experienced as of equal or greater important than relief from one's oppressive situation. As Nietzsche stated, "any meaning is better than none at all."

Adina Dreksler points out that in the ghettos, the concentration camps, and even in the extermination camps there was an ongoing religious life for particular Jews and for the community as a whole. In the underground in hidden bunkers, for example, there were *hederim* and *Talmudei Torah* (religious academies) where Yeshiva students learned. Dreksler further notes that there is ample evidence of the community's success in organizing public worship, kindling the Hanukah candles, wearing *[t]zitzit* (fringes), even observing *kashrut* (dietary laws) in the concentration camps under great danger.[19]

The contributions of Yaffa Eliach, Eliezer Berkovitz, and Daniel Landes, primarily focusing on the Hasidic and Orthodox communities, indicate the powerful need on the part of incarcerated devout victims to maintain their humanity by reaffirming their boundless belief in God, in the integrity of the Jewish people, and the goodness of mankind.[20] Rabbi Ephraim Oshry's extraordinary *Questions and Responses from Out of the Depths*, written on scraps of paper in the Kovno ghetto, is a seminal work of emergency rulings on both ritual law and Jewish ethics. His book describes his own religious activities and the efforts of his fellow inmates to observe their Judaism.[21] In this book and Robert Kirschner's *Rabbinic Responsa of the Holocaust Era*, we see the religious community's attempt to apply traditional precepts to a catastrophe of unprecedented proportions.[22] One illustrative question put to a rabbi was about a man who smothered a child inadvertently, to avoid detection of a group of Jews hiding from the Nazis. The ruling was that the man had acted lawfully, even though a pious and holy course of action would have been to suffer death rather than take an innocent life.

These and other responsa written during the Holocaust reflect the struggle of religious Jews to preserve life and integrity under the most

extreme conditions, that is, the need to affirm the self in thought and action--
to give one's own personal stamp to self and world as well as the profound
ontological need to be rooted in a self-transcending power source mediated
by a significant other.

Thus, the Jews who were deeply involved in Judaism generated a
meaningful order of existence for themselves, who without this sheltering
cosmos would have experienced the horror and chaos even more sharply. It
is furthermore clear that the religious factor is only one of the crucial
elements that enhanced the inmates' probability of survival. Other
circumstances, such as one's age at the time of incarceration, the particular
conditions in the camp where one was imprisoned, one's pre-Holocaust
personality, and whether one was lucky--are all important considerations
when trying to understand the reasons for an inmate's survival. But we
believe the religious dimension in some cases was also a very important
element of survival.

It also seems important to emphasize that any person, religious or
otherwise, who had a well-organized symbolic world to which he strongly
adhered was somewhat more likely to survive camp experience.[23] Anna
Pawelczyńska has pointed out that if an inmate had values and models that
were deeply internalized, the strength derived from these values greatly
contributed to resisting any alien system that denied those values.[24] Primo
Levi and Frankl point out that people with strong religious convictions, like
the Jehovah's Witnesses and Orthodox Jews, coped better than most under
the hardships of the concentration camps.[25] These people, says Christopher
Lasch, found strength in the revealed word of an absolute, objective, and
omnipotent creator, as they saw it, not in personal values meaningful only to
themselves. Survival, says Lasch, must have some purpose external to
ourselves that gives us a reason to live or to die.[26] Such deeply internalized
convictions enhance psychological resilience in situations of extremity.

AFTER LIBERATION

Many survivors went into displaced person camps following the war,
while others returned to their homes only to find death and destruction.

Many survivors' religious beliefs seem to have gone through an initial period of disorganization and confusion after liberation.

The most basic physical and psychological needs were more pressing, and there was often a temporary pause in grappling with religious questions. In addition, when survivors found out about the deaths of loved ones and the destruction of their communities, a deep depression usually ensued, sometimes taking many years before it receded; at other times a significant residue lasted for a lifetime. Other survivors reacted quite differently; they too were often depressed but dealt with this by throwing themselves into the recreation of the Jewish community, helping establish synagogues, conducting religious services, and acquiring kosher food for religiously observant survivors. Still others tried to maintain their sense of continuity and Jewish life by becoming involved with Zionism and other Jewish self-help movements.

A very significant influence on whether a survivor remained religious immediately after the war was the response he received from the host community he went into.[27] For example, one survivor, who prior to the war was a cantorial student at a prominent academy in Germany recontacted the head rabbi of that academy, who had left Europe before the Holocaust and was now living in the United States, and requested help in continuing his training there.

The survivor was extremely angry when the first question the rabbi asked him was if he kept a kosher kitchen and if his wife went to the *mikvah* (ritual bath) regularly. But more to the point, and underlying this anger, was the survivor's pain at the realization that there was no longer any continuity between his pre-Holocaust world and his present one, with its very different needs, wishes, and sensibilities. Compounding this jarring realization was the painful and disappointing feeling of being misunderstood by a former role model and the further realization that the gap between his post-Holocaust world and the rabbi's was unbridgeable. The consequence of this interchange was that the survivor's wish to continue his cantorial studies and practice Judaism was irreversibly ruptured. He worked in the garment district for 30 years and died a bitter old man.

A further influence on the survivor's religious beliefs was his own internal need to have an extreme response to God. A choice that felt less than extreme appeared grossly inadequate and unworthy of what one had experienced. Hence, a total rejection of God or absolute piety were the two options most available to survivors.[28]

A plausible reason for this is suggested by a long tradition of theory in social psychology that argues that we are motivated to keep our attitudes and experiences in order.[29] Specifically, we are motivated to avoid contradictions and inconsistencies within our attitudes and between our attitudes and behavior. When inconsistency does occur we are often motivated to overcome it. Inconsistency or dissonance is a negative state (experienced as tension or discomfort) we may seek to avoid. For the survivor, his Holocaust experience was viewed as profoundly dissonant with much of what he believed, knew, and did prior to the war, and it was therefore necessary after the war either to change radically one's beliefs or to recommit oneself to the former beliefs--both being ways to bring a sense of order, coherence, and harmony to one's world. The survivor had a great need to maintain intact the logical structure of his symbolic meaning framework, and only an extreme reaction one way or the other could achieve this goal.

SURVIVORS WHO REMAINED RELIGIOUSLY COMMITTED

The Holocaust has been viewed as a transformational event by most survivors; nevertheless, there were those individuals whose faith and/or religious behavior remained largely unchanged (at least manifestly), although in many instances there were subtle ways in which their Holocaust experiences affected their religious world both positively and negatively. That there were as many survivors who remained more or less religiously committed after the Holocaust speaks to the fact that humans struggle against the loss of their world, the whole range of action and objects that they so laboriously and painfully fashioned during their lives. They fight against the subversion of themselves in the only world they know.[30]

Among those survivors who remained religious after the war there were a variety of responses to their suffering, and these different responses are as numerous as there are survivors. We therefore will draw from a few examples to show that survivors tried very hard to maintain and/or recreate their symbolic world, in order to preserve their own sense of being part of a meaningful order, with its consequent feeling of self-cohesion and continuity. That is, as Berger has shown, a theodicy legitimates the marginal and alienating experiences that constantly threaten a person's existence. Sickness, injury and death are interpreted as events in a larger cosmic history, and as such are given an ultimate significance. In the course of everyday life theodicy allows a person to carry on life after the death of a significant other and to anticipate his own demise without being paralyzed in his daily routines by the terror of it.[31] Thus, to the extent that a person is able to make sense of the pain of life, so is he able to feel that he is securely moored in the world, with a past worth remembering, a present worth living, and a future worth facing.

Among the survivors who remained committed to their religion, there were those who severely doubted the assumptions underlying their beliefs and behavior and who were generally less comfortable with themselves. There were also those who were less questioning and tended to make sense of their suffering in light of their belief in the traditional God of the Hebrew Bible. These people drew from the well-tried classical theodicies that Jews have used for thousands of years to account for national catastrophies and personal tragedies. The point to keep in mind is that all of the theodicies used by survivors are ways of maintaining their world.

One response by some survivors to the Holocaust was to view the event like any other tragedy, in that the cataclysm and their suffering during it put into sharp focus the problem of evil. However, it did not, they believe, profoundly change the problem or add anything new to it.[32] This attitude may also have been reinforced by the many personal tragedies that challenged their faith in God (e.g., loss of parent or a child, etc.) prior to the war. They thus had seriously struggled with their belief in a just, compassionate, omnipotent, and intelligible God. The Holocaust was fitted into this interpretive framework with the event viewed as a worst case example of the problem of evil without traumatic discomfort.

Other survivors interpreted their Holocaust experience as the extreme of human evil, the price humankind has to pay for human freedom. They believed that the Nazis were human, not gods, and that Auschwitz reflects shamefully on humans but does not touch God's existence or perfection.

This belief often manifests itself in the unwillingness of the believing survivor to contemplate the problem of God's seeming indifference in the first place. "I do not allow myself to think about it," said one survivor. The contemplation of God's role during the Holocaust is too painful, while the best way to deal with these feelings is to avoid the problem altogether. Often this attempt to deny the issue is accompanied by manic-like activity in another sphere, such as work, in order to strengthen the defenses against examining God's silence and lack of intervention in ending Jewish suffering. Furthermore, when doubts about God are evoked, the religious survivor can draw from traditional sources that demand ridding oneself of alien thoughts that could foster irreligious behavior or attitudes, since one has not acquired the wisdom to truly decipher the significance of the doubts. The unwillingness to judge God may be an aspect of pious resignation rooted in the rabbinic view that God in His perfect wisdom and goodness knows best.

In other words, writes Berger, the problem of theodicy becomes the problem of anthropodicy.[33] The question of God's injustice becomes a question of man's sinfulness. There is a submission to God's omnipotence--a submission to the totally other who can neither be seriously questioned nor challenged, and who, by his very nature, is sovereignly above any human ethical standards. The religious survivor, like all of us, fights against being uprooted and disorganized; he thus tenaciously clings to the cosmic perspective and unified vision which assures him a secure place in a universe of known dimensions and definite purposes. To refrain from aggressively challenging God's inaction during the Holocaust by focusing on human cruelty becomes a way for the survivor to maintain the self-transcending meanings for which he and all humans hunger.

A third response from devout survivors was to view the Holocaust as an unfathomable mystery. It is a modern *akedah* (binding of Isaac), a test of one's faith. However, like all of God's ways, the Holocaust transcends human comprehension and requires faith and silence. These survivors felt that the Holocaust tested their faith as God has always tested His people, and although it is not always clear that one is being challenged or why, it is one's obligation to rise to the challenge in faith and devotion. This view, although seemingly dogmatic, actually reflects a philosophical acceptance of the lack of explanatory certainty one has in the face of God's behavior during the Holocaust. It is an attitude that in whole or in part underlies many of the diverse survivor theodicies and all religions, namely, the awareness that for a religious person the heart of the matter is always mystery, especially the riddles of suffering in an assumed ethically caring universe. Perhaps Spinoza best captured this sentiment when he said, "simple faith is the path to salvation."

Such a theodicy may be augmented by a fourth perspective: the belief that the Holocaust is an example of the temporary "Eclipse of God." That is, there are times when God is inexplicably absent from history or unaccountably chooses to turn His face away.[34]

These religious survivors often feel a compelling need to challenge God about His lack of presence during the Holocaust. For them it is a way of venting their anger at Him without being passive. And yet there is a need to preserve their God, despite the numerous questions and debates frequently raging in their minds:

> It is all I think about....My life is a running, nagging dialogue with God...He is always on my mind. Why? Why? I sometimes find I have been walking the lonely, crowded streets of Tel Aviv, wandering aimlessly, conducting a question and answer session with Him--with no satisfactory answers forthcoming. I believe in Him with the same certainty as ever. The Holocaust couldn't change that. But I find I want very much to keep after Him and try to the best of my ability to overcome the obscurity of His ways and I can't escape Him, however much He may have wished to escape us. I will do this to my last breath. I know it. More than this, I believe this is precisely what a Jew must do, to keep after Him for answers. And it brings me a measure of repose and comfort to conduct these conferences, to be God's interlocutor, to keep after Him by creating and inventing, like the traditional Jew of the past in history, new arguments against Him, and new justifications for Him. For me it is the entire Torah, the Etz Chayyim [Tree of Life]. Although I have no choice to the contrary, I am happy to hold fast to it.[35]

One significant aspect of this vignette is the fact that this debate with God provides the survivor with an existential drama, giving a post-Holocaust purpose to his existence. The survivor in this example never has peace, something always has to be questioned, something always has to be recapitulated; but in these repetitions there is embedded a structure with which he can organize his life. Thus, this man's religion serves to maintain the reality of that socially constructed world within which he exists. Moreover, this survivor feels that he is involved in a debate that is condoned by Jewish tradition and through this identification with the group he thereby feels that there is continuity with his personal and Jewish past.

Finally, in this illustration we see the survivor being capable of relaxing his individualistic self-assertion, and rooting himself in a secure self-transcending framework. That is, the survivor in this mode of being is able to sustain his self-esteem by fashioning a self-transcending mythic drama.

A fifth rather disturbing perspective on the meaning of the Holocaust was articulated by devout survivors. They viewed the Holocaust in terms of *mipenei hata'einu* ("because of our sins we were punished"). According to this view, the Jewish people were sinful and the Holocaust was its just punishment.

The tendency to blame oneself for one's problems is a characteristic defensive reaction to the passivity inherent in externally imposed suffering. Indeed there is such a line of thought in Jewish liturgy (e.g., Leviticus 26) that has probably helped condition religious Jews to interpret their suffering as a result of their sin and transgression to God. Said one survivor,

> The Holocaust was saying that Jews who keep the mitzvot are doing the right thing and Jews who do not are doing the wrong thing, a terribly wrong thing, but we will all suffer and be punished alike. The innocent and guilty together until we all become religious and observant Jews.[36]
>
> The six million died because of their sins towards God and towards man
>
> --a survivor.

This is a retributive God similar to a child's view of an angry father, who disciplines and punishes his children for not obeying his rules. This view also does something to one's view of the victims. In psychological terms it allows one to view the fate of the victims as their own fault. One does not have to feel so bad for them, a distancing can take place. Also, one's survival can be interpreted as due to one's greater piety, while God metes out strict justice, and each person is dealt with according to what he deserves.[37]

A very interesting sixth theodicy articulated by some survivors goes like this: The Holocaust is the ultimate in vicarious atonement. The Jewish people are the "suffering servant" of Isaiah--Israel suffers and atones for the sins of others. Some Jews die so that the Gentiles might be purified and live. Said one very observant Jewish woman, "The six million perished for the sins of the rest of the world. When they sin we suffer." A variation on this view is that sometimes survivors feel that the death of the 6 million resulted from the sins of less religious Jews around the world, something like a burnt offering. The good Jews suffered to save the sinful ones.

The belief in messianism is one important consideration here and warrants a brief diversion. According to this belief, there will be a resurrection of the dead upon the arrival of the Messiah. It follows, therefore, that the martyrs who died and those who survived honorably will be reborn and enjoy eternal bliss with the Messiah within God's kingdom.

As Berger points out, the belief in messianism permits one to relativize the suffering of the present in terms of it being overcome in a glorious future. "The anomic phenomena are legitimated by reference to a future nomization, thus reintegrating them within an over-all meaningful order." By articulating such a theodicy, the survivor feels the comfort of knowing that in the final analysis the sufferer will be comforted, the good man rewarded, and the evil punished. This perspective permits the survivor to maintain his messianic hopes, but at the same time, says Berger, transposes such beliefs to a mysterious, empirically inaccessible sphere safe from the vicissitudes and challenges of history.[38]

A seventh perspective on the Holocaust, although not technically a theodicy, was articulated by many survivors: Remain religious in order not to give Hitler a posthumous victory. In this view, the Holocaust is revelation, it issues a call for Jewish affirmation. As Emil Fackenheim has written, from Auschwitz comes the command: Jews survive![39] Said one survivor:

> Before this Holocaust I was a simple observant Jew. Today I'm an observant Jew but very complex....I have now a clear reason in my mind and very deep motives for practicing Judaism whereas before it was not as clear. Besides everything else, it's my revenge against Hitler and the Nazis...it is a spitting on their grave. My way of getting even is by practicing my religion with fervor and enthusiasm. Serving God and the Jewish

people and carrying on my father's and my grandfather's and ancestors' traditions.[40]

In this example we see among other things a survivor's attempt to transform narcissistic rage into mature self-assertion rooted in the need for inner continuity with one's personal and traditional past. A by-product of viewing their suffering in this way is the feeling that through their survival, God was telling them that there was some higher purpose for their survival. This was usually interpreted as a mandate to reinforce their faith in Him and do His commandments.

We can also see how the Holocaust is interpreted in the survivor's religious frame of reference, and how a feeling is generated that one should be more committed to religion. It was construed that because of this commitment, one was saved, and thus greater loyalty to God was evoked.

Some survivors appear to have remained observant after the war, and indeed on a behavioral level this is so. However, the cracks in their symbolic world are deeper than implied in those survivor theodicies already mentioned. Sometimes it is the extensive need for disavowal that indicates the severe challenge that the survivor's Holocaust experiences have posed to his symbolic world. For example, another way that survivors maintained their religious faith and continued their religious behavior was to view their Holocaust experience as belonging to another long lost alienated period of their lives without any connection to their present concerns. These individuals view the Holocaust as a weird detour in their personal lives, without significance for the present. They pursue one of the ways to preserve one's world in the face of a deeply disturbing challenge by acting as if that challenging experience is completely unrelated to one's current world. Through exiling one's jarring experience to psychological and biographical irrelevance, one can preserve the integrity of one's world construction.

We have reviewed prevalent ways that survivors were able to maintain their world in the face of the great anomaly--the Holocaust. We have also seen that people have a tremendous need to consciously and/or unconsciously maintain their symbolic world in the face of overwhelming suffering. The reason for this, says Hannah Arendt (writing in another context), is that when one loses one's sheltering "sacred canopy," then one finds oneself without a guide in the wilderness of bare facts, "for when man is robbed of all means of interpreting events he is left with no sense whatsoever of reality."[41]

SURVIVORS WHOSE FAITH WAS LOST OR DIMINISHED AFTER THE HOLOCAUST

There were survivors who were not able to sustain their religious worldview during the Holocaust. Without God their world began to fall apart and lost its plausibility, its personal sense of reality. As Berger points out, for the religious person, "The subjective reality of the world hinges on the thin thread of conversation"[42] (i.e., maintaining an ongoing dialogue with God, significant others, and, more broadly, active involvement with the religious community and tradition). In the camps, religion filled the inmates' need to be rooted in a sustaining source of self-transcending power grounded in a divine person and/or divine world. Traumatic disruption, however, occurs when the dialogue ends or is interrupted as was the case for many religious inmates. For the survivor, when a religious framework no longer served as an all-embracing sacred order against the dread of physical and/or psychological annihilation, he was left alone against the threats of chaos, meaninglessness, and death. That is, his entire world began to lose credibility.

In the concentration camp the fear of death predominated. Perhaps nothing undermines human meanings, and threatens the very foundations upon which humans erect their self-esteem, more than the fear of death.[43] Furthermore, when a person observes the death of a significant other and anticipates his own death, he is strongly compelled to question the ad hoc cognitive and normative operating procedures of his "normal" life in society.[44]

For the religious survivor, then, the loss of religious perspective is experienced as becoming worldless. His orientation in experience becomes tenuous, and in extreme cases he loses his sense of reality and identity. When a person can no longer make sense of his life, he also loses his "moral and cognitive orientation" with debilitating psychological ramifications.[45] These consequences will be discussed later. In this section we want to describe the reasons why many survivors gave up their faith (in whole or in part), their religious beliefs, and/or religious behavior.

The relinquishing of faith in a just God by survivors in some ways is the most expected reaction after the Holocaust. Brenner reports that as a general rule faith declined as a consequence of the devastation, and during it as well. Moreover, belief in the major articles of faith never recovered to their pre-Holocaust level.[46] The survivors to be described in this group tended to view the Holocaust and their suffering during it as an anomaly that could not be easily assimilated into their interpretive world. For these survivors, none of the previously mentioned theodicies was satisfactory in making sense of the cataclysm; there was an absence of a synthesized, coherent worldview that adequately explained and/or justified the Holocaust.

Many survivors consciously view their lack of faith as based on a rationale that goes something like this: The Holocaust is proof that "God is dead." If there were a God, He would certainly have prevented Auschwitz; if He did not, then He does not exist. In *After Auschwitz*, Richard Rubenstein argues that after the Holocaust the belief in a redeeming God, who is active in history and who will redeem mankind from its troubles, is no longer possible. Belief in such a God, and a loyalty to the rabbinic theodicy that attempted to justify Him, would imply that Hitler was part of a divine plan and that the Jewish people were being punished for their sins. This belief is not plausible in a post-Holocaust world, says Rubenstein.[47]

However, survivors had great difficulty speaking about a God who is dead. Rather they preferred to speak about God's total absence. The idea that "God was dead" and never to reappear in their lives was experienced with tremendous anxiety.

That God could have done something to prevent the Holocaust but chose not to is a more disturbing feeling for the survivor than the declaration that He does not exist. If God is the master of the universe and stood idly by while his chosen people were destroyed, then this would make Him what Rubenstein calls a "cosmic sadist." Most survivors prefer not to believe in God rather than to view Him in this satanic manner.

Survivors also find belief in God impossible because they view the victims as entirely innocent. What makes God's absence more distressing is that the victims were totally undeserving of their fate. They were a pious and decent group, and the death of so many innocent children made faith in a God that allows this to happen seem untenable. That is, when good people offer good prayers for good purposes and God remains silent amidst the horrific cruelty, there can be a loss of basic trust, and the relinquishing of faith is understandable.

For the religious survivor, perhaps the predominant internal reaction to the loss of their world was a terrible sense of abandonment by God. Nowhere is this agonizing sense of radical abandonment better described than by Elie Wiesel in the often-quoted passage from *Night*. In this powerful episode, the S.S. decided to publicly hang three camp inmates for sabotage, one of them being a young child with a refined and beautiful face like that of a "sad angel." Wiesel continues:

> The three victims mounted together onto the chairs.
>
> The three necks were placed at the same moment within the nooses.
>
> "Long live Liberty!" cried the two adults. But the child was silent. "Where is God?
>
> Where is He?" someone behind me asked.
> At a sign from the head of the camp, the three chairs tipped over.
>
> Total silence throughout the camp. On the horizon, the sun was setting.
>
> "Bare your heads!" yelled the head of the camp. His voice was raucous. We were weeping.
>
> "Cover your heads!" Then the march past began. The two adults were no longer alive. Their tongues hung swollen, blue-tinged. But the third rope was still moving; being so light, the child was still alive....
>
> For more than an hour he stayed there, struggling between life and death, dying in slow agony under our eyes. And we had to look him full in the face. He was still alive when I passed in front of him. His tongue was still red, his eyes not yet glazed. Behind me, I heard the same man asking:
>
> "Where is God now?" And I heard a voice within me answer him: "Where is He? Here He is--He is hanging here on this gallows...."

That night the soup tasted of corpses.[48]

What follows from such an experience of God's abandonment in the face of such brutality is rage, despair, and hopelessness, in short, the loss of trust in the plausibility of one's world. Says Wiesel, "Never shall I forget that nocturnal silence which deprived me, for all eternity, of the desire to live. Never shall I forget those moments which murdered my God and my soul and turned my dreams to dust."[49]

Rage at God in particular is centrally connected to feeling abandoned by Him in the most critical hour of need, especially because this abandonment led to such personal suffering and loss of loved ones. As Brenner points out,[50] it is important to emphasize that the survivor who blasphemes God, curses Him, denies Him, hates Him, menaces Him, and/or threatens to withhold faith in Him is doing so in part because of this terrible narcissistic hurt he experienced while incarcerated, when God was absent. "God, if you don't do something I'm going to stop believing in you..." was the way many survivors confronted God during imprisonment. When there was no help given by Him, this feeling of abandonment *by* God was transposed and became abandonment *of* God. As Brenner further indicates, of those individuals who were seeking to punish God by shouting His nonexistence to His face, they were reacting as if they were a deserted lover crying out in pain, "I don't love you anymore: for me you no longer exist." In other words, for many survivors, God's nonexistence is often proclaimed as a way of punishing God for concealing Himself when He was desperately needed.

We have seen why it was that survivors lost their faith, as well as the significance of this for their ability to maintain themselves as a locus of primary value in a world of meaning. In the following section we will look at some of the psychological problems that this loss generates and its impact on the psychotherapeutic experience. We will also offer some suggestions as to how psychotherapists can best facilitate reconstruction of the survivor's symbolic world.

TREATMENT ISSUES WITH SURVIVORS

Regardless of theoretical orientation, most people agree that psychotherapy with the Holocaust survivor is an enormously difficult task.

Psychoanalysts in particular have attempted perhaps more than any other professional group both to treat survivors and to theorize about the origin of their symptoms and their problems in living.[51] Regrettably, their success in treating survivors, as with most other approaches, has been rather limited. Thus, Kurt Eissler has serious doubts that survivors can be helped by psychoanalytic psychotherapy since the trauma of persecution remains incomparable and incomprehensible.[52] Moises Kijak and Silvio Funtowicz stress the difficulties of treating survivors because their incarceration led to "irreversible deterioration of the ego."[53] Barocas despondently claims that hardly anyone could have emerged from the Nazi death camps without having been scarred, scars "which will never be removed by psychotherapy."[54] Henry Krystal stresses the limitations of psychoanalytic psychotherapy with elderly survivors, primarily because their ability to grieve effectively has been impaired by the enormity of their suffering and losses.[55] He elsewhere grimly concludes that "the therapist has to be satisfied when the patient is restored to his chronic survivor syndrome state with its symptoms, handicaps and problems."[56]

We believe that one of the reasons survivors have been so difficult to treat is that the models being used to understand and conceptualize their problems have not adequately considered the awesome significance of the survivors' loss of their symbolic world: "When a man is so utterly stripped of life meaning [as was the concentration camp inmate] he has no furnishings for his inner life, he is as good as dead, even though his organism gropes blindly towards life."[57] Therapists need to understand that conceptualizing the survivor's symptoms solely in terms of classical psychoanalytic theory does not sufficiently account for the core of the survivor's experience nor illuminate the significance of this pain.[58] Viewing the survivor's symptoms primarily in terms of the product of conflict between a repressed impulse and the repressing agency (compromise formations) or in terms of Freud's theory of trauma or its variations[59] fails to grasp the significance of the survivor's symptoms for his overall functioning.

According to Ernst Becker, neurosis as a clinical problem can be seen in part as an existential failure to create a personal drama in a world of meaning that supports self-affirmation.[60] Man becomes neurotic when vital living bogs down. There must be the capacity and the confidence to thrust oneself into active participation in the world. Clinical neurosis testifies to a behavioral poverty, to the blocking of the forward momentum of action and the restriction of experience. For the survivor in particular, it is the experienced result of the failure to develop patterns of behavior that allow the individual to merge successfully with the demands of a sustaining cultural drama. Only such a merger allows for the development of an assured sense of self-respect, and gives a person the courage to open himself to a reality that is both inviting and terrifying.

Such a framework for psychopathology helps us better understand the often reported symptoms associated with survivorship embodied in the so-called "survivor syndrome." The survivor has been described as having chronic depressive states, a tendency to isolation and withdrawal, reappearing manifestations of anxiety, some disturbances of cognition and memory, guilt, and psychosomatic complaints.[61] Perhaps the underlying reason why survivors develop this way of being-in-the-world has to do with the trauma of the loss of loved ones and the inability to mourn them during and following the Holocaust. For the survivor who abandoned his faith, this trauma may be because it also meant the loss of identity as it was reflected in membership in the religious community, since the survivor's religious world was the world of meaning that provided the framework for a sense of self-value. The survivor who was once deeply religious and who no longer defines himself as God's rational partner has, perhaps more than any other kind of survivor, to come to terms with the painful and disorganizing consequences of losing his symbolic world.

It is not by chance that depression and isolation and withdrawal are repeatedly cited as key symptoms of the survivor who comes to therapy. Depression can be precipitated by the loss or removal of anything that the individual values. To the extent that one's sense of well-being, safety, and meaning is dependent on love, social position--or God--to that extent one will be threatened by its loss. When the reliance is preponderant, the person despairs of survival and gives up. It is this despair that we call depression, and this was a common reaction for many survivors.

Hopeless and helpless, the survivor may give up the struggle. It is this abandonment which makes depression different from other psychological conditions. The ego is paralyzed because it feels incapable of meeting life's demands.[62] Edward Bibring's ego theory of depression which points to the importance of loss of self-esteem (as opposed to viewing depression as self-directed aggression) allows us to broaden our understanding of the religious survivor's depression to include the entire range of social phenomenon:

> Since the ego is rooted in social reality, since self-esteem is composed of social symbols and social motives, depression becomes a direct function of a cognitively apprehended symbolic world.[63]

The religious survivor's depression is concerned with more than object loss, but fundamentally includes the loss of norms or rules for significant action that were embodied in religious observance and community. These "social rules and objects provide an individual with a staged drama of significance which is the theatre of his action."[64] To lose a loved one is to lose someone to whom one has made appeal for self-validation. To lose one's norms or rules for significant action is to lose a performance part in which identity is fabricated and sustained.[65] The survivor is thus unable to feel that he is an object of primary value in a world of meaning.

The survivor's depression has other dimensions that can be more deeply understood when viewed from a model that stresses man's need to be a center of personal significance in a meaningful world. As with other survivors, the survivor who has lost his religious world often has a restricted and closed life-style. Indeed, a depressed person builds himself firmly into his cultural world such that he is imprisoned in his own narrow behavioral mold. Becker, in his brilliant essay on the *Pawnbroker*, calls this fetishization "the organization of perception and action, by the personality, around a very striking and compelling--but narrow theme."[66] Becker points out that the reason a survivor would artificially inflate a small area of the world and overvalue it (in the pawnbroker's case it was money) is because it represents an area that he can firmly hold on to, can skillfully manipulate, use easily to justify himself--his actions, his sense of self, his option in the world. As Becker writes, "the fetish, in word, is an arbitrary focus for your derivation of self-value."[67]

The religious survivor who lost the sense of meaning, who views the richness of his past life as unrelated to his harrowing present, needs to reorient his personality around a narrow and compelling source of meaning, of self-sustenance. Without organizing his self-concept around such a theme the survivor feels that he has no justification for his entire life, no justification for going on.

The often-cited guilt of the survivor can also be conceptualized more broadly when using this new perspective. In the early theorizing survivor guilt was assumed to occur in relation to the feeling of not deserving to live when all or most relatives and friends were murdered during the Holocaust. Survivor guilt was classically viewed as a result of early hostility and death wishes to the lost love object.[68]

Ornstein, however, views survivor guilt rather differently. She believes it is related less to having survived while others had died than to survivors' difficulty in reconciling the alteration in their behavioral and moral conduct during the Holocaust with their conduct and behavior under civilized conditions.[69]

Developing Ornstein's conception somewhat differently, we suggest that survivor guilt reflects the survivor's difficulty in having lived in one symbolic world which is accepted for the purpose of survival, that is, "l'universe concentrationnaire," and then moving into another post-Holocaust symbolic world that is experienced as morally discontinuous with the previous one. An example of this is the inmate who survived in the camp by bribing a Kapo to remove his name from the list of those to be gassed and replacing it with someone else's name. Elie Wiesel offers another example, writing that when incarcerated he had the thought that he wished his father was dead so as not to be an additional burden to his own survival. The difficulty after the Holocaust in coming to terms with this behavior, behavior that made sense at the time within the camp context, is obviously awesome because it demands a way of integrating the survivor's Holocaust experience into the value structures that he now judges himself by. Since most of these values reside outside the reflective capacity of most people, the survivor's attempt at integration is extremely difficult and complex.

Likewise the survivor's psychosomatic complaints make more sense when we consider the degree to which bodily complaints focus one's mind and behavior around the ache or pain. The survivor who narrows his concerns to sorting out the vagaries of his physical condition actually has a project that anchors him in a "fetishized" world of meaning. Through such a creation of meaning the survivor does not have to face a sense of helplessness at piecing together a world of reciprocal relationships and a world that integrates the past and present.

The survivor's reappearing anxiety is a complicated matter and is tied in part to his symbolic difficulties. One often-cited characteristic of survivors is alexithymia--the inability to identify, symbolize, and express feelings and fantasies.[70] As Becker points out, "For the symbolic animal, anxiety derives largely from lack of words--lack of conventional reasons for action."[71] That is, the symbol gives focus and reality to vague feelings of restlessness and tension. For the survivor, having abrogated a religious framework has meant the near discontinuity of existence on a symbolic level. This discontinuity of identity fosters a sense of anxiety about the future, anxiety about the task of redefining oneself anew in an unfamiliar context. Thus, when an individual loses his ability to symbolize and articulate his meaning in the world, the world begins to lose its credibility and one's everyday life feels pointless.

The survivor's situation is further complicated by their jarring memories, sometimes expressed in their difficulties in sleeping and nightmares. The task for the survivor is twofold: on the one hand, he has to come to terms with the brutal and painful memories associated with camp internment and suffering. On the other, and perhaps more agonizing than the memories of being physically tortured, are the rich, meaning-saturated, life-affirming pre-Holocaust memories that intrude into his life, disrupting it and rendering his current life valueless and meaningless by contrast.

Said one survivor when walking into a synagogue many years after liberation.

> My eyes filled with tears but my lips wouldn't quiver with prayer. It was as if I have a paralysis of the mouth. My mind began racing toward past times of joy in the synagogue with my father and my grandfather and the other Jews of our town; happier times and happier places.[72]

When the past is experienced as so overwhelmingly painful, it is extremely difficult for the survivor to feel meaningful aliveness in the present. The past is not experienced as a positive resource but rather a negative influence pulling the survivor backward into the painful and debilitating memories.

We have tried to suggest another way of articulating and understanding some of the survivor's symptoms as described in the psychological literature. We hope it is clear that when a survivor's religious framework, his symbolic world, can no longer "make sense" of his life, and he can't recognize his own identity, his psychological world begins to crumble. The survivor's symptoms thus broadly signify the rupturing, if not loss, of his symbolic world. The specific symptoms, especially as they are compromise formations, are to be regarded as the person's attempt to preserve self-cohesion, self-continuity and self-esteem[73] in a tottering symbolic world. It is within this context that the survivor may seek out psychotherapy, and it is to this subject that we now turn.

PSYCHOTHERAPY WITH THE RELIGIOUS SURVIVOR

We have divided religious survivors who come to therapy into two different groups: those who have maintained their faith, although in a problematic way, and those who have lost their faith. The usefulness of this somewhat simplified categorization resides in the fact that these two groups of survivors present the therapist with different clinical problems.

In the former group are survivors who still consider themselves as God-focused and members of a religious community. They still observe the *halakhah*; however, their faith has weakened and most importantly the ontological security derived from the "sacred canopy" has lessened. Perhaps the most salient characteristic of a survivor from this group is his attitude towards the *mitzvot* (commandments) he performs. Said one survivor:

> you could not tell from my religious behavior what I have undergone, what the Holocaust has done to me, but in my soul where my beliefs reside there has been a tremendous transformation. My faith has been crushed and I am nearly a non-believer...you may say I've been changed philosophically, and religiously in connection with beliefs about God, but not

changed at all where for a Jew it counts most--in actions. In this respect I'm still a pious Jew.[74]

Such survivors may feel that they must perform mitzvot because they fear God--His retribution and power. But they are not able to serve Him in love like they once were. It is as if their symbolic world has lost its capacity to energize and propel them. Even with this loss of vigor there is still the understanding, familiarity, predictability and safety derived from being in their religious framework with its many behavioral obligations and so it is not abandoned even though one's faith has been severely undermined.

With the survivors from this group the fundamental viability of their religious framework still exists, yet there are modifications in their symbolic world, sometimes radical ones, that are necessary to maintain the plausibility of their world.

The second group of survivors alluded to earlier are those who have lost faith and no longer consider themselves as active relational partners with God; they no longer feel part of a faith community. These individuals require a replacement for their demolished religious symbolic world. Such survivors generally experience more anomie, anxiety, and meaninglessness than the group already described.

The basic focus of psychotherapy with religious survivors ought to be the rebuilding of viable human meaning formations in their lives. That is, the survivor needs help in constructing a revised or different plausible symbolic world. Following George Atwood and Robert Stolorow we believe "that the need to maintain the organization of experience is a central motive in the patterning of human action."[75] When that organization of experience loses its narrative coherence, as was the case of survivors who lost their religious world, there is a subjective sense of "self-dissolution" and "self-loss." That is, the survivor no longer feels himself to be a "locus of primary value in a world of meaning." The aim of psychotherapy with the survivor becomes the resurrection and/or creation anew of world structures which generate a feeling of meaning, continuity, self-cohesion and overall narrative coherence. This is accomplished, say Atwood and Stolorow,[76] by having the therapist focus on the illumination of meaning in the survivor's personal experience and conduct. The goal of psychoanalytic therapy with the survivor thus becomes the unfolding, clarification and transformation of personal subjective worlds. The above goals of psychotherapy are not easy for the religiously inclined survivor to achieve, in part because the loss (or near loss) of basic trust that came about due to the Holocaust makes faith and trust in the benevolence of an omnipotent God seem implausible.[77] Therapists need to be aware that for survivors the rupturing in the dialogue with God is experienced as traumatic. One of the ways to strengthen the survivor's religious framework, especially when the survivor wants a God-focused life, is to help him broaden the conception of God from a somewhat narrow notion of Him.

This can be achieved by helping the survivor to create a replacement attitude. Indeed, survivors have accomplished this when the personal conventional God of the Bible is replaced by an impersonal God who is not actively involved in their lives. This modified view of God often stresses the idea that there is some kind of order and design in the universe, but avoids assigning to God the capacity to intervene in history. Other survivors revised their conception of God somewhat differently--God is still all-good but He is no longer all-powerful. By the therapist's helping the survivor (who is so inclined) to reconstruct a viable post-Holocaust God, the survivor is given the opportunity to feel linked, albeit with modifications, to his religious community.

The loss of basic trust in God, in the orderly and ethically caring nature of the universe, is a major problem for the survivor, and it manifests itself quite dramatically sometimes in the transference--or rather more accurately, in the survivor's difficulty in developing a transference. The profound anger and sense of abandonment and loss (of loved ones and of God) that the survivor may harbor due to his Holocaust experience makes the emergence of an intense, intimate relationship very anxiety provoking if not impossible. The idea of trusting another human being, a member of the species that did him so much harm, is terrifying for the survivor, as is the loss of control and the associated regression implied in a transference.

Likewise, the capacity of the survivor to build himself back into a world of significance is seriously truncated by this impairment in his human relationships. The capacity to recreate new relationships of personal meaning and/or the capacity to deepen previous ones is perhaps the main way a survivor can recenter himself in the world.

The survivor's difficulties in basic trust also have bearing on the therapist's potential counter-transference. The fact that the survivor may seem to have a truncated capacity for intimacy must not be interpreted by the therapist as an indication that the survivor is too damaged for in-depth psychotherapy. Rather the therapist needs to empathize with the fact that the survivor's Holocaust experience, with its loss of loved ones and loss of God, also involved the rupturing of the taken-for-granted ways of being-in-the-world, that is, the survivor's modes of perception, expression, and participation with other human beings have been changed, fostering a new order of consciousness. Thus, therapy with survivors involves quiet listening and patience on the part of the therapist until some sort of trusting relationship can evolve, until the survivor can construct a hopeful image of a human person.

The issue of continuity for the survivor is of considerable importance primarily because it highlights the felt disharmony between life before, during, and after incarceration. Without the feeling that there is an essential sameness about him--even though he was in *l'universe concentrationnaire*--there is only a small possibility that recovery can take place. For the therapist, the survivor needs to be encouraged to focus on his mode of adaptation during incarceration with all its implied strengths and resources.[78] Only in this way will he be able to understand that indeed something did endure amidst the horror, qualities of strength, and courage or whatever, which existed before the Holocaust, which were expressed in the camps and can now be used to create a new world of meaning. Many survivors, for example, who come for treatment, have married or remarried and have had children. Sometimes these families are viewed almost completely in terms of the past. Wives and husbands and especially the children are seen as replacements for lost loved ones to such an extent that the present and past merge. The survivor lives in a kind of strange double-world heavily colored by Holocaust imagery and themes. Indeed the focus of therapy has to be on helping the survivor separate these images, to ascribe a contemporary meaning to his new family, such that he appreciates them on their own terms.

Only in this way will he feel himself anchored in a world of present significance.

Last, survivors have also replaced their religious symbolic world with other perspectives, often secular commitments such as Zionism, Jewish survival, Jewish culture, fighting anti-Semitism, Holocaust scholarship, and/or commemoration. Such a focus gives the survivor a feeling of active mastery of his environment, especially in light of a possible feeling of victimization during the Holocaust. Also, survivors who are involved with such replacement activities often feel that there is a powerful truth in what they are doing which is similar to the religious person's sense of overriding truth and validity to his faith in God and his religion.

CLOSING REMARKS

As the religious survivor reaches old age, many of the psychological problems already described are experienced more sharply. Most importantly, however, the survivor has to evaluate his life within the broader context of the vicissitudes of senescence, with the inevitable awareness that one is getting closer to the end. This coming of age has all the problems usually associated with this phase of the life cycle; however, the goals of integrity[79] and integration[80] in old age are especially problematic for the Holocaust survivor. Psychotherapists are by and large working with survivors who are now in old age. An awareness on the part of therapists of some of the special difficulties that Holocaust survivors have to struggle with as they reach the last phase of the life cycle seems to be an appropriate coda to our chapter. This subject is especially relevant to psychotherapy with the survivor, since as Terrence Des Pres has pointed out,

> One of the principal discoveries to come out of follow-up studies of Jewish and Armenian catastrophes is that the impact of historical trauma does not lessen but rather *grows* with time, both in the memory of aging survivors and in the passions of subsequent generations, if, that is, no way to reconciliation presents itself.[81]

In addition, in a recent survey of 275 survivors, it was found that a very high percentage of them at a later age were suffering from nervousness, fear, chronic tiredness, feelings of loneliness, inability to concentrate, depression, insomnia, and psychosomatic complaints, problems often related to a fall back on the memories of the past.[82]

In our view the problems of the aging survivor can best be conceptualized by using Erik Erikson's life-cycle framework. Erikson[83] has called the last stage of the epigenetic process of development "integrity." It can be described as a state one arrives at after having taken care of things and people, products and ideas, and having adjusted to the successes and failures of one's life. This is accomplished, says Erikson, when the individual is able to accept his life cycle "as something that had to be and that, by necessity, permitted no substitutions....For he knows that an individual life is the accidental coincidence of but one life cycle with but one segment of history...."[84] Through such accomplishments individuals may reap the benefits of the previous stages of life, and perceive that their life has some coherence and meaning within a larger order. When one has achieved integrity, one maintains with dignity his own lifestyle and defends it from potential threats.

Erikson further says that when the individual is unable to accept his life cycle as the ultimate and one and only meaning that living embodies, he feels despair. Despair of what has been implies that what has been, has been meaningless. Despair is the protest of a person who is not yet satisfied with a life that has fundamentally been unsatisfying. Despair indicates an unwillingness, paradoxical as it may be, to end a life that has failed to achieve fulfillment and that now culminates in the sum of a thousand little miseries.

For the aging Holocaust survivor, achieving integrity and its corresponding ego attainment--wisdom ("detached concern with life itself, in the face of death itself"[85])--is a complex and difficult problem requiring lengthy analysis. We, however, will only mention a few of the difficulties for the aging survivor to achieve integrity.

The process of the survivor's reviewing his life is often terrifying and anxiety producing, primarily because so much energy has been devoted to fending off intrusive painful and disorganizing memories. This avoidance of one's history makes psychotherapy quite difficult, since facing the past is such an important factor in psychotherapeutic experience. Klein has commented on why so many aging survivors avoid their past. The "sensitivity to cleavage and dissonance" which "reaches its crest...in the twilight years when irreversible finitude is finally to be faced and the effort to bring together past, present and the shrinking future into a self-justifying meaning is especially poignant and difficult."[86]

For the survivor, acceptance of the Holocaust "as something that had to be" part of his life cycle is painfully paradoxical. As Krystal points out, acceptance on the part of survivors that what happened to them was justified by its causes implies an acceptance that Nazism was also justified by its causes. This acceptance, says Krystal, is too closely reminiscent of the submission to persecution:

> The process of making peace with oneself becomes impossible when it brings back the helplessness and shame of the past. Many survivors would experience the self-healing as "granting Hitler a posthumous victory," and therefore angrily reject it. To them, self-integration appears antithetical to the only justification for their survival: to be angry witnesses against the outrage of the Holocaust.[87]

According to Krystal, a final obstacle that prevents survivors from reaching integrity and self-acceptance is their incomplete mourning. Many survivors have had to grapple with the premature, absurd, and grotesque deaths of parents, spouses, and children. This is especially difficult because of the awareness that their loved ones were murdered simply because they were Jews who were living in the wrong place at the wrong time, while the world stood idly by. The capacity to sustain such multiple losses within such a bizarre context--without surrender to despair and hopelessness--requires great inner strength. This is poignantly true when we remember that the human capacity to endure psychic pain and guilt is limited.

Religious survivors must grapple with many of the same issues that nonreligious survivors struggle with. They too have to wrestle with integrity and despair. Indeed, the religious survivors who come to psychotherapy may have great difficulty coming to terms with the overall quality of their lives and with their God. The survivor may find that the previously useful theodicies no longer make sense as he reaches old age. A strong feeling of God's injustice begins to stir uncomfortably in his mind. Many of the related painful existential questions that were in sharp focus during and after the war return to haunt the survivor. He begins to feel that he was cheated by God, he feels rage and sadness and doesn't understand why he was chosen to suffer, why his life was mercilessly derailed.

Sometimes religious survivors come to therapy because of a sudden onset of problems rooted to old age (e.g., loss of a spouse, illness), whereas in other situations the circumstances relate to a more chronic sense of unhappiness. Regardless of the reason for coming to therapy, the aging religious survivor usually directly or indirectly links these current problems with his Holocaust past, and it is this constellation which poses a profound threat to the plausibility of his symbolic world.

Psychotherapists who work with aging religious survivors need to focus on helping them find a way to integrate this threat into their religious world. The therapist needs to help the survivor shake up his protective "sacred canopy," since there is not enough time left for the survivor to create a new world meaning.

For the therapist to aid the religious survivor in the above task, always within the context of the survivor's coming to terms with his life, with integrity, means, among other things, supporting the survivor's need to assess his accomplishments and failures from the perspective of an ideal of total commitment, unconditional and unqualified, to the service of God. To the extent that he was able to live life, bear pain with spiritual self-awareness, self-assertion, and self-creation--all within the context of the demands of tradition and community--then can the religious survivor review life and say to himself that it was dedicated to the sacred; that it had meaning worthy of God's benign judgment.

For the aging religious survivor in psychotherapy to achieve this kind of life-affirming self-evaluation requires that the therapist help expand the survivor's religious worldview. Religious survivors at their best, perhaps more than any other religious personality, recognize that the key to religious self-acceptance and the acceptance of God is the awareness:

> That faith is a life response of the whole person to the presence in life and history. Like life, this response ebbs and flows. The difference between the sceptic and the believer is frequency of faith and not certitude of position.[88]

Becker has amplified the significance of the above notion in a way that points to the ultimate aim of psychotherapy with the religious survivor, namely, that meaning and conviction ought to be grounded in "a sense of intimacy with the cosmic process" which would provide a perfect closure of human striving. Becker continues:

> Genuine heroism for man is still the power to support contradictions, no matter how glaring or hopeless they may seem. The ideal critique of a faith must always be whether it embodies within itself the fundamental contradictions of the human paradox and yet is able to support them without fanaticism, sadism, and narcissism, but with openness and trust. Religion itself is an ideal of strength and of potential for growth, of what man might become by assuming the burden of his life, as well as by being partly relieved by it.[89]

For the survivor, as with us all, strength for creation of liberatory meaning is most firm when rooted in a personal dialogue that calls forth one's spontaneous powers and encourages their development in terms of a shared ideal of human potential. Ultimately, this ideal for the religious survivor must be grounded in a religious community oriented toward an open and nondogmatic God-personal-experience, usually, but not always, within a traditional context.

Finally, as the religious survivor begins to move toward achieving some modicum of integrity, it is important for the therapist to appreciate the survivor's evolving attitude towards what is generally regarded as a person's greatest fear--his own death.

For the religious survivor, the deepening of his faith in God, which is often the consequence of the therapist working effectively within the survivor's frame of reference, allows him to view his own death as a return to his beloved Maker. Life is a borrowed treasure and it must be reclaimed by its Owner. In this way, he links his existence back into a higher ground of meaning, which allows him to view his suffering and his achievements in terms of God's purpose for creation,[90] in terms of religious group continuity, and in terms of ultimate judgment. As a result of this, death loses some of its terror, as there is the hope and comfort in final redemption. At this point the religious survivor can surrender his life not in fear and trembling but in love, trust, and fellowship with God.

As for the secular psychotherapist who may view death very differently, often with extreme anxiety, the genuinely religious survivor may seem like a naive anomaly. However, if he is to be able to empathize with and ultimately help the religious survivor, there must be the recognition, acceptance, and support of the integrity of the survivor's symbolic world.

ENDNOTES

[1]For example, the *Chicago Psychoanalytic Literature Index*, as well as the most recent and comprehensive research bibliography on The psychological effects of Nazi persecution on survivors, does not have any entries that deal with the religious dimension of survivorship. See Leon Eitinger, Robert Krell, and Miriam Rieck, *The Psychological and Medical Effects of Concentration Camps and Related Persecutions on Survivors of the Holocaust* (Vancouver: University of British Columbia Press, 1985).

[2]This point is illustrated in remarks made by Henry Krystal, perhaps the seminal thinker in The field: "Desperate attempts are made by survivors to restore and maintain their faith in God. However, since problems of aggression and the destruction of basic trust that resulted from the events of the Holocaust make true faith and trust in The benevolence of an omnipotent God impossible, the yearning for the comfort of religion only results in a piling up of rituals." "Integration and Self-healing in Post-traumatic States," in Steven Luel and Paul Marcus, eds., *Psychoanalytic Reflections on the Holocaust: Selected Essays* (New York: KTAV and University of Denver, 1984), p. 129. Krystal's generalization does not seem to take account of the large theological literature and survivor testimony which sharply challenges his conclusion. Also see Paul Marcus, "Jewish Consciousness after the Holocaust," in *Psychoanalytic Reflections on the Holocaust: Selected Essays*, pp. 179-196; Paul Marcus and Irene Wineman, "Psychoanalysis Encountering The Holocaust," *Psychoanalytic Inquiry* 5 (1985): 85-98.

[3]This essay is based on three data sources: first, 30 focused interviews with Jewish concentration camp survivors from Orthodox Eastern European families. Their ages and educational and socioeconomic levels varied. Second, Paul Marcus' work in psychoanalytic psychotherapy with survivors for a number of years. Third, secondary sources including diaries, novels, and the very helpful raw data from Reeve R. Brenner's *The Faith and Doubt of Holocaust Survivors* (New York: The Free Press, 1980), which contains a survey of 780 survivors.

[4]Robert Wuthnow, James Davidson Hunter, Albert Bergesen, and Edith Kurzweil, *Cultural Analysis* (Boston: Routledge and Kegan Paul, 1984), pp. 37, 75.

[5]Peter Berger, *The Sacred Canopy* (Garden City: Doubleday, 1967).

[6]*Ibid.*

[7]Ernest Becker, *The Revolution in Psychiatry* (New York: The Free Press, 1964), p. 44.

[8]Roy Shaefer, *A New Language for Psychoanalysis* (New Haven: Yale University Press, 1976); also Anna Ornstein, "Survival and Recovery," *Psychoanalytic Inquiry* 5 (1985): 99-130.

[9]Jacob Robinson, "Holocaust," *Encyclopedia Judaica*, VIII (1972): 827-906.

[10]Brenner, *Faith and Doubt*, p. 37.

[11]Lucy Dawidowicz, *The War Against the Jews 1933-45* (New York: Holt, Rinehart and Winston, 1975), p. 248.

[12]Daniel Landes, "Spiritual Responses in the Camps," in *Genocide: Critical Issues of the Holocaust*, Alexander Grobman and Daniel Landes, eds. (Chappaqua: Rossel Books, 1983), p. 272.

[13]Joseph B. Soloveitchik, *Halakhic Man* (Philadelphia: The Jewish Publication Society, 1983).

[14]Aharon Lichtenstein, "Joseph Soloveitchik," in Simon Noveck, ed. *Great Jewish Thinkers of the Twentieth Century* (Washington, DC: B'nai B'rith Books, 1985).

[15]Paul Marcus and Alan Rosenberg, *Faith During the Holocaust: A Psychological Inquiry* (New York: Praeger, forthcoming).

[16]Ornstein, "Survival and Recovery."

[17]Berger, *The Sacred Canopy*, pp. 54, 58.

[18]Our position is similar to Viktor Frankl's (*Man's Search for Meaning* [New York: Pocket Books, 1963]) insofar as we believe that meaning constitutes the major problematic for understanding the human condition. We fundamentally disagree with Frankl in that he believes that meaning is "given," that it is something that one "finds." We, however, believe that meaning is a social construction, that human beings collectively create and develop their "locus of primary value in a world of meaning."

[19]Adina Dreksler, "Holocaust, Spiritual Resistance in the Ghettos and Camps," *Encyclopedia Judaica*, 17, Supplement (1982): 311-313.

[20]Yaffa Eliach, *Hasidic Tales of the Holocaust* (New York: Avon Books, 1982); Eliezer Berkovitz, *With God in Hell* (New York: Sandhedrin Press, 1979); Daniel Landes, "Spiritual Responses in The Camps."

[21]Ephraim Oshry, *Questions and Responses from Out of the Depths* (New York: Judaica Press, 1983).

[22]Robert Kirshner, *Rabbinic Responsa of the Holocaust Era* (New York: Schocken Books, 1976).

[23]Viktor E. Frankl, *Man's Search for Meaning*; Hillel Klein, "The Survivor's Search for Meaning and Identity," *The Nazi Concentration Camps: Proceedings of the Fourth Yad Vashem International Historical Conference* (1984): 543-554; Terence Des Pres, *The Survivor* (New York: Pocket Books, 1976); Primo Levi, *The Drowned and the Saved* (New York: Summit, 1986). Jean Améry, in *At the Mind's Limits: Contemplations by a Survivor on Auschwitz and its Realities* (New York: Schocken, 1986), makes the subtle point that in Auschwitz an intellectual background and/or basic disposition was of little help in survival primarily because the intellectual was alone with his intellect and no social reality that could confirm or support it. Moreover, if the intellect was not centered around a religious or political belief, it was more or less useless. The religious and political prisoners, says Améry, survived better or died with more dignity than their irreligious or unpolitical intellectual comrades.

[24]Anna Pawelczyńska, *Values and Violence in Auschwitz* (Berkeley: University of California Press, 1979).

[25]Levi, *The Drowned and the Saved*; Frankl, *Man's Search for Meaning*.

[26]Christopher Lasch, *The Minimal Self* (New York: W. W. Norton and Company, 1984).

[27]Paul Marcus and Alan Rosenberg, "A Philosophical Critique of The 'Survivor Syndrome' and some Implications for Treatment," in Randolph Braham, ed., *Psychological Perspectives of the Holocaust and of its Aftermath* (Boulder: Social Science Monographs, 1988). Distributed by Columbia University Press.

[28]Brenner, *Faith and Doubt*, p. 122.

[29]Leon Festinger, *A Theory of Cognitive Dissonance* (Stanford: Stanford University Press, 1957).

[30]Ernest Becker, *The Revolution in Psychiatry* (New York: The Free Press, 1964).

[31]Berger, *The Sacred Canopy*; Withnow et al., *Cultural Analysis*.

[32]We have generously drawn from the very useful book by Steven T. Katz, *Post-Holocaust Dialogues* (New York: New York University Press, 1983), in our enumeration of the basic strategies and models used by survivors and theologians to account for God's "behavior" during the Holocaust. Furthermore, it should be clear that survivors usually use these explanatory frameworks in a variety of interrelated and complementary ways.

[33]Berger, *The Sacred Canopy*, p. 74.

[34]See Martin Buber, *Eclipse of God: Studies in the Relation Between Religion and Philosophy* (New York: Harper Torchbooks, 1957).

[35]Brenner, *Faith and Doubt*, p. 98.

[36]*Ibid.*, p. 58.

[37]It should be pointed out, however, that 72 percent of the 780 survivors contacted in Brenner's study thought that the 6 million were destroyed not because of sin, but only because of man's relationship to man, with no connection whatsoever to God, *Faith and Doubt*, p. 225.

[38]Berger, *The Sacred Canopy*, pp. 69, 71.

[39]Emil Fackenheim, *God's Presence in History* (New York: New York University Press, 1970).

[40]Brenner, *Faith and Doubt*, p. 59.

[41]Hannah Arendt, *Hannah Arendt: The Jew as Pariah*, Ron H. Feldman, ed. (New York: Grove Press, 1978), p. 24.

[42]Berger, *The Sacred Canopy*, p. 12.

[43]Becker, *The Revolution in Psychiatry*.

[44]Berger, *The Sacred Canopy*.

[45]*Ibid.*, p. 22.

[46]Brenner, *Faith and Doubt*, pp. 162, 201-202.

[47]Richard L. Rubenstein, *After Auschwitz: Radical Theology and Contemporary Judaism* (Indianapolis: Bobbs-Merrill, 1966). Other scholars agree with the theological dilemma that Rubenstein has sharply raised, however, they do not share his conclusion that "God is Dead." See Katz, *Post-Holocaust Dialogues*, for an overview of the varying responses to the problem of belief in God after the Holocaust.

[48]Elie Wiesel, *Night* (New York: Avon Books, 1958), p. 76.

[49]*Ibid.*, p. 44.

[50]Brenner, *Faith and Doubt*, p. 100.

[51]Martin S. Bergmann and Milton E. Jucovy, *Generations of the Holocaust* (New York: Basic Books, 1982).

[52]Kurt Eissler, "Die Ermordung von wievielen seiner Kinder musi ein Mensch syndrom-,frei, ertragen könen, um eine normale Kunstitution zu haben?" *Psyche* 1 (1963-64): 197-241.

[53]Moises Kijak and Silvio Funtowicz, "The Syndrome of the Survivor of Extreme Situations," *International Review of Psycho-Analysis* 9 (1982): 25-33.

[54]Harvey Barocas, "Children of Purgatory: Reflections on the Concentration Camp Survival Syndrome," *International Journal of Social Psychiatry* 21 (1974\5): 87-92.

[55]Henry Krystal, "Integration and Self-Healing in Post-traumatic States," in Luel and Marcus, eds., *Psychoanalytic Reflections on the Holocaust: Selected Essays*, pp. 113-134.

[56]Henry Krystal, ed., *Massive Psychic Trauma* (New York: International Universities Press, 1968). There are a few psychoanalysts who have reported more favorable results in their work with survivors. See, for example, Ornstein, "Survival and Recovery"; Klein, "The Survivor's Search"; Emmanuel Dewind, "Persecution, Aggression and Therapy," *International Journal of Psychoanalysis* 53 (1972): 173-178; Edith Gyomroi, "The Analysis of a Young Concentration Camp Victim," *Psychoanalytic Study of the Child* 18 (1963): 484-510.

[57]Ernest Becker, *Angel in Armor: A Post-Freudian Perspective on the Nature of Man* (New York: Braziller, 1969), p. 80.

[58]Ornstein, "Survival and Recovery"; also Frankl, *Man's Search*.

[59]Henry Krystal, "Trauma and Effects," *Psychoanalytic Study of the Child* 33 (1978); Krystal, *Integration and Self-Healing: Affect Trauma and Alexithymia* (Hillsdale: The Analytic Press, 1988).

[60]Becker, *Revolution in Psychiatry*.

[61]William G. Niederland, "The Survivor Syndrome: Further Observations and Dimensions," *Journal of the Psychoanalytic Association* 29 (1981): 413-426.

[62]Edward Bibring, "The Mechanism of Depression," in Phyllis Greenacre, ed., *Affective Disorders* (New York: International Universities Press, 1953).

[63]Becker, *Revolution*, p. 111.

[64]*Ibid.*, p. 112.

[65]*Ibid.*, p. 113.

[66]Becker, *Angel*, p. 85.

[67]*Ibid.*

[68]Henry Krystal and William G. Niederland, eds., *Psychic Traumatization* (Boston: Little Brown and Company, 1971).

[69]Ornstein, "Survival and Recovery," p. 128.

[70]Krystal, "Integration and Self-Healing."

[71]Becker, *Revolution*, p. 178.

[72]Brenner, *Faith and Doubt*.

[73]Ornstein, "Survival and Recovery."

[74]Brenner, *Faith and Doubt*, p. 49.

[75]George Atwood and Robert Stolorow, *Structures of Subjectivity: Explorations in Psychoanalytic Phenomenology* (Hillside: Analytic Press, 1984).

[76]*Ibid.*

[77]Jean Améry, in a powerful essay, comments on the effect of torture on the Holocaust survivor. What is lost in torture, Améry contends, is trust in the world. "At the first blow...this trust...breaks down. The other person, *opposite*...with whom I can exist only as long as he does not touch my skin surface as border, forces his own corporeality on me with his first blow. He is on me and thereby destroys me." *At the Mind's Limits: Contemplations by a Survivor on Auschwitz and its Realities*, p. 28.

[78]Ornstein, "Survival and Recovery."

[79]Erik E. Erikson, *Childhood and Society* (New York: W. W. Norton and Company, 1963).

[80]Krystal, "Integration and Self-Healing."

[81]Terrence Des Pres, "Preface," in Richard G. Hovannisian, ed., *The Armenian Genocide in Perspective* (New Brunswick: Transaction Books, 1986), p. 17.

[82]*Internet on the Holocaust and Genocide* (Jerusalem, 1987), p. 5.

[83]Erikson, *Childhood and Society*.

[84]*Ibid.*, p. 268.

[85]Erik E. Erikson, *Insight and Responsibility* (New York: W. W. Norton and Company, 1967), p. 133.

[86]George S. Klein, *Theory of Psychoanalysis* (New York: International Universities Press, 1976), p. 231. Quoted in Krystal, "Integration and Healing," p. 122.

[87]*Ibid.*, p. 123.

[88]Irving Greenberg, "Judaism and Christianity After the Holocaust," *Journal of Ecumenical Studies* 18 (1963): 534.

[89]Ernest Becker, *The Birth and Death of Meaning* (New York: The Free Press, 1971), p. 198.

[90]Becker, *Angel in Armor.*

BAPTISTS, JEWS, NAZIS: 1933-1947

Robert W. Ross

The two largest Baptist denominations in the United States in the period 1933-1947, were the Northern Baptist Convention and the Southern Baptist Convention. Both were active members of the Baptist World Alliance, a Congress of worldwide Baptist groups. Both denominations held annual meetings, and participated in the meetings of the Baptist World Alliance, held every five years. Three such meetings were held in the period 1933-1947, in Berlin (1934), in Atlanta, Georgia (1939), and in Copenhagen (1947). The Berlin meeting was delayed one year because of the uncertainties caused by the Nazi party, and Hitler.[1]

This paper will examine what was reported in the minutes of the meetings of these three Baptist organizations regarding the plight of the Jews in Germany under Hitler, and in Europe during Nazi occupation. The Baptist World Alliance was a worldwide network of Baptists; both the Northern and Southern Baptists had missionary workers and connections throughout Europe. Further, the Southern Baptists had a full-time missionary assigned to "Jewish Work." The Reverend Jacob Gartenhaus gave reports of this work to the annual convention of Southern Baptists, 1933-1947.

The General Secretary of the Baptist World Alliance, John H. Rushbrooke from England, had both personal and professional connections throughout Europe. An international statesman, he represented all Baptists, and travelled extensively.[2] Given the connections possible in these three organizations, it may be assumed that they had information available regarding Jews in Germany and Europe during the Nazi era. Two questions may then be asked; what was reported in the conventions? What, if anything was done if there were reports?

In the annual meeting of the Northern Baptist Convention for 1933, there appeared the following statement.

> We deplore the outbreak of race hatred and discrimination, as seen in our own country, and in the persecution of the Jews in Germany, and we call on followers of the Son of Man to show forth his spirit of justice and goodwill to all.[3]

In 1934, a committee report was made in relation to Northern Baptist participation in the Federal Council of Churches of Christ in America. The subject was the Church struggle in Germany, involving Protestant ministers. The report includes the following:

> Vigorous support has been given to the group of protesting pastors in Germany who have insisted upon maintaining the freedom of the church and who are resisting the application of the so-called Aryan paragraph to the church. The encouragement given by the American churches through the Council to the German pastors in their heroic struggle is heartening evidence of the growing world solidarity of Protestantism.[4]

At the same convention in 1934, a resolution was adopted under the heading of "Church and State" which included a general reference to "Christians and Jews." There was nothing more specific.[5]

From this year through the year 1938, there is no mention of Jews in the minutes of the annual meetings of the Northern Baptist Convention. In 1939, the subject of the plight of the Jews reappears, in two contexts. The first is in relation to anti-Semitism in the United States, and in the same resolution, in conjunction with Christians in Germany and Russia "...who suffer disabilities for religions' sake;..." to which is added "...Jews in Germany and other lands, who are enduring sore persecution." A report was made to the 1939 Convention on race, but no mention of Jews is to be found in the report. It concerns only Negroes.[6]

In 1940, the Northern Baptists in Convention received a long report on Race, and on Moral Issues. Later, a long statement on International Relations appeared. In none of these reports is there mention of Jews, though an appeal is included to aid refugees. The silence about Jews continued in 1941. Reference to race refer only to Negroes.

In 1942, the minutes of the Northern Baptist Convention contain references to the internment of Japanese Americans on the West Coast, Chinese students stranded in the United States because of the war, and concerns about post-war issues, but no mention of Jews is included either in the United States or in Europe. While addressing many issues brought on by WWII in 1943 such as food shortages, the needs of children in occupied Europe, the problems caused by rationing and relief to suffering people generally, again no mention is made of Jews either in the United States or in Europe. This is interesting because it is now known that this information was readily available in newspapers and in the religious press.[7] 1944 is equally devoid of any mention of the plight of the Jews and again, such information was widely dispersed in the press and elsewhere.

Because of wartime restrictions on travel, there was no Convention in 1945. Instead there was a meeting of the General Council in Chicago, May 21-23, 1945. The war in Europe was over. Information about the Concentration Camps in Europe was being published dramatically in news magazines and newspapers and by radio. The feelings of horror and revulsion were filling editorial pages, news columns and photo pages which were filled with scenes from the Camps. Gas chambers, unburied dead, emaciated bodies and crematoria were there for all to see. Yet the minutes of the General Council are silent. No mention is made of the plight of the Jews. The minutes of the first post-war meeting of the denomination do mention the cooperation with the Baptist World Alliance in relief work in Europe, but it is May, 1946. Social ills, race relations, peace-time conscription, conscientious objection, food for the starving, the United Nations, the atomic bomb, atomic energy, and relations with the Vatican are issues that appear in these minutes, but no mention of Jews anywhere. Why, in the crucial years immediately after WWII was there no mention of Jews? It is possible to speculate, but the truth is plainly evident. As reflected in its minutes, the Northern Baptist Convention had nothing official to say about what had happened or what was happening to Jews in Europe, victims of the Nazi regime. The silence speaks for itself. Comparisons can be made with other denominations and nonreligious groups; the silence remains its own commentary for Northern Baptists, now the American Baptist Churches of the USA.[8]

The Southern Baptist Convention also met annually, and published the minutes of its meetings. In 1933, a brief mention of Jews appeared as a part of a discussion on International Relations. The reference is to what is called a "counter-revolution" in Germany "...resulting in the unwarranted persecution of Jews, and other distracting conditions -- these are some of the disquieting conditions prevailing throughout the world."[9] In 1934 Southern Baptist missionaries in Syria/Palestine reported

> The influx of German Jews within the past year has opened another door of service for our Master. The suffering of these people has made them more ready to listen to the truth. We have already come in contact with these people and feel that their hearts are good soil for the seed.[10]

No mention of Jews in Germany was made by Jacob Gartenhaus, missionary to the Jews in his report to the convention in 1934. Nor was there mention of Jews in the reports to the Convention in 1935, or in 1936. It should be noted at this point that the widely publicized resignation of James G. McDonald as High Commissioner for Refugees (and Others), in relation to the League of Nations is mentioned neither in the Northern nor Southern Baptist Convention minutes for 1936.[11] 1937 continues the silence concerning Jews.

In 1938, concern for Jews in Germany appears in the report of Gartenhaus, Field Secretary for Jewish Work for the Southern Baptist Convention. Under the title "Praying for Jerusalem," Gartenhaus quoted a text from Jeremiah 37.3, then wrote,

> If there ever was a time when Israel needed the prayers of God's people it is today. As I pen these lines they are passing through one of the greatest tragedies in their history, as if their cup of sorrow has not already been filled with millions starving in Poland and the fate of hundreds of thousands in Germany hanging in the balance, not to mention their suffering in Rumania and Palestine. Now, overnight these brutalities have

extended into Austria. Complete elimination of the Jews from the life of the community is launched. 'Perish Judea' is the cry there with increasing frequency, and perishing indeed they are.

Gartenhaus then goes on to describe suicides in Vienna, and the Jews in Austria as "destitute, undernourished, despised, afflicted and disconsolate." He then explains how the situation in Austria relates to Jewish evangelism. Wherever he goes, Gartenhaus states, this is the subject he must face. Further, he refers to the "manifesto signed by several hundred clergymen, calling on Christians to oppose the sin of anti-Semitism." He then quotes extensively from the Manifesto.[12]

It is surprising then to note that Gartenhaus does not mention Jews at all in his report for 1939 in light of his fervent statements in 1938. In 1940 this changes. The Reports on Jewish Work will refer to Jews in Germany and Europe with increasing frequency, usually as opening statements. His report for 1940 focuses on what he calls the change in attitude of Jews toward Christ.

> I have been asked the reason for this remarkable change in attitude and I answer: 1. the unprecedented persecution which has caused widespread destruction of Jewish communities throughout Europe leaving millions homeless, starving, tens of thousands slaughtered like cattle, all of which has shattered their hopes for a universal brotherhood.

He then goes on to refer to the many Christian responses to such inhumane treatment, and to Christian organizations formed to aid such refugees.[13]

In 1941, Gartenhaus reported that there was an "Israel awakening" which he attributed to the fact of the Jews' suffering. "Persecution has not relaxed in intensity. Ever increasingly Jews are being annihilated, starved and tortured."[14] In 1942, Gartenhaus reports of "Satanic fury...in all its intensity seeking to wipe the Jews from the face of the earth." He speaks of children dying in the arms of their mothers, and includes a long quotation from the *London Jewish Chronicle* detailing the burying of Jews alive, the ghettoizing of Jews, slave labor for Jews and the unwillingness of nations to take in Jews.[15] In 1943, there was mention of Jews other than in Gartenhaus' report. Noting that race was a problem throughout the world, the "Germanic superiority over all other races and the right and duty of the superior race to dominate, subordinate, or exterminate the inferior races" along with anti-Semitism present in America and race issues concerning both Negroes and Jews were called a continuing problem.[16]

This report concluded with recommendations, one of which calls for "safeguarding the rights of Jews, Negroes and all other minorities."[17] Gartenhaus highlighted what was happening to Jews in his report for 1943. He writes of millions of Jews who have been left homeless and starving and that 2,000,000 Jews will be exterminated "...before the end of the year." He also reports an eyewitness account of the massacre of Jews in Minsk, 72,000 in all, 35,000 in one day.

His report also includes a long quotation from one W. W. Gauld, delivered before the General Assembly of the Church of Scotland in which Gauld describes Jews as "...; the scapegoat of tyranny and the perplexity of democracy,..."[18]

In 1944, Gartenhaus makes a very strange statement in his report, by indirection. There is no detailed account as before, but a quotation from Habakkuk 1:5, then ("If God's people sin they must expect punishment.") The implication is, that God is punishing the Jews, particularly in Europe for "their sin." In support of this idea, Gartenhaus states, "In their four thousand year history has God ever dealt with Israel as He is now dealing with them?" He then says, "Newspapers, magazines and the radio tell of the cold-blooded systematic murder of hundreds of thousands of Jews."[19]

In 1945, a report on race was again presented to the Convention. The report identifies four groups, under "race." They are Jews, Indians, Japanese and Negroes. These are racial groups "...sharply distinguished from the rest of the population,..." After generalizations about religion, and physical differences the report then states that the real concern is with Negroes. No more mention is made of Jews, particularly Jews in Europe. As for Gartenhaus, his 1945 report mentions the continuation of mass killings, mentioning Nazi doctors who were using injections as a killing method. "Some four million Jews have been disposed of in one way or another and those who have not been able to escape the clutches of the enemy await a similar fate." He does mention the Christians of Holland, Belgium and

Norway who worked hard to save Jews and to hide Jews from the Nazis at great risk to themselves.[20]

The minutes of the 1946 Southern Baptist Convention are interesting, simply because it seems as though WWII had never happened. No mention is made anywhere of the conditions under which Jews were living in Europe, nor to DP's, refugees or to post-war problems for Jews. The subject of race was once more addressed, but only concerning Negroes. The Gartenhaus report dealt entirely with the fact that he had completed twenty-five years as a missionary to Jews for the Southern Baptist denomination.[21]

The meeting of the Congress of the Baptist World Alliance for 1934 was held in Berlin, August 4-10. It was widely reported in the religious press in the United States.[22] The minutes were published. Each item of procedure or business was assigned a number. Item #163, was a resolution presented on August 10, by Professor A. T. Ohrn of Norway on Racialism. One part reads,

> This Congress deplores and condemns as a violation of the law of God the Heavenly Father, all racial animosity, and every form of oppression or unfair discrimination toward the Jews, toward coloured people, or toward subject races in any part of the world.[23]

Commission #1 reported on Nationalism at some length. There was no mention of Jews. Commission #2 reported on Racialism. Jews were mentioned in relation to the Arab-Jewish tension in Palestine, in relation to anti-Semitism, and in relation to Christianity. "...among all the other faiths in the world, there is none for which we have more reverent honour than for that of the Jew,..." The speaker went on to condemn "...the record of ill-usage of Jews on the part of professedly Christian nations."[24]

The Rev. F. Fullbrandt of Germany in his address, "The Religious Situation in Russia" included the following.

> Perhaps none have seen more clearly the dangers of Bolshevism for the church and for democracy than have the National Socialists in Germany. Adolph Hitler from a purely political standpoint, has entered upon the tasks and solved the problems in a way which shames us as members of the Churches. What the churches ought long ago to have done, a politician has taken from our hand, inasmuch as he has dealt with conditions which the energy of a strong inner light ought to have tackled and overcome.[25]

In no other reports or speeches to the Congress was the subject of Jews addressed, other than in the report mentioned above on Racialism. There seems to have been a sort of tacit agreement that no one would raise questions about Jews in Germany under the Nazis thereby embarrassing the German Baptists who had worked so hard to bring the Congress to Berlin.[26]

The Sixth World Congress of the Baptist World Alliance was held July 22-28 in Atlanta, Georgia. It was a different world, and a different location. Among the resolutions adopted by the Congress was one on Racialism. A part of this resolution reaffirms the statement adopted by the 1934 Congress held in Berlin:

> This Congress deplores and condemns as a violation of the law of God the Heavenly Father, all racial animosity, and every form of oppression or unfair discrimination toward the Jews, toward coloured people, or toward subject races in any part of the world.[27]

#109 in the Minutes reads, "The Rev. J. Cocutz of Rumania delivered an address on 'The Best for Christ.'" #110 reads, "At the close of the address, the chairman called on the audience to rise in support of a message of sympathy for the Rumanians, and especially the Christian Jews."[28]

John H. Rushbrooke, the General Secretary addressed the Congress, his official report. His was titled, "Between Berlin and Atlanta. Five Years of the History of the Baptist World Alliance." In recalling Berlin, he said,

> Nor can we forget the effect of our resolution on racial discrimination. The Jews of America and Britain and other lands publicly thanked us; in Eastern Europe they went further by thanking God in their synagogues for the witness Baptists had borne. It means much when a great religious communion finds itself able spontaneously, without ifs or buts, without tacit reserve or compromise, to utter its judgment in the hearing of the world.[29]

Dr. Gilbert Laws of Norwich, England addressed the Congress on "The Present Crisis and Evangelical Religion." He spoke first of the limitations imposed in Russia on religious practice, then, he said, "In another great country the church has been in the gravest difficulties through its connection with the state." Without ever naming Germany, the context makes it clear that this is who he was referring to.

> Moreover, this permitted and tolerated church must be limited by race-barriers. It must be closed against the very people (the

Jews) through whom the gospel first came to us, and of whom, according to the flesh, Christ himself came. A doctrine of racial pride and racial hatred entirely forbidden by the gospel is imposed on the minister of Christ. Any refusal to tune the pulpit to these unchristian notes of pagan conceit and race-hatred can bring condign punishment upon the preacher bold enough to make such refusal. Any contention for the full authority of the Lord Jesus Christ in the church called by His name lands the preacher in a concentration camp.[30]

In his address on the Totalitarian State, the Rev. M. E. Aubrey of London mentioned Martin Niemoller twice, as well as German pastors who resisted the Nazis and the Church Struggle. He did not mention Jews.[31]

A brief glimpse of the problems of Baptists in Germany in 1939 was given in an address by Prediger Paul Schmidt. In his "liberalism, Collectivism and the Baptists" he made the classic argument from Paul's letter to the Romans about being subject to the authority under which one lives.

Thus Paul did not meddle with the affairs of the Graeco-Roman world or empire, but asked the Christians individually and the Church collectively to be subject to the existing order in state and nation within the Graeco-Roman empire as unto God ordained powers.

He then went on to say,

The dilemma which results from this fact is world destiny; it is the fulfillment of the Biblical view of history. These insights will not lead us to a position of resignation, but we shall firmly face the facts and do what the doctor does, who even then tries his best when he sees the catastrophe before his eyes.

He then stated that the Baptists in Germany had little choice but to accept these principles.

Our Baptist brethren should not look on this attitude as being narrow or insignificant. The Churches of Baptists in Germany assume this attitude, and they stand forth in missionary power and are entering through open doors.[32]

The next address was entitled, "Civil and Religious Freedom, World Peace." Professor William A. Mueller of the United States spoke about the Baptists in Germany and Europe. He compared the current situation to what he thought Oncken and the founders of the Baptist Church in Germany might have done. "I wonder if this early passion is still alive." He went on,

Today it seems to us on this side of the Atlantic that the Baptists of Germany have too easily adapted themselves to the prevailing spirit....Thus far, we have not heard a clear word from our Baptist brethren in Germany concerning the racial problem that is a burning issue in your land as well as ours.[33]

There were other criticisms as well, but this one spoke directly to the racial policies in Germany in 1938-1939.

Finally, in his address to the Young People's Business Meeting of the Sixth Congress, the Rev. T. G. Dunning told of a German Jewish man who was about to enter a concentration camp. He secured a permit to go to Belgium as a refugee, but had no funds. "But he was known to the young Baptists of another land, who, on hearing of his peril, wired £10 to him, and ultimately brought him to their own land and provided employment and a good home for him." He cited another case where young Baptists assisted a family to leave Germany for South America by raising £200. The subject of his address was, "International Contacts Through the Youth Committee of the Alliance."[34]

In 1947 the Baptist World Alliance once again met in Copenhagen, Denmark. Denmark had been directly under Nazi domination during the occupation, and had gained special recognition for her rescue of Jews. The memory of the occupation lingered on with a number of the welcoming addresses making reference to the five years under the Nazis.[35] The first reference even vaguely related to Jews appears on page 47 of the Minutes. The reference is to "race hatred and pride," and then mentions the DP camps. This raises the interesting question that I. F. Stone and Helen Warin raised at the end of WWII, that is the inability of the Allies to deal with Jews as Jews.[36] They became DP's, refugees, internees, never Jews. The person mentioning the DP's was the new General Secretary, Walter D. Lewis, who succeeded Rushbrooke who was deceased.

The Rev. J. Pious Barber of Chester, Pa. addressed the Congress on "The Colour Bar in the Light of the New Testament." He referred to Jews twice. He states, "With the Jew it is a race question, but not a colour question." Later he mentions a visit he made to Palestine. "I saw men and women refugees emaciated, crushed."[37] Nothing more. The report of the General Secretary for Baptist relief efforts after WWII mentions only relief provided to needy Baptists in Europe, including "Baptist displaced persons."

Dr. Edwin A. Bell, Representative in Europe of the American Baptist Foreign Missionary Society spoke on "conditions in Europe." His opening paragraph was devoted entirely to Displaced Persons.

> They have been living in camps in Germany, Austria, and Italy for four, five and some of them six years. I cannot describe their plight in detail, but they are victims of circumstances which they did little or nothing to create....They are in virtual bondage, and tragically illustrate further, that the battle for human liberties is yet to be won, and that the Christian doctrine of man faces as serious a challenge in our times as it has ever faced in human history.

The remainder of his report details the needs in Germany and Poland, and the assistance coming from groups in and outside of Europe and how much remained to be done.[38]

At this point in the proceedings, the name of Dr. Jacob Gartenhaus appears. As a delegate to the Congress he presented a resolution "moved seconded and passed unanimously." #155 was a "Resolution concerning Jews." It reads in part,

> Aware of the unprecedented suffering through which the people of Israel have passed in recent years, millions of them being exterminated by the most inhuman means; aware also that these sufferings are not yet at an end, but that hundreds of thousands are still in concentration camps or wandering homeless from land to land; aware further, that the poisonous propaganda and destructive designs of antisemitism are still at work in many lands: this Congress puts on record its sense of sorrow and shame that such conditions prevail.

The resolution calls on Baptists for aid, for open doors from the nations of the world for refugees, and "...upon Jewry everywhere to refrain from provocative acts and to restrain those among them who would resort to violence." It closes with an appeal to support missionary work among Jews. Gartenhaus was consistent with his personal call.[39]

The most touching address was that of Director Eberhard Schroeder. A Baptist layman from Germany, he spoke on "The Responsibilities of Baptist Laymen." He opened "...by starting with the present situation in Germany." He continued,

> First of all, however, I cannot but thank you that a German representative is allowed to speak at all. The whole world has suffered so much from the terrible war of which our nation is

guilty that we are outlaws everywhere. I thank you that I am able to speak here as a brother in Christ.

It must be said that his address contained nothing about Jews, but it vividly reflected the condition in Germany at the time.[40] His statement was one of the few expressing the feeling of guilt and shame felt by Germany for her part in WWII. That Schroeder is a layman speaking for laymen is evident. He had been asked to speak by Rushbrooke. All of his internal references are to what laymen were doing as active Baptists in post-war Germany.[41]

The questions asked at the beginning can now be addressed, though the answers might be less than satisfactory. To the first one, what was reported in the annual minutes of the three Baptist organizations, the answer is quite a lot, but not nearly enough. The Northern Baptist Convention for several years reported nothing about what was happening to Jews in Germany. In fact, from 1935 through 1938, it was as though neither Hitler nor Germany existed. Issues of race were addressed by both major Baptist denominations in their annual conventions. But race meant Negroes, seldom if ever were Jews included.

As the years of the war came, more information did appear in the minutes about Jews, but never as a major issue central to the Conventions. This is best illustrated by the reports of Gartenhaus to the Southern Baptists, beginning in 1938. A Jew, and a convert to Christianity, he was responsible for Jewish work, or the Jewish Department in the denomination. In 1946 he reported that he had been in this position for twenty-five years. Yet, reading his reports, the information given about what was happening to Jews in Germany and Europe from 1938, was always subordinated to his main concern, evangelism among Jews in the United States. At one point, as noted above, Gartenhaus suggests that what was happening to Jews was punishment from God "for their sins." That Gartenhaus does not mention either the Jews in general or the 6,000,000 who were victims of the Nazi years in his report in 1946 is startling. Equally shocking is his lack of attention to the incredibly difficult time post-war European Jews were having at the hands of the Allied governments, in their efforts either to find refuge either in the West or in British-held Palestine.

And what about the Southern Baptists without Gartenhaus? Even less would have been reported than was reported to the Northern Baptists. Yet Gartenhaus must be placed in context. He was a convert to Christianity. This made it difficult for him to have access to the Jewish community, as he acknowledged. Further, his appointment within the Southern Baptist denomination was specifically for evangelistic work among Jews. He was totally committed to attempting to win Jews to personal faith in Jesus Christ through literature distribution, personal contact, public meetings and evangelistic meetings to which Jews would be invited. He travelled widely, missing attendance at one Convention because he was travelling. This meant speaking to Southern Baptist congregations, also to gain support for his work.

This meant that what he reported about the plight of the Jews in Germany and Europe was always secondary to the major purposes for his reports, to engender interest in and support for his work among Jews in the United States. This is not unusual. In some religious periodicals published in the period 1933-1946, there were paid advertisements from missionary agencies involved in "Jewish evangelism" both in the United States and in Europe. These paid ads included information concerning the Jewish plight in Germany and Europe. Invariably, however, the main purpose for the ads was to raise funds for continuing missionary effort.[42] The purpose for Gartenhaus was similar, to encourage denominational support for this effort. He asked for more workers from time to time; he requested more funds. Did he include information about the plight of the Jews, particularly after 1942? Yes he did. What were the results? As with the Northern Baptists, resolutions were passed and calls for prayer were made. Additionally, both denominations linked the Jews with minority problems worldwide, generalizing the problem thus blurring the focus on Jews in Germany and Europe.

No specific course of action was ever presented to either Convention. When it would have been possible to intervene even slightly, 1933-1938, there is no indication of concern. The minutes of both denominations are silent. Further, the Northern Baptist Convention was a member denomination of the Federal Council of Churches of Christ in America. This Council made many attempts to intervene in the early Nazi years, but no mention of this fact appears in the minutes.[43] The Southern Baptists were not members of the Council.

As for the Baptist World Alliance the situation was somewhat different. First, it met only every five years. Second, it was a Congress of all Baptist groups, with no direct jurisdiction over any member. Third, its General Secretary was resident in England. He was much more attuned to situations developing in Europe than were Baptists in America. Fourth, a close reading of the reports of John Rushbrooke, the General Secretary in 1934 and 1939, reveals that he had a large personal network throughout the world. He was a frequent visitor to European nations. In the memorial addresses given at the 1947 Congress, mention was made of his high standing throughout Europe. Fifth, elsewhere, it can be shown that Rushbrooke made special efforts to learn what he could about the accuracy of what he was hearing about Jews under the Nazis, particularly in 1941-1942.[44]

As for reports to the Congress, it can be shown that the question of persecution of Jews by the Nazis was a delicate one, particularly in 1934 when the meeting was held in Berlin. In a series of articles in *The Christian Century* Conrad Moehlman raised questions about whether Baptists in Germany could speak freely on the subject of Jews and persecution.[45] German Baptists, as evidenced in their remarks to the Congress, seemed especially sensitive to this issue, but they did not want it raised prominently. After the Congress ended, this issue was discussed at length in a number of articles in the religious press in the United States.[46]

In Atlanta in 1939, the situation in Europe was much different. The problem of location did not hinder or preclude discussion as had happened in Berlin. The issue was then raised quite directly. One speaker, Professor Mueller, spoke to his German Baptist brethren directly about their acquiescence to German racial policies.[47] It is true that Rushbrooke, in his Atlanta report, went to some lengths to speak about what he believed to have been a strong stand for Jews in the Berlin Congress. He cited responses from the Jewish community to support his contention.[48]

But again, while the Atlanta discussion was more direct, the offered solutions did not change. Resolutions were adopted; prayers made. That more direct action was near impossible at this late stage is correct; that nothing could have been done at all is more problematical. Jews were being ghettoized; concentration camps were being enlarged and filled; slave labor was in place. Euthanasia was being practiced in Germany, and the situation for Jews in Germany had deteriorated beyond anything yet experienced prior to July, 1939 when the Baptist World Alliance was meeting in Atlanta. These things were known in more detail than was thought at the time.[49] Yet the Congress seems not to have made the Jewish plight a central issue. The speech critical of German Baptists for the failure to speak out in behalf of Jews, is even more critical of German Baptists for their failure to speak out against restrictions on literature distribution, freedom to speak in the streets, to witness in public places and participate in public life as Baptists. They were accused of being more accepting of Nazi-imposed restrictions than Baptists are traditionally supposed to be.[50]

By 1947 the evidence was in. The Nazi terror was over. Hitler was dead, Germany was defeated and devastated, and the whole world was reeling from the war and its consequences. Among the greatest casualties were 6,000,000 Jews, and among the living there were Jews still confined to concentration camps because there was no place for them to go. But Jewish identity was not specified because the term Displaced Person had become the common identifier for all still in the camps.

The problem of DP's was a subject that was discussed in the Congress of the Baptist World Alliance in 1947. But Jews were not specified, or particularized as having special needs. There was expressed concern for some 10,000 Germans returning to Germany, *Volkdeutsche* who were said to be Baptists.

Dachau, Lidice, the Gestapo prison in Prague and Warsaw are mentioned in an address to the Congress on "Conditions in Europe" but there is no mention of Jews as Jews in relation to the above-named sites. The Gartenhaus resolution that was adopted, does make specific reference to Jews, including noting those still in camps, and wandering as homeless throughout Europe. Yet even these mentions are subordinated to Gartenhaus and his commitment to evangelization among Jews.[51]

Here then are the official records of these three Baptist organizations, meeting in Convention. For two of them the meetings were held annually;

for the third, once every five years. The official minutes recorded in these meetings reflect the official business and concerns of these three Baptist groups. What these minutes convey is a singular lack of concern for Jews under the Nazis. When direct action might have been possible early in the Nazi era, nothing was done. No effort to influence official policy by governments, contact agencies of the United States government or put pressure on the Congress in behalf of Jews was made. Intervention in behalf of Jews just was not done, early or late.

ENDNOTES

[1]See Robert W. Ross, *So it was True, The American Protestant Religious Press and the Nazi Persecution of the Jews.* Minneapolis, Minnesota, The University of Minnesota Press, 1980, pp. 49-67.

[2]*The Baptist World Alliance, Official Report,* "Report of the General Secretary," 1934, 1939, various.

[3]*Annual of the Northern Baptist Convention,* 1934, p. 238.

[4]*Ibid.,* p. 174. The Aryan paragraph refers to paragraph 4 of the decree announced on April 7, 1933, "Law for the Restoration of the Professional Civil Service," which removed Jews from their Civil Service positions. This was the first of some 400 such anti-Jewish decrees. See "Lucy S. Dawidowicz, *The War Against the Jews,* 1933-1945. New York, Holt, Rinehart and Winston, 1975, pp. 58ff; Raul Hilberg, *The Destruction of the European Jews.* New York, Harper Colophon Books, 1961, pp. 5ff; Ross, *So it was True,* p. 3 and various.

[5]*Ibid.,* p. 194.

[6]*Ibid.,* 1939,pp. 270, 271.

[7]See: Ross, *So it was True*; Deborah Lipstadt, *Beyond Belief: The American Press and the Coming of the Holocaust,* 1933-1945. New York, Free Press, 1986; David S. Wyman, *The Abandonment of the Jews: America and the Holocaust,* 1941-1945. New York, Pantheon Books, 1984.

[8]The Northern Baptist Convention became the American Baptist Convention in 1950, and the American Baptist Churches of the USA in 1972, (ABC/USA).

[9]*Annual of the Southern Baptist Convention,* 1934, pp. 107-108.

[10]*Ibid.,* p. 238.

[11]See Ross, *So it was True,* pp. 84-87.

[12]*Annual of the Southern Baptist Convention,* 1938, pp. 292-293.

[13]*Ibid.,* 1940, p. 296.

[14]*Ibid.,* 1941, p. 312.

[15]*Ibid.,* 1942, p. 274.

[16]*Ibid.*, 1943, p. 107.

[17]*Ibid.*, 1943, p. 109.

[18]*Ibid.*, 1943, pp. 245, 248.

[19]*Ibid.*, 1944, p. 304.

[20]*Ibid.*, 1945, pp. 96-97, 291-292.

[21]*Ibid.*, 1946, pp. 326-329.

[22]Ross, *So it was True*, pp. 49-67.

[23]*Fifth Baptist World Congress: Official Report*, 1934, 17.

[24]*Ibid.*, 1934, p. 41.

[25]*Ibid.*, 1934, pp. 154-159: see 159.

[26]For a discussion of this matter, see: Ross, *So it was True*, pp. 48-69.

[27]*Sixth Baptist World Congress: Official Report*, 1939, p. 15.

[28]See Glossary, Ross, *So it was True*, p. 311, for an explanation of the term "Christian Jew" or "Hebrew Christian."

[29]*Sixth Baptist World Congress: Official Report*, 1939, p. 38.

[30]*Ibid.*, p. 191.

[31]*Ibid.*, pp. 198-199.

[32]*Ibid.*, pp. 204-205.

[33]Professor William A. Mueller, "Baptist Emphasis East and West of the Atlantic" in *Ibid.*, 1939, pp. 207-209, 208.

[34]*Ibid.*, 1939, pp. 240-241.

[35]*Seventh Baptist World Congress: Official Report*, 1947, p. 7.

[36]*Ibid.*, 1947, p. 47. See also: Leonard Dinnerstein, *America and the Survivors of the Holocaust*. New York, Columbia University Press, 1982; Helen Warin, *The Buried Lie Screaming*. New York, The Beechhurst Press, 1948; I.F. Stone, *Underground to Palestine*. New York, Pantheon Books, 1946 and 1978.

[37]*Seventh Baptist World Congress: Official Report*. 1947, p. 78.

[38]*Ibid.*, 1947, p. 79.

[39]*Ibid.*, 1947, p. 99.

[40]*Ibid.*, 1947, pp. 124-128.

[41]*Ibid.*

[42]See "Paid Advertising" in a number of places in Ross, *So it was True.* Example, p. 161.

[43]Ross, *So it was True.* See under Federal Council, Index, p. 368.

[44]Ross, *So it was True,* the letter from Rabbi J. H. Hertz to John Rushbrooke, p. 163.

[45]Ross, *So it was True,* pp. 48-50.

[46]*Ibid.*, pp. 55-67.

[47]*Sixth Baptist World Congress: Official Report,* pp. 208-209.

[48]*Ibid.*

[49]See: Ross, *So it was True*; Lipstadt, *Beyond Belief*; Wyman, *The Abandonment of the Jews;* A. D. Morse, *While Six Million Died: A Chronicle of American Apathy.* New York, Random House, 1968.

[50]*Sixth Baptist World Congress: Official Report,* 1939, p. 191.

[51]*Seventh Baptist World Congress: Official Report,* 1947, p. 80.

GYÖRGY KÁDÁR'S DRAWINGS AS ARTISTIC NARRATIVE

Beverly Asbury

György Kádár, the Hungarian Jewish artist who survived Auschwitz and four other camps, has stated time and again that his drawings speak for him. He prefers not to discuss the Holocaust. "My art speaks," he says, and he insists that its nature is "documentary." By that, he surely means, at least, that he sees his drawings as representational in style. Though the art that he has done professionally since 1946, is, for the most part, abstract and non-representational, he reserves the representational/documentary style for expressing the Holocaust. That is true of his Holocaust narrative of 1945-46, as well as the second one he finished in 1989. As a survivor, he seems to have known from the time of his liberation that the "facts" of the Holocaust had to be "documented," they had to be communicated. It was as "natural" for him to turn to art as it was for Elie Wiesel or Primo Levi to turn to memoir or fiction or essay. Kádár's expression is one of artistic narrative, a representation of experience: it is not a rational or historical analysis. He sees his drawings documenting the ways in which he and others experienced the Holocaust.

He depicts several events which were not directly experienced by him. These drawings, of which there are seven or eight in the total collection of fifty-seven, are based on what he was told or on what was commonly believed, or a matter of general knowledge in the camps. For example, he made his way from Buchenwald back to Budapest just over three months after V.E. Day, and he searched relentlessly and persistently for information about his family. What he learned is reflected in three drawings: #6 *My Relatives Are in the Gas Chambers*; #39 *My Wife and Her Parents Were Executed on the Banks of the Danube in Budapest*; and #57 *My Brother Was Killed in the Last Hours before Liberation*.

#6 "My Relatives Are in the Gas Chamber"

#39 "My Wife and Her Parents Were Executed on the Banks of the Danube in Budapest"

#57 "My Brother Was Killed in the Last Hours before Liberation"

There are also drawings which are not matters of documenting objective facts. Instead, they represent inner states; they reveal the subjective feelings of those experiencing the incomprehensible reality. One drawing presents his own recurring nightmare; #24 *Selected for Death.* Another drawing documents the shock of liberation while still in the camp and before a return to whatever world of life is left "out there," "somewhere," "maybe." #55 *And Where Now?*

Kádár gives us an artistic narrative. Much of it can be correlated with historical documents. That is, some of his drawings have a factuality about them, and they can be verified to the satisfaction of historians and other research scholars. But the real power of his drawings derives from more than factuality. The power lies in his story, in artistic narrative, in the ways facts have been filtered and mediated through his eyes, his seeing.

Kádár's drawings both permit and compel the viewer to come to see the Holocaust, because the drawings make credible what might be otherwise incredible if left to factual presentation. Kádár depicts events that most of humanity, born since 1950, would be largely unable to imagine. His work contains evidence of the Holocaust, but its greatest contribution to our understanding comes from his portraying what he and others experienced. His artistic narrative complements and extends written narratives, and it adds a dimension to our understanding, a dimension for which it is difficult to find a word.

What is it, then, that we have here? While Kádár rarely depicts himself, it is surely Kádár himself who imparts power to this narrative. The fact of his experience gives a context of actuality and authenticity. The power comes from what he as survivor and artist creates in this story. The artist has created from his experiences as a victim a story into which we, the viewers, can and do enter.

Take note of the fact that Hungarians were open to his narrative in the winter of 1946, and demanded a second exhibit in the spring of 1947. It is, in a sense, a tribute to how compelling Kádár's narrative is that the Hungarian political climate did not permit another exhibition after that time. His drawings were kept on the floor of a dark closet in his Budapest flat for forty years. The authorities of that nation and others of the Soviet bloc had

#24 "Selected for Death"

#55 "And Where Now?"

replaced an openness to the Holocaust with four decades of denial of the murder of European Jewry. Even now, anti-Judaic feeling persists in Hungary, but official attitudes have begun to change. Surely, it is no accident of history that the Kádár collection became available to Vanderbilt University in 1987. Kádár had become free again to share his personal understandings, to admit that his Holocaust experiences continued to torment him, and to return to the subject in his art.

However, we have to note some limitations that accompany the depictive power of Kádár's artistic narrative. His is not primarily a Jewish story. Some signs of his being a Jew are present, and there is no denial that it was Jews who were singled out for extermination. Yet, we must depend on other narratives, other memoirs, for understandings of the experiences of Hungarian Jews who were less assimilated and more devotedly observant than Kádár and his family.

Such a caveat is meant only to illustrate how Kádár's narrative is "filtered" or mediated, as all narratives are. In his case, the goal of his narrative is not factuality. What he documents are the experiences of the Holocaust. What he draws has been shaped, edited, explained by his perception, and his perception is, like all human perception, culturally influenced. Therein lies his creativity, his use of personal eyewitness testimony as an artist to filter and mediate experience in such a way as to draw the viewer in as his own contemporary. Kádár has an artist's eye, an inner eye as well as an external one, to see and to allow us to see what he and others have experienced.

Kádár's drawings link facts and experiences into a visionary narrative into which we can enter. There is an intensity about his drawings, and it is worth recalling that he drew from memory, that he drew all fifty-seven within a few months of his liberation while he was still a desperately ill man. There can be no doubt that he was driven to draw by the need to depict, to document, as he would say, what was imprinted so deeply in his memory. Kádár had a will to survive, to give witness, to bear testimony. He was determined to speak, as it were, for those who were no longer alive to tell the story. Kádár seems to have felt that a failure to give us this artistic narrative would be a crime that he could not commit. Kádár's authority arises from his having survived, and he gives that authority to his drawings, an authority and authenticity seemingly more powerful than photographs because of the very subjectivity of his experiences.

Here we might contrast Kádár's drawings with Bruce Carter's excellent "Warsaw Woodcuts." Carter is an American nonwitness who took the narratives of victims and survivors and produced a number of woodcuts that depict scenes from the Holocaust. Carter's work lacks Kádár's immediacy and intensity. It is documentary also, but it is more impersonal. The contrast is analogous to a contrast between a diary and a history text which has used the diary as a source. Carter's work surpasses most attempts in various media to portray the Holocaust, but it illustrates by contrast the power of Kádár as survivor creating an artistic narrative that reaches souls as well as minds.

In writing about survivors in an essay entitled "Survivor As Creator", *The American Poetry Review*, Jan/Feb., 1973, Robert Jay Lifton defines a survivor as "one who has come into contact with death in some bodily or psychic fashion and has himself remained alive." Kádár was immersed in death and was marked in his very existence by it. Out of that immersion he presents a narrative that makes us know and feel that our own existence has also been marked by death. In Lifton's terms, Kádár permits and in fact invites us to become survivors too, and as Lifton so clearly sees, we become "survivors not only of holocausts which have already occurred but of those we imagine or anticipate as well."

Following Lifton, it seems to me that Kádár struggled with his hard-won knowledge of death and gave it shape, grasped his experiences and rendered them significant. He drew for himself as an act of survival. He drew to become free of the death imprint and the death guilt. By reordering his own experiences, he contributes to our seeing the need to reorder our own lives and our own society. His experiential, artistic narrative imparts a special knowledge that can reach everyone. In Lifton's words,

> ....the painful wisdom of the survivor can, at least potentially, become universal wisdom. What I am suggesting is that to 'touch death' and then rejoin the living can be a source of insight and power, and that this is true not only for those exposed to holocaust, or to the death of a parent or lover or

236

friend, but also for those who have permitted themselves to experience fully the 'end of an era,' personal or historical. (Page 40, *American Poetry Review*)

Kádár as artist has given us a narrative, artistic form, for entering and understanding the survivor's struggle with total immersion into death. We are invited to recognize this "death or near-death, pursue it, record it, and enter into it...to learn the truth about ourselves." Lifton goes on to say that such a

capacity for intimacy with (and knowledge of) death in the cause of renewed life is the survivor's special quality of imagination, his special wisdom. (Page 42)

What Kádár has done is not only to call forth powerful imagery but in some degree has mastered it and given it a place in our moral and aesthetic imagination. Having seen Kádár's drawings, having entered his artistic narrative, it is futile to try to dismiss Holocaust imagery from our consciousness. Instead, the Holocaust and Kádár's experiences of it become part of our history, of what we are, and our imagination is stimulated to make the leaps it must make to reorder our lives and to live beyond but not without the curse of mass murder and the vision of total annihilation.

A. M. KLEIN AND MORDECAI RICHLER: THE POETICS OF POST-WAR SELF-EDUCATION IN CANADIAN JEWISH LITERATURE

Rachel Feldhay Brenner

John Milton's *Paradise Lost,* spells out the poem's monumental undertaking to "assert Eternal Providence and justify the ways of God to men."[1] As God's spokesman, the poet, proclaims his absolute trust in the perfection of the divine. In that sense, Milton adheres to Sir Philip Sidney's view of poetry as "an art of imitation ... of the inconceivable excellencies of God," and of the poet as the creator of "a speaking picture" designed to "teach and delight."[2] The poetic tradition pictures the poet as the reader's inspired teacher of God's ways.

This classical view of the poet as a "seer" and interpreter of providence in history highlights the problematics of post-Holocaust poetics. The post-Holocaust poet struggles with the notion of history divested of the divine. Consciousness of history's meaninglessness disqualifies the poet's *raison d'être* of "delightful teaching." In view of the Holocaust, the poet can neither justify God, nor rebel against God's incomprehensibility. The function of poetry is transformed: no longer certain of providential presence, the poet sets out on a path toward self-reeducation.

Wesley A. Kort argues that the crisis in "the religious understanding of history" is "particularly felt by Jewish thinkers for whom the holocaust marks the end of history as the unfolding of divine intention."[3] Alan L. Berger, in his analysis of post-Holocaust Jewish theologians - Emil Fackenheim, Irving Greenberg, and Richard Rubinstein - and their diverse responses to the tragedy, also discerns the ending of an historical era. Berger maintains that "the Holocaust was unique and, consequently, the history of the world must be clearly demarcated into pre- and post-Holocaust periods."[4]

Events of the Holocaust explode the certainty of man's moral progress because they replaced the sacredness of human life by consciousness of human dispensability. The new awareness signals a breach in the poetic tradition. Literature emerging from the consciousness of unprecedented mass-murder has estranged itself from, in Lawrence Langer's terms, "the noble figure that has inspired man's dreams--and his art--for centuries."[5]

The centuries-old narrative of "the noble figure," struggling to implement the ideals of goodness, justice, and morality, has been shattered by another narrative: the story of the Holocaust victim. In view of Holocaust testimony, "the noble figure" has become a meaningless figure of speech and the victim of the atrocity assigns the artist the task of fearful learning rather than that of "delightful teaching." The prophetic teacher of God's truth has become a humble student of a reality which no longer aspires to imitate the divine.

The profundity of the post-Holocaust moral crisis has effected a literary response in communities which did not experience Nazi victimization. Canadian Jewish literature, especially the work of A. M. Klein and Mordecai Richler, offers instructive insight into the painful process of post-Holocaust poetic self-search.

The two writers project polarized ideological and artistic tendencies. A. M. Klein (1909-1972), a prominent Montreal poet, novelist, journalist, and critic, considered the father of Canadian Jewish literature, attempted, in a truly humanistic fashion, to establish viable connections among the Jewish, French, and English ethnic milieux in Quebec. The universal intent of his poetic message and the erudite complexity of his style gained wide recognition in the Canadian literary world. Klein was viewed as the spokesman of the Jewish tradition. Due to illness, Klein ceased to write in the early 1950's, at the time when Mordecai Richler (born in 1931) was starting his writing career. Richler's work has not always elicited approval from his readership. In fact, Richler has often been considered the *enfant terrible* of Canadian letters. His satiric portrayals of Jewish characters have not endeared him to his Jewish compatriots, whereas his dismissive view of Canadian cultural achievements has earned him a controversial status on the Canadian literary scene.

The generational gap and disparate worldviews notwithstanding, both Klein and Richler demonstrate the need to explore the function of art in post-Holocaust reality. For both authors, the legacy of the "banality of evil" forebodes the paralysis of artistic expression: in their work, Holocaust consciousness filters through the theme of arrested creativity and poetic silence. Society, rendered insensate by the extent and form of the catastrophe displays hostile indifference to the artist's need to reaffirm the "forgotten" message of moral sense in human existence. The insistence on exploring the moral ramifications of the Holocaust manifests the desire to restore meaningfulness of art and thus to counteract the nihilistic tendency to obliterate the spiritual.

Both Klein and Richler react to the sense of futility in a world which no longer endorses the principles of justice and compassion. Their work delineates a spectrum whereby the response to post-war nihilism moves from despair to a heroic affirmation of hope and, finally, to an uneasy adjustment couched in compromise. Klein outlines progression from grief and moving into a vision of redemption of the post-war world; Richler's initial global vision of restored human brotherhood eventually reemerges as a possibility of co-existence on a limited, personal level. Whereas Klein's protagonist is able, through a painful confrontation with the reality of suffering, to reconstruct the sense of meaningfulness in history, Richler's protagonist's emotional inability to internalize the history of suffering invalidates the attempt to reestablish faith in humanist values.

Klein's poem "Talisman in Seven Shreds" written in 1932 as a response to the rise of the Nazi party in Germany portrays a world in which God has been replaced with an unfeeling golem. Traditionally, the legendary figure of the golem projects the persecuted Jew's desire for self-defence.[6] Klein, however, uses the golem metaphor to portray the overpowering forces of brutality which threaten the world. The poet conveys a terrifying vision of a soulless, earthy golem as the tyrannical ruler of the world. Man's creation of the idol has invalidated the ideals of justice and beauty; the arrogant assumption that "God is myth"[7] proclaims the world as "the work of golems." (*CP* 135).

In a world that worships brutality and physical strength, the victory of spirituality is by no means certain. In the closing lines the poet conjures a scene which not only depicts the devastation of tyranny, but also outlines the future role of the poet:

> But I will take a prong in hand, and go
> over old graves and test their hollowness:
> be it the spirit or the dust I hoe
> only at doomsday's sunrise will I know.
>
> (*CP* 136)

The Holocaust proved that Klein's pre-Holocaust grotesque picture of the world governed and destroyed by a monstrous tyrant has indeed materialized. In the aftermath of the Holocaust, Klein seems to gravitate toward despair. In "Elegy," written in 1947, (*CP* 291-294) the graveyard scene is poignantly reenacted: the poet, reaching from across the ocean, searches for the dead:

> Oh, through a power of ghosts I walk:
>   through dust
> Seraphical upon the dark winds borne;
> Daily I pass among the sieved white hosts,
> Through clouds of cousinry transgress,
> Maculate with the ashes that I mourn.

Perhaps even more intensely, desparately, the grieving poet seeks God who is "thought-lost" and whose throne is "abstracted." The pleading for "a sign" (*CP* 292) of vengeance remains unanswered; the reference to the Egyptian and Babylonian returned exiles highlights, through an ironic contrast, the absence of divine justice in recent history. In a series of powerful images, Klein registers the fading presence of God in the victims' unanswered cries for help:

> A world is emptied...
> There where Thy people praised
> In angular ecstasy Thy name, Thy Torah
> Is less than a whisper of its thunderclap.
> Thy synagogues, rubble. Thy academies, are silent,
> dark.
> ....
> there
> Is nothing, nothing...only the million echoes
> Calling Thy name still trembling on the air.

Following the long tradition of "Jewish Protestantism," Klein pleads the cause of his people. Like the Chasidic Rabbi Levi Itschak of Berditshev, who drew a circle and promised not to stir from it before God hears him plead his people's innocence,[8] the poet intercedes for his murdered brethren:

> Hear me, who stand
> Circled and winged in the vortex of my kin...

The striking self-image of the poet enveloped in the whirling mass of the dead communicates the intensity of the need to reaffirm God. Furthermore, the image implies total fusion with the dead. In another post-Holocaust lamentation, "Meditation upon Survival" (*CP* 288-289), the poet re-emphasizes his identification with the dead:

> At times, sensing the golgotha'd dead
> run plasma through my veins, and that
>   I must live
> their unexpired six million circuits, giving
> to each of their nightmares my body for a bed
> ....
> I feel their death-wish bubbling the
> channels of my blood-
> ....
> and would almost add my wish
> for the centigrade furnace and the
>   cyanide flood.

The tragedy thus effects not only immense grief and mourning, but a sense of ending for those who survived. God's silence marks all Jews as Holocaust victims. Since the Holocaust demonstrated the worthlessness of human life, the poet feels, both as a human being and a Jew, that he too has been reduced to an inanimate object. In a moment of despair, the poet sketches a bitterly ironic picture of himself as

> "a curio;/
> the atavism of some old coin's face/
> ...What else, therefore, to do

> but leave these bones that are ash to fill-
> O not my father's vault - but the glass-case/
> some proud museum catalogues *Last Jew*." (*CP* 289)

Lament and the sense of ending characterize, however, only one aspect of Klein's response to the tragedy. As a mourner, he is overwhelmed by grief; yet, as a morally accountable spokesman and teacher of both his people and humanity at large, he cannot succumb to despair. Despair signifies creative atrophy, a surrender to the mindless golem.

In *The Hitleriad*, a long satire written in 1942, when the tragedy was beginning to unfold, Klein eloquently reestablishes the role of the poet as a visionary who maps out humanity's road to redemption. The poet sees himself as "the grandson of prophets" who can not "seal his lips against iniquity." (*CP* 186) The poem's opening as a rewritten intertext of Milton's apostrophe to the Muse, however, signals the shifting consciousness of the poetic role vis-á-vis the unprecedented manifestation of human bestiality:

> Heil heavenly muse, since also thou must be
> Like my song's theme, a sieg-heil'd deity,
> Be with me now, but not as once for song:
> Not odes do I indite, indicting Wrong!
> Be with me, for I fall from grace to sin,
> Spurning this day thy proffered hippocrene,
> To taste the poison'd lager of Berlin!
>
> (*CP* 186)

By associating with Milton's epic and dissociating from it at the same time, Klein communicates the break-up of the pre-Holocaust world picture. While Milton concentrates on the formative stages of man's relationship with Providence, Klein focuses on the disintegration of this relationship. The rise of Nazism heralds the emergence of pre-covenantal lawlessness: the destruction of the Jewish people manifests regression to the age of savagery.

In post-Holocaust reality, man can redeem himself and history only through a self-implemented act of justice. Such an act is predicated upon the victim's testimony. The humanist vision of history will continue to unfold only if the testimony of man's both unspeakable inhumanity and unspeakable suffering is acknowledged:

> And let them speak. And let the dead attest
> Their murder and its manner and its cause--
> ....
> Speak out, or neither we, nor they, again
> know rest.
>
> (*CP* 207)

In *The Hitleriad* Klein arrives at the understanding that the future of humanism depends upon the battle waged against silence. Paradoxically, the atrocity which has destroyed the sense of meaningfulness in history must be articulated for meaningfulness to be restored. The victim's silence signifies the victory of the golem; the victim's voice contravenes destruction and reasserts the continuity of both humankind and humanism.

The victim's speech, therefore, performs a crucial educational function; the voice of suffering restores the hope for justice to prevail and thus carries the promise of redemption for the post-Holocaust world. At the same time, the voice vindicates the dead in that it reasserts the viability of Jewish national heritage.

The redemptive function of the testimony is stressed in Klein's only novel, *The Second Scroll* (1951). The novel is based on Klein's own journey to Israel, Europe, and North Africa in 1949. It is a first-person narrative of a young Canadian Jewish poet who sets out to the newly established State of Israel to collect and translate the new Hebrew poetry. At the same time he searches for his European uncle, a Holocaust survivor. On the eve of his departure, however, he gets a letter from his European uncle who, as a Talmudic scholar, disenchanted communist, and Holocaust survivor, characterizes the Jewish Everyman. In a letter sent from a D. P. Camp, Uncle Melech depicts the horrible destruction of the Jewish community in Kamenets, annihilated and buried in a communal grave. At the same time, the letter identifies the Canadian Jew as a Holocaust survivor. Melech tells his nephew that

> ...we were all in that burning world, even you
> who were separated from it by the Atlantic--
> that futile bucket.[9]

The letter sets the nephew on a quest for his Uncle, a quest which eventually not only brings him to Israel, but also makes him realize his own ethnic roots and history. Arthur A. Cohen, who acknowledged Klein's poetic prescience among the authors who "were writing well before the historical and theological categories of understanding the Holocaust had even been described," claims that "all Jews are survivors."[10] In a sense, Klein subscribes to Cohen's dictum not only in his poetry of lamentations and his satire, but also in the characterization of the narrator in *The Second Scroll*. The first person narrative presents the search for Uncle Melech as the process of self-redefinition via-á-vis the post-Holocaust victim. The nameless narrator is identified only as Uncle Melech's nephew. The Canadian Jew defines himself by his European kinship; the constant presence of the Holocaust survivor sustained through letters, literary pieces, and testimonies communicates Klein's conviction that the redemption of the post-Holocaust world is predicated upon the reception of the victim's story. Indeed, the narrator's recital of the *kaddish* at his uncle's grave signifies restored father-son ties; the persistent desire to assert loving human relations restores hope for the future.

The vision of regeneration in *The Second Scroll* is not limited to the survival of the Jewish people; hope of spiritual revival is extended to the world at large. Uncle Melech's message transcends divisions among religions while focusing on the humanistic principles that bind them together. In the Sistine chapel, Melech discovers a humanist message in Michelangelo's Christianity: "Since Adam is created in the image of God, the killing of man is deicide (*TSS* 51); and in Melech's one-act play, "The Three Judgements," the Jewish character asserts his brotherly ties with the Moslem Cadi: "Oh, of the same sire descended,/Are we not all one kin, one tribe, one race?" (*CP* p. 134.

Despite Melech's violent death at the hands of Arab infiltrators, the novel does not end on a tragic note; rather, it refocuses on the Canadian nephew who accepts his uncle's spiritual legacy of the "new alphabet" (*TSS* 93) which will write the history of a better future world. Redemption, for Klein, is no longer predicated upon Miltonic assertion of "Eternal

Providence"; it is incumbent upon the new alphabet shaped out of the victim's story in defiance of silence and despair.

Mordecai Richler's first novel maintains the vision of redemptive humanism. *The Acrobats* (1954) highlights the educational significance of the generational encounter. Chaim, the European-born Jew, reaffirms, like Melech Davidson, his faith in human brotherhood: coming back to Europe from the United States after the war, Chaim gives his American passport to a "young survivor of the camps, "the thin frightened boy, with a number and a symbol on his arm." Chaim thus assumes the identity of both redeemer and Holocaust victim: a man without papers, he is the prototypical Wandering Jew. Despite his knowledge and experience of suffering, however, Chaim, like Melech, is capable of discerning the ideal of humanism inherent in both Jewish and Christian religions:

> Without Hillel there couldn't have been Christ...For hundreds of years men have murdered in the name of Christ. It's a contradiction, isn't it? Killing *for* God? (*TA* 76)

In Spain, Chaim meets André, a young Canadian artist. André seems unable to atone for his anti-Semitic treatment of his Jewish lover which inadvertently caused her death. Despite Chaim's fatherly support, the increasingly depressed young man seeks death at the hands of Kraus, an ex-Nazi officer, as a symbolic act of moral self-purification. Chaim, however, will not be deterred by André's nihilism and despair: by assisting to raise Kraus' son, he counteracts death and desperation through affirmation of life. As a wise teacher and spokesman of the old tradition of Jewish hamanism, Chaim imparts the hope for the future. Like *The Second Scroll*, Richler's first novel concludes with a vision of a world in which order and harmony are about to be restored. Both novels foreground the notion that the Jew, the victim of brutality, is also the source of redemption. The victim's assertion of human brotherhood despite suffering and loss confirms the validity of the heroic struggle against despair.

Richler's following novel, *Son of a Smaller Hero* 1955, no longer sustains the humanist vision of redemption. Written only a year after *The*

Acrobats, the novel takes place in Richler's native Montreal "ghetto" which the protagonist, Noah Adler, wishes to flee. In his attempts to assimilate into the Gentile world, Noah, a Jewish young man, carries the humanist principle of equality *ad absurdum* when he insists on comparing the moral flaws of his fellow-Jews with those of their worst persecutors:

> At last Noah understood about the concentration camps....The Germans have told the truth when they said that they hadn't known. They couldn't cope with knowing. Neither could the Goldenbergs. Their crimes varied in dimension but not in quality.[12]

Noah uses, or rather abuses, the universality of the humanist ideal in an attempt to renounce his Jewish identity. The abstracted story of the Holocaust victim as a representation of universal suffering becomes an ideological argument proffered to affirm Jewish equality in the Gentile world. Such argumentation reveals an emotional predicament grounded in an unacknowledged fear of Jewish vulnerability: the abstraction of recent Jewish victimization foregrounds anxiety as a significant motive for Jewish assimilation in the post-Holocaust world. The desire to avoid the seemingly inescapable fate of suffering, rather than a quest for universal redemption, seems to underscore Noah's adherence to the humanist ideal. Unlike Chaim in *The Acrobats* and Uncle Melech's nephew in Klein's *The Second Scroll*, Noah foreshadows Richler's subsequent protagonists, all of whom tend to distance themselves from situations which may implicate them as potential victims of Jewish identity.

The need of Richler's North American Jew to dissociate himself from Jewish suffering seems to originate in Richler's own childhood experience in the Montreal "ghetto" of the 1940's. An episode in Richler's 1969 collection of memoirs, *The Street*, recounts a complex relationship between a Montreal Jewish boy and Herr Bambinger, one of the few European refugees who arrived in Montreal in 1942. In what emerges as a parodic inversion of the impulse to identify with the victim, as demonstrated both in Klein's work and Richler's first novel, the boy obstinately rebuts every attempt to establish contact with the European Jew. His derogatory exclamation discloses the emotional underpinnings of the rejection:

> Why'd you run away from Hitler, you chicken?
> Couldn't you have stayed behind and fought in
> the underground?[13]

The refugee's plight undermines the fantasy of a Jewish Superman fighting against the Nazi enemy and demonstrates the extent of Jewish weakness and inferiority. Indeed, in another memoir, "The Great Comic Heroes," Richler recalls that "they [the comic heroes] were invulnerable, all-conquering whereas we [the Jewish boys] were puny, miserable and defeated."[14]

The allusion to the comic hero in relation to suffering and defeat communicates a conscious desire to dissociate from those who do not fit into the patterns of popular heroism and, at the same time, projects the suppressed fear of victimization. The author's astute observation of the North American response to the European tragedy counteracts his earlier reaffirmation of hope against despair.

The centrality of the victim's story in humanist re-education foregrounded in *The Acrobats* is displaced in Richler's later work: the Holocaust story of victimization becomes the stigma of Jewish impotence, and the failure of the Jew to transform into a glorious superman portends another Holocaust. Richler's protagonist becomes increasingly obsessed with the simplistic notion that an act of physical courage will avenge the Holocaust and thereby obliterate the foreboding story of Jewish victimization.

The prevailing ironic mode in Richler's two latest novels, *St. Urbain's Horseman* (1971) and *Joshua Then and Now* (1980), teaches the futility of redemption sought in an anxiety-induced act of violence. In Northrop Frye's definition, the ironic figure, the *pharmakos* or scapegoat isolated from society, "is guilty in the sense that he is a member of a guilty society, or living in a world where...injustices are an inescapable part of existence."[15] Richler's protagonists aspire to correct the irony of Jewish exclusion by assuming the heroic stance of a rebellious social reformer. Their eventual social reintegration signifies renunciation of this unrealistic self-image as well as an attitude of compliance with the morally unredeemed post-war world.

Unlike Chaim in *The Acrobats*, Richler's later protagonists consider their ethnic identity an obstacle which blocks both artistic spontaneity and sense of well-being. Similarly to Noah Adler in *Son of a Smaller Hero*, Jake Hersh, the protagonist of *St. Urbain's Horseman*, rebels against the Jewish environment in Montreal. Subsequently, he emigrates to England, marries a Gentile woman, and becomes a successful television film director. The developing frustration and neurotic fear, however, bring on a crisis in terms of his career and family life. The recurring recollections of Nazi atrocities against the Jews disrupt Jake's self-satisfied complacency:

> Then there obtrudes the familiar photograph of a bewildered little Jewish boy, wearing a cap, a torn pullover, and shorts, his eyes aching with fear as he raises his arm over his head. There are other Jews huddled together on this street in Warsaw....All of them, with arms raised....Then, in Jake's Jewish nightmare, they come. Into his house. The extermination officers seeking out the Jew vermin. Ben is seized by the legs like a chicken and heaved out of the window, his brains spilling to the terrace. Molly...is raised in the air...to be flung against the brick fireplace. Sammy is dispatched with a pistol.[16]

Consciousness of Holocaust atrocity in Richler's work engenders a sense of identification. Unlike Klein, however, who deeply empathizes with the victim, Richler's protagonist appropriates, so to speak, the experience of suffering: his prefiguration of the Jewish future presents a reenactment of the recent history of horror, a reenactment in which now he becomes the victim. In Jake's view of history, Providence manifests itself paradoxically in the diabolical cycle of Jewish persecution. Such historical determinism precludes the possibility of anxiety-free Jewish existence.

Joshua Then and Now, demonstrates a similar attempt to terminate the whirligig of Jewish victimization. Like his predecessors, Noah and Jake, Joshua escapes the constricting boundaries of the Montreal "ghetto." An aspiring writer, young Joshua wishes to commemorate through his art the extraordinary dedication of the Spanish volunteers to the ideal of human brotherhood. On his arrival in Spain, however, the consciousness of Spanish Jewish history interferes with his plans:

The next morning he was in Madrid...when once more his Jewishness obtruded. Descending on him unbidden. Like press. Some four hundred years ago, during the Inquisition, they used to burn Jews here, right here, for sport.[17]

"Jewishness" is ineluctably defined in terms of ever-present, imminent suffering. Joshua's subsequent encounter with Dr. Mueller, the ex-Nazi officer, on the Spanish Island of Ibiza makes the spectre of victimization unbearably real. The experience undermines Joshua's faith in human brotherhood as represented by the International Brigades. Mueller who represents the threat of castration, forces Jake to flee the island. In view of Joshua's shameful escape, the contemptuous, provoking question of the German: "Are you a man or a mouse?" (*JTN* 190) brands him as yet another powerless victim of anti-Semitic hatred. For the next twenty-five years the unresolved rage and desire for revenge will undermine Joshua's creativity, jeopardize his career, and nearly ruin his family life.

Both *St. Urbains Horseman* and *Joshua Then and Now* focus on revenge as an act of emotional liberation and restoration of potency. Unrealized revenge manifests Richler's ironic view of the precariousness of Jewish relations with the post-Holocaust world. When Joshua finally returns to the island to confront Mueller, he learns that his enemy is dead. The death of him tormentor highlights the absurdity of his obsession. Joshua's subsequent reconciliation with his Gentile wife indicates that the possibility to restore Jewish pride and dignity is limited to the domestic scene. The restricted nature of harmonious personal relations in *Joshua Then and Now* as opposed to the global vision of redemption in *The Acrobats* demonstrates Richler's consciousness of pervasive vulnerability and anxiety which underscore the need to assimilate.

In *St. Urbain's Horseman*, Jake Hersh projects his sense of helplessness in his fantasy of his Cousin Joey, the Horseman, galloping on his white stallion somewhere in Paraguay in search of Dr. Mengele. The avenger of the Holocaust is, in Jake's fantasy, "a Jewish Batman..." a replica of the legendary "golem" (*SUH* p. 252). Joey becomes Jake's imaginary mentor, forever elusive, even in his death in an airplane crash in Paraguay.

Interestingly, both Klein and Richler use the golem legend: their parodic interpretation of the myth represents the loss of faith in history's providential scheme. In Klein's vision, the Nazi golem, the man-made brutal automaton, deposes God, the Creator of man:

> If golem is the effigy of man, and man is the simulacrum of the Lord, the sequitur--I blanch to mouth the word, the blasphemous equation framed to span the chasm between the Lord and Caliban! (*CP* 133)

In Richler, Jake's obsession with a brutal act of physical revenge as an act of liberation turns the avenging golem, the "body without soul," into an absolute master, an object of idolatry, his "moral editor" (*SUH* 290). In his comment on the novel, Richler explains the golem as a rejection of divine morality and truth:

> There *is* a strong religious note at the end [of the novel]...the Horseman is a Golden Calf that [Jake has] made for himself.[18]

Through the manipulation of the old text, both writers delineate the distance that separates the post-Holocaust world from the Miltonic notion of providential order. Man seems to have reverted to the pre-Revelation, pre-humanist condition, whereby spirituality and moral choice are sacrificed in the worship of a brutal, mindless emblem of power. Both Klein and Richler attempt to forestall the increasing dominance of a golem-like mentality. Both seem to indicate that courageous confrontation of the moral deterioration in the post-war world may start the redemptive process.

The victim's story of the Holocaust seems to empower Klein's vision of redemption. The lesson of victory over despair that Uncle Melech conveys to his Canadian nephew reestablishes the links with the past and indicates the possibility of spiritual regeneration. Conversely, Richler's darkening vision of the future indicates the complexity of his lesson. The ironic failure of the golem fantasy signals the futility of physical revenge. Dissociation from the golem, however, does not signify moral regeneration. When Jake finally joins the world, he seems to have exchanged one idol for another, rather than recognize the need for self-actualization. His resumption of work as a television film director marks his comic-ironic reintegration into a "guilty society," as Frye terms it, whose immorality is clearly spelled out in his Gentile friend's cynical perception of the post-war world:

> Look here, baby. We're on the *Titanic*. It's going down.
> Everything, everybody. Me, I've decided to travel first class.
> (*SUH* 238)

The Gentile world, thus, cannot offer moral guidance to the Jew who has transferred the pursuit of justice into the sphere of fantasy and dream. In his ironic exposure of the disintegration of moral values in the post-war world, Richler seems to dissociate from Klein's process of moral re-education. At the same time, however, some hope of redemption is conveyed in the failure of Richler's protagonists to remain in the sphere of fantasy. Richler's ironic treatment of his protagonists' escapism signals a considerable extent of the younger writer's identification with Klein's notion of the courageous confrontation of history in the Holocaust victim's story.

Some historical lessons are harder than others; as the progression from Klein's to Richler's world picture teaches us, the problematics of the post-Holocaust reality are becoming increasingly complex; however, the courage of both writers to confront the post-Holocaust crisis in their art communicates the value of self-examination in the struggle against despair. In contrast with the Miltonic view of history, the works examined here show that it is not the assertion of "Eternal Providence" that will offer hope for the post-Holocaust world, but rather it is man's conscious acceptance of the painful past that holds hope for a meaningful future.

ENDNOTES

[1]John Milton, *Paradise Lost and Selected Poetry* and *Prose* (New York: Rinehart & Co., Inc., 1951, p. 6.

[2]Philip Sidney, *An Apology for Poetry*, ed Geoffrey Shepherd (Manchester: Manchester Univ. Press, 1979), p. 101.

[3]Wesley A. Kort, *Narrative Elements and Religious Meanings* (Philadelpohia: Fortress Press, 1975), p. 81-82.

[4]Alan L. Berger, *Crisis and Covenant: The Holocaust in American Jewish Fiction* (Albany: State University of New York Press, 1985), p. 28.

[5]Lawrence L. Langer, *The Age of Atrocity: Death in Modern Literature* (Boston: Beacon Press, 1978), p. 4.

[6]For further resources on the golem legend see Gershom Scholem, *Kabbalah* (New York: Dorset Press, 1974), pp. 351-355.

[7]A. M. Klein, *The Collected Poems of A. M. Klein*, ed. Miriam Waddington (Toronto: McGraw-Hill Ryerson, 1975), p. 135. All further references to this work (*CP*) appear in the text.

[8]For further explanation of the tradition of Jewish protestantism see: Byron L. Sherwin, "Wiesel's Midrash" in *Confronting the Holocaust: The Impact of Elie Wiesel*, eds. Alvin H. Rosenfeld and Irving Greenberg (Bloomington: Indiana University Press, 1978), pp. 122-124.

[9]A. M. Klein, *The Second Scroll* (Toronto: McClelland and Stewart, 1969), p. 30. All further references to this work (*TSS*) appear in the text.

[10]Arthur A. Cohen, *The American Imagination After the War: Notes on the Novel, Jews, and Hope*, The B. G. Rudolph Lectures in Judaic Studies, March 1981, pp. 29, 31.

[11]Mordecai Richler, *The Acrobats* (London: Sphere Books, 1970), p. 30. All further references to this work (*TA*) appear in the text.

[12]Mordecai Richler, *Son of a Smaller Hero* (Toronto: McClelland and Stewart, 1969), p. 70. All further references to their work (*SSH*) appear in the text.

[13]Mordecai Richler, *The Street* (Harmondsworth: Penguin Books, 1977), p. 73. All further references to this work (*TS*) appear in the text.

[14]Mordecai Richler, "The Great Comic Heroes" in *Notes on the Engendered Species and Others* (New York: Alfred A. Knopf, 1974), p. 119.

[15]Northrop Frye, *Anatomy of Criticism: Four Essays* (Princeton: Princeton University Press, 1971), p. 41.

[16]Mordecai Richler, *St. Urbain's Horseman* (Toronto: Bantam Books, 1972), p. 67. All further references to this work (*SUH*) appear in the text.

[17]Mordecai Richler, *Joshua Then and Now* (New York: Bantam Books, 1981), p. 162. All further references to this work (*JTN*) appear in the text.

[18]John Metcalf, "Black Humour: An Interview: Mordecai Richler," *Journal of Canadian Fiction* (Winter 1974), p. 76

MARY BERG'S *WARSAW GHETTO:* A DIARY

Susan Lee Pentlin

On April 19, 1944, thousands gathered at the Warsaw Synagogue in New York and marched to the city hall in commemoration of the first anniversary of the Warsaw Ghetto Uprising. They carried signs reading: "We appeal to the conscience of America to help save those Jews in Poland who can yet be saved," "Avenge the blood of the Polish ghetto" and "Three Million Polish Jews have been murdered by the Nazis! Help us rescue the survivors." Heading the marchers that day were the Wattenberg family, Shya and Lena and their daughters Mary (Miriam) and her younger sister Ann.[1]

The Wattenbergs had arrived in the United States as repatriates only four weeks earlier on the exchange ship "Gripsholm." Mary had brought a diary of their experiences in the Warsaw Ghetto with her in twelve small notebooks. She began to rewrite her abbreviated notes immediately. She had only used the initials of people she wrote about and she had always referred to the Nazis as "they." In October and December of 1944, S. L. Shneiderman[2] published selected pages from the diary in English translation in the periodical *The Contemporary Jewish Record.* The diary was titled *Pages from a Warsaw Diary* and the author's name was shortened to Berg.[3] In February, Mary Berg's full work, *Warsaw Ghetto: A Diary*, was published by L. B. Fisher in New York with Norbert Guterman and Sylvia Glass as translators.[4]

In the foreword to a special edition of the diary, Berg and Shneiderman's purpose in publishing her diary is clearly outlined. Joseph Thon, the President of the National Organization of Polish Jews which sponsored a special edition of the diary, explained:

> The leaders of the United Nations have declared that they would resort to poison gas and bacteriological warfare only if the Germans used these inhuman methods first. The Germans have used these methods to slaughter millions of Jews in Treblinka, Majdanek, Oswiecim, and other camps. But even today the civilized world does not fully realize this fact. It is therefore our duty to make known the horrible truth, to publicize documents and eye-witness accounts that reveal it beyond any doubt.[5]

It is important to note that Berg's diary was published before the war was over, before people in the United States and abroad and even Mary herself could have known the enormity of the German crimes and the details of the Final Solution. Moreover, we should remember that as a witness to the German crimes against humanity, Mary Berg had arrived in New York before the summer of 1944 when the Hungarian Jews, the last of the European communities, were gassed at Auschwitz.

Of course, Berg was not the only witness of these events to testify. Initial selections of her diary were published at nearly the same time Jan Karski's report, "My Visit to the Warsaw Ghetto," appeared in the *American Mercury* magazine. Karski, a courier for the Polish underground, had visited Warsaw in 1942 and met with three of the ghetto leaders. He reported on their conversation:

> The first thing they made clear to me ... was the absolute hopelessness of their predicament. For the Polish Jews, this was the end of a world. There was no possible escape for them or for their fellows....'Do you mean that every one of those presumably deported was actually killed?' 'Every last one.'

One of the Bund leaders had told him: "The Germans are not trying to enslave us as they do other people; we are being systematically murdered."[6] Like Karski, Berg intended to inform America of the Nazi atrocities against the Jews of Europe.

However, Berg's diary is a full and detailed account of these experiences, from the ghetto's establishment through the first deportations from July through September of 1942. It is the first published eyewitness testimony from an inhabitant of the ghetto and the first account to testify that gas was being used to kill the Jews at Treblinka. In a preface to the diary, Shneiderman had pointed out that:

> At some future time, we hope, chronicles hidden by writers in the ruins of the Warsaw ghetto will be discovered. Other survivors may be found to give additional testimony to this heroic episode of the war...for the time being, Mary Berg's diary is the only existing eye-witness record.[7]

Fortunately, the diaries and chronicles of Adam Czerniakow, Janusz Korczak, Chaim Kaplan and Emanuel Ringelblum who perished in the Holocaust and of the ghetto policeman Stanislav Adler who killed himself in 1946 are available to us today in English,[8] along with many memoir accounts by the survivors of the Warsaw ghetto. Since only one percent of the ghetto inhabitants survived the war, even accounts written after 1945 remain rare.[9]

Berg's unique contribution was already recognized in reviews during the winter of 1945. The *New Yorker* reviewer wrote: "This is a grim book, full of darkness and horror, and, because of the picture it gives of the courage and humanity of the people of the Warsaw ghetto, it is also a brave and inspiring one."[10] The *Kirkus Review* called it "a moving record of terrorism"[11] and the *New York Times* recommended it as reading for everyone "without qualification."[12] The *Saturday Review* concluded that Berg's diary notes "bear the imprint of sincerity and authenticity, and apparently are not 'glamorized' by editorial treatment."[13]

A Hebrew translation of the diary also appeared in Tel Aviv in 1945 and in 1946 an Italian edition was published in Rome. A French translation came out in Paris in 1947.[14] A Polish translation also appeared in Poland in 1983 on the fortieth anniversary of the ghetto uprising. It includes several drawings Mary Berg made in the ghetto.[15] Her diary is listed in the bibliography of many important works on the Holocaust available to scholars and students, including Lucy Dawidowicz's *The War Against the Jews*, Nora Levin's *The Holocaust: The Destruction of European Jewry, 1933-1945* and Yisrael Gutman's *The Jews of Warsaw, 1939-1943*. Martin Gilbert's recent study *The Holocaust* draws extensive quotes from the diary in discussing the Warsaw Ghetto.[16] However, the diary has not been re-issued in English since 1945. Consequently, it is difficult to locate and therefore not generally used in Holocaust education today.

Of course, we value the diary for the rarity of its testimony alone. However, a closer study also establishes the uniqueness of Berg's testimony, quite aside from the fact that the diary was the first one in print. First of all, the other diary and chronicle accounts were usually written by adults, men such as Ringelblum and Czerniakow who had reached maturity and were considered successful members of the community. In the ghetto, they realized the hopelessness of their situation and recorded the events around them as a chronicle for the future.

Kaplan felt this strong commitment to record what he saw happening. He explained in one entry:

> I sense within me the magnitude of this hour, and my responsibility toward it...continuing this diary to the very end of my physical and spiritual strength is a historical mission which must not be abandoned.[17]

They had little hope that they would survive, so they wrote public accounts to be read after the war as testimony of the destruction of the Jewish community.

Unlike these accounts, Berg's diary is that of a young girl, who was fifteen when the Germans attacked Poland. Alvin Rosenfeld in his work *A Double Dying* concludes that diaries of the Holocaust written by children or young adolescents "seem almost to constitute a distinctive subgenre of the literature of incarceration."

This is in part because children look in wonderment at the violence of the adult world and at the world's apparent indifference. He points out "a heavy premonition of human finitude is usually no part of childhood awareness," but these diarists became increasingly aware that, although they could indulge in dreams of adulthood, in fact the future might not include them.[18] In a July 1941 entry, Berg expressed this passionately, writing with bitterness:

> Where are you foreign correspondents? Why don't you come here and describe the sensational scenes of the ghetto? No doubt you don't want to spoil your appetite....Is the whole world poisoned? Is there no justice anywhere? Will no one hear our cries of despair?[19]

Rosenfeld explains that, unlike the adult diarists and chroniclers, these young people wrote mainly for private reasons. Often, they wrote, like Anne Frank, for companionship and for consolation. He suggests that their principal purpose was to "exorcise their unwanted sense of dread, to find some means of coping with the unexpected but very tangible fearfulness all around." They needed to "control (their) experience in a measurable space"[20] and as children mature, they typically seek privacy as a way of learning about themselves and of defining themselves as individuals.

Berg shared her diary entries with friends in the ghetto. After a party when friends from Lodz helped celebrate her seventeenth birthday, she wrote:

> We spent a few pleasant hours together, transported into a completely different world....We talked a great deal and discussed our plans for after the war. I had to read several passages from my diary, which everyone praised, and several of my friends brought me nicely bound little notebooks to continue my journal.[21]

Thus the diary had a social function and Mary's friends must have felt it a collective effort that expressed their youthful confrontation with horror and deprivation.

In many of the entries, Mary recorded the experiences of her friends which she learned either from what they told her or later from letters she received in internment. In the first months of ghetto life, Berg realized they all had begun to change, explaining that it is "that precocious war maturity which is so characteristic of so many of us. It is really a psychological rather than a biological maturity."[22]

Rosenfeld suggests that in diaries and other Holocaust writing "the individual cry is always recognizable, but as it echoes across a continent it is the assemblage of pain and rebellion that impresses itself upon us more than anything else."[23] As the experiences of the ghetto became more bitter, Mary knew her mother's being an American citizen gave her at least a greater chance of survival than her friends and she called the American flag on their door "that miraculous sign."[24] At first Mary wrote for her own memory and comfort. But mature beyond her years, she may also have begun to write about her relatives and youthful friends for other purposes as well.

Eventually she began recording ghetto scenes about her as an adult chronicler or witness. In February 1941, standing at the window and watching a snowfall, she dreamed of "a sled driving over the snow, of freedom." With adult understanding, she wrote:

> For the time being I am still warm and have food, but all around me there is so much misery and starvation that I am beginning to be very unhappy...sometimes I quickly snatch my coat and go out into the street. I gaze at the faces of the passers-by, blue with cold. I try to learn by heart the look of the homeless women wrapped in rags and of the children with chapped and frozen cheeks.[25]

Marlene Heinemann in her study *Gender and Destiny: Women Writers and the Holocaust* explains that: "Holocaust memoirs are also often affected by differences in the present time situation of the writer, which help to determine how the past will be recreated."[26] Berg's work has a freshness, a naiveté that cannot be found in memoirs where the authors frequently try to remember or recreate their childhood experiences. She also did not write the diary with the intent to publish as most memoirists do. While the diary was eventually published to inform America about the destruction of European Jews, this was apparently not her conscious purpose.

In terms of perspective, the reader also must recognize that in the ghetto Mary was considered an "American." Although the family's hope often wavered and their rescue was never a certainty or at times really even probable, the possibility remained. Mary had at least the hope of being saved, whereas her friends did not. This undoubtedly made her an objective, careful observer of ghetto life, but at the same time her family was spared the harshest of ghetto experiences.

As a young girl, she was also protected by her family and friends more than a young boy might have been. However, when her boy friend Romek said to her condescendingly: "Little, girl, it is good that you don't understand too much. I am happy that you don't suffer as I do," she wrote: "Tears choked me, because I do know and understand everything, but I am powerless and cannot help anyone."[27] If anything, this made her more intent as an observer and more determined to be independent in her outlook.

Mary began her account on October 10, 1939 which was her fifteenth birthday, although she had apparently kept a diary before. She wrote that day:

> Today I am fifteen years old. I feel very old and lonely....I have not written my diary for such a long time that I wonder if I shall ever catch up with all that has happened. This is a good moment to resume it. I spend most of my time at home. Everyone is afraid to go out. The Germans are here.[28]

At that time, she was with her family in Warsaw. They had decided to flee from Lodz in early September, as the Germans broke through the Polish lines.

They fled on bicycles, travelling through countryside already ravaged by the Germans. Mary's father was a prosperous art dealer who owned his own shop in Lodz, so the sisters had grown up in a comfortable, pleasant home. This was their first experience with devastation and death. Weakened by hunger, her mother had collapsed on the road. Horrified, Mary began to cry and her sister Ann remained standing still in the road as if in a daze.[29]

Being a young girl, rather than a public figure, Mary recorded only those experiences which she and her family encountered, but free from adult responsibilities, she may also have had more time and opportunity to bear witness to daily life on the streets of Warsaw. As a Jew in German-occupied Poland, these experiences were soon defined by Nazi racial policy. The first atrocity she witnessed was in November after the family had returned to Lodz to find their home and shop looted. From behind the curtain of their apartment, she witnessed for the first time German brutality against Polish Jews.

A man whom she recognized as Jewish was standing on the street curb when a German soldier approached him. After giving him an order, which the man apparently did not carry out, the soldier and several others began beating him. The Germans then tied his feet to the back of a cab and ordered the driver to start. The stones of the pavement were dyed red with blood, as the cab went down the street.[30] Resolutely, Mary reported, a few weeks later that "moreover everyone wonders whether the Nazis will even let him live much longer."[31]

With youthful uncertainty, however, her mood often shifted. One minute, she confessed to knowing that the chances that any of them would survive was minimal. In the next entry, she enjoyed being with her friends and with them continued to plan for the future. One day she wrote: "...but who worries about what will happen in eight months? By then the war may be over."[32] But then in a few weeks, she admitted to herself again that "...there is no hope for anyone within the ghetto walls."[33]

On the whole, the diary is a strong testimony to the vitality and perseverance of the human spirit, even on the brink of disaster. *The Library Journal* review of the diary in February 1945 remarked: "This is not a pleasant book, neither is it entirely depressing for the courage of this young person shines through the Nazi atrocities."[34] The *Horn Book* reviewer also concluded that: "This is a grim, unpleasant record, but it is shot through with the heroism of youth. Our young people need it to show them in human terms what oppression has meant and to give them a stake in the peace to come."[35]

In September 1940, before the ghetto was sealed off from the rest of Warsaw, Berg, with a group of young friends from Lodz, formed a theater group to raise relief funds. Calling themselves the Lodz Artistic Group, or the LZA in Polish abbreviation, this group acquired its own theater and gave musical performances nearly every week. Mary soon grew to enjoy performing and sang English songs for the ghetto audience, ignoring the prohibition against public use of French or English.

Although the first performances were quite successful and the friends enjoyed being together, it could not keep their minds from the ghetto's omnipresent oppression and horror. Realistically, Mary wrote:

> Our little group is having a lively time and is finding preparations for the show absorbing. But one look outside the window is enough to awaken us to reality. At any time one can see tangible evidence of the terror that reigns in the city. The man hunt goes on without interruption. We always have to leave our meetings one by one.[36]

They were proud to be able as young people to make a contribution in the ghetto and gave half of their proceeds to welfare institutions, including Janusz Korczak's children's home.

Amidst the fear and horror around them, the young people realized
that "life goes on."[37] In the ruins of Warsaw, they planted gardens, attended
illegal *Gymnasium* classes and courses in graphic and manual arts and
entertained themselves imaginatively. A favorite pastime was sunbathing on
the roofs. Mary even described a garden cafe called "Bajka" or "Fairy Tale"
in the Little Ghetto:

> This cafe covers the site of a completely bombed-out house.
> To one side stands a wall with burned window openings. This
> is an excellent backdrop. Near by is a "beach"--a piece of
> ground on which a few deck chairs have been placed. For two
> zlotys one can bask in the sun here for an entire day. Bathing
> suits are obligatory, apparently in order to create the
> atmosphere of a real beach.[38]

She recognized this momentary happiness was merely an illusion. Even
children in the ghetto knew they had little prospect for the future.

With a growing sense of foreboding though, they found it more and
more difficult to shut out "the sad world" around them. In the summer of
1941, Mary described a recurrent dream or nightmare:

> I am full of dire forebodings. During the last few nights, I have
> had terrible nightmares. I saw Warsaw drowning in blood;
> together with my sisters (sic) and my parents, I walked over
> prostrate corpses. I wanted to flee, but could not, and awoke
> in a cold sweat, terrified and exhausted. The golden sun and
> the blue sky only irritated my shaken nerves.[39]

In face of the poor health conditions and the stress they were living under,
friendship and companionship with others their own age was very important.

The group of young entertainers from Lodz continued their
performances until January 1942, when typhus and labor details had taken so
many of the members that they agreed there was no reason to continue.
They came to this decision on New Year's Eve 1942. Mary's parents had
moved to a new apartment and the young people came together in the old
one. Instead of champagne, they drank lemonade by the light of a carbide
lamp and ate little sandwiches of pickled fish.

Mary wrote the next day: "I feel completely empty, as though I were
suspended over an abyss. Last night was a mixture of entertainment and
nightmare." As a clock from a nearby church chimed in the New Year,
Romek went to the piano. Romek, a talented pianist, was no longer able to

play; his hands were so damaged from the work he did maintaining the ghetto wall for the Germans. To everyone's surprise, he began to play Chopin's Funeral March. As he finished playing, he whispered "I have a strange premonition on this New Year's Day, mark my words."[40]

The year 1942 did, of course, mark the beginning of the end of the Warsaw Ghetto's existence. With premonition that New Year's Eve she recalled that while Romek was playing: "Sad ideas flashed through my mind. Was not all this symbolic? Was there not something terrible in store for me, something that would separate me from my friends?" Soon Mary's path did begin to turn from that of her friends, although as a survivor she remained full of despair and guilt. She often asked herself: "Have I the right to save myself and leave my closest friends to their bitter fate?"[41]

Unbelievably, a very small number of Polish Jews with American or British passports or with papers from South American Republics at war with Germany were singled out shortly before the mass deportations began. Mary's mother had not registered with the Gestapo, so the Bergs were not interned for the first exchange in April 1942.[42] Czerniakow's diary confirms that he received word from the Germans on June 3, 1941 that "foreign Jews will be allowed to leave, to be exchanged, provided their foreign documents are in order."[43]

Mrs. Berg wrote to the representative of the American colony in the city of Warsaw, who helped her contact Nikolaus, a member of the Gestapo in charge of foreign affairs in the General Government. At first, it was unclear if Mary and her father would be regarded as citizens and allowed to leave with Mrs. Berg and the younger daughter Ann. On July 15 they received news that all foreign citizens should report on July 17.[44]

The next days were emotionally draining for the family. In desperation, friends came to their apartment with addresses of relatives and friends in America, pleading for Mrs. Berg to ask their help. Mary recalled: "All of them pour their troubles out to my mother--they have nothing left to sell, nothing to live on, in another few months they will perish."[45] Everyone recognized the ghetto was doomed and rumors about deportations were heard everywhere. A neighbor, Captain Hertz who was a ghetto police commander, sensed the significance of the moment. He told the Bergs:

"Now you'll see that I was right. We are all doomed. The foreign citizens are being removed because the Germans do not want them to witness what they are preparing for us."[46]

Accompanied to the gate by their tearful friends and relatives, the Berg family left the ghetto and were interned in the Pawiak Gestapo prison right outside the ghetto walls. Czerniakow reported in his diary on July 15 that:

> Nikolaus arrived at the community and issued orders for (over) 80 foreign Jews to be brought to Pawiak (prison) on Friday morning from where they are to be sent abroad. Schmied came. He declared that prisoners would be released in exchange.[47]

The next week on July 22, the day before his suicide, Czerniakow's diary entry notes "we were told that all the Jews irrespective of sex and age, with certain exceptions, will be deported to the East."[48]

Among the seven hundred foreign citizens in Pawiak, there were only twenty-one United States citizens, including the Berg family. These internees remained in the Pawiak prison throughout the summer of 1942. They witnessed from prison windows the mass deportations to the east, primarily to Treblinka death camp. By the end of September the ghetto population had been reduced to a remnant of about 60,000 compared to its 1940 population of 500,000. Mary Berg continued to record what she saw from the prison, reporting news of the ghetto received by the prisoners.

Mary stood at the prison window in August and watched the Germans surround Korczak's children's home and saw the determined doctor marching with his orphans down the street.[49] Throughout the fall, she heard the shootings and cries from the street and watched columns of workers march down the streets under heavy guard as, over and over, their departure date from Pawiak was postponed.[50] In December, Dita, a new arrival at the prison told the internees what she had learned about Treblinka.

At Gestapo headquarters, Dita had become acquainted with an official from the death camp. Not knowing she was Jewish, he had bragged about how the deported Jews were murdered there. Mary carefully recorded what she learned about the transports and the "actual death house of Treblinka." Dita told them that "after the bathhouse is entirely filled, strongly concentrated hot steam is let in through the windows. After a few minutes the people begin to choke in horrible pain." She also reported that "various gases" were used.[51]

On January 18, 1943, the internees left Warsaw by train. Until the last minute, the Bergs feared they would be sent to Auschwitz. From the train, Mary wrote: "I cannot believe my eyes, and I still do not know whether I am dreaming or waking. Our train is moving in the direction of Poznan, not of Oswiecim."[52] At the internment camp in Vittel, France, she still received letters from her friends in the Warsaw ghetto. The last one from Romek told her how many of their acquaintances were already gone. He advised Mary: "Do not think of me, my dear. I know my days are numbered."[53]

Without her friends' companionship, she quit writing in her diary. But several months later, when she heard of the Ghetto Uprising, she opened her notebook again with this entry:

> I have not written anything here for a long time. What good does it do to write; who is interested in my diary? I have thought of burning it several times, but some inner voice forbade me to do it. The same inner voice is now urging me to write down all the terrible things I have heard during the last few days.

In despair, she asked: "God, why must there be all this cruelty? I am ashamed. Here I am, breathing fresh air, and there my people are suffocating in gas and perishing in flames, burned alive. Why?"[54]

On March 1, 1944, the Bergs miraculously were evacuated from Vittel. In a little-known chapter of Holocaust history, a train of internees crossed the Spanish border several days later and on March 4 reached Lisbon where the Swedish exchange ship, the "Gripsholm" was docked.[55] On March 16, the ship arrived at Jersey City, New Jersey with over 600 wartime internees, including thirty-five American prisoners of war, an American diplomatic party from Vichy France and 160 internees from Vittel, many of whom were not Jewish. The ship had earlier carried about 750 Germans to Europe for the exchange.[56]

As one of the rare testaments of the Warsaw Ghetto, Mary Berg's diary is an important Holocaust document. Although her testimony may have come too late to change America's priorities in World War II, her record is a unique contribution to our knowledge about daily life in the Warsaw ghetto. It is an affirmation of the human will to survive and a tribute to human dignity and initiative. It will enrich any study of women in the Holocaust and of children in extreme situations. Its authenticity and its detail are striking and one can only hope it will be re-issued in the near future in English, so that it can have a wider readership and become integrated into contemporary American courses of study on the Holocaust.

ENDNOTES

[1]"Thousands Mourn Victims of Ghetto," *New York Times*, 20 April 1944, p. 10. In her diary, Mary refers to her sister as Ann. The family's names are confirmed in S. L. Shneiderman's introduction to a recent Polish translation: Mary Berg, *Dziennik z Getta Warszawskiego*, tr. Maria Salapska (Warsaw, 1983), pp. 5-10. English trans. by L. Literman.

[2]Berg, (Warsaw), pp. 7-8. Shneiderman is an American journalist who was born in Poland. As a reporter, he first met Mary Berg at the arrival of the "Gripsholm." He lives in New York today.

[3]Mary Berg, "Pages from a Warsaw Diary," *Contemporary Jewish Record*, 7 (October-December, 1944): pp. 497-510; 616-625.

[4]Mary Berg, *Warsaw Ghetto: A Diary*, ed. S. L. Shneiderman (New York: L. B. Fisher, 1945); special edition sponsored by the National Organization of Polish Jews.

[5]Berg, special edition, foreword by Joseph Thon.

[6]Jan Karski, "My Visit to the Warsaw Ghetto," *American Mercury*, 59 (November, 1944): pp. 567-575.

[7]Berg, p. 9.

[8]Adam Czerniakow, *The Warsaw Diary of Adam Czerniakow: Prelude to Doom*, eds. Raul Hilberg, Stanislaw Staron and Josef Kermisz (New York: Stein and Day, 1968, 1979); Janusz Korczak, *Ghetto Diary*, and Aaron Zeitlin, *The Last Walk of Janusz Korczak* (New York: Schocken, 1978); Chaim Kaplan, *Scroll of Agony: The Warsaw Diary of Chaim A. Kaplan*, ed. Abraham I. Katsh (London, 1966); Emanuel Ringelblum, *Notes from the Warsaw Ghetto: The Journal of Emanuel Ringelblum*, tr. and ed. Jacob Sloan (New York, 1958); Stanislav Adler, *In the Warsaw Ghetto, 1940-1943. An Account of a Witness. The Memoirs of Stanislav Adler* (Jerusalem: Yad Vashem, 1982).

[9]Janina Bauman, *Winter in the Morning: A Young Girl's Life in the Warsaw Ghetto and Beyond 1939-1945* (New York: Free Press, 1986). For comparison, this is a particularly interesting account. Bauman, born in 1926, also kept a diary in the ghetto. Unfortunately, most of her text was lost after the war, but she includes some entries from her original diary.

[10]Review, *New Yorker*, 21 (February 24, 1945): 77.

[11]Review, *Kirkus*, 13 (February 15, 1945): 24.

[12]Marguerite Young, "First Hand Report of a Nightmare," *New York Times Book Review*, 18 February 1945, p. 6.

[13]F. Weiskopf, review, *Saturday Review*, 28 (March 3, 1945): 34.

[14]Mary Berg, *Geto Varshah*, (Tel Aviv, 1945/1947); *Il ghetto di Varsavia: diario di Mary Berg*, ed. S. L. Shneiderman, tr. Maria (Martone) Napolitano (Rome: De Carlo, 1946); *Le ghetto de Varsovie, journal de Mary Berg*, ed. S. L. Shneiderman, tr. Baillon de Wailly (Paris: A. Michel, 1947).

[15]Telephone interview, Ben Shneiderman, 28 February 1989.

[16]Lucy Dawidowicz, *The War Against the Jews, 1933-1945* (New York: Bantam, 1975, 1976); Nora Levin, *The Holocaust: The Destruction of European Jewry, 1933-1945* (New York: Schocken, 1973); Yisrael Gutnma, *The Jews of Warsaw, 1939-1943*, tr. Ina Friedman (Bloomington: Indiana University, 1982); Martin Gilbert, *A History of the Jews of Europe during the Second World War* (New York: Holt, Rinehart and Winston, 1985).

[17]Kaplan, p. 104.

[18]Alvin H. Rosenfeld, *A Double Dying: Reflections on Holocaust Literature* (Bloomington: Indiana University, 1980), p. 50.

[19]Berg, p. 87.

[20]Rosenfeld, p. 51.

[21]Berg, p. 107.

[22]*Ibid.*, p. 35.

[23]Rosenfeld, p. 34.

[24]Berg, p. 29.

[25]*Ibid.*, p. 47.

[26]Marlene E. Heinemann, *Gender and Destiny: Women Writers and the Holocaust* (New York: Greenwood, 1986), p. 38.

[27]Berg, p. 92.

[28]*Ibid.*, p. 11.

[29]*Ibid.*, p. 13.

[30]*Ibid.*, p. 20.

[31]*Ibid.*, p. 21.

[32]*Ibid.*, p. 30.

[33]*Ibid.*, p. 65.

[34]Review, *Library Journal*, 70 (February 15, 1945): 162.

[35]Review, *Horn Book*, 21 (May, 1945): 210.

[36]Berg, pp. 35-36.

[37]*Ibid.*, chapter heading, ch. 3, pp. 52-65.

[38]*Ibid.*, p. 61.

[39]*Ibid.*, p. 81.

[40]*Ibid.*, pp. 125-127.

[41]*Ibid.*, p. 162.

[42]*Ibid.*, pp. 154-155; see The American Federation for Polish Jews, *The Black Book of Polish Jewry: An Account of the Martyrdom of Polish Jewry Under the Nazi Occupation*, eds. Jacob Apenszlak et al. (n.p., 1943), p. 52 for a short account by Mrs. R., the wife of an American citizen who died in the ghetto. She had been able to leave the ghetto in early April 1942. She had then been interned with other Americans in Pawiak Prison and allowed to leave Europe by way of Lisbon.

[43]Czerniakow, p. 362.

[44]Berg, p. 158.

[45]*Ibid.*, p. 156.

[46]*Ibid.*, pp. 158-159; see Adler, p. 75.

[47]Czerniakow, p. 380.

[48]*Ibid.*, p. 384.

[49]Berg, p. 174.

[50]See David Wyman, *Abandonment of the Jews: America and the Holocaust 1941-1945* (New York: Pantheon, 1984), pp. 276-280.

[51]Berg, pp. 208-209.

[52]*Ibid.*, p. 216.

[53]Letter from Romek Kowalski quoted in Berg, p. 224.

[54]Berg, p. 227.

[55]*Ibid.*, p. 251.

[56]"List of Americans Returning from Europe aboard the Liner Gripsholm," *New York Times*, 12 March 1944, p. 26; Stanley, Lena, Mary and Anna Wattenberg, Long Branch, New Jersey on list; "35 Soldiers, ill but Happy First to Leave Gripsholm," *New York Times*, 16 March 1944, pp. 1, 4.

CHALLENGED TO RESPOND--
NEW POLISH NOVELS ABOUT THE HOLOCAUST

Iwona Irwin-Zarecka

In Polish literature, writing about the Holocaust has long been dominated by works of survivors. Beginning with poetry and eyewitness accounts produced *during* the war, and through nearly four decades that followed, non-Jewish voices were a rarity.[1] Today, this pattern appears to be changing, as more and more Polish writers assume the task of reflecting on the Holocaust through fiction. Together with a large number of previously unpublished historical sources and survivor testimonies, there is now a growing body of work presenting the events from a unique perspective--that of *witnesses*, the closest of witnesses to the 'Final Solution.'

Can these new works add to our understanding of the Holocaust? Yes, as long as the analytical focus remains on this unique perspective they both adopt and illuminate. Within the by-now extensive and extensively analyzed "Holocaust literature," writings by Poles comprise a rather special category; their value lies with what they tell us about *Poles and* the Holocaust, about remembrance and forgetting, about feelings then and rationalizations now. Quite apart from the intentions of the writers themselves, which often parallel those of their Western counterparts--to bring a fresh understanding of the Holocaust--the interpretive strategy here is not to judge just how accomplished these works are. Close attention to the texts, although a prerequisite, does not suffice. What is needed, and what I will concentrate on is a reading which brings the readers themselves into the foreground. To write about the Holocaust in Poland today is to join in a widening public debate on Polish-Jewish relations.[2] While speaking of the past, the authors in fact speak to the present, their works resonating with other statements on the public agenda.

For the first time since the Holocaust, Poland's public agenda accords a prominent position to the Jew; Jewish culture, Jewish history, Judaism itself, have gained wide exposure since 1982. In contrast, then, to previous years when works dealing with the Holocaust were the exception to a general rule of silence surrounding things Jewish, today's fiction is but a small component in a veritable deluge of public discourse treating a great variety of themes, from Hasidic tales to Bundist philosophy. Whether it is genuine interest or fashionable fascination, the public's response to this growing stock of Judaica has been very positive. Films and exhibits attract large audiences, books are rapidly sold out, private initiatives in the area of remembrance multiply. Discussions of Polish-Jewish relations, especially those during the Holocaust, are heated, but they *are* taking place, again breaking a long-held silence.

Admittedly an elite phenomenon, these shifts in public discourse *are* important. For the young and the educated especially, the new exposure offers an opportunity to learn about a part of their country's history they could have totally ignored otherwise. Even ten years ago, it was possible (and likely) to grow up in Poland without any sense of the Jewish presence there; today, it is becoming difficult to avoid some form of an encounter with the Jew.

It is against this background of an intensive effort to bring the Polish-Jewish past within the realm of Poland's collective memory that one must view any recently published writings on the Holocaust, but particularly the works by contemporary Polish authors.[3] Of such works, two books--Andrzej Szczypiorski's *The Beginning* (1986) and Jaroslaw Marek Rymkiewicz's *Umschlagplatz* (1988)--deserve particular attention. Both are authored by prominent writers, both first appeared in the independent publishing network (underground in Poland as well as under the auspices of Paris' emigré journal *Kultura*), both adopt nonconventional form to convey the texture of Polish and Jewish experience during the Holocaust. Where the two radically differ is in their public presence; *The Beginning* became a national and then an international event, and a best-seller in West Germany; *Umschlagplatz*, published close to two years later, stirred little debate in Poland and is only now gaining wide recognition in France. These differences are not accidental (or products of marketing); rather, they are indicative of the position each work could and apparently did assume within the larger context of discussing Polish-Jewish relations. In other words, when closely reading the two texts, we must keep in mind that one captured widely shared sentiments, the other one did not. What may account for this?

The Beginning is a work of reassurance, a quasi-didactic presentation of Germans-Poles-Jews-in-the-trying-times. Although the author's voice is clearly heard at certain key points here, it is a voice of a detached observer, who otherwise gives his characters center stage. The composition resembles that of a film script rather than a novel; in a short time, scenes change rapidly, too rapidly for a reader to gain a deeper sense of the people involved. Each scene tells its own story, indeed, each scene works like a miniature "morality play," with the characters symbolizing ethical choices rather than struggling to make them. This narrative strategy does not allow for stopping to contemplate human nature or the historical complexities--or the characters' "non-essential" qualities. There is a certain economy of expression perfected here, but also a flattening of situations into tableau-like "messages" which should be immediately comprehensible to the reader.

Szczypiorski does not say why he wrote the book, or why he decided on the particular cast of characters. Why, then, presume as I did that he was "challenged to respond"? The key here lies with the very structure of his book, with that didactic quality of each and every scene, and, of course, with the 'lessons' themselves. Practically all of these lessons, including the ones coded as reflections rather than parts of the plot, can be juxtaposed with an opinion about Polish-Jewish relations, primarily those of Western critics,[4] secondarily those shared by Poles themselves. The "challenge" in question is not then the Holocaust itself, but rather that of the impact the events had on how Poles are being perceived in the world. Implicitly but quite directly, Szczypiorski sets out to draw a 'correct' picture of the past, a picture which obviously proved appealing both to Poles and to West Germans.

One of the first misconceptions to be set straight is the one touching on the very act of writing about the Holocaust, in Poland, forty years after the fact. Szczypiorski goes beyond the frequently used assertion that it was the government's censorship which had prevented writings about Jews from being published (an assertion indeed least applicable to works on the Holocaust which did *not* disappear). Instead, he makes a strong statement about the destruction of Polish Jewry being a loss to Poles and Poland--a statement very much in agreement with the recently heard appeals to remember the Jews. The near-absence of Polish voices is said to reflect the emotional burden of witnessing a great trauma, and that of coming to terms with loss.

The reasoning is convincing; it is also reassuring. Historical records available today, especially of the events immediately after the end of the war, do not support this vision of general traumatization.[5] In other words, even if Poles *today* might genuinely feel a sense of loss towards their country's Jewish heritage, any projection of this feeling back into the past remains problematic, intellectually as well as morally. Such projection, however, is a prerequisite for the rest of the narrative here to work at all. Within the context of the Nazi occupation, when the final results of the "Final Solution" were not yet known, when indeed there was still a possibility some Jews would be spared, the feeling of loss translates into its more active counterpart--solidarity with the victim. And Poles in *The Beginning* feel, express and (often) act upon sympathy for the Jews and their plight; the exception to the rule are the thugs hunting for Jews outside the ghetto walls (*szmalcownicy*), but they are an exception. Everyone else, in a matter-of-fact way, treats Jews as fellow citizens, as neighbours in trouble, as human beings in need of help. And when another exception to the rule is introduced, this time in the figure of a woman watching the flames in the ghetto with unabashed satisfaction, the scene is quickly balanced with one of the strongest images Szczypiorski provides--that of an older man whose heart literally breaks when he overhears the woman's comments, a man who dies in anguish, so close to the ghetto walls.

What *The Beginning* does, then, is to reclaim the Poles' good name through a purported objectivity of the account. The negative characters, as if flashed across the screen, provide an assurance of balance; the positive ones, who occupy most of the time and space here, are not heroic or otherwise extraordinary. Taken together, they allow the reader to formulate the "average" of Polish attitudes during the Holocaust in terms of warm, unreflective, thus natural human bonds with the Jews.

To further balance the picture, Szczypiorski introduces another key element to his morality play--the figures of a "good German" and a "bad Jew." Central to the narrative is a story of Irena, a refined and Polonized Jewish woman, with strong chances of surviving on the "Aryan" side, who is recognized and given to the German authorities by a Jewish "head hunter." A Jew living off the persecution of his fellow Jews is not Szczypiorski's invention, of course; the prominence accorded to him within the text can, however, easily translate into a more general thesis on Jewish complicity, a thesis again supported by the long-standing tradition in Polish history textbooks to present victims as cooperating in their own destruction.[6]

Irena is rather rapidly rescued; a chain of good will (and good luck) created by her Polish friends and people she had never met culminates with a German officer whose task becomes to convince the German in charge of the prisoners that Irena's case is one of mistaken identity. Cool nerves and a dose of good luck, together with the obvious imbalance between the word of a German and that of a Jew, set Irena free. Once again, the figure of a German who helps the Jews is not Szczypiorski's invention; in this case, the credibility of the character is further enhanced by introducing his past attachment to Poland and Poles. The other German--the one who needs to decide whether Irena is or is not Jewish--emerges as a typical bureaucrat, following orders without much reflection on their significance. In a clear departure from the usual portrayal of the Nazis in Polish literature, we do not encounter evil, bestiality or obsessive nationalism. Both German characters, the ordinary and the extraordinary one, fall within a very human range between banality and compassion.

That *The Beginning* became very popular with West German readers and critics is not surprising, considering this particular cast of characters. Equally significant here, and speaking to both Poles and Germans, is the voice of the author-as-historian. Szczypiorski, as noted, generally avoids the subjective approach, and that makes the long passage where he does adopt it truly stand out. Reflecting directly on the Holocaust, he tells the reader to consider just how crude and unperfected the Nazi methods were--compared to those of the *Gulag*. Mass killings may have been a technological and organizational feat, but what of the unmatched capability of the Soviet system to instill fear, to destroy the moral fibre, to hold the *whole* society captive? For a Polish reader, in 1986, this attack on Soviet totalitarianism sounds perfectly reasonable; by that time, the exposure given in the underground publishing network to facts and analyses of the Soviet oppression would offer strong support indeed to the claim of "superiority of evil." A West German reader, confronted with this view in the midst of a highly publicized historians' debate, could easily fit it into a larger framework of efforts to deemphasize the uniqueness of Nazism. Coming from a Polish writer, the soothing of German conscience is undoubtedly even more effective.

Szczypiorski does not stop with a Nazi/Soviet comparison either. He moves closer to the present, citing recent atrocities committed in Cambodia and Biafra and the world's indifference to genocide as representative of a historical pattern--of which the "Final Solution" is but one component.

The Holocaust as "a genocide among many" challenges Man, it no longer challenges the Germans, and it does not even begin to challenge the Poles, co-victims of the Nazi policies.

Umschlagplatz, in sharp contrast, does challenge the Poles, Poles-as-passive-observers. Rymkiewicz writes from a very personal perspective, so the challenge too is a personal one. His whole work is in effect a response to a photograph in the family album, that of himself as a carefree little boy on summer holidays; the picture was taken in 1942, in Otwock, a resort town near Warsaw, popular with both Poles and Jews. Rymkiewicz asks himself--and the reader--how was it possible for him and his sister simply to enjoy the sun and the water, to play and laugh, at the very time that the Jews in

Otwock, two or three miles away, were being herded for deportation to the death camps. He does not allow himself the comfort of childhood innocence absolving him of responsibility; rather, he treats the photograph as a symbol of something much larger than his own past experience, yet no less private and troubling--the Poles' indifference to the fate of the Jews. His is one of the strongest voices in the current debate on Polish-Jewish relations, and one of the rare reflections on the very meaning of "responsibility."[7] Through a dialogue with his wife, Rymkiewicz rejects the idea that "responsibility" is a notion applicable solely to concrete action and specific persons. His own is an understanding of "responsibility" closely paralleling the one contained in Western discussions of the Holocaust--a sense of shared moral and cultural burden. Yet while he adopts this universalized conception of the challenge posed by the Holocaust, Rymkiewicz is also careful not to let it overshadow the particular questions he wishes to ask of the Poles.

Indeed, the universal-yet-specific quality of the challenge his book is a response to emerges at the very beginning of *Umschlagplatz*. Rymkiewicz asks the reader to think of the real *Umschlagplatz*, the site of deportation of over 300,000 Warsaw Jews, as a place which holds the key to understanding modern history, a unique place.[8] The history is universal, but the place is very concretely in the middle of Warsaw. What happened there calls upon humanity's conscience, but only Poles lived--and live--next to it. Theirs is a special memory obligation, an obligation Rymkiewicz translates into a private effort at memory reconstruction. His *Umschlagplatz* is an attempt to visualize, in minute detail, what the real *Umschlagplatz* looked like. The author realizes that somewhere in the West, perhaps in Israel, there must exist a record of the physical setting of the deportations, a part of Jewish memory. His task, though, is to bring *Umschlagplatz* within the lexicon of Polish memory, to make concrete what is behind a short inscription of a commemorative plaque now on site.[9] Through the work, Rymkiewicz aims to fulfill his obligation, that of a little boy who could enjoy playing in the summer of 1942.

In the text, the duality of purpose acquires yet another dimension--that of reconstruction of the pre-Holocaust Jewish presence. Intertwined on the pages of *Umschlagplatz* are then three quite distinct themes: a search for an accurate description of the place, an inquiry into Polish attitudes during the Holocaust, and, a portrait of a group of Warsaw Jews vacationing in Otwock in 1937. A collage of serenity and brutal detail, of debate and reflection, of simplicity and symbolization crosses time zones as well as space; we move from the past to the present, from Warsaw to Otwock to New York and back to Warsaw. A reader expecting an orderly narrative will find that he is continuously forced to switch interpretive gears; it is as if the very structure of the text was designed as a challenge, a break from the comforting convention of drama and resolution.

As much as this collage-like composition prompts an active reading, it also has the effect of smoothing the edges of Rymkiewicz's critique of Polish attitudes. The reflection on indifference and responsibility, on forgetting and idealizing the past, when surrounded by the fiction-and-fact remembrance of the Jews, provides for escape routes.

A more serious problem, however, as far as the text's resonance within the larger debate on Polish-Jewish relations, lies with a certain "Judaization" of perspective. By 1988, when the book appeared, issues discussed by Rymkiewicz were no longer new in the public forum; in late 1985, Claude Lanzmann's *Shoah*, selectively screened on Polish television, provoked a wide debate about Poles and the Holocaust, to be followed, in early 1987, by another sharp exchange of views, this time in response to a Polish literary critic's essay on moral responsibility, published in the key Catholic weekly.[10] The two debates made rather apparent the difference between being challenged by a Jew and by "one of our own"--*Shoah* was successfully neutralized,[11] while the second voice generated both a great deal of protest and a substantial amount of serious reflection.

Umschlagplatz, though clearly a work of a Polish writer, contains just enough Jewish "parentage" to make it potentially suspect for the readers. First, there is the author's wife, a partner in some of the most revealing discussions, who is Jewish. Her voice is in effect *less* challenging, but her presence is what ultimately explains the writing itself; Rymkiewicz tells the reader that he has no choice, married to a Jew, but to confront the troubling past. Then, there is a long passage in the book where we learn that the author himself was for quite a few years after the war "suspected" of being a

Jew.[12]   The story carries some poignance--and some humor--but it also makes clear that Rymkiewicz might not be an "average Pole." His is an experience allowing for a degree of empathy with the Jews well above that possible with generalized concern. At one point, in fact, he speculates on what *kind* of a Jew he would have been were he born a Jew, engaging his assimilated wife in a bitter debate on the merits of traditionalism and Orthodoxy.

Within the context of autobiographical reflection, Rymkiewicz's emphasis on his closeness to the Jews is not unwarranted. Within the context of recent discussions on Polish-Jewish relations, however, the Jewish dimension of *Umschlagplatz* weakens its potential to engage readers in a self-critical inquiry into the past.

Despite the drawbacks of this highly personal approach to the question of empathy with the Jews, the question itself retains its centrality-- and its formulation as a challenge. Rymkiewicz does not read his own present sentiments into the past--the little boy in 1942 remains oblivious to the fate of the Jews. He does not project his empathy on other Poles either; the book intends to generate a better understanding of the Jewish experience, not to serve as a confirmation that empathy had been prevalent before. The "Jewish experience" too loses its quasi-monolithic quality of victimization, with the introduction of a diverse group of pre-war vacationers, whose conversations are set to mirror at least some of the complexity within the Jewish community. For Rymkiewicz, then remembrance is *work* and so is empathy. The challenge, for Poles, is to engage in the work without forgetting that it is work, to feel closer to the Jew without forgetting the past indifference.

In *The Beginning*, as we have seen, empathy with the Jews is treated as a given, and not as a feeling yet-to-be-acquired. There is one exception, though, to this general pattern, an exception revealing just how much Szczypiorski's work is informed by the need to enlighten. Irena, the Jewish woman rescued with the help of the Poles and the German officer, survives the war and becomes a devoted member of Poland's ruling elite. In 1968, together with so many other Jews, she is forced to emigrate. We meet her again in Paris in 1981, still unforgiving and bitter, traumatized by Poland's rejection of her. Szczypiorski, in a deliberately didactic voice, speaks of Irena's memories of 1968 as obliterating the earlier ones, of her apparent ingratitude as an understandable result of the pain of rejection. The reader is now being educated on the dynamics of anti-Polish discourse in the West in general, and asked to empathize with the Jews in their biases.

This "update" on Polish-Jewish relations brings into the foreground one of the key elements of the current debates--the connection between Jews and Communism. Rarely explicit in officially approved publications, but strong nevertheless is an effort to "balance" Polish past wrongdoings with those of Jewish Communists.[13] The idea that all of post-war antisemitism can be explained by the widely shared perception of Jews as agents of foreign oppression gives the "Jew-Communist" image a great deal of additional strength. Szczypiorski does little more than to remind his readers of this dimension of the past; he does not need to do more for the overall tone of his reflection to fall within the standard range.

Once again, Rymkiewicz's work stands in sharp contrast to *The Beginning*. Here, the Jewish Communist belongs to the patiently reconstructed gallery of political options, to the world of discord and debate within the pre-war Jewish community. Though given more exposure than historically warranted, the appeal of Communism to Polish Jews becomes a topic for quasi-sociological reflection on its origins rather than any kind of explanation for what was to follow. Given the still scant knowledge of the Jewish political scene, Rymkiewicz too might be said to "enlighten" the reader, his lesson, though, is not a comforting one. Fitting in the overall pattern of remembrance-as-work, the connection between Jews and Communism is made to lose its mythological quality, or at least to lose its power of neutralizing questions of responsibility.

Umschlagplatz, despite its novel approach to then widely discussed issues, did not arouse much controversy. The few generally positive reviews which appeared did not take up Rymkiewicz's challenge. Among Polish intellectuals with a strong interest in the Jewish issues, the book provoked little public (or private) debate. According to Krystyna Kersten,[14] a prominent historian of the post-war era, *Umschlagplatz* failed to stir emotions largely because of its timing. In 1988, after two "rounds" of discussion about Poles and the Holocaust, the subject appeared exhausted.

The Beginning also did not provoke a debate. It was not designed to do so. The book's popularity and high praise for its author is a good indication that Szczypiorski's views were both acceptable and accepted. Considering how much comfort he provides, this is not at all surprising. Challenged to respond by Western criticism, Polish readers found in Sczczypiorski an excellent advocate for their sense of injustice such outsiders' critique perpetuates.

Umschlagplatz is not a comforting work. Its inability, so far, to generate wider reflection on the questions it poses may indeed not be related to just how troubling these questions are. However limited its impact, the book's very presence *is* significant for its departure from the well-established patterns of rendering the Polish-Jewish past morally unchallenging. An examination of conscience does not automatically follow a voice of conscience. Yet without such voices--and Rymkiewicz's is not alone[15]--it cannot even begin.

When read against the background of the wide public exposure recently given to Poland's Jewish heritage, the two books examined here acquire an "indexical" quality. Behind *The Beginning*, there is by now a vast terrain of remembrance which allows solace and self-justification; *Umschlagplatz*, on the other hand, stands for a small-yet-growing group of self-critical inquiries into the past. The declared obligation to remember the Jew which joins the two works is also shared across the current efforts to retrieve Poland's Jewish heritage, reminding us, in turn, that remembering may serve as a way to forget as much as a way to honor.

ENDNOTES

[1]For an analysis of Polish Holocaust literature, see Henyk K. Grynberg (1984). On the larger issue of memory of the Holocaust in post-war Poland, see Iwona Irwin-Zarecka (1989).

[2]Dating back to about 1978, the subject of Polish-Jewish relations has been taken up by more and more writers from across the political spectrum, becoming especially prominent within the independent Catholic media. [The present paper draws on an earlier study of the current discourse; see Irwin-Zarecka (1989).]

[3]Within this body of writings, Stanislaw Lem's (1984) reflections on the Holocaust would also very much warrant a separate study; his work is a rare instance of approaching the subject from a general perspective, i.e. without calling upon a "Polish question."

[4]Although few of the Western voices reach Poland directly, local media have long accorded a prominent position to summarizing them, usually within the framework of "anti-Polishness." The television series *Holocaust*, for example, was in its time widely criticized for its portrayal of Poles (and not screened in Poland).

[5]Of particular importance here are studies of anti-Jewish violence during the first years following the war; see Yehuda Bauer (1970), Lucjan Dobroszycki (1973), Marc Hillel (1985).

[6]As late as 1987, a survey of most widely used textbooks (Marian Marek Drozdowski) showed that the theme of the Jews' passivity is both prevalent and exclusive of other interpretations.

[7]In Polish discourse on the Holocaust, "responsibility" is generally reduced to the facts-and-figures of what happened at the time. The most important historical actor who is thus absolved is the Catholic church, with neither pre-war attitudes nor post-war violence entering the picture.

[8]The idea is, in my view, very much worth reflecting on. Auschwitz, which so often serves as a symbol of the Holocaust in the West, was also a camp for non-Jewish prisoners. *Umschlagplatz* in Warsaw, on the other hand, is where Europe's largest Jewish community--and no one else--met destruction.

[9]Since the book was written, a more extensive memorial along the road to *Umschlagplatz* was erected, on the initiative of a group of volunteers.

[10]The English translation of Jan Blonski's "Poor Poles watched the ghetto" (*Tygodnik Powszechny*, Jan. 7, 1987) appeared in *POLIN*, vol. 2, 1988.

[11]The fact that *Shoah* was used by the Polish government in its own long-standing argument with the Catholic Church did not help matters. Critical reflection, when coming almost exclusively from "court Jews," resulted in an ever-stronger defensive posture on the part of Catholic intellectuals.

[12]The language of "suspicion" is best exposed by Slawomir Mrozek (1985), another prominent Polish writer who had experienced it himself.

[13]During the debate around *Shoah*, both the Catholic press in Poland, and the emigré journal *Kultura* carried several examples of this "balancing" strategy.

[14]Interview with the author, February 25, 1989.

[15]Considering the importance of events *after* the Holocaust (see Irwin-Zarecka, 1988), the film *Witnesses*, independently produced in 1988, represents the most significant development to date. Composed of interviews with the inhabitants of Kielce, it is a chilling portrait of people taking the murder of Jews (in the 1946 pogram) as "natural."

REFERENCES

Bauer, Yehuda. 1970. *Flight and Rescue: BRICHAH.* New York: Random House.

Blonski, Jan. 1987. "Biedni Polacy patrza na getto." *Tygodnik Powszechny* (Jan. 11).

Dobroszycki, Lucjan. 1973. "Restoring Jewish Life in Post-War Poland." *Soviet Jewish Affairs*, no. 2:58-72.

Drozdowski, Marian Marek. 1987. "Dzieje najnowsze w maturalnych klasach." *Tygodnik Powszechny* (May 17).

Grynberg, Henryk. 1984. "Holocaust w literaturze polskiej." *Archipelag* (West Berlin), nos. 1(6) and 2(7).

Hillel, Marc. 1985. *Le massacre de survivants. En Pologne après l'holocauste (1945-1947).* Paris: Plon.

Irwin-Zarecka, Iwona. 1988. "Poland, After the Holocaust." Paper presented at *Remembering for the Future*, Oxford, July 11-14.

_____. 1989. *Neutralizing Memory: The Jew in Contemporary Poland.* New Brunswick, N.J.: Transaction Books.

Lem, Stanislaw. 1984. *Prowokacja.* Krakow-Wroclaw: Wydawnictwo Literackie.

Mrozek, Slawomir. 1985. "Podejrzenie." *Kultura*, no. 11/458:42-44.

Rymkiewicz, Jaroslaw Marek. 1988. *Umschlagplatz.* Paris: Instytut Literacki.

Szczypiorski, Andrzej. 1986. *Poczatek.* Paris: Instytut Literacki.

DATING THE *SHOAH:* IN YOUR BLOOD SHALL YOU LIVE

Zev Garber

On April 12, 1951, the Knesset of Israel decreed *Nisan* 27 to be the official date for observing the Holocaust and Ghetto Revolt Remembrance Day (*Yom ha-Shoah u-Mered ha-Getaot*). The date is commemorated worldwide by all who wish to recall the Great Catastrophe, honor its victims and heroes, and pledge that the devastation caused by the Nazis will never again be repeated.

The eminent Jewish philosopher and prisoner of Sachsenhausen concentration camp, Emil Fackenheim, has observed, "We cannot give meaning to Auschwitz with Jerusalem. Still less is it possible, however, to give meaning to the catastrophe without Jerusalem: Indeed, we cannot give meaning to Auschwitz at all."[1] Yet the decision of the Knesset has insured the meaning of Auschwitz for eternity.

However, the choice of *Nisan* 27 as the date of record to recall the most significant event of the twentieth century disappointed religionists and secularists alike. To understand the "Day of Remembrance" decision is to disclose contemporary Jewish thinking on the *Shoah:* is it an act of providential design, history, or a combination of both?

Asarah b'Tevet is one of four fast days in the Jewish calendar which recalls the end of the first Jewish Commonwealth, signified by the destruction of the First Temple (*Churban)* and the Babylonian Exile of the Jewish People from Eretz Israel (586-539 B.C.E.).

To label the destruction of European Jewry as a *Churban* is to link it with a past devastating event, but, in the words of Neo-Orthodox thinker, Rabbi Irving Greenberg, this does not come to grips with the awesome emotional, historical, and theological weight of the Holocaust; the *Shoah* as a category-shattering event.[2] In addition, it can be said, classical *Churban* catastrophe takes place within the Land of Israel; *Shoah* outside of the Land.

Tishah b'Av. This major fast day in midsummer is *the* day of reflection on catastrophes of Jewish History in *and* outside the Land of Israel: Destruction of the First and Second Temples, the expulsion of Jews from Spain in 1492, the Chmielnicki murder of Polish Jewry in 1648-49 (in addition, Sivan 20 is specifically set aside to remember these massacres), and all other major atrocities committed against Jews.

To remember *Shoah* on *Tisha b'Av* is to teach that the causes, reasons, and politics of genocide past have repeated themselves in the Nazi destruction of six million Jews, and to suggest that learning the proper responses to *Churban*, depicted in Jewish literature and *Halachah* (Jewish law), could have averted or diminished the evil decree unleashed on millions of innocents during World War II.

However, to observe *Shoah* on *Tisha b'Av* (day of *Jewish* tragedies) could make the event parochial and not universal--lest we forget, millions of others were murdered in Hitler's inferno. Also, if *Shoah* were recalled with other Jewish calamities, then the uniqueness of Hitler's war against the Jews would be dramatically diminished.

Never in history was a people so radically abandoned, dehumanized, and murdered. Emil Fackenheim puts it well:

> ...to lump the Holocaust with all the others would be to act as if nothing new had happened in the history of horror when the attempt was made to "exterminate" the Jewish people, that is to murder saints as well as sinners, new born babies as well as adults, and no exception was made even for those already near the grave; and the attempt was successful beyond the wildest nightmares of anyone.[3]

Furthermore, *Tisha b'Av* in the minds of many is of biblical origin and its observance is dictated by *Halachah*. Would the non-religious feel comfortable observing *Shoah* on a day guided by minutiae of rabbinic guidelines?

April 19. On this day in 1943, the liquidation of the Warsaw Ghetto began, and Mordechai Anielewicz led the Warsaw Ghetto revolt; the liquidation was completed on May 16. Secularists, Yiddishists, Bundists, among others, feel that this freedom fighter image--the revolt of the few against the many--is the proper way to record the *Shoah*.

Opposition to "April 19," however, was mounted on three major ideological points.

(1)   The Warsaw Ghetto uprising was by no means the only revolt against the Germans; why then should this act of heroism be singled out?

(2)   Not all moments of heroism took place with gun in hand. Many simple Jews who participated not in "uprisings" did exceptional, courageous feats, usually at the risk of life and limb, over and above the sorts of acts that "ordinary" individuals ever do. These Jews and others who endured sufferings at the hands of Nazis were heroes on a much more basic human level; for certainly it is correct to view their endurance itself as something of heroic proportion.

(3)   "April 19" is a solar date; issues of Jewish destiny demonstrate permanence only when they are commemorated in the Jewish lunar year (providential calendar).

Nisan 15 is the Hebrew date on which the Warsaw Ghetto uprising began. Setting aside the objections mentioned above, *Nisan* 15 is the first day of Passover. Many would agree that the birthday of the Jewish people (Hebrew tribes became a nation on the first Passover) is a time for joy and celebration, not a time for pain and remembering destruction.

Others say if there is no Jewish people there can be no celebration as Jews; hence, *Shoah* should take precedence over Passover. Curiously, this argument may be supported by a reading from the Book of Esther, and a midrash (rabbinic hermeneutical pronouncement) thereupon:

> In the first month, that is, the month of Nisan, in the twelfth year of King Ahasuerus, *pur*--which means "the lot"--was cast before Haman concerning every day and every month, (until it fell on) the twelfth month, that is, the month of Adar.

> On the thirteenth day of the first month, the king's scribes were summoned and a decree was issued, as Haman directed...to destroy, massacre, and exterminate all the Jews, young and old, children and women, on a single day, in the thirteenth day of

the twelfth month--that is, the month of Adar--and to plunder their possessions.

(Esther 3:7, 12-13)

When told of this evil decree by her wise and informed cousin, Mordechai, Esther bids the Jews of Shushan and her court maidens to fast for three days and three nights (Esther 4:15). The rabbinic view is that the fast followed immediately after Esther heard Mordechai's report on the 13th of Nisan. According to the midrash, the fast embraced *Nisan* 13, 14, and 15.

The fast days, proclaimed to avert the decree of extermination, coincided with and took precedence over Passover (*Nisan* 15). The text records, *va-Ya'avor Mordechai*/"And Mordechai went his way (in the city)" (Esther 4:17), but the talmudic sage Rav takes *va-Ya'avor* (= he violated) to mean, "transgressed the Passover law by fasting on a festival day."[4] The Sages' embellishment of this account presents Mordechai as protesting to Esther, "But these three fast days include the first day of Passover," and Esther as replying, "If there is no Israel, how can there be a Passover?"

Rabbinic legislation permits the cancellation or minimization of joy due to pain or shame. The Talmud speaks about God's anger at angels for singing a song of victory after the pursuing Egyptians drowned in the sea: "The work of My hands are drowning in the sea, and you sing my praises?" (BT Megillah 10B). Consequently, Jews intentionally curtail their Passover joy by not reciting the complete Hallel (Psalms 113-118) during Passover week, by diminishing the second cup of wine at the Seder, and by the Fast of the First Born on the eve of Passover, out of empathy for the dying Egyptians.

In the midrashic account, Esther's decision to cancel Passover may be seen as an act of *Pikuah Nefesh* ("saving life"), and Jewish law permits the suspension of Jewish practice if life is at stake. Esther's cancellation of Passover was an act *before* destruction in order to avoid it; *Shoah* observance, however, is an act of obedience *after* destruction in order to lament and learn from it.

Today on 'erev Passover many read Holocaust selections during the recitation of the "Pour Out Thy Wrath" paragraph accompanying the Cup of Elijah. But reference to *Shoah* here does not dominate the Passover tiding of freedom and birth. Rather they are part of a liturgical message invoking the Judge of all the earth to deal justly with the murderers, and on another level, the nations of the world, who did nothing to condemn Nazism and do nothing to abolish the cry that Zionism is racism, as He continuously judges Israel. Only then, can the complete messianic fulfillment of the future, a brotherhood of man under the fatherhood of God and inspired by the Torah way, be realized swiftly in our days.

On this point, we should note that the anthem of many Jews as they were led to extermination was the 12th article of the Maimonidean Creed ("I firmly believe in the coming of the messiah, and although he may tarry, I daily wait his coming"). These helpless victims of Nazism sang of a better day for humanity--a humanity that chose to be silent at the hour of their destruction. This is an authentic Jewish understanding of hope and *Heilsgeschichte*, conducted without politics, politeness, and paternalism. The message: The major traits of Hitlerism--isolation, vilification, expulsion, slavery, and extermination--are not the will of heaven but the act of every man, the bitter fruits of the freedom he has abused.

Shoah cannot cancel Passover because the latter is transformed by Sinai (providence), and the former is the leaven waste of cyanide (history).

On the 12th of April 1951, the Knesset arrested Heaven and Earth and declared *Nisan* 27 as the national holiday commemorating the Holocaust. The declaration (see Appendix) recalls antecedents to the Nazi brutality done to Ashkenazi Jewry in European lands; chooses biblical proof texts that narrate exile, plight, mercy, justice, return, redemption, and responsibility; maintains that in the month of *Nisan*, many communities were destroyed by the forebears of the Nazis, the Crusaders; and offers a fable emphasizing some useful truth:

> A man and his son were walking along the path. The son tired and asked the father: "Father, where is the state?" The father replied: "Son, this should be your sign, if you see a cemetery close by, the state is near."

In our day, the catastrophic destruction of the Jewish people is the Holocaust ("cemetery"), which is forever linked to the rise of Israel ("state"). Indeed, Israel Independence Day is celebrated on *Iyar* 5, showing a connection between *Yom ha-Shoah* and *Yom ha-Atzmaut*.

Thus on April 12, 1951, the Knesset read first the declaration on *Yom ha-Atzmaut* followed by the declaration on *Yom ha-Shoah*. The order of the readings is important; it suggests that only a relentless commitment to life and hope (Zionist dream and hope) can withstand the pain and grief of remembering the *Shoah*. The reverse is unthinkable.

So we count the days from *Yom ha-Shoah* to *Yom ha-Atzmaut* and we compute nine. Who knows nine? Nine, in the words of the Passover Haggadah, "are the months of pregnancy." Pregnancy means life and life is ushered in by covenant. And in the covenant of Abraham, Jews recite this prophetic utterance:

> And I pass by thee (Jerusalem) and
> I (God) saw thee wallowing in thy blood,
> And I said unto thee
> In thy blood live. Yea, I said unto thee,
> In thy blood live.
>
> (Ezekiel 16:6)

The cited verse is found in the Knesset statement on the *Shoah*.

At the Wannsee Conference in January 1942 the blueprint for the "Final Solution" was unveiled in 58 minutes. In less than 20 minutes on April 12, 1951, people, history, God, *Shoah*, and Zion were sealed in an eternal manifesto committing a post-Holocaust age to life, hope, and action.

On 6 *Nisan* 5711 (April 12, 1951), clouds gathered over Auschwitz, Poland, and in Jerusalem the Golden, the sun rose over Zion.

"In your blood, Israel, in your blood shall you live."

ENDNOTES

[1]Fackenheim, Emil L. *What is Judaism?* New York: Summit Books, 1987, p. 37.

[2]An insightful summary of Rabbi Irving Greenberg's thinking on *Shoah* is his "The Shattered Paradigm: Yom Hashoah," in *The Jewish Way*. New York: Summit Books, 1988, pp. 314-372.

[3]Fackenheim, *loc. cit.*, p. 37.

[4]See S. Goldman's comment on Esther 4:17 in *The Five Megilloth*. London: Soncino Press, 1961, p. 218.

APPENDIX

The Decision Regarding the Establishment of a National Holiday Commemorating the Holocaust and Ghetto Revolt Remembrance Day.

Chairperson Yosef Sprinzak:

I request the subcommittee chairperson of the House Committee, Knesset member Nourok, to present us with the decision regarding *Yom ha-Shoah*. Mordechai Norouk (in the name of the House Committee):

The Heaven weeps, the Land weeps, and Israel weeps.

High Court, sisters and brothers in suffering. On behalf of the House Committee, I am honored to present to you an important and significant proposal. Six years have passed since the removal of the iron bars enclosing the European countries occupied by Nazi Germany during World War II, when we finally realized the awful truth, that our expectation was in vain and our hope was nought, and our worst fears came to be: Six Million of our people were murdered, a third of our nation, most of our sons, in cold blood were killed, with frightening brutality, using a system horrifying in its completeness, fathers and sons, women and children, a million two hundred thousand Jewish children, the Jewish youth, the hope and future of a nation, who could have become the pride of our people and a beacon to the nation.

The significant thousand-year period of European Jewry came to a tragic end. Carved in our minds is the intricate and complete social and political life of the various Jewish communities in the European diaspora. A wide network of schools teaching in other languages, from pre-school through higher education, supported by the state and local authorities, encouraged by the cultural, national autonomy; the large yeshivas, their reputation preceding them throughout the Jewish world; splendid institutions cultural, financial, philanthropic; various organizations, rich daily newspapers, libraries, publishing; parliament representatives elected by Jewish parties, who continuously protected equal rights for all, with integrity and respect of Jewish values; tens of thousands, study halls and prayer quorums, hundreds of thousands of Jewish books and millions upon millions of worshippers--"a wind passes by and it is no more"[1]--this is, the Third Destruction (*Churban*) of the House of Israel.

We hear the voice of the blood of our brethren screaming from the earth: "Earth, do not cover my blood,"[2] so that all future generations will know the horrendous acts done by the vicious animals disguised as human beings.

We hear the cry of our beloved sons: raise the flag which is drowning in blood and tears, that fell from our hands, and carry it with pride and reverence. If we mourn on *Tisha b'Av* for the communities of Magneza, Vermiza, and Smyrna, that were destroyed by the ancestors of the Nazis, then we must know how many Jews these communities numbered - five thousand at the most. And yet now we have witnessed communities such as Warsaw, which numbered during the war as much as half a million residents, Lodz, Lamberg, Cracow, Lublin, Tzintuchov, Pinsk, Luzak, Rona, Vilna (the Jerusalem of Lithuania), Kovna, Grodna, Brisk, Bialistock, Riga, Mitaov, Lvov, Berlin, Frankfurt, Hamburg, Breslau, Vienna, Strasburg, Budapest, Bucharest, Kishinev, Tzernovitz, Belgrade, Zagreb, Thessalonica, Prague, Odessa, Charson, Kiev, Vitvask, Mohil, and many, many more, who is able to count them? In all these communities there were no less than 50,000 Jews.

"When I think of this, I pour out my soul."[3]

"Oh, that my head were water
My eyes a fount of tears!
Then would I weep day and night
for the slain of my poor people."[4]

"For how can I bear to see the disaster
which will befall my people! And how can I
bear to see the destruction of my kindred!"[5]

I am a prayer to the God of our ancestors: "Before our eyes let it be known among the nations that You avenge the spilled blood of Your servants!"[6] When the Romans found Rabbi Hananya ben Teradyon, one of the Ten Martyrs, who gathered unto him crowds and Torah in public, they sentenced him to burn at the stake. And as he took his last breath, he declared: "The parchments are burning, but the letters of The Torah soar upward." Our enemies can destroy us in body, the parchments are burning, but the spirit of Israel, the infinite treasure, lives on forever, the letters soar from country to country, from one part of the earth to another.

Those that remain, the survivors, who were subjugated to incomprehensible suffering, do not know where the ashes of the holy and pure have spread: "And no man knows their sepulchre unto this day."[7]

Every Jew has a proper memorial day, a day he commemorates the memory of his dear beloved ones. They died a natural death, we know when they left us; we ourselves buried them and we have always opportunity to shed tears on their graves. On days that we rejoice and on days of sadness, when we stand at their graves, we can almost see our dearly beloved, we can practically hear their voices, and our hearts warm to the sound.

However, dear Knesset members, brothers and sisters in suffering, different is the other kind, the uncommon; we have no knowledge of neither the day or the year of death of the innocent souls of all the martyrs, nor any idea to where their ashes were spread.

Even this small consolation, the vicious animals, posing as humans, take from us.

Even in our history, submerged in blood and tears, which knows Pharoah, Nebuchadnezzar, Vespasian, Titus, Hadrian, the Crusades, the Poisoning of The Wells, Blood Libels, the Inquisition, the Pogroms--there is no equivalent to the annihilation of a third of our people in such a form.

And we feel compelled to commemorate the memory of our loved ones, but we must designate a day that will be commemorated by all, to remember all The martyrs. On this day the unity of the nation in its entirety will be reflected for "there was no house where there was not someone dead."[8]

It is our national duty to designate for the generations to come a memorial day for our martyrs. We are proud of the ghetto uprisings, and of our brothers and sisters who saved the honor of Israel with miraculous feats accomplished in great courage, and they showed the vicious animals that the people of Israel will not be led like sheep to slaughter, and that it will die heroically, the death of righteous and courageous people. So that all future generations will know how to honor and respect the memory of these sacrificial victims of our nation. This is our consolation.

Our forebears have dedicated days of fast and mourning to certain events, such as the 20th of *Sivan*,[9] etc., which cannot be compared in any shape to this modern tragedy.

We must choose a significant day which will reflect the days of slaughter and the days of uprising that took place in the month of *Nisan*. Therefore, the House Committee has chosen the end of the month of *Nisan*, in The days of *Sefirah*,[10] during which many sacred communities were destroyed by the ancestors of the Nazis, the Crusaders.

The commemoration of the victims of the Holocaust is an issue in and of itself. I hope we will do so when the people of Israel will dwell secure in our country, and by the grace of God, we will achieve a normalized state. In evidence is an elaborate plan conceived by Yad VaShem and sponsored by the World Jewish Congress with the participation of the Jewish Agency and the National Committee.

The people of Israel have always excelled in the commemoration of their departed. Our forebears carried Joseph's coffin 40 years in the desert in order that he be buried in the Land of Israel.

Let us commemorate the memory of our martyrs and the future generations will pass down from generation to generation the glory and honor of our martyrs, and from them they will draw the strength and courage to continue the chain of generations. Our martyrs have a significant part in the building of our people and the land. And we ask with pain gripping our hearts: Why didn't our dear and beloved ones live to see their hopes and dreams, from which they dedicated their lives, come to be?

I take the liberty to find the answer in a fable. A man and his son were walking along the path. The son tired and asked his father: "Father, where is the state?" The father replied: "Son, this shall be your sign, if you see a cemetery close by, the state is near."

Honored Knesset: We too have seen a cemetery before us, a graveyard of Six Million of our sisters and brothers, and perhaps by the merit of their blood spilled like water, we achieved a state and the beginning of redemption, as in the words of the prophet spoken from the hills of Zion: "And when I passed by you, and saw you wallowing in your blood, I said unto you: In your blood live; yea, I said unto you: In your blood live!"[11] In other words, my oppressed and persecuted people--do not despair! You will rise to a new life, to an independent life, to a glorious life.

I have the great pleasure to present to the Knesset the following legislation formulated by the House Committee:

The First Knesset declares and states that the 27th day of the month of *Nisan* of every year will be the Day of the Holocaust and Ghetto Revolt Remembrance--an eternal day of memory for Israel.

Honored Knesset, the elected of the Land, with the permission of the chairperson, we will stand for a moment of silence in the memory of our martyrs. (The Knesset stood at attention.)

I hope,[12] that at this moment, when the images of the martyrs and their communities appear before us, we will think of them with respect, with sympathy and admiration, and we will decide unanimously to commemorate their memory on this established day, this year and forever. And we call to the sacred communities destroyed, as Jonathan called to David: "You will be missed when your seat remains vacant."[13]

We will not forget you, you who have left an empty space in the Jewish world.

Chairperson Sprinzak:

I declare the decision.

The First Knesset declares and establishes the 27th day of the month of *Nisan* of every year as the Holocaust and Ghetto Remembrance Day--an eternal day of memory for the House of Israel.

The meeting adjourned at 9:20 A.M.

The meeting resumed at 10:35 A.M.

Translation by Zev Garber

ENDNOTES

[1]Psalm 103:16.

[2]Job 16:18.

[3]Psalm 42:5.

[4]Jeremiah 8:23.

[5]Esther 8:6.

[6]Psalm 79:10b.

[7]Deuteronomy 34:6b. Text speaks of "his sepulchre," i.e., Moses; likewise, an unknown burial place is the fate of millions of Holocaust victims.

[8]Exodus 12:30b.

[9]The Council of the Four Lands, the central institution of Jewish self-government of Poland and Lithuania from the middle of the 16th century until 1764, decreed the Fast of Sivan 20, the day upon which the Chmielnicki massacres began in Nemirov (*Gezeirot Tah ve-Tat*).

[10]*Sefirah* = count; the counting of the Omer (a measure of grain) for seven full weeks starting from the second day of Passover to the beginning of Shavuot (Pentecost); see Lev 23:9-15. In addition, rabbinic memory has changed this biblical season of joy to one of pain as it remembers the slaughter of Rabbi Akiva and his students for the "crime" of teaching Torah in Eretz Israel against the wishes of Rome.

[11]Ezekiel 16:8.

[12]Error in text; word should read *mekaveh* and not *tikvah*.

[13]I Samuel 20:18b. The prooftext has the verbs in the singular, understandably changed to the plural in the Knesset quotation.

JOHN BEATY'S *THE IRON CURTAIN OVER AMERICA:* ANTI-
SEMITISM AND ANTI-COMMUNISM IN THE 1950's*

Richard V. Pierard

The early 1950's were a profoundly trying time in American history.
China had just fallen under Communist rule, spy scandals rocked the country,
the Soviet Union now had the atomic bomb, the House Un-American
Activities committee was busily ferreting out alleged subversives, and the
intensive FBI effort to break the back of the Communist Party USA was
proving successful.   In 1950 the conviction of Alger Hiss elevated
congressman Richard M. Nixon to national status, opening the way to a
Senate seat and eventually the vice presidency, while an obscure senator
from Wisconsin, Joseph McCarthy, captured headlines with his free-wheeling
accusations that the State Department was honeycombed with Communists.
The United States took up arms against Communists in Korea, but got
bogged down in a standstill war of attrition and national passions were stirred
when President Truman dismissed Gen. Douglas MacArthur from his
command. Passed over Truman's veto was the McCarran Internal Security
Act, a far-reaching assault on civil liberties which required federal
registration of "Communist-action" groups whose members were then denied
passports and federal jobs, made political belief a standard for admission to
and deportation from America, and provided for concentration camps to
detain alleged subversives "in time of national emergency." Around the
country the American Legion was busily promoting "Americanism" through
its meetings and publications. Due to the combination of McCarthy, Korea,

and corruption in his administration, Truman decided not to seek re-election in 1952.

One of the most vicious aspects of this ubiquitous anti-Communism was hatemongering. Numerous speakers and writers linked Communism with the Jews, charging that Jewish Communists had infiltrated key government positions and that Communists and Zionists were one and the same. For example, Conde McGinley's *Common Sense*, one of the worst hate rags of the era, called itself "The Nation's Anti-Communist Newspaper," and Gerald L. K. Smith made anti-Communism a major plank in his demagogic platform.[1] This kind of thinking was especially pervasive in the Southwest, as Don Carleton brings out in his study of right-wing hysteria in Texas,[2] and it was here that an obscure English professor gained national notoriety through a book entitled *The Iron Curtain Over America*.

Dr. Beaty's Book

In December 1951 *The Iron Curtain Over America* was published by the Dallas-based Wilkinson Publishing Company.[3] The author, Dr. John O. Beaty, a senior professor of English at Southern Methodist University, affirmed in the preface that he would not only exhibit the external and internal dangers threatening the survival of the country but also would show how they developed and why they continued to plague us.

The book opened with a thoroughly positive assessment of the Teutonic Knights' role in German history. Then Beaty turned to Russia and developed the tendentious thesis that a people called the Khazars adopted Judaism in the eighth century and remained in tension with the Slavic peoples throughout the middle ages and modern times. According to his interpretation of history, these "Judaized Khazars" functioned as both an indigestible mass in the Russian body politic and a formidable anti-government force. They were responsible for the Russian Revolution and Communism in general, and they carried out the secret efforts of the Soviet regime to undermine freedom elsewhere in the world. Khazar Jewish immigrants to the United States served in the vanguard of the Communist advance here, especially as they penetrated the Democratic party. These persons of Eastern European stock rose to many of the most strategic spots in the Roosevelt and Truman administrations and they exercised great power in shaping U.S. policy

Their influence was particularly evident when the country was dragged into "the unnecessary war" against Hitler's Germany. The Jewish clique around Roosevelt was responsible for his "silly infatuation for Stalin and the accompanying mania for serving the interests of world Communism" (68), and for his interest in "weakening the British Empire while strengthening the Soviet Empire" (70). The U.S. undertook the war against Germany to please this dominant Eastern European element in the Democratic party who regarded with enthusiasm "the killing of as many as possible of the world-ruling and Khazar-hated race of 'Aryans'" (74). Our alien-dominated government sought to annihilate Germany, "the historic bulwark of Christian Europe" (77).

We were unaware of what was happening because "a black mask of censorship" hid the identity and purpose of the enemies of the American way of life who were undermining the Constitution and our heritage of Christian civilization (80). The "blackout of truth" was carried out by the executive branch of the U.S. government and by the media. "Marxism and other alien ideas" were propagated by people who controlled public opinion and the "infiltration of aliens" into the publishing industry, libraries, and schools (101).

In particular, they tossed "the label of anti-Semitic" at those who mentioned Jewish Communists by name and opposed government ventures which were Jewish-sponsored or endorsed (105). The "Khazar Jew" equated anti-Communism with anti-Semitism, an action which was patently unfair to loyal American Jews. Moreover, the Khazar Jews were really not even Semites as such. The blood of Abraham, Isaac, and Jacob did not flow in the veins of the East European Jews but in those of the Palestinian Arabs. "Perhaps the truest seed of Bible Jews," the Palestinians were in fact "refugees today from the barbarity of non-Semitic Khazars!" (106).

The "mistakes" of the Truman administration's foreign policy were due to ineptitude and disloyalty. These included the "sell-out" of China to the Communists, a Palestinian policy which alienated our Arab allies and placed the area under the control of the Communist, Zionist, Khazar Jews (he used the terms interchangeably and always used quotation marks when referring to the state of "Israel"), and the draconian treatment of defeated Germany. Having set the stage for possible disaster by these three "colossal" mistakes, "we awaited the enemy's blow which could be expected to topple us to defeat" (144). It came in Korea where "the State Department and Presidential coterie" did all they could to prevent the victory of our troops (147). The controllers of the national Democratic Party clearly wanted war because this would safeguard their power.

The only hope for America was a cleansing of "the Augean stables." His commentary on the famous parable of Hercules was perhaps the most colorful passage in the book:

> King Augeas is Mr. Truman. The sacred bulls are those high and mighty individuals who control and deliver the votes of minority blocs. The filth is the eighteen-year accumulation of Communists and fellow-travelers in the various departments, executive agencies, bureaus, and what not, of our government. There can be but one Hercules--an aroused American people (172).

The cleansing could be carried out by the election of strong, patriotic, and able candidates in a national election, bringing public pressure to bear on Congress, and ousting the "high-placed leftists and their dupes" from their places in the government (186, 191).

"America can still be free" if immediate steps were taken against the "insidious forces working from within" that were "opposed to all our great traditions" (193). This would require lifting the iron curtain of censorship, utilizing the rights guaranteed by the Constitution, and working "in the spirit of humane Christian civilization" to develop some method which would prevent "our unassimilable mass of aliens and alien-minded people" from exercising so much power over our culture and shaping policies that were against the national interest in such vital matters as war and immigration (197). The government must act against Communism in the United States by arresting and deporting or placing under surveillance all known Communists. Our military policy must be totally separated from the influence of minority voting blocs. We should withdraw from and dismantle the UN. We should view Russians positively as Christians and make common cause with them in their struggle to get out from under the yoke of the Judaized Khazars.

Finally, all subversives should be removed from the executive departments and agencies in Washington. Carrying out this program of action would free our people at last from the haunting nightmare of fear.

The Author

John Owen Beaty hardly seemed the person to be destined to such notoriety.[4] Born in Crow, West Virginia on December 22, 1890, he earned a B.A. and M. A. from the University of Virginia and a Ph.D. from Columbia University. He was an army officer in World War I, reaching the rank of captain. He joined the Southern Methodist University faculty in 1919 and spent his entire professional career there. From 1927 to 1940 he was head of the English department. In 1926-27 he traveled in Europe on a grant from the Albert Kahn Foundation. His literary output was quite respectable, with a scholarly monograph, *John Esten Cooke, Virginian* (Columbia University Press, 1922), two novels, *Swords in the Dawn* (Longmans, Green, 1937) and *Crossroads* (Wilkinson, 1956), textbooks in English composition (Crofts), English poets (Dial), drama (Macmillan), and poetry (Macmillan), and numerous other minor works. He belonged to a variety of professional and social organizations, including the American Legion, Veterans of Foreign Wars, and the Dallas Army and Navy Club. Politically, he identified with the Republican party.

A reserve officer, Beaty was recalled to active duty in 1941 and assigned to the General Staff where he worked in military intelligence, engaged in historical studies and interviewed persons who had returned from overseas assignments. When at the end of 1946 he left the army to return to teaching, he had risen to the rank of colonel. The army experience only stimulated an already existing bent toward right-wing politics, and at once he went on the political lecture circuit. Many of the ideas that were to appear in *Iron Curtain* were expressed in his speeches, and the Southwestern Jewish Community Relations Council monitored his activities.[5] He also was faculty sponsor of the Baptist students at SMU, and in a Christmas letter to them urged the "Christians of America" to stand together and courageously meet the evil stalking among us.

Buy as a Christian, vote as a Christian, give as a Christian, pray as a Christian, and you will do your part toward reversing America's current trend toward immorality and paganism. If you do your part the old decencies and the old virtues may be enthroned again in our society, and the heritage which we call Christian or Western civilization may yet be saved.[6]

With the appearance of *Iron Curtain*, a storm of controversy arose over Beaty. The Jewish community was deeply disturbed about the allegations contained in it, and the March 1952 issue of the Anti-Defamation League *Facts* and the April 1952 *ADL Bulletin* focused on his work. *Iron Curtain* was condemned in the January 11, 1952 issue of the SMU student newspaper, and an article in the Autumn 1953 number of the university's scholarly journal, the *Southwest Review*, charged him with "positive falsehoods" and being part of "the Protestant underworld." President Umphrey Lee publicly dissociated himself and the university from the English professor's views in a major address on February 12, 1953, and calls went out for Beaty's dismissal but academic freedom concerns precluded such drastic action. He in turn hurled various countercharges at his critics, including a pamphlet in January 1954 entitled *How to Capture a University* which accused "a certain powerful non-Christian element in our population" of trying to dominate SMU. This sparked a faculty investigation which categorically rejected the professor's contention.[7]

Because he was nearing retirement, the university was content to wait out the crisis. After receiving emeritus status in 1957, Beaty returned to Virginia where he spent his last years at Barboursville, near Charlottesville, and died on September 9, 1961.

The Reception of the Book

Although controversial, Beaty's tome became an instant success and quickly went through nine printings. A number of modifications were made in the eighth printing (June 1952), primarily changes within the text that reflected current events, but the book was not lengthened.[8] By the end of the year, 39,000 hard-back copies of the 268-page book had rolled off the presses, and by 1961 over 60,000 were in print. It eventually reached a 25th printing, and it continues to be available today on the lists of extreme right-wing booksellers.[9]

The religious and political right greeted the book with enthusiasm. The Kansas-based fundamentalist preacher Gerald Winrod urged that "Christians and all other patriotic Americans lose no time in ordering and circulating it among friends and neighbors," while Methodism's most famous fundamentalist, "Fightin' Bob" Shuler in Los Angeles, labeled it "the most startling and sensational book of this generation." Allen A. Zoll, well-known anti-Semitic educational theorist, called it "the most important book in the last 50 years," while gossip columnist Hedda Hopper asserted it was "the most revealing and frightening book that's come to my desk in ages."[10]

A former American Legion National Commander and U.S. Ambassador to several European states, Alvin M. Owsley, endorsed it as "one of the great documents of our times....It is a 'must' on every reader's list....[I]t should become the first reading of every patriot in the land. Read it and you will be a better American." Gerald L. K. Smith called it the "the most sensational book ever to be written on a college campus" and "the greatest book of its kind ever to appear in print." Beaty was "an erudite gentleman" who was "one of the nation's better historians," and he could not "be dismissed as a rabble rouser or a leader of the lunatic fringe." Smith's scholarly biographer Glen Jeansonne points out that *Iron Curtain* was his favorite book on communism because it discussed the "Jewish question" and Beaty pretended to be a scholar. Smith sold more copies of *Iron Curtain* than any other book he peddled outside of *The Protocols of the Elders of Zion* and *The International Jew*.[11]

One of the principal boosters of the book was millionaire J. Russell Maguire, who in 1952 took over the moribund *American Mercury* and turned it into the foremost right-wing magazine of the 1950's. He personally purchased several thousand copies of *Iron Curtain* and gave them away. One amusing anecdote concerns the Rev. Henry Darlington, retired rector of the Episcopalian Church of the Heavenly Rest in New York and Chaplain of the Military Order of Foreign Wars of the Untied States. Maguire, a former parishioner, gave him 113 copies of the book to pass on to fellow clergymen. Darlington noted in his cover letter of March 25, 1952 that it "shows the anti-Christian and the anti-American 'conspiracy' in our beloved country" and that "a Christian patriot" paid for the books. When the American Jewish

Committee persuaded the Rev. Mr. Darlington to read the book carefully, he quickly repented and apologized to each recipient, admitting that it attempted "to engender religious hostility" and as such it was "scarcely worthy of your attention."[12]

More perceptive commentators immediately recognized the danger of the work. The oldest Methodist periodical in the country, *Zion's Herald* of Boston, editorialized: "Beaty is a recent 'intellectual' addition to the lengthening list of outspoken bigots across the country; and his volume appears to be the most extensive piece of racist propaganda in the history of the anti-Semitic movement in America." Methodist minister Ralph Lord Roy deftly dissected it as a piece of racist bigotry.[13] A noted libertarian scholar, Orval Watts, subjected the book to a withering review in *Faith and Freedom* (the organ of James W. Fifield's Spiritual Mobilization, a politically and economically conservative group headquartered in Los Angeles), declaring that "the myths, distortions, and deficiencies of his main thesis make the book far more a source of harm than of good to the cause of freedom."[14]

From the standpoint of scholarship, *Iron Curtain* is a disaster. Although it abounds with references and gives the appearance of being a scholarly work, it is in reality a masterpiece of mediocrity. Beaty quotes extensively from encyclopedias, textbooks, magazines, and secondary works and frequently distorts even these sources. Also, he relies heavily on right-wing sources, such as the *American Legion Magazine*, the *Freeman*, and books from the Regnery and Devin-Adair publishing houses. Like the writer of a freshman term paper, Beaty gives elaborate documentation for details that are commonly known while in other places he makes totally unsubstantiated assertions. Again and again he draws the most contorted conclusions from the evidence he cites, and he is not beneath outright falsehoods, such as, Lenin appeared on the scene in Russia in 1917 "after his exile in the Bronx (New York City) and elsewhere" (27). A full examination of Beaty's use of evidence, twisting data to make it fit his preconceptions, fabricated theories, and prevarications would require a lengthy essay.

Significance

Although this seems like an aberration of the Cold War era that can be quickly ignored and forgotten, *The Iron Curtain Over America* deserves to be taken seriously. One useful lesson it provides is how to deal with such a situation. The strategy adopted by agencies in the Jewish community was to draw as little attention to it as possible.[15] At the same time, the groups applied pressure on those occasions when it seemed fitting. The Darlington case was one example: another was the ADL's successful effort to persuade H. L. Hunt to remove the book from the circulating library of his *Facts Forum* radio and television show.[16]

Moreover, the book is important because it was the most scholarly appearing of all the 1950's-era anti-Semitic/anti-Communist works. It did have rather wide distribution, given the fact that it was a ponderous tome and was published in hardback. The far right embraced it with enthusiasm and promoted it in their organs. And, it is still being sold today.

Finally, because of its ready availability, *Iron Curtain* will continue to be a source of the Khazar legend for those anti-Communist anti-Semites who are looking for pseudoscientific straws which they can grasp. Thus, we will have to be alert for the appearance of this canard and be ready to counter it with solid historical arguments. When it comes to anti-Semitism, old ideas never seem to die--they just keep surfacing over and over again.

ENDNOTES

*The author acknowledges with gratitude grants from the Research Committee of Indiana State University and the Vidal Sassoon International Center for the study of Antisemitism, Hebrew University of Jerusalem, which assisted him in the preparation of this essay.

[1]See the superb biography by Glen Jeansonne, *Gerald L. K. Smith: Minister of Hate* (New Haven: Yale University Press, 1988). Noteworthy contemporary discussions are Margaret L. Hartley, "The Subliterature of Hate in America," *Southwest Review* 37 (Summer 1952): 177-190; and Ralph Lord Roy, *Apostles of Discord: A Study of Organized Bigotry and Disruption on the Fringes of Protestantism* (Boston: Beacon Press, 1953), PP. 26-91.

[2]Don E. Carleton, *Red Scare: Right-wing Hysteria, Fifties Fanaticism and Their Legacy in Texas* (Austin: Texas Monthly Press, 1985).

[3]All page references are to the 3rd printing, February 1952.

[4]Biographical data from *Who's Who in America* 29 (1956-57): 174; and *Who Was Who in America* 4:69.

[5]Memorandum, Southwestern Jewish Community Relations Council, Houston, Tex., Jan. 18, 1952, Library, American Jewish Historical Society, Waltham, Mass., contains biographical data not found in *Who's Who* and summarizes some of his speeches. A clipping from the *Daily Oklahoman*, Oct. 28, 1948, reports Beaty's address in Oklahoma City where he criticized immigration from Eastern Europe, urged Christians to stick together to defend Western civilization, and expressed other ideas later found in *Iron Curtain*. Beaty file, Blaustein Library, American Jewish Committee, New York.

[6]"A Christmas Message, 1948," Beaty file, AJC.

[7]Memorandum, Southwestern Jewish Community Relations Council, Houston, Feb. 27, 1953; *How to Capture a University*, Jan. 20, 1954; Report of the Beaty Committee to the Board of Trustees, May 6, 1954; Beaty file, AJC: *Time*, Apr. 12, 1954, p. 57.

[8]I determined this by comparing the first and sixth printings of the book which are in the collection of the AJHS Library.

[9]Memorandum, Southwestern Jewish Community Relations Council, Houston, Apr. 3, 1953; brochure advertising book from Beaty's personal firm, Chestnut Mountain Books, Barboursville, Va., May 1961; undated leaflet from Gerald L. K. Smith (early 1970's); Blaustein Library, American Jewish Committee, New York. Bibliographical information in the OCLC computer

database indicates that Noontide Press reprinted the book in 1970 and Gordon Press in 1980.

¹⁰Quotations documented in Roy, *Apostles of Discord*, pp. 89, 383.

¹¹Brochure, *At Last!* (Los Angeles: Christian Nationalist Crusade, 1954); Gerald L. K. Smith, *Editors Confidential* (St. Louis: Christian Nationalist Crusade, 1952, pp. 28-29; Jeansonne, *G. L. K. Smith*, p. 138.

¹²*Time*, Dec. 8, 1952, p. 42; copies of correspondence and memorandum of AJC, August 4, 1952, AJC Library.

¹³Roy, *Apostles of Discord*, pp. 84-91.

¹⁴Orval Watts, "Communism Is Not a Jewish Conspiracy," *Faith and Freedom*, December 1952-January 1953, and also reprinted as a pamphlet. Quotation on page 13 of the January installment and page 21 of the pamphlet.

¹⁵Memorandum, Southwestern Jewish Community Relations Council, Houston, Tex., Apr. 8, 1953, Beaty file, AJC. After noting that sales of the book had fallen off markedly since the fall of 1952, the author of the memorandum made the point that "our tactics were basically correct. Any additional publicity at this point or any further frontal attack on Beaty would probably restimulate the entire situation with an increase in the sales of the volume."

¹⁶"McCarthy, Hunt, and Facts Forum," *Reporter* 10 (Feb. 16, 1954): 20-21.

THE *SHOAH* AND THE AFFIRMATION OF THE RESURRECTION OF JESUS: A REVISIONIST MARGINAL NOTE

A. Roy Eckardt

The birth, life, crucifixion, and resurrection of Jesus ordinarily furnish the determining content of Christology. However, the final item in the list distinctively perpetuates debate within Christian theological and scholarly circles at a decisive point: Ought the resurrection be treated or accepted as a historical event, or ought it be received or placed within some alternative category? Is the resurrection part of the worldly history of Jesus, or is it to be construed as metahistorical?[1]

In Christian scholarship and testimony upon the resurrection of Jesus we immediately face two extreme positions, not to mention additional viewpoints that fall between the extremes. For analytical purposes, the two extremes may be identified as indicative of subjectiveness and of objectiveness.

J. K. Elliott represents the former extreme. He concludes that "whereas we can assert with conviction that the resurrection belief founded the church, we cannot readily assert as fact the resurrection itself ....[The] resurrection of Jesus was an event only in the minds and lives of Jesus' followers. It cannot be described as an historic[2] event. The Easter story is a faith legend, not an objective eye-witness report; but it is a myth that the Christian church through the centuries has found to be a continuing inspiration."[3] (Elliott's book is published by the Student Christian Movement Press.)

At the opposite extreme is the point of view of objectiveness. This position is represented in the Gospels, wherein "the Easter stories are all told as if they were historical events on the same basis as, say, the crucifixion."[4] In the Gospel of Luke the post-resurrection Jesus replicates the pre-crucifixion Jesus. For it is the risen Jesus himself who protests to the eleven disciples and to "those who were with them," "See my hands and my feet, that it is I myself; handle me, and see; for a spirit has not flesh and bones as you see that I have." Jesus then proceeds to eat "a piece of broiled fish" (Luke 24:33, 39-40, 42). However, within the Gospels as in the Apostolic Writings as a whole there are differences and conflicts respecting the form and content of the objectiveness.[5] Thus, in contrast to the Gospel of Luke the apostle Paul maintains that when the dead are raised, the body in question differs from the body that has died: "It is sown a physical body, it is raised a spiritual body" (I Cor. 15:35-50). The only way to reconcile Luke and Paul would be to treat the risen Jesus as a special and different case within the abstract or generic category of those persons who have been dead.

Why is the claimed event of the resurrection to be singled out as *the* issue within the Christian-Jewish encounter, or more precisely within the problem of Christian triumphalism and supersessionism? The reason is that in the Christian *Anschauung* the resurrection constitutes a class by itself. To turn for a moment to the general history of religions: Under the rubric of sacred or numinous events as such, we are apprised of certain events that concentrate univocally upon the action and power of the *divine*; certain others that emphasize the action and power of *humans* (the Hinayana Buddhist paradigm, for example); and finally those that exhibit synergism, a *combination* of the action and power of both kinds of agents (the human and the divine, perhaps with Moses and God at Sinai as an example *par excellence*). Objectively stated, the resurrection of Jesus boasts the first of the three eventualities: God alone is the agent--this upon a most rudimentary and (humanly) anxiety-inducing experiential foundation: human beings can do nothing whatever to extricate themselves from death. It is this that puts the resurrection of Jesus (and of course *any* alleged resurrection) in a singular class.

I am going to recount and assess the stages through which my own thinking and conviction upon Jesus' resurrection have passed. To this end, I shall apply a Hegelian form of dialectic:

Thesis: Pedestrian Acknowledgement

Antithesis: Critical Questioning upon Moral Grounds

Synthesis: Antitriumphalist Affirmation

It will be recalled that while in Hegel's theoretical schema "thesis" is reputed to reveal one aspect of things, and "anti-thesis" a contrasting aspect, the two are then raised (*aufgehoben*) to the higher synthesis of a third stage.[6] What I mean by this allusion when applied to my own situation--and I mean nothing else--is that I do not now wholly repudiate either the thesis of pedestrian acknowledgment or the antithesis of critical questioning upon moral grounds; each of these is--I hope--gathered up, for their partial truths, into the third stage.

I. Thesis: Pedestrian Acknowledgment

As I look through my earlier writings, I am struck by the rather casual and unthinking way in which, over a number of years, I received and handled the resurrection. I remained quite oblivious to such moral issues as the promulgation of that doctrine might raise. In my first book I ignored the subject entirely, though in an avowal of "loyalty to Christ as the transcendent Truth who stands above the relativities of history," I was obviously giving voice to a high Christology. In another book I unabashedly equated the "incarnate and resurrected Christ" with "the Word of God," though I did add that the resurrection of Jesus "stands at the apex of the Jewish-Christian *Auseinandersetzung*," and I did recognize that the resurrection entails "fundamental transformation of Messianic expectations." In a later book I continued to agree that "the uniqueness of Christianity is its faith in the resurrection of Jesus as the Christ," although I did supplement such bald statements as this with an awareness that "from a Jewish point of view the Christ has not come and was not raised from the dead." Further along in the same study I seemed to hint at future misgivings in and through counsel to

316

the church "to proclaim the death of the resurrected Christ, in the name of
the Christ who may one day come"--counsel the wording of which strikes me
today as somewhat on the incoherent side.[7]

All in all, my "thesis" stage appears in retrospect to mirror a prosaic,
unreflective attitude.

II. Antithesis: Critical Questioning on Moral Grounds

This second stage requires a background, autobiographical note: My
personal and scholarly interest in the overall relation between Christian and
Jewish thinking and life, and more especially in the human evil and
destructiveness fabricated by Christian triumphalism and absolutism, did not
result from a confrontation with the *Shoah* (Holocaust) as such, but preceded
the latter concern, a concern that did not develop until considerably later.
However, the *Shoah* was subsequently to exercise salient influence upon me--
particularly through the mediation of Elie Wiesel, Irving Greenberg, Emil L.
Fackenheim, and Eliezer Berkovits--and the *Shoah* has been the single most
determining element in my encounter with the resurrection of Jesus. The
phenomenon that originally nurtured my interest in the Christian-Jewish
relation, beginning in 1944-1945, was Christian antisemitism as such. But
since that phenomenon and the *Shoah* are ineluctably bound together, there
is no point in disjoining the *Shoah* from my original work and its motivations.
Nevertheless, it was the anti-Jewish problematic within Christianity and
Christian history that finally led me, and also my wife, to the subject of the
Shoah.[8] I speak of all this here only in order to underscore the fact that the
question of Christology and its moral/immoral potentialities is much more
than a modern or contemporary issue. It has ancient and abiding and tragic
roots.

By way of further clarification of my antithetical stage: The nature of
the confrontation (to the death?) between the *Shoah* and Christian
theological doctrine is elementary and transparent: It is the issue of
transhistoricalness. For the way to try to shelter or shield Christianity as
something transhistorical is to turn it into a faith that, as Alan T. Davies has
maintained, "does not see history as open to God's presence in the way
Judaism does." Upon this view, such happenings as the crucifixion and the

resurrection become transhistorical events that rule out "further orienting experiences...."[9] Yet to any such view the *Shoah* as a fully historical consequence of Christian praxis (and of course of other influences as well) answers: No, you cannot turn your back upon such orienting experiences.

My antithetical stage developed at a time of shattering unrest and a searching of conscience among Christian scholars and theologians (a period that remains with us). For Jean Daniélou, among many others, had expressed the final logic of Christian anti-Jewishness: The offense of the Jews is that "they do not believe in the *risen* Christ."[10] The citations that follow may be set in polemical juxtaposition to Daniélou's claim.

The Canadian Catholic churchman and theologian Gregory G. Baum declared: "What Auschwitz has revealed to the Christian community is the deadly power of its own symbolism." The "anti-Jewish thrust of the church's preaching" is not a historical, psychological, or sociological matter; "it touches the very formulation of the Christian gospel." Baum was speaking here of Christian triumphalism and supersessionism respecting the Jews and Judaism, the sort of thing that "assigns the Jews to the darkness of history," rejected by God and all peoples, in ways that could only end in the murder camps. In the Nazi *Endlösung* "The theological negation of Judaism and the vilification of the Jewish people" within the Christian tradition were, at the last, translated into the genocide of the Jews. "The message of the Holocaust to Christian theology ... is that at whatever cost to its own self-understanding, the church must be willing to confront the ideologies implicit in its doctrinal tradition."[11]

Baum's judgments were paralleled by the Episcopalian theologian, Paul M. van Buren: "The roots of Hitler's final solution are to be found in the proclamation of the very *kerygma* of the early Christians....[The command out of Aushcwitz] is that we accept a judgment on something false lying close to the very heart of our tradition...."[12]

And the United Methodist historian-theologian Franklin H. Littell wrote:

> The cornerstone of Christian antisemitism is the superseding or displacement myth, which already rings with the genocidal note. This is the myth that the mission of the Jewish people was finished with the coming of Jesus Christ, that "the

old Israel" was written off with the appearance of "the new Israel." To teach that a people's mission in God's providence is finished, that they have been relegated to the limbo of history, has murderous implications which murderers will in time spell out. The murder of six million Jews by baptized Christians, from whom membership in good standing was not (and has not yet been) withdrawn, raises the most insistent question about the credibility of Christianity.[13]

To all these colleagues, there is a common foe: supersessionist elitism. Before the fact of the *Shoah* the question emerges: Is the Christian message morally credible? In the post-*Shoah* world many Christian spokespersons have expressed a readiness to "rethink" Christian teaching, to avoid Christian imperialism. Yet for more times than we ought to allow, such expressions of concern appear as no more than nice or pleasing sentiments lacking any concreteness. When a demand is made for specifics, the reformer may back off. And whenever a critic from within the Christian community raises the moral question concerning *specific* Christian teachings, viz., Christological teachings, he or she may be dismissed as a "radical" who is undermining the faith. It is as if the *critic* were on trial, and not the Christian message.[14] Until the self-identified reformer does something concrete to reconcile the resurrection of Jesus and the apodictic requirements of human morality, he or she can hardly take refuge in objections respecting what is or is not the *sine qua non* of the Christian faith. Unless and until calls for post-*Shoah* Christian reform are implemented in specific measures or specific advice, these calls remain mere words, noisy gongs and clanging cymbals.

In the frame of reference of the resurrection, the overall moral-psychoanalytic issue may be formulated as follows: On the one hand, a consummated resurrection of Jesus may be said to constitute a basic theological (Christological) threat to or indictment of Judaism and the Jewish people; on the other hand, any denial of Jesus' resurrection may be said to comprise a life-and-death threat to the Christian faith and the Christian community. On the one hand, "once the resurrection is identified as a special act of God, a divine event or divine fact, how can Christian vilification, imperialism, and supersessionism vis-à-vis Judaism and the Jewish people ever be vanquished? For the issue between the two sides is seen to be, not a relatively harmless disparity of mere human symbolism, spiritual conviction, or 'religious experience'--probably amenable to the soothings of 'relativization' or 'confessionalism'--but a matter of saying Yes or No to God himself, Sovereign of all things."[15] Yet on the other hand, are we then compelled to identify the Christian as visited by forlornness, as lost and without hope in this world? (cf. Eph. 2:11-22).

In checking over my own writings I note that it was back in 1976 in a critical analysis entitled "Jürgen Moltmann, the Jewish People, and the Holocaust" that I first made more than passing reference to the problematic of the resurrection. The context of the passage that follows is Moltmann's explanation that while his book *Theology of Hope* begins with "the *resurrection* of the crucified Christ," his succeeding work *The Crucified God* turns back "to look at the *cross* of the risen Christ."[16] Here is my response:

> We may have the temerity to envisage a next step: the non-resurrection of the crucified Jesus, and the crucifixion of the non-resurrected Christ. This potential development may be formulated in at least two alternative ways: (i) Absolute Godforsakenness (until the still-future resurrection, which means the future resurrection of Jesus, as of others). (ii) The pure faith of Christian Judaism (not to be confused with Jewish Christianity, which is the faith of Jews and not of Gentiles). If we are to "turn back" with radical and total resoluteness, then we must really turn back: to the crucified Jew, and thereby to the suffering Jews (of whom Jesus remains, to be sure, in a real sense the *Stellvertreter*).[17]

However, in the remainder of the above source I did not follow up upon the subject of the resurrection but concentrated instead upon the issue of the crucifixion and the *Shoah*[18]--although at the end I did suggest that ultimate Christian liberation from complicity in the Nazi *Endlösung der Judenfrage*, "Final Deliverance from the Jews," necessitates "the total secularization, demythologization, and humanization" of Christian theology.[19]

In 1977 I read a paper that may clarify a little--though hardly do anything to authenticate--the above-cited materials vis-à-vis Moltmann. My presentation took as its point of departure the historical-moral finding, for some time now a truism of scholarship, that Christian teachings and ideology helped prepare the way for the coming of the *Shoah*. (None of this is to forget that the Christian gospel, insofar as it incarnates the love of God and neighbor, retains an opposite consequence of fostering human solidarity and justice.) In the 1977 piece I declared that "the all-decisive avowal of Christianity is the resurrection of Jesus Christ," citing Paul's word to the church in Corinth, "if Christ has not been raised,...your faith is vain" (I Cor. 15:14), and adding that to my knowledge the possible vainness of the Christian faith has never been linked to the denial of any other church doctrine.[20] I continued that some in the Christian community fancy that they can oppose anti-Jewishness "while holding fast to the central Christian dogma, the consummated resurrection of Jesus Christ." In a word, I was maintaining that the teaching of Jesus' resurrection cannot be separated from other Christian doctrines that Jules Isaac gathers under the rubric of the "teaching of contempt."[21] But then I concluded on a note of faith or trust or hope--falling, as I now look back upon the essay, into something of a *non sequitur* or at least a superfluity--by affirming a resurrection yet in the future:

> The man from the Galilee sleeps now. [I wonder how I knew that.[22]] He sleeps with the other Jewish dead, with all the distraught and scattered dead of the murder camps, and with the infinite dead of the human and nonhuman family. But Jesus of Nazareth shall be raised. So too the young Hungarian children of Auschwitz shall be raised. Once upon a coming time, they shall again play and laugh. The little ones of Terezín shall see another butterfly.[23] "The wolf shall dwell with the lamb, and the leopard shall lie down with the kid, and the calf and the lion and the fatling together....They shall not hurt or destroy in all my holy mountain; for the earth shall be full of the knowledge of the Lord as the waters cover the sea" (Isa. 11:6, 9). The last enemy, death, shall be sentenced to death (I Cor. 15:26; Rev. 21:3, 4). One day we shall be together in the regnancy of God, so hope tells us, the hope that lives upon faith and love. We shall sing and we shall dance. And we shall love one another. Accordingly, it is not assured that we shall read and write theological papers to each other.[24]

I have not completely given up the above stress upon the future. Here is a comment of mine upon Ulrich E. Simon's declaration that without the resurrection, the *Shoah* is pure hell:[25] "He is right--in principle. But for the sufferers, as for the survivors and descendants, the only way that hell can be defeated is through a future resurrection, when God will be victorious over every satanic and evil power, including death itself. *For no past event, however holy or divine, could ever redeem the terror of the present; only a future happening can do this.*[26]

Shattering questions remain: How can the resurrection of Jesus be proclaimed as a special act of God without the Christian triumphalism that paved the way to Belzec and Sobibor? Is not the resurrection in and of itself a form of Christian supersessionism? How can the Christian church escape supersessionism and triumphalism while continuing to proclaim as a realized fact the resurrection of Jesus Christ? In its claim that the resurrection of Jesus concretely means God's triumph over death, is not the church inevitably implying its own triumph over non-Christian faith? In the resurrection does not God (reputedly) *confirm* the Christian gospel in the sense of a definitive embodiment of objective truth? Does not the resurrection appear as a divinely wrought displacement event? Is it possible, or how is it possible, to proclaim Jesus' resurrection in a nontriumphalist way?

The above questions come forcibly to mind as one consults many Christian advocacies of the resurrection. One example is a study by John Frederick Jansen: "In the resurrection and vindication of Jesus the earliest church saw the completion and goal of Israel's faith in God." That faith "finds its ultimate expression" in the Easter faith of Christianity. "The whole of God's story with his people" is "fulfilled in the resurrection of Jesus....All people do not yet accept Easter's pledge, but one day 'every eye will see him, every one who pierced him' (Rev. 1:7)....Ultimate vindication includes ultimate judgment. The risen Jesus 'is the one ordained of God to be judge of the living and the dead' (Acts 10:42)." The New Testament message "sees in Easter the surety of the future of Jesus Christ as Lord of all and Lord forever." The Easter faith reminds us that "the future of Jesus includes the future of Israel....Israel's future is bound up with the future of Christ."[27]

Subsequent writings by me carry forward the moral critique of the proclamation of a consummated or triumphalist resurrection of Jesus. for example, in 1978 I developed that critique in and through an assessment of Wolfhart Pannenberg. Pannenberg contends that "through the cross of Jesus, the Jewish legal tradition as a whole has been set aside in its claim to contain the eternal will of God in its final formulation."[28] The "law" is consummated and fulfilled in Jesus. For support, Pannenberg calls upon Jesus' resurrection: Jesus came into basic conflict "with the law itself, that is with the positive Israelite legal tradition which had become calcified as 'the law' after the exile." But through the resurrection "the emancipation from this law" takes place. Jesus' claim to authority, in replacement of the "law" and through which he put himself in God's place, "has been visibly and unambiguously confirmed by the God of Israel...." In a word, the resurrection of Jesus Christ serves to abolish Judaism.[29]

Pannenberg's exposition points up the way in which

> the teaching of an achieved resurrection can lie at the center of Christian opposition and hostility to Judaism and the Jewish people. For only with that teaching does Christian triumphalism reach fulfillment. Only here are the various human and divine-human claims making up the church's dogmatic structure furnished with the capstone of an event that is said to be exclusively God's and that in this way vindicates every other claim. The representative of this ideology declares, in effect: "It is not the Christian theologian to whom you Jews are to listen. The theologian is, after all, a fallible and sinful human being. Rather, let us have God decide the matter. But God's decision proves to be on the Christian side, not yours. *God* raised Jesus from the dead. Thus is the Christian shown to be right and you are shown to be wrong. In the resurrection God himself *confirms* the Christian gospel, the Christian cause."[30]

Those who affirm the resurrection of Jesus but who oppose Wolfhart Pannenberg's assimilation of that event to Christian imperialism are challenged to make clear how, if at all, their own affirmation avoids supersession.[31]

In our joint work, *Long Night's Journey Into Day*, first published in 1982 and revised for publication in 1988, Alice L. Eckardt and I included an intensive critique of Christian supersessionist elitism. The integrity of the Christian faith was avowed, but it was also characterized as problematic: "Through the continuous and contemporaneous asserted truth that in Jesus Christ the eschatological domain entered into human history in definitive, salvational form, Christianity has legitimized historically-theologically its supersessionism and triumphalism over Judaism and the Jewish people, as well as its exclusivism toward other faiths." If Rosemary Ruether is right that "the Christian historicizing of eschatological reality is the foundation of

Christian antisemitism, and if we are correct that the center and proof of Christianity is the event of the resurrection, then any continued advocacy of the resurrection appears to represent in clear and authoritative form the fateful, culpable union of the Christian message and the murder camps."[32]

To conclude this review of my antithetical stage, during that period (in 1986) I referred in at least two places to the hope that a nontriumphalist apprehension of the resurrection might yet gain a place in Christian teaching.[33] These references may be received as a kind of transition to stage three of my thinking.

III. Synthesis: Antitriumphalist Affirmation

To recall to mind a point made early in this essay: A synthesis beyond both the thesis of pedestrian acknowledgment and the antithesis of critical questioning upon moral grounds need not abandon or wholly repudiate the other alternatives. The synthesis may gather up, assimilate, but also subject to critical judgment the thesis and the antithesis.

I have come at least tentatively to the view that a moral-theological remedy for Christian resurrectionist supersessionism, elitism, and triumphalism is to apprehend the resurrection of Jesus in the frame of reference "Spirit of God" (to apply the terminology of Marcus J. Borg[34]) within the special and continuing history of Judaism and the Jewish people. It is within the reality of Israel that the all-decisive meeting place or convergence of religious faith and historical event takes place. Once Christian confessions are deideologized,[35] i.e., monotheized, they may be enabled to become the spiritual implementation of what might be called "Jesus-historicity." A primary Christian challenge in the shadow of the *Shoah* is not just to demythologize the Christian tradition but to deideologize it, viz., to wage war upon its supersessionist elitism.

The above "remedy" is no mere pragmatic or political move calculated to make the Jewish people or other people happy. Its character as a responsible position derives from its grounding in historical experience. The resurrection, part and parcel of the nascent world of Christian faith, is yet continuous with, even integral to, the social world of Judaism--or, in theological phrasing and following Paul van Buren, to the covenant with

Israel. Accordingly, against John Frederick Jansen's conclusion that "Israel's future is bound up with the future of Christ," we may propose that Christ's future is bound up with the future of Israel.

A few current illustrations may be adduced. Each of these can be treated as tacitly rejecting the triumphalist views of such analysts as Jansen and Pannenberg.

If only to get it out of the way I reproduce first my own, somewhat mischievous midrash upon a spiritual (= Spirit of God) rendering of the resurrection, the date 1987:

> We are given to understand that the Sadducees insisted that there is no resurrection (e.g., Matt. 22:23)--contra Pharisee teaching. To introduce a light note (and perhaps therefore an especially serious one): We are advised that the One who sits in the heavens is not above laughing certain parties to scorn (Ps. 2:4). What would be a better joke on those reactionary Sadducees than for God to raise her own Pharisee-liberal Son from the dead! She would be having a go at one of her dearest truths, and would also be giving at least a few of her people a foretaste of the things that are to come. Maybe best of all, she would be reminding the Sadducees exactly what she thought of them, meanwhile assuring her good friends the Pharisees that she was on their side.[36]

The Dutch Protestant theologian Jacobus Schoneveld provides broader and deeper conceptualization:

> The resurrection means the vindication of Jesus as a Jew, as a person who was faithful to the Torah, as a martyr who participated in Jewish martyrdom for the sanctification of God's name. What else can this mean than the validation of Torah and vindication of the Jewish people as God's beloved people? The resurrection of Jesus confirms God's promises as well as God's commandments to the people Israel....I see the Jewish people's survival throughout the centuries in the light of what the resurrection means: the affirmation of the Torah, of the people of Israel, and of Jewish existence....
>
> It is not true that the church has replaced Israel or taken over its vocation. Both Israel and the church await the fulfillment of the Torah, when the image of God will be visible in the whole of humanity. The Jews await this final Day incorporated in the people of Israel, the Christians incorporated in the body of Christ....Jews have expressed their faithfulness in a "no" to Jesus as his church tried to take the Torah away from them. Christians may express their faithfulness in their "yes" to Jesus who embodies the Torah,

and therefore also in a "yes" to his brothers and sisters, the Jewish people.[37]

From a point of view such as that of Schoneveld, the resurrection may be legitimately and morally restored to Christianity once the poison of victimization is drained from it.

Paul M. van Buren is at one with Schoneveld in construing the resurrection (and perforce each and every authentic Christological attestation) as indigenous to God's unbroken (unbreakable?) Covenant with Israel. In this connection van Buren works to counteract (at least upon a theoretical level) the linkage between Christian resurrection doctrine and anti-Jewishness:

> The fact of Easter that matters absolutely for the church is that Jesus once more proved effective in standing for God and God's cause, that, in the cause in and for which he had lived before, he was alive again....[This] claim of Easter faith cannot be itself the root of the church's anti-Judaism. [I should want to qualify this: cannot be allowed to remain the root....] That root we have seen to consist of the subtle and not-so-subtle transformation of the original witness to Jesus as a Jew committed to the renewal of his people in their covenant with God, into a witness to an anti-Judaic Jesus in deepest conflict with his people. If Easter faith concerns this one who, as Paul wrote, became a servant of the Jewish people (Rom. 18:8), if the event of Easter is preached, as Paul claimed he had both learned and practiced, "in accordance with the Scriptures" (I Cor. 15:3-4), then it undercuts the anti-Judaism that developed in the church....Indeed, the Resurrection only stands in the way of anti-Judaism, since it underscores the continuity of the risen one with the Jew from Nazareth.[38]

With acknowledgment to Paul van Buren and others, I rather think now that a refusal to entertain the option of an extrabodily or spiritual resurrection of Jesus, together with a failure to insist upon the Jewishness of the resurrection (as in *Long Night's Journey Into Day*[39]), are overdrawn and probably not right. Furthermore, I now recognize a substantive discrepancy between triumphalist resurrectionism and nontriumphalist or antitriumphalist resurrectionism. Can the Christian church achieve the latter? I believe so. Or at least I hope so.[40]

I submit a concluding comment upon the resurrection in its place as an ongoing challenge but also an enigma to Christians.

We know that among the earliest followers of Jesus, as represented in the Apostolic Writings, doubt of his resurrection was present. "The resurrection is impossible"--Is not that the shattering conclusion to which especially rationalistic and/or burdensomely despairing moments sometimes drive the Christian? The rationalist and the cynic join hands in propagating the grim proposition that within the rules with which this world is "run," dead people do not become living people Against such a conclusion, advocates of a strictly or minimally somatic resurrection continue to array themselves. John 20:27 is among their proof texts: "Then he [the risen Jesus] said to Thomas, 'Reach your finger here; see my hands. Reach your hand here and put it into my side. Be unbelieving no longer, but believe.'" Yet we moderns tend to turn aside from somaticist explications of the resurrection. The Christology of many Christians also has problems with them. But at the same time many such persons are not happy with modernist reductionism, which restricts the resurrection to the moral and religious influence of a "great teacher" as continuing on in the world. A new and increasingly widespread Christology appears to be seeking out a resurrectionist position that navigates between and thence beyond both the Scylla of somaticism and the Charybdis of modernism. Thus does Paul van Buren proffer a synergist-covenantal viewpoint that involves a living parallel between the resurrection and the event of Sinai. To some, the resurrection

> was a pure act of God; the recipients of the act were purely recipients. Or, on the contrary, it has seemed to others that the appearances were the subjective experience of believers, so that it could be said that Jesus rose into the *kerygma,* the preached faith of the disciples. Each of these conclusions misses the covenantal character of Easter: it was at once an act of God and an act of the disciples, of the nascent church. Without a doubt the witness to Easter, consistent with the witness to Sinai, insisted on the priority of God's initiative but, as in the case of Sinai, the action of those who bore witness to it was [also] constitutive to the event.[41]

To return to a distinction made at the beginning: From van Buren's standpoint the resurrection partakes of both objectiveness and subjectiveness.[42]   In the vocabulary of our own day, the expression "resurrection of Jesus" may become, if you will, a spiritual--*not* "spiritualized"--metaphor or a transcending metaphor that presents us with a particularly epochal renewal of God's covenant with Israel. I suggest that van Buren's proposal may be buttressed through the Pauline persuasion of a transformed risen body (I Cor. 15:35-44), since in that case the historically discrete aspect of the resurrection is retained as at the same time literalist-somaticist difficulties are avoided. For to separate the resurrected one from all somatic identity would be to divorce the risen Christ from Jesus of Nazareth.

The sum and substance of this position of synthesis is that the imperialization of the resurrection is definitely fightable from within the Christian community by those Christians who, just because they will to live and die in historical-moral solidarity with the Jewish people to whom the resurrection in the first instance belongs, are thereby allowed to witness to the resurrection themselves.

At the last, there is the assurance that if the God of Israel has defeated death in her son Jesus, she may will to do the same again and again--for Christians, in and through the Body of Christ; for others, in and through her Spirit as it blows wherever she wills (John 3:8). In either case, the question to Mary of Magdala and the other women--the first Christian believers were evidently women--is fitting: "Why do you search among the dead?" (Luke 24:5). For is not Jesus, the Jewish *hasid* from the town of Nazareth, loose (again) in the special world, amidst all the anguish and all the joy of human events?

ENDNOTES

[1]See Paul M. van Buren, *A Theology of the Jewish-Christian Reality*, Part III--*Christ in Context* (San Francisco: Harper & Row, 1988), chap. 5.

[2]By "historic" Elliott means "historical"; he does not deny the historic, i.e., significant, quality of the resurrection.

[3]J. K. Elliott, *Questioning Christian Origins* (London: SCM Press, 1982), pp. 78, 92. Elliott's equation of "legend" and "myth" is somewhat careless. Legends are suffused by falsehood in a way that is not perforce the case with myths.

[4]*Ibid.*, p. 77.

[5]Mark (chap. 16) and Matthew (chap. 28) are not as somaticist as Luke and John.

[6]See William Kelley Wright, *A History of Modern Philosophy* (New York: Macmillan, 1941), pp. 327ff.

[7]A. Roy Eckardt, *Christianity and the Children of Israel* (New York: King's Crown Press, Columbia University, 1948), p. 149; *Elder and Younger Brothers* (New York: Scribner, 1967; Schocken, 1973), pp. 127, 88, 140; but cf. pp. 139-140; *Your People, My People* (New York: Quadrangle/New York Times, 1974), pp. 225, 238, 248.

[8]Alice & Roy Eckardt, "Christentum und Judentum: Die theologische und moralische Problematik der Vernichtung des europäischen Judentums," *Evangelische Theologie* 36 (1976): 408.

[9]Such is the claim of Alan T. Davies, as reported in David Glanz, "The Holocaust as a Question," *Worldview* 17 (Sept. 1974): 37.

[10]Jean Daniélou, *Dialogue With Israel* (Baltimore: Helicon, 1966), p. 99 (italics added).

[11]Gregory Baum, *Christian Theology After Auschwitz* (London: Council of Christians and Jews, 1976), pp. 8, 9, 11, 12; Introduction to Rosemary Radford Reuther, *Faith and Fratricide: The Theological Roots of Anti-Semitism* (New York: Seabury, 1974), p. 8.

[12]Paul M. van Buren, "The Status and Prospects for Theology," address to the Theology Section, American Academy of Religion, Chicago, Nov. 1, 1975, as cited in A. Roy Eckardt, "Christians and Jews: Along a Theological Frontier," *Encounter* 40 (1979): 93.

[13]Franklin H. Littell, *The Crucifixion of the Jews* (New York: Harper & Row, 1975), p. 2.

[14]An illustration of this attempt to dismiss one or more Christian post-*Shoah* theologians for "going too far" or being "too radical" is Michael B. McGarry's review of A. Roy Eckardt, *Jews and Christians* in the journal *America* (May 23, 1987): 428-429.

[15]A. Roy Eckardt, *For Righteousness' Sake: Contemporary Moral Philosophies* (Bloomington: Indiana University Press, 1987), pp. 304-305.

[16]Jürgen Moltmann, *The Crucified God*, trans. R. A. Wilson and John Bowden (New York: Harper & Row, 1974), p. 5.

[17]A. Roy Eckardt, "Jürgen Moltmann, The Jewish People, and the Holocaust," *Journal of the American Academy of Religion* 44 (1976): 686.

[18]Subsequent paragraphs of the appraisal of Moltmann question whether his attribution of absolute evil to the crucifixion, "the very torment of hell," can stand up in the presence of the *Shoah* (p. 687). The analysis concludes with a recognition and critique of changes in Moltmann's thinking in his subsequent volume, *Kirche in der Kraft des Geistes*.

[19]Eckardt, "Jürgen Moltmann," p. 691.

[20]Some of those who are loudest in their zeal for the resurrection are sometimes prepared to pass over and tacitly to cast aside other elements that are equally indigenous to the Apostolic Writings, e.g., Satan or Jesus' birth by parthenogenesis. In effect, most of us pick and choose between beliefs. We practice "selective Christianity." Among the most woefully discretionary, and hence anticatholic, of all Christian bodies is the Vatican, which, at the level of praxis, consistently chooses the rights of males over the rights of females-- and upon what is for the Catholic hierarchy invincible grounds: Jesus Christ was a male and he chose only males for his disciples.

[21]Jules Isaac, *The Teaching of Contempt: Christian Roots of Anti-Semitism*, trans. Helen Weaver (New York: Holt, Rinehart, and Winston, 1964).

[22]There is no absolute "guarantee" against a bodily resurrection of Jesus. Cf. Eckardt, *For Righteousness' Sake*: "How could we ever dub [any] supposed event 'impossible' when we remain in the vulnerable position of not being able to establish final criteria for adjudging what can and cannot occur in history as in nature? In point of truth, no human being can say absolutely what is possible and impossible in our world" (pp. 306-307).

[23]Cf. *...I never saw another butterfly ...: Children's Drawings and Poems from Terezín Concentration Camp 1942-1944*, ed. Hana Volavková, trans. Jeanne Nemcová (New York: McGraw-Hill, 1971).

[24]A. Roy Eckardt, *Proceedings of the 2nd Philadelphia Conference on the Holocaust, Feb. 16-18, 1977*, ed. Josephine Knopp (Philadelphia: National Institute on the Holocaust, 1977), pp. 39-45 (slightly emended).

[25]Conversation with Ulrich E. Simon, London, 20 Feb. 1976.

[26]Eckardt, "Christians and Jews," p. 125.

[27]John Frederick Jansen, *The Resurrection of Jesus Christ in New Testament Theology* (Philadelphia: Westminster, 1980), pp. 22, 84-85, 89, 92, 91.

[28]Pannenberg here misrepresents the Jewish claim. The majority, ongoing point of view of Jewish scholars and rabbis is that the legal tradition must be continually rethought and reformulated.

[29]Wolfhart Pannenberg, *Jesus--God and Man*, trans. Lewis L. Wilkins and Duane A. Priebe (Philadelphia: Westminster, 1968), pp. 67, 257, 258. The second English edition of this study by Pannenberg published in 1977 (translation from the 5th German edition) differs from the 1968 English-language edition only in the inclusion of an eleven-page afterword taking note of Pannenberg's critics. His strictures against Judaism and "the Jewish law" remain.

[30]Eckardt, "Christians and Jews," pp. 106-108. Other writings of mine in this period that bear upon the issue of a supersessionist or triumphalist resurrection include "*Ha'Shoah* as Christian Revolution: Toward the Liberation of the Divine Righteousness," *Quarterly Review* 2 (1982): 52-67; "Contemporary Christian Theology and a Protestant Witness for the Shoah," *Union Seminary Quarterly Review* 38 (1983): 139-145; and "Antisemitism is the Heart," *Theology Today* 41 (1984): 301-308.

[31]Eckardt, *For Righteousness' Sake*, p. 305.

[32]Alice L. Eckardt and A. Roy Eckardt, *Long Night's Journey Into Day: A Revised Retrospective on the Holocaust*, revised and enlarged (Detroit: Wayne State University Press; Oxford: Pergamon Press, 1988), pp. 136, 139, 140 (slightly emended).

[33]A. Roy Eckardt, "Is There a Way Out of the Christian Crime? The Philosophic Question of the Holocaust," *Holocaust and Genocide Studies* 1 (1986): 121-126; *Jews and Christians: The Contemporary Meeting* (Bloomington: Indiana University Press, 1986), p. 156.

[34]Marcus J. Borg, *Jesus: A New Vision* (San Francisco: Harper & Row, 1987); "A Renaissance in Jesus Studies," *Theology Today* 45 (1988): 280-292.

[35]If Christian ideology is recourse to certain ideas and idea-systems in the service of collective self-interest, deideologization is the struggle against ideology.

[36]Eckardt, *For Righteousness' Sake*, p. 310.

[37]Jacobus (Coos) Schoneveld, "The Jewish 'No' to Jesus and the Christian 'Yes' to Jews," *Quarterly Review* 4 (Winter 1984): 60, 63 (slightly emended).

[38]Van Buren, *Christ in Context*, p. 110.

[39]Cf. Eckardt and Eckardt, *Long Night's Journey Into Day*, rev. ed., pp. 142, 143. The effort is made in the original edition of that book to limit the possibilities to either a fully somatic resurrection or no resurrection at all. In the rev. ed. the possibility of other alternatives is raised (pp. 140-141).

[40]There are criticisms by me still applicable to my new position on the resurrection--written, of course, before my shift--in *For Righteousness' Sake*, pp. 313-315.

[41]Van Buren, *Christ in Context*, p. 111; see also Tom F. Driver, *Christ in a Changing World* (New York: Crossroad, 1981), p. 8.

[42]A response of subjectiveness to the resurrection is still, in a sense, an objective datum of human history.

MEMORY AND TRIUMPHALISM

Dr. Eugene J. Fisher

I wish to draw your attention to some recent official Catholic teaching which relates to the theme of this conference, "Bearing Witness." These are one statement of the Holy See and two issued by committees of the National Conference of Catholic Bishops (NCCB).

All three of these documents need to be read within the context of the reassessment of official Catholic thought regarding Jews and Judaism begun by the Second Vatican Council.[1] Although the Second Vatican Council's declaration on the Jews, *Nostra Aetate*, No. 4, was very much precipitated by Catholic reaction after the *Shoah*, it was not until 1974, in its implementing document for *Nostra Aetate*,[2] that this crucial context for the Conciliar debate was first officially acknowledged at this level:

> ...the step taken by the (Second Vatican) council finds its historical setting in circumstances deeply affected by the memory of the persecution and massacre of Jews which took place in Europe just before and during the Second World War.[3]

It was not, in turn, until 1985, that the "Notes" issued by the same Commission[4] for the first time universally mandated that Catholic religious education (properly, "catechesis") "should help in understanding the meaning ...of the extermination (of Jews) during the years 1939-1945, and its consequences," though Pope John Paul II had begun addressing the subject in depth some years earlier.[5]

It can be said, then, that many of the themes and issues first raised at these Annual Scholars' Conferences on the Holocaust over the years are only now becoming embedded in the official teaching of the Roman Catholic Church. The other side of this same statement, however, is that these crucial themes *are* becoming embedded in the very heart of the teaching of the Church, filling the catechetical "gap" left by the concurrent attempt to remove the vestiges of the old, pernicious "teaching of contempt" condemned by the Second Vatican Council.

While perhaps relatively slow to act, the Church's institutional memory is long and, once committed, correspondingly deep.

The first statement is primarily historical and moral, though it does rebut rather effectively one lingering element of the theology of contempt, the pernicious dichotomy between so-called Jewish particularity and Christian universalism. Both elements are to be found in both traditions, of course. The Pontifical Commission on Justice and Peace statement, "The Church and Racism,"[6] is, in many ways, a remarkable document for the Holy See to issue. It offers a survey of "racist behavior throughout history" that does not seek "to gloss over the weaknesses and even, at times, complicity of certain Church leaders ...in this phenomenon," but rather analyzes the growth of intergroup antipathy to its apotheosis in modern antisemitism. Indeed, it calls antisemitism "the most tragic form that racist ideology has assumed in our century," citing specifically the Holocaust in this context (Section No. 15).

Nor does "The Church and Racism" shirk from including the teaching of contempt in its pre-history of modern racial antisemitism, acknowledging that "within 'Christendom' the Jews, considered the tenacious witnesses of a refusal to believe in Christ, were often the subject of serious humiliations, accusations and proscriptions" (Section No. 2). It distinguishes, properly, this *religious* polemical stance from modern racial ideology as it appeared in the eighteenth and nineteenth centuries. It devotes a major section to the development of National Socialism in the twentieth century, citing it as "responsible for one of the greatest genocides in history." "This murderous folly," the statement continues, "struck first and foremost the Jewish people in unheard-of proportions," thus acknowledging the historical uniqueness of the *Shoah*, while also calling to memory Nazism's genocidal attacks "on the Gypsies and the Tziganes and also categories of persons such as the handicapped and the mentally ill."

The Holy See's document recalls the opposition to these Nazi policies by Pope Pius XI (which has never been a subject for scholarly contention) and by Pope Pius XII (which has, though perhaps unfairly). "The Church and Racism" is a timely statement that will be immediately of use to Catholic teachers not only in history, but in ethics and religion courses as well, providing them with the beginnings of a framework for the development of Holocaust education on all levels, as Pope John Paul II called for during his visit to Miami on September 11, 1987.[7] I say "beginnings," because the Holy See's document on the *Shoah*, also promised by the Pope in Miami, is still forthcoming. This latter will be drafted, however, as is most appropriate, after "serious studies" on the subject have been undertaken *jointly* by Christians and Jews through the mechanism of the International Catholic-Jewish Liaison Committee.[8]

The two American documents were issued by different Committees of the U.S. Bishops' Conference. In June of 1988, *Criteria for the Evaluation of Dramatizations of the Passion*, by the Bishops' Committee for Ecumenical and Interreligious Affairs (BCEIA), was published in both Spanish and English. This document centers on depictions of Christ's death and spells out, in some detail, how it can be portrayed dramatically without having the implication, as in the past, of "collective guilt" of Jews for Jesus' death.[9]

In this, as with the second document to be discussed below, one can see how the Church is moving into a new stage in its implementation of *Nostra Aetate*'s effort to eradicate antisemitism from Catholic teaching, reaching even the level of local passion plays and media presentations.

The second document, *God's Mercy Endures Forever: Guidelines on the Presentations of Jews and Judaism in Catholic Preaching*, published just this January, is a statement by the NCCB Committee on the Liturgy. Designed for homilists, it covers the entire spectrum of the Church's liturgical calendar. Bishop Joseph P. Delaney of Fort Worth, who chairs the Bishops' Committee on the Liturgy, begins his Preface to the document with the following words:

> Even in the twentieth century, the age of the Holocaust, the Shoah, the "scouring Wind," God's mercy endures forever.

The Holocaust drew its fiery breath from the ancient, sometimes latent, but always persistent antisemitism which, over the centuries, found too large a place within the hearts of too many Christian men and women. Yet, since the Holocaust and since the Second Vatican Council, Christians have struggled to learn the reasons for such irrational and anti-Christian feelings against that special people for whom "God's mercy endures forever," to deal with those feelings, and to overcome them through knowledge, understanding, dialogue, and love.[10]

The purpose for these liturgical guidelines, Bishop Delaney continues, is thus "to see to it that our (Catholic) liturgical celebrations never again become occasions for that anti-Semitic or anti-Jewish sentiment that sometimes moved the liturgy in the past."

Drawing on the 1974 Vatican *Guidelines*, the 1985 Vatican *Notes* and a wealth of recent liturgical and biblical scholarship, *God's Mercy* offers historical perspective and hermeneutical clarification to Christian preachers. It begins by noting the "Jewish roots of the Liturgy," not only biblically but also in the synagogue and post-biblical Jewish forms of worship. It rejects explicitly the false notions "that the New Covenant 'abrogated' or 'superseded' the Old, and that the Sinai covenant was discarded by God and replaced with another" (Section 6), as well as the decide charge (Section 7).

God's Mercy denounces "triumphalism" and instead frames a positive understanding of the Gospel message that affirms unequivocally the Church's teaching about Christ while affirming also the continuing validity of God's covenant with the Jewish people. It does this, it should be noted, on specifically *Christian* theological grounds:

> The Christian proclamation of the saving deeds of the One God through Jesus was formed in the context of Second Temple Judaism and cannot be understood thoroughly without that context. It is a proclamation that, at its heart, stands in solidarity with the continuing Jewish witness in affirming the One God as Lord of history. Further, false or demeaning portraits of a repudiated Israel may undermine Christianity as well. How can one confidently affirm the truth of God's covenant with all humanity and creation in Christ (see Rom. 8:21) without at the same time affirming God's faithfulness to the Covenant with Israel that also lies at the heart of the biblical testimony? (Section 8).

God's Mercy tackles the often-abused "fulfillment" theme of the Advent liturgy, noting that the biblical prophecies are not to be understood as "merely temporal predictions," but are also "profound expressions of eschatological hope." They are "fulfilled (i.e., irreversibly inaugurated) in Christ's coming," but preachers must also note that "that fulfillment is not completely worked out in each person's life or perfected in the world at large." Hence, it concludes, "with the Jewish people, we await the complete realization of the messianic age" (Sections 11-12).

Similarly, *God's Mercy* affirms traditional Christian applications of biblical texts, such as typology, but notes that such interpretations, while valid, do not exhaust the "unfathomable riches" and "inexhaustible content" of the Hebrew Bible. The association of the *Akedah* with Christ's sacrifice, for example, is a natural one for Christians. But this does not invalidate traditional Jewish applications of the same biblical text, from which Christians can continue to learn (Section 14).

In these areas, I believe, *God's Mercy* is moving toward a positive, non-triumphalist form of Christian *anamnesis* ("memory") within the very understanding of the Church's worship. Since, for Catholics, *lex orandi* is indeed *lex credendi*, the significance of such liturgical hermeneutics is quite apparent.

God's Mercy, as does the Vatican *Notes*, stresses that the conflict scenes in the Gospel between Jesus and "the Pharisees" often reflect later Christian-Jewish disputes "long after the time of Jesus" (Sections 16-20) and, like the BCEIA *Criteria*, takes particular care with the passion narratives of Holy Week (Sections 26-28). The document concludes with a summary listing of nine "general principles" applicable to all homilies throughout the year. I would like to see this list posted on the bulletin boards of every Catholic seminary and parish rectory in the country.

Finally, the bishops, for the first time that I know of in any official Church statement at this level, recommend joint Jewish/Christian memorial services for the victims of the Holocaust and offer specific examples of prayers to be said at Mass on the Sunday closest to *Yom ha Shoah*:

> 29. Also encouraged are joint memorial services commemorating the victims of the *Shoah* (Holocaust). These should be prepared for with catechetical and adult education programming to ensure a proper spirit of shared reverence. Addressing the Jewish community of Warsaw, Pope John Paul

II stressed the uniqueness and significance of Jewish memory of the *Shoah*: 'More than anyone else, it is precisely you who have become this saving warning. I think that in this sense you continue your particular vocation, showing yourselves to be still the heirs of that election to which God is faithful. This is your mission in the contemporary world before...all of humanity' (Warsaw, June 14, 1987). On the Sunday closest to *Yom ha Shoah*, Catholics should pray for the victims of the Holocaust and their survivors. The following serve as examples of petitions for the general intercessions at Mass:

- For the victims of the Holocaust, their families, and all our Jewish brothers and sisters, that the violence and hatred they experience may never again be repeated, we pray to the Lord.

- For the Church, that the Holocaust may be a reminder to us that we can never be indifferent to the sufferings of others, we pray to the Lord.

- For our Jewish brothers and sisters, that their confidence in the face of long-suffering may spur us on to a greater faith and trust in God, we pray to the Lord.

ENDNOTES

[1]See my, "The Evolution of a Tradition: From 'Nostra Aetate' to the 'Notes'," in *Fifteen Years of Catholic-Jewish Dialogue 1970-1985* (Rome: Libreria Editrice Lateraneuse, 1988), pp. 239-254.

[2]Pontifical Commission for Religious Relations with the Jews, "Guidelines and Suggestions for Implementing Nostra Aetate, No. 4," December 1, 1974, contained in *ibid.*, pp. 293-298.

[3]*Ibid.*, p. 294.

[4]Text and commentary in *ibid.*, pp. 306-318.

[5]For collections of the papal texts, with commentary, Eugene Fisher, *John Paul II and the Holocaust* (Washington, D.C.: USCC Publications, 1988) and E. Fisher and Leon Klenicki, *John Paul II on Jews and Judaism, 1979-1987* (USCC Publications, 1987).

[6]"The Church and Racism: Toward a More Fraternal Society," *Origins*, Vol. 18, No. 37: (Feb. 23, 1989) 613-626.

[7]*John Paul II on the Holocaust*, p. 10.

[8]For previous papers from the International Catholic-Jewish Liaison Committee, see *Fifteen Years of Catholic-Jewish Dialogue*, cited above (footnote 1).

[9]Copies are available from the USCC Office of Publishing and Promotion Services, Washington, D.C., Publication No. 211-X.

[10]*God's Mercy Endures Forever* (Washington, D.C.: USCC Publishing and Promotion Services, 1989, Publication No. 247-0), p. 1.

BEARING WITNESS BY HOLOCAUST SURVIVORS: IMPLICATIONS FOR MENTAL HEALTH THEORY AND PRACTICE

Maria Rosenbloom

For a long time after liberation, a period often referred to by survivors as the zero hour in history, there was only silence. We survivors who crawled out of camps, forests and hiding places resisted not only talking but even thinking about what we had witnessed. We would answer inquiries in a perfunctory manner, in response to questions by "authorities" (e.g., Immigration officials) or, in response to hesitant questions from fellow survivors who were still looking for kin. We did not talk.

Many reasons contributed to this circumstance. People around us were trying to reestablish their lives and did not want to be reminded of the past. The Cold War and the fear of alienating the Germans prematurely brought the Nuremberg Trials of Nazi war criminals to an end, and with it the opportunity and responsibility for citizens of the world to learn what happened.

Survivors took notice. Even if we were willing to talk--despite the extreme pain in confronting the awesome truth--there was no one to listen. A conspiracy of silence set in and continued for decades. But words could never fully express, anyway, what we felt. Even tears could not be shed or, if shed, bring relief.

However, I remember two occasions when we let go in a spontaneous, albeit non-verbal way. Both times, the expression of the emotion was facilitated by a special and symbolic event and by being with a group of fellow-survivors.

The first event of collective mourning which I remember took place on the site of the Bergen-Belsen Camp, a few months after liberation--and was occasioned by dedication of a monument to the victims, donated by the Jewish Community in Palestine. As a staff member, then, of the American Jewish Joint Distribution Committee I was invited to attend.

Suddenly with the Rabbi's recital of the Kaddish prayer, a collective moan came thru with such enormous depth and resonance that it seemed as if every corner of the world was picking up the echo.

In my memory, the second event is associated with my departure from Germany in September, 1947 on the S.S. "General Hershey", filled with displaced persons seeking a new homeland in America. Suddenly and precisely at the moment when the anchors were cut and the boat began to move away from the shores, a powerful, collective sigh went up, signaling the depth of emotion for which words could never be found. This probably was the moment of direct emotional confrontation with the final separation from the soil of Europe, the continent soaked with the blood of our people and with horrors we were fated to witness and outlive.

I share these two vignettes, both as an expression of my own unending need to "bear witness" and as a brief introduction to the theme of "witnessing" which has found expression in a myriad of ways, both during the Holocaust, and in the decades that followed.

"The testimony of those who survived constitutes the main record of what was done to the Jews during those years."[1] However, considerable testimony has also been provided by many of the victims who did not survive. Under the most brutal conditions, inmates of ghettos and camps kept diaries, wrote poems and created art--depicting the reality of a world of agony--in the hope that these materials would survive and tell the world what happened.

More than death, they feared that the world would never know what they were enduring and, worse, that they would not be believed. For some, the need to record and witness was as elemental as hunger and therefore worth risking our life for. Some of these works survived, though most of their creators perished. The most distinguished writings are those of Emanuel Ringelblum[2] who kept a diary of the crucial events and described in somber details the experience of the Jews incarcerated in the Warsaw ghetto.

Less known, yet worth attention are the diaries authored by a group of Jewish Doctors who kept a daily record of the impact of starvation on the Ghetto inhabitants. Hungry themselves, and anticipating their own death (they were, indeed, deported to Treblinka in 1943) these doctors placed their manuscripts in milk cans to be smuggled out to the Aryan side of the city. Buried there for the next twenty-five years, these documents were accidentally discovered and eventually brought to America. In English translation, they were edited by Myron Winick under the title *Hunger Disease*.[3]

In the early years after the war only a few survivors had the wisdom and emotional strength to become chroniclers of the events that took place during the Holocaust. A few books appeared describing in chronological detail and somber terms the people and the communities that were systematically destroyed by the Nazis. Written in native languages, often Polish or Yiddish, these materials remained unknown and unavailable to the public at large. Under the sponsorship of the *Landsmanschaften* and titled "Yiskor books" (memorial books), some eventually found a home in the Judaica department of the New York Public Library. English excerpts of these writings can be found in the book *From a Ruined Garden*.[4] Among the best known books of this period are those by Elie Weisel,[5] Victor Frankel,[6] and Primo Levi.[7]

Within the last few years we have seen an outpouring of testimonies authored by Holocaust survivors. Far from being professional writers; most are plain folks who are determined to leave a record. This witnessing appears in the form of books, diaries, recorded oral histories, poems and songs. There is an ever-growing number of works of art. Some of these materials are of excellent quality, others are not. Their significance lies primarily in their role as witnesses to history.

What is their contribution to the field of mental health? What lessons do they teach?

First and foremost, that professional knowledge and skill are hollow, even dangerous, unless embodied in human values. Too many gruesome details in these survivor memoirs attest to the unbelievable deception and cruelty on the part of these well-educated and skilled engineers, lawyers, doctors and psychologists.

Survivor testimonies establish the Holocaust firmly in the realm of history. Thus, they sharpen our awareness of the role of history in the lives of our clients and patients and of our responsibility to integrate a historic perspective into our processes of assessment and treatment.

They challenge and extend our perception of human behavior, particularly behavior under extreme stress. From the thousands of pages of testimony the victims emerge not as heroes or bundles of psychopathology but as human beings, capable of a wide range of behavior, even in environments of hell. We find those (probably the majority) who relied on some degree of "psychic numbing" to get through the days of hard labor, hunger, terror and the excruciating pain of seeing their kin executed or go up in smoke. Others are depicted as coping with their ordeal by extreme selfishness, even cruelty, toward fellow inmates.

But we also find among the victims those who were capable of self-sacrifice, fundamental human decency and altruism. We find prisoners who shared their starvation diets, cared for the sick and consoled the bereaved. These survivors' testimony challenge earlier stereotyped clinical notions that emphasized regression, dehumanization and Jewish passivity which brought them like "sheep to the slaughter." These materials reflect myriads of examples of resistance, selflessness and courage and explicitly illuminate how these activities enabled victims to transcend their suffering and achieve some emotional relief.

While describing the emotional benefits of altruistic behavior and resistance, these testimonies never imply that biological survival was insured by these activities. In fact, they make clear that the Gestapo, and the Gestapo only, determined who should live and who should die or, more accurately, when one would die. The role of accident comes across loud and clear and offers an important lesson to mental health workers who tend to view human victory and survival in terms of "ego strength" or other positive personality characteristics. Under the weight of thousands of survivor-chronicles, the vital role of accident in biological survival is clearly established as a historic fact.

a. *Child Survivors*

There are other important challenges to our cherished psychological concepts and theories. Of particular significance may be the emerging autobiographical writings by those survivors who were children or adolescents during the Holocaust.

The mere existence of child-survivors is a miracle, since in the Nazi extermination program, the old and the children were the first priority. The memoirs of these child survivors include tragic scenes of separation from parents, a range of experiences in living incognito with Christian families, unbelievable cruelty suffered at the hands of peasants as they wandered around the countryside, orphaned and abandoned, suffering hunger and freezing weather. Some remember their imprisonment in Death Camps.

At the time of liberation, the very young did not know their names, countries of origin, or even their first language. Through efforts of international agencies, unclaimed children were sent to live with families abroad in foster or adoptive arrangements. Unlike adult survivors who gravitated toward the same communities and kept in touch with each other, child-survivors did not have such contact and did not know of each other. Characteristically, they wanted to lead ordinary and normal lives, undistinguished from their contemporaries. Curiously, their development and adaptation does not reflect the immense trauma they suffered in the formative years of their lives.

Many completed college, engaged successfully in careers and established stable family situations. Some say that memory of the parents was helpful; others credit their spouses for the stability of life they are enjoying (Judith Kestenberg,[8] Flora Hogman[9]).

This growing body of literature should be studied and followed up as it significantly broadens our understanding of human development, particularly in identifying those adaptive-integrative forces that help people grow into productive members of society despite extreme early life traumatization.

b.   *The Second Generation*

The sons and daughters of survivors born after the war have also become chroniclers of their formative years in Holocaust families. Some focus on problems they experienced growing up in these dismembered and overprotective families. Here the emphasis is on the emotional scars they still carry as a result of this background. Others seem to have used their tragic legacy to achieve a purpose in life, a strong sense of identity and sensitivity to human suffering (Helen Epstein,[10] Eva Fogelman[11]).

In one way or another, it is clear that the experience of genocide casts a long shadow and affects succeeding generations. This is also evident among the second generation of Hiroshima survivors, many of whom have suffered nightmares of the atomic devastation (R. J. Lifton,[12]). And, some descendants of the Armenian victims in the 1915 massacre still seek revenge in random killings of Turkish officials.

c.   *Aged Survivors*

Holocaust survivors may offer unique insights into the process of aging. Most are now aging or aged. As such, they share with their contemporaries the blessings and vicissitudes which accompany this stage in life. And yet, there are two characteristics in their background that may uniquely affect their process of aging and dealing with illness and death.

Holocaust survivors have "no models for aging in their family backgrounds...(they) have not seen their parents grow to an old age. The mothers and fathers were often killed in the fourth and fifth decade of their lives. While all Jews were meant to die and indeed most were eventually annihilated, the parental generation of the current survivor was selected for death immediately and precisely because its middle-age marked the generation as old and useless even for full labor as slaves."[13])

> "Each survivor has outlived a sentence of death. Facing death at this time is dying the second time around. Old, frightening memories may come back and there may be a reversal of the coping strategies of that earlier, prolonged period of immersion in the death experience....While such reactions are not common, they are known to occur and need to be understood within the context of the historic trauma. All efforts must be made to help the survivor-patient separate the

now from the then and cut short the process of retraumatization."[14]

Among the commonly observed dynamics in Holocaust survivors are an exaggerated sense of family, a continuous sense of loss and guilt, and a persistent need to bear witness.

Family is a loaded concept for survivors because of the total or near total destruction of all their pre-war family members. There are unique bonds in Holocaust families.

> Children have often been perceived by survivor-parents as the meaning for survival and the reason to be. In turn, the second generation is known to have experienced intensive conflict in breaking away because of guilt in imposing pain on parents who had suffered such cruel and multiple separation....No wonder that illness, institutionalization or death of an aging parent may elicit in the son and daughter a set of complicated grief reactions that are related to the ever-present issues of loss and mourning that binds and transcends generations of Holocaust victims.[15])

It is incumbent for mental health professionals who often treat members of the second generation to be familiar with these complex, dynamic issues, particularly the agony of separation in Holocaust families.

Survival Guilt. Survival guilt may re-emerge with potency at times of crisis, particularly around loss of family and friends. New insights into survival guilt suggest that it is not necessarily a pathological phenomenon as often assumed in the field of mental health. Clearer differentiation is needed between psychological and moral aspects of guilt. As Hillel Klein[16] suggests, survival guilt may serve as a reparative, humanizing function and help in maintaining a connection to the past.

Most survivors readily admit that a sense of loss and guilt are continuing themes in their lives. Nevertheless, many have functioned well, raised wholesome families, achieved economic success and made a contribution to society in general. How this was possible is still an unanswered question and only recently has there been some research in this area (S. Davidson,[17] Z. Harel, E. Kahana and K. Boaz[18]).

Finding a meaning in life seems to have aided many in the adaptation process. Meaning was found in a variety of ways. Some found a meaning in re-establishing families, in bonding with others, in supporting humanitarian, religious, cultural and historical causes, and in "bearing witness."

Bearing Witness. Aware of their advancing age and encouraged by societal interest in the Holocaust, survivors are now engaging en masse in the task of leaving a record of their Holocaust experiences and of their pre-Holocaust family and community life.

To an unprecedented degree in human history, survivor-witnesses are writing the history of the Holocaust (M. Gilbert[19]), influencing the media (C. Lanzman[20]) and speaking in schools, universities and professional organizations. In large numbers they participate in oral history projects and have produced volumes of tapes for use by museums, libraries, and other institutions.

Although remembering is painful and is often avoided, survivors now show a unique drive to overcome that natural resistance to reliving the pain which necessarily accompanies the act of reminiscing about the Holocaust. Multi-motivational psychological forces--not always explicit--are probably involved in this strong sense of mission to leave a record.

Survivors want to make sure that the Holocaust not be forgotten and that it be remembered in ways that are not distorted. They are enraged by societal tendency to trivialize, universalize and commercialize the facts of the Holocaust.

The act of bearing witness and documenting in some orderly fashion the painful and chaotic fragments of their past, may help survivors (and the following generations) give some coherence to the unimaginable and incomprehensible events of the Holocaust.

Survivors want their children to know about their pre-Holocaust ancestors and about the communities in which they lived. Undoubtedly, such knowledge offers the children and their children's children a bridge to the past, and a sense of roots. Specific information about parental experiences during the Holocaust may also correct inaccurate assumptions about the parents' role in survival:

Remembering the dead, giving them a name, a face and a place may represent an obsessive effort to rescue them from oblivion and insure that they will be remembered as individuals, with identity, and not as an amorphous six million. Survivor testimony may also represent--in a symbolic way--the rituals of mourning and an effort to replace the missing graves, headstones and burial places which were so cruelly denied to the victims. Unquestionably, the acts of remembering and committing the memories to paper facilitates the mourning process which is never complete. In working with Holocaust survivors and victims of other mass destruction these needs must be understood creatively and harnessed for they may help in restoring a meaning to survival and may mercifully promote an integration of brutally fragmented lives....For survivors, the Holocaust remains a source of unending trauma. a Trauma of such depth can never be worked through. Instead, our efforts may be directed toward improving the quality of their lives, including relationships with kin. We can help the sons and daughters retain bonds with the survivor parent(s) and yet retain the right to autonomy and separateness. We can join survivors in their process of mourning and assist them in their quest for meaning, particularly their need to "bear witness." And lastly, as mental health professionals, we can use the lessons of the Holocaust to strengthen our commitment to sensitive, compassionate and ethical practice.[21]

ENDNOTES

[1]Martin Gilbert, *The Holocaust*, (N.Y.: Holt, Rinehart and Winston, 1985). (Book Jacket)

[2]Emanuel Ringelblum, *Notes from the Warsaw Ghetto*, (McGraw Hill, 1958).

[3]Myron Winick, *Hunger Disease* (N.Y.: John Wiley & Sons, 1979).

[4]Jack Kugelman and J. Boyarin, *From a Ruined Garden* (N.Y.: Schocken, 1984).

[5]Elie Wiesel, *Night* (N.Y.: Avon Books, 1958).

[6]Victor Frankel, *Man's Search for Meaning* (N.Y.: Simon and Schuster, 1964).

[7]Primo Levi, *Survival in Auschwitz* (N.Y.: Collier Books, McMillan, 1958).

[8]Judith Kestenberg, "Child Survivors of the Holocaust," *Journal of the American Academy of Child Psychiatry*, 24 (4) (1985): (special section), pp. 378-412.

[9]Flora Hogman, "Role of Memories in Lives of World War II Orphans," *Journal of the American Academy of Child Psychiatry* 24 (4) (1985): (special section), pp. 378-412.

[10]Helen Epstein, *Children of the Holocaust* (N.Y.: B. P. Putnam's Sons, 1979).

[11]Eva Fogelman, "Therapeutic Groups for Children of Holocaust Survivors," *International Journal of Group Psychotherapy* (April 1979): 211-235.

[12]Robert J. Lifton, "Observations of Hiroshima Survivors," in *Massive Psychic Trauma*, (eds.) Henry Krystal and William Niederland (N.Y.: International Universities Press, 1968), pp. 168-189.

[13]Maria Rosenbloom, "The Holocaust Survivor in Late Life," in *Journal of Gerontological Social Work*, Vol. 8, 314 (Spring 1985): 187.

[14]Maria Rosenbloom, "Lessons of the Holocaust for Mental Health Practice," in *Psychological Perspectives on the Holocaust*, ed. Randolph L. Braham, Holocaust Studies Series, the Graduate School and University Center, New York, 1988, pp. 145-159.

[15]*Ibid.*, p. 157.

[16]Hillel Klein, "Children of the Holocaust: Mourning and Bereavement," *The Child and His Family*, (eds.) James Anthony and Cyrille Kompernick (N.Y.: John Wiley & Sons, 1973).

[17]Shamai Davidson, "Human Reciprocity Among the Jewish Prisoners in the Nazi Concentration Camps," *Proceedings of the Fourth Yad Vashem International Historical Conference* (Jerusalem: Yad Vashem, 1984).

[18]Zev Harel, Kahana Boaz and Eva Kahana, "Psychological Well-Being Among Holocaust Survivors and Immigrants in Israel," *Journal of Traumatic Stress*, Vol. 1, No. 4 (1988).

[19]Martin Gilbert, *ibid.*

[20]Claude Lanzman, *Shoah* (Film).

[21]Rosenbloom (1988), p. 15.

CONTRIBUTORS

Dr. Beverly Asbury has served Vanderbilt University since 1967 as University Chaplain and Director of Religious Affairs. He also chairs the Tennessee Commission on the Holocaust and serves on the education Committee of the U.S. Holocaust Memorial Council.

Alan L. Berger directs the Jewish Studies Program and teaches in the Department of Religion at Syracuse University. His books include *Crisis and Covenant: The Holocaust in American Jewish Fiction* and *Methodology in the Academic Teaching of the Holocaust* (Associate Editor). His articles on Jewish literature and theology have appeared in numerous publications.

Rachel Feldhay Brenner is the author of *Assimilation and Assertion: The Response to the Holocaust in Mordecai Richler's Writing* (Peter Lang, 1989) and *A. M. Klein, The Father of Canadian Jewish Literature* (Edwin Mellen, 1990). She teaches at York University in Toronto. This article was completed during her post-Doctoral Fellowship awarded by Social Sciences and Humanities Research Council of Canada.

A. Roy Eckardt is Professor of Religion Studies Emeritus at Lehigh University and a Senior Associate Fellow of the Centre for Postgraduate Hebrew Studies at the University of Oxford. His latest book is *Reclaiming the Jesus of History* (Fortress Press, 1991).

Jack Fischel is chair, Millerville University History Department and co-editor of the *Encyclopedia of Jewish-American History and Culture.*

Dr. Eugene J. Fisher is Director of Catholic-Jewish Relations for the National Conference of Catholic Bishops and, since 1981, Consultor to the Holy See's Commission for Religious Relations with the Jews. He has published over 200 articles and a dozen books in the field, including *Jewish Roots of Christian Liturgy* and *In Our Time: The Flowering of Jewish-Catholic Dialogue* (both Paulist Press, 1990).

Zev Garber is Professor of Jewish Studies, Los Angeles Valley College, and Visiting Professor of Religious Studies, University of California at Riverside. The author of numerous scholarly articles and reviews, he is also the main editor of *Methodology in the Academic Teaching of Judaism* (1986), *Methodology in the Academic Teaching of the Holocaust* (1988), and a new series, *Studies in Shoah.*

Gershon Greenberg is a research fellow for the Institute of Holocaust Research at Bar Ilan University. His work on the Holocaust in Jewish Thought (especially Orthodoxy) has appeared in *Simon Wiesenthal Annual, Holocaust and Genocide Studies, Tradition, Modern Judaism, Keshev, European Judaism* and numerous conference proceedings.

Herbert Hirsch, Ph.D., is Professor and Chairperson of the Department of Political Science at Virginia Commonwealth University. He is the author or editor of several books including: *Poverty and Politicization; Comparative Legislative Systems; Violence as Politics; Learning to be Militant; The Right of the People;* and *Persistent Prejudice: Perspectives on Anti-Semitism;* as well as articles in *The American Political Science Review, Social Science Quarterly, Western Political Quarterly, Holocaust and Genocide Studies,* and *The Educational Forum.*

Iwona Irwin-Zarecka is the author of *Neutralizing Memory: The Jew in Contemporary Poland* (Transaction Books, 1989). She is an Assistant Professor of Sociology and Communication Studies at Wilfrid Laurier University in Waterloo, Ontario (Canada).

Roberta Kalechofsky is a writer, publisher, and lecturer, whose articles and fiction have appeared in many quarterlies and journals. The recipient of Fellowships in Creative Writing from the National Endowment for the Arts and the Massachusetts Council on the Arts, her biography is included in the volume of American Jewish Writers in the *Dictionary of Literary Biographies.*

Steven T. Katz is Professor in the Department of Near Eastern Studies at Cornell University. His three volume study *The Holocaust in Historical Context* will be published by Oxford University Press beginning in 1992.

Paul L. Marcus, Ph.D., has written a number of scholarly articles and has co-edited *Psychoanalytic Reflections on the Holocaust: Selected Essays* (1984) and *Healing Their Wounds: Psychotherapy with Holocaust Survivors and their Families* (1989). He is the Secretary of the New York Psychoanalytic Society's Group for the Psychoanalytic Study of the Effects of the Holocaust on the Second Generation.

Robert Melson is Associate Professor of Political Science and former Chairperson of the Jewish Studies Program at Purdue University. He has been a research scholar at Harvard, MIT, and the Hebrew University of Jerusalem. His publications have appeared in *The American Political Science Review, Comparative Studies in Society* and *History, and Holocaust and Genocide Studies.* He has recently completed *Revolution and Genocide: Comparative Perspectives on the Armenian Genocide and the Holocaust.*

Susan Lee Pentlin has her doctorate from the University of Kansas. She is an Associate Professor of Modern Languages at Central Missouri State College where she teaches a course "The Holocaust in Memory."

Richard Pierard, Professor of History, Indiana State University, also Fulbright Professor, University of Halle, Germany, 1989-1990. His most recent book is *Civil Religion and the Presidency* (1988). His essays appear in numerous works including *Liberty and Law, Covenant Quarterly* and *Remembering for the Future.*

Alan Rosenberg is the author of a number of articles and reviews that have appeared in a variety of journals and books, including *Modern Judaism* and

The Simon Wiesenthal Center *Annual*. He is the co-editor of *Echoes from the Holocaust: Philosophical Reflections on a Dark Time* (1988) and *Healing Their Wounds: Psychotherapy with Holocaust Survivors and Their Families*. He is a lecturer in the Department of Philosophy, Queens College of the City University of New York.

Maria Rosenbloom, a native of the Polish Ukraine, experienced the Holocaust in ghettos, in hiding, and by living as an "Aryan." She is Associate Professor at the Graduate School, Hunter College School of Social Work, is involved in the clinical counseling of survivors, teaches about Holocaust implications to mental health professionals, and writes extensively on the subject.

Robert W. Ross, retired from the University of Minnesota, is currently Adjunct Professor in the Bay Area Extended Education, Fuller Theological Seminary; he is also a member of the Associated Faculty, the Starr King School for Ministry, the Graduate Theological Union, Berkeley, California. He is the author of *So it was True: The American Protestant Press and the Nazi Persecution of the Jews*.

Richard L. Rubenstein is Robert O. Lawton Distinguished Professor of Religion at Florida State University and President of the Washington Institute for Values in Public Policy, a public policy research institution in Washington, D.C. A greatly enlarged and revised twenty-fifth anniversary edition of *After Auschwitz* is to be published by Johns Hopkins University Press.

Roger W. Smith is Professor of Government at the College of William and Mary, where he teaches courses on Political Philosophy and the Comparative Study of Genocide. He is a contributing editor of *Internet on the Holocaust and Genocide*.

Emanuel Tanay, M.D., is a Clinical Professor of Psychiatry at Wayne State University, College of Medicine, Detroit. He is a Holocaust survivor from Poland.

Nechama Tec is a Professor of Sociology at the University of Connecticut in Stamford. Since 1977 she has been conducting research about compassion, altruism and the rescue of Jews during World War II. Her fifth and latest book, *In The Lion's Den: The Life of Oswald Rufeisen*, Oxford University Press, 1990, was nominated for a Pulitzer Prize. For 1991-1992, she was awarded a National Endowment For the Humanities Fellowship to conduct research and write her sixth book.